The Copyright-Competition Interaction within the EU

Dino Gliha

The Copyright-Competition Interaction within the EU

Springer

Dino Gliha
Zagreb, Croatia

ISBN 978-3-031-94401-7 ISBN 978-3-031-94402-4 (eBook)
https://doi.org/10.1007/978-3-031-94402-4

This Springer imprint is published by the registered company Springer Nature Switzerland AG
The registered company address is: Gewerbestrasse 11, 6330 Cham, Switzerland

Preface

The intersection of copyright and competition law presents one of the most intricate challenges in the modern legal landscape, at least from my perspective, which comprehends a mixture of law, business and technology. As society transitions into an era defined by digital innovation and globalization, the balance between fostering creativity and ensuring fair market practices has become increasingly pivotal. This book explores this evolving terrain, offering a structured approach to address the nuanced conflicts that arise when copyright law intersects with competition law.

The initial inspiration for this work stemmed from the growing number of high-profile cases and the lack of consistent methodologies to address such conflicts effectively. Landmark judgments within the European Union, from *Magill* to *Microsoft* and beyond, have underscored the need for a more coherent framework—one that respects the unique principles and rules of both copyright and competition law while adapting to the dynamic challenges of the digital age.

Through a rigorous analysis, this book delves into the foundational principles of copyright and competition law, tracing their historical development and examining their nature and roles in a rapidly changing economy. Special attention is given to the application of competition rules, particularly Articles 101 and 102 of the TFEU, as they pertain to copyright. The discussion expands to specific scenarios, focusing on prohibited agreements and abuse of dominance concerning the exercise of copyright, and culminates in a proposed structured framework for the assessment. This approach is designed to ensure legal predictability and market clarity, both at the EU and national levels.

The book also addresses the emerging challenges posed by digital platforms and the EU Digital Single Market. These platforms, while fostering unprecedented creativity and market access, have introduced new complexities in addressing competition and copyright issues. As the global economy becomes increasingly platform driven, the framework proposed here seeks to navigate these complexities and provide actionable insights for policymakers, practitioners and scholars.

Acknowledging the profound impact of technological advancements, this work envisions a future where copyright and competition law coexist harmoniously. The proposed guidelines aim not only to resolve existing issues but also to anticipate and address the legal challenges of tomorrow.

This book is intended for academics, legal practitioners, policymakers and anyone interested in the confluence of intellectual property and competition law. It is my hope that the insights offered here will contribute to a deeper understanding of these intertwined fields and serve as a foundation for further scholarly exploration and practical application.

This book is a consequence of my doctoral research at the University of Zagreb, Faculty of Law, and research stays at the Max Planck Institute for Innovation and Competition, where I spent my most fruitful days working on the subject. Thus, I extend my gratitude to my doctoral supervisors, Izv. Prof. Dr. Silke von Lewinski and Prof. dr. sc. Siniša Petrović, and my family, who supported me along the way. Finally, I would like to thank Springer Nature for their support in bringing this work to light.

Zagreb, Croatia Dino Gliha

Competing Interests The author has no competing interests to declare that are relevant to the content of this manuscript.

Contents

Chapter 1
General Introduction, Research Questions and Scope of the Research

1.1 General Introduction

The interaction between copyright and competition law is an interdisciplinary and complex issue in law. Already in 1970, Hay and Oldekop wrote that the Court decisions on this matter "have been one of the most controversial topics of the EC law, perhaps even more so than its decisions on such fundamental issues as the direct effect of Community law within the legal system of the Member States or the supremacy of Community law over national law."[1]

The specific nature of the copyright-competition issue emanates from the complexity of market relations. This causes interaction between two completely different and independent fields of law, which needs to be harmonised and balanced without disturbing the substance of those laws. Benabou describes the relationship between copyright law and competition law as "the stormy love affairs."[2] Thus, cases concerning the copyright-competition interaction must inevitably consider the understanding of several divergent fields. Besides copyright law and competition law, dealing with the issue also requires an understanding of economics and at least sufficient knowledge of industry, recognition of (anti-)competitive effects on the market, etc.

However, for now, that remains only a theoretical observation. In practice and among scholars, the issue of copyright-competition interaction is far from settled, starting from the very relationship between copyright law and competition law. Both decision-makers and scholars tend to discuss matters stemming from this issue without previously acknowledging the fundamentals of the two laws that govern

[1]Hay and Oldekop (1977), pp. 121–122.

Choi and Heinemann also state: "(…) the issue of the intersection between competition law and IP is one of the most difficult and heavily debated areas of the law." Choi and Heinemann (2016), p. 413.

[2]Benabou (2005), p. 663.

D. Gliha, *The Copyright-Competition Interaction within the EU*,
https://doi.org/10.1007/978-3-031-94402-4_1

the issue, resulting in solutions that are not sustainable and theoretically founded. Consequently, discussions on this matter often neglect the particularities of copyright and economic argumentation. Moreover, even if that is put aside, we still lack a structured analytical framework for dealing with copyright-competition interaction situations, required to secure the consistency of case law and the legal and economic security of stakeholders caught by the copyright-competition interaction issue.

Within former case law, especially in the European Union, it appears that the competent authorities neglected the substance of copyright law and competition law, and the essential specificity of the copyright-competition interaction issue. In a paper on compulsory licensing, Temple Lang picturesquely described the situation in the EU in the following way: "(...) the law has developed piecemeal without any explicit framework or general principle, and the Court has never explained the principles comprehensively."[3] The reason for that can be found in previously elaborated criticism—mainly, the competent authorities tend to diminish the importance of particularities of copyright and neglect the need for a comprehensive economic analysis. Furthermore, there has been no defined structured analysis or uniform approach to such cases, creating inconsistency and legal insecurity. The situation is not much better in comparative systems, except that some legislations have introduced guidelines to preserve at least somewhat uniform dealing with cases of copyright-competition interaction.

Nevertheless, in the academic society, there is a sense that something has to change in relation to the copyright-competition interaction issue. The view is still widespread that there is a need for an appropriate framework and (possibly) guidelines to deal with the copyright-competition interaction matter.[4] There is no specific guidance about drawing a careful balance between copyright law and competition law in EU legislation. The only trace of the copyright-competition interaction issue can be found within the soft law. Thus, Guidelines on the application of Article 101 of the Treaty on the Functioning of the European Union to technology transfer agreements[5] and Guidance on the Commission's enforcement priorities in applying Article 82 of the EC Treaty to abusive exclusionary conduct by dominant undertaking[6] in a way partially deal with the issue in hand, however, surely not comprehensively. Thus, something clearly must change.

Particularly nowadays, when the new economy is driven more and more by creation and originality, technological complexity has increased significantly. Thus, the importance of dynamic competition has overcome the need for a static

[3] Temple Lang (2010), p. 411.

[4] See Choi and Heinemann (2016), pp. 407, 418.

[5] Communication from the Commission—Guidelines on the application of Article 101 of the Treaty on the Functioning of the European Union to technology transfer agreements, OJ C 89, 28.3.2014, pp. 3–50.

[6] Communication from the Commission—Guidance on the Commission's enforcement priorities in applying Article 82 of the EC Treaty to abusive exclusionary conduct by dominant undertaking, C 45, 24.2.2009, pp. 7–20.

competition.[7] Copyright underlies the development of digital and software technologies, and artificial intelligence. With the ongoing digital revolution and an increase in the importance of intangible assets in the overall economy, the interaction between copyright and competition has been growing in prominence. Therefore, it is essential to set up a uniform and comprehensive set of ground rules for proceedings in cases concerning copyright-competition interaction.

1.2 Research Questions

The main research questions to which the research endeavours to provide the answers are the following:

- What is the relationship between copyright law and competition law? Can the copyright-competition interaction issue be observed through limitations to the exercise of copyright, and as a specific situation in view of dynamic competition?
- In which situations could the exercise of copyright constitute an infringement of competition law?
- Which method of assessment is appropriate for the copyright-competition interaction issue, particularly regarding the competition rules on prohibited agreements and abuse of dominance?

1.3 Scope of the Research

The focus of this research is limited to the interaction between copyright law and competition law. This matter is often discussed as the interaction between intellectual property rights in general and competition law; however, due to the specific nature of the particular intellectual property right, such an approach does not seem appropriate. Each right encompassed by the notion of intellectual property should be observed individually in relation to competition law. Compared to the interaction of other intellectual property rights with competition law, a large part of the scarce case law deals with copyright. Also, in view of the future, with the development of digital and creative technologies, it is likely that the importance of copyright will continue to grow and that more and more competition concerns may arise. Thus, it is crucial to define the relationship between copyright law and competition law and settle the issue of copyright-competition interaction timely to avoid potential future issues.

Within copyright-competition interaction, research is narrowed to focus on the exercise of copyright under the competition rules on prohibited agreements (which mainly concern licensing agreements) and the exercise of copyright under the

[7] See Choi and Heinemann (2016), p. 418.

competition rules on abuse of dominance (which commonly concern the refusal to license situation). Other specific situations that are also caught up by this issue, such as concentrations and collective organisations, are not covered by this research. Nevertheless, the main findings from this research may be adequately applied to those situations as well, particularly concerning the relationship between copyright law and competition law and the general approach to the copyright-competition interaction issue.

Regarding copyright, the findings from this research are believed to be applicable to all the different objects of copyright, including the neighbouring rights.[8]

References

Benabou V-L (2005) Neutral or harmful effects of competition law on copyright or Liaisons Dangereuses (Dangerous Love Affairs) on the *Carte du Tendre*, Exploring the Sources of Copyright. Paper presented at the ALAI Congress, Paris, 18–21 September 2005, pp 648–663

Choi YS, Heinemann A (2016) Restrictions of competition law in licensing agreements: the worldwide convergence of competition laws and policies in the field of intellectual property. Eur Bus Organ Law Rev 17(3):405–422

Hay P, Oldekop D (1977) EMI/CBS and the rest of the world: trademark rights and the European communities. Am J Comp Law 25(1):120–151

Temple Lang J (2010) European competition law and intellectual property rights—a new analysis. ERA Forum 11(3):411–437. https://doi.org/10.1007/s12027-010-0157-9. Accessed 25 Oct 2024

[8]However, within the work, for practical reasons, the right involved shall always be referred to as copyright.

Part I
The Copyright-Competition Interaction Issue: General Part

Chapter 2
Copyright Law and Competition Law: Nature, Characteristics and Objectives

The issue of the copyright-competition interaction generated many discussions in the academic society all around the world. Although this specific issue is not a novelty, no appropriate approach to it has been produced. The reason for this could be that in most of the discussions on this matter, there is often neglect of the fundamental laws that this issue concerns. Namely, the copyright-competition interaction issue inevitably comprises copyright law and competition law, each with its individual development, principles, rationales and regulation. Hence, to demystify the copyright-competition interaction issue, it is in the first place necessary to take into consideration the fundamentals of copyright law and competition law and clearly distinguish the elements of those laws that concern this specific interdisciplinary issue. Only when there is a fundamental understanding of the copyright law and the competition law will it be possible to comprehensively analyse the situations in which they interact and discuss how to approach such situations.

Therefore, a brief history, nature and objectives of copyright law and competition law are presented separately to provide grounds for understanding the historical development and the essence of the interaction between copyright law and competition law. Since this thesis focuses primarily on the copyright-competition interaction in the EU, the elaboration on copyright law and competition law in this chapter is given mainly from the perspective of the European Union and its Member States.

2.1 Copyright Law

2.1.1 A Brief History of Copyright Law

Copyright has a complex, subtle and rich history. Although the development of modern copyright law commenced during the eighteenth century and was later

D. Gliha, *The Copyright-Competition Interaction within the EU*,
https://doi.org/10.1007/978-3-031-94402-4_2

formulated through the nineteenth and twentieth centuries,[1] the origins of copyright law can be traced back in earlier history.

Some sources and literature even indicate that traces of copyright law can be found far back in ancient times.[2] Still, discussing copyright in ancient times, which is

[1] See Dock (1974), p. 126; von Lewinski (2008), pp. 36–37.

[2] Thus, Bappert indicates that even in the earliest human societies, some recognition of the right to intellectual creations can be found (for instance, in cave paintings, dances, etc.); Bappert (1962), pp. 7–8.

Some researchers consider that in ancient Norse culture, there was an awareness of the value and particularities of at least literary art and a poetical 'know-how' which would be acknowledged (or tolerated) by Kings. The same can probably be concluded from the Irish respect for letters at the beginning of the Middle Ages; see Strömholm (1967), p. 47; Gieseke (1957), p. 17.

Others indicate that, in accordance with certain anthropological research, even some of the early African tribes had some notion of literary property. Thus, among the so-called Negrito ethnic groups, allegedly, only the author of a song was entitled to sing it, the author of a poem to recite it. Among Bushmen, nobody could handle a lithic painting as long as its author or family members were known to exist; see Dock (1974), p. 128, referring to Dekkers, Rapports Généraux au V Congres international de droit comparé, Brussels, 1960, Vol. 1, p. 13.

There are some indications that there were sanctions for unauthorised oral or written replication of sacred rituals in ancient Egypt. Ploman and Hamilton (1980), p. 6.

Some studies of Jewish law consider that traces of copyright can be found in principles and rules of Talmudic law, including the rules for citation and traces of distinction between moral and economic rights; see Hazan (1970), pp. 23–28, 24–28; Ploman and Hamilton (1980), pp. 6–7.

Even in ancient Greece, where there was no genuine recognition or regulation of copyright, some scholars consider that the particular origins of copyright can be found, especially in poetry and art. The 'authors' of creative content received some acknowledgement for their work and protection from piracy, and could even earn their livings from subsidies received from the state or *mecenaes*. Hauser (1962), pp. 65–66; May and Sell (2006), pp. 45–56; Dock (1974), p. 130; Kohler (1880), p. 326.

In ancient Rome, there was a developed publishing and book trade. Also, it seems that there were advocates for the better protection of authors, such as Seneca, Martial, Cicero, Pliny, Septicus and Arrian, whose works point to a particular recognition of certain copyright principles. There are even some indications that Roman authors were aware that publishing and exploitation of works comprise both intellectual and moral interests, and that they distinguished the right of the author to the integrity of the work from the rights acquired by the purchaser of a manuscript (including the right to reproduce the work). Furthermore, it seems that there was a need for some kind of authorisation of the publishing of works. Moreover, plagiarism was condemned, at least morally; Boytha (1991), p. 71; Geller (2000), p. 213; Ploman and Hamilton (1980), p. 7; Seneca (1935); Martialis (1976); Dock (1974), pp. 144–146; Ploman and Hamilton (1980), p. 7; Ciceronis (1999), pp. 320, 327; Plinius (1910); Dock (1974), pp. 146–152; Martialis (1976); Ploman and Hamilton (1980), p. 7.

In medieval times, there is also an indication that there was some sense of what may be considered copyright awareness—mostly in connection with monasteries and universities, the only places where such activities could practically be conducted; Bappert (1962), pp. 83–88; Bowker (1912), pp. 9–10; Dock (1974), pp. 154–158; Ploman and Hamilton (1980), p. 8.

debatable per se,[3] would not contribute to understanding the development of the copyright-competition interaction. However, in later times, when the printing industry started to develop, the privilege system, as a predecessor of copyright law, might have some relevance in finding the first signs of the interaction between (pre-)copyright law and (pre-)competition law.

The overall history of copyright is intertwined with technological development and social occurrences; thus, the further development of copyright awareness is linked with the invention of the printing press in the mid-fifteenth century.[4] De Wolf states: "Copyright law is the child of the printing press."[5] Printing enabled the creation of cheap multiple copies of literary works and provided incentives for developing the book market. Despite all the benefits of the development of the printing industry, it also brought certain problems to publishers and authors who invested great efforts to create and produce works. In the first place, to compensate publishers primarily for their publication overhead costs and their house commercial risks; to avoid free-riding; and later, as well, to control the printing trade (censorship)—different state-related bodies started to interfere and grant commercial monopolies ('privileges'), mainly to the

---

[3]Thus, commentators firmly consider that there are no indications that copyright was protected or even recognised in ancient times. One explanation for this can be found in the belief of those times that knowledge and the ability to make it manifest to man was a gift from a god and as such, should be freely given (such a belief can also be recognised in other great civilisations, such as Chinese, Islamic, Jewish and Christian, and was present practically until the eighteenth century). Starting from the premise—"Only when media technology and market conditions made piracy profitable could copyright arise"—another explanation considers that in those times, piracy was not yet lucrative enough to set grounds for the development of the copyright system. Thus, in some more developed legislations, such as ancient Roman, 'ownership' of a work was practically equalised with traditional ownership—an owner of the material was also the owner of the work; see Bowker (1912), p. 8; Hesse (2002), pp. 26–29; Alford (1995), pp. 26–29; Geller (2000), pp. 210–214; Dzlatzko (1894), pp. 568–569; Gaius (2024); Iustinianus (1998a), pp. 204–205; Iustinianus (1998b), pp. 4–5; Visky (1987), p. 19; Rintelen (1958), p. 4.

[4]See Bowker (1912), p. 10.

[5]De Wolf (1925), p. 1; however, in the following text, De Wolf also notes that for the recognition of their right to the fruits of their labour, the creator of intellectual works actually had to wait two and a half centuries longer since the first copyright law (Statute of Anne in 1710).

publishers (and some to the authors).[6] The oldest known privilege dates back to 1469 and was granted in Venice to Johannes of Speyer.[7] Later on, the system of privileges spread all over Europe, to countries such as England,[8] France,[9] Germany,[10]

---

[6]See Dock (1974), pp. 158–166; Grosheide (2010), pp. 84–87, 95–96; Ploman and Hamilton (1980), p. 9; Rose (1993), pp. 9–10.

[7]Printing monopoly granted to a German master printer, Johannes of Speyer, conceding a 5-year exclusive right to print in Venice and its dominions, Venice (1469). Primary Sources on Copyright (1450–1900). eds L. Bently & M. Kretschmer. www.copyrighthistory.org. Accessed on 23 October 2024. See Prager (1944), pp. 712–720.

According to some sources, exclusive privileges to print and sell were granted in China during the Sung dynasty (960–1179), although such privileges were more of a grace of the authority, revocable at any time; see Hesse (2002), pp. 29–30; see also Geller (2000), p. 214.

Also, according to some sources, even in Venice, granting of such privilege does not seem a novelty or an exceptional concept in the economic life and legal tradition of Venice. Namely, "ever since the thirteenth century, the Venetians led Europe in their efforts to attract foreign expertise by granting monopoly rights to immigrants who brought with them new skills and techniques to the city." Thus, de Spira's privilege can be seen as a part of the general framework of governmental support for industry, and of regulation of industry (and books were more or less treated as any other piece of merchandise); see Kostylo (2010), pp. 23–25.

[8]John Day's Privilege for the Catechism, Westminster (1553). Primary Sources on Copyright (1450–1900). eds L. Bently & M. Kretschmer. www.copyrighthistory.org Accessed on 23 October 2024; Robert Calve's printing privilege for the 'Holsome and Catholick Doctrine' (30 April 1558), Westminster (1558). Primary Sources on Copyright (1450–1900). eds L. Bently & M. Kretschmer. www.copyrighthistory.org. Accessed on 23 October 2024; Thomas Phayer's lifetime privilege for Virgil's Aeneid in English (6 May 1558). Primary Sources on Copyright (1450–1900). eds L. Bently & M. Kretschmer. www.copyrighthistory.org. Accessed on 23 October 2024.

In relation to the privilege system in England, Godson considers that the occurrence of (pre-) copyright was inevitably related to the formation of the Stationers' Company; see Godson (1840), pp. 307–308.

[9]Privilege granted to Eloy d'Amerval for his poem 'Le Livre de la deablerie' (1507), Primary Sources on Copyright (1450–1900). eds L. Bently & M. Kretschmer. www.copyrighthistory.org. Accessed on 23 October 2024; Privilege granted to the printer Galliot Du Pré for 'Le Grand Coutumier de France' (1515). Primary Sources on Copyright (1450–1900). eds L. Bently & M. Kretschmer. www.copyrighthistory.org. Accessed on 23 October 2024; Patent of 'Music Printers to the King', awarded by Henri II to Messrs Adrien Le Roy and Robert Ballard (orig. Brevet d'Impression du Roy pour la musique accordé par Henri II aux Sieurs Adrien Le Roy et Robert Ballard). Paris (1552). Primary Sources on Copyright (1450–1900). eds L. Bently & M. Kretschmer. www.copyrighthistory.org. Accessed on 23 October 2024; etc. See Pfister (2010), pp. 118–126.

[10]Privilege granted by Rudolf of Scherenberg, Prince-Bishop of Würzburg for the Printers Reyser, Dold and Beckenhub in a Breviary for the Würzburg Diocese (orig. Breviarium Herbipolense) (1479). Primary Sources on Copyright (1450-1900). eds L. Bently & M. Kretschmer. www.copyrighthistory.org. Accessed on 23 October 2024; Title, Dedications and Colophon with Reference to a Privilege of the Imperial Senate in Favour of the Sodalitas Celitica for an Edition of Works of Hrotsvit, Nuremberg (orig. OPERA HROSVITE ILLVSTRIS VIR||GINIS ET MONIALIS GERMANE GEN||TE SAXONICA ORTE NVPER A CONRA||DO CELTE INVENTA.||) (1501). Primary Sources on Copyright (1450–1900). eds L. Bently & M. Kretschmer. www.copyrighthistory.org. Accessed on 23 October 2024; Title, Dedications and Colophon with Reference to a Privilege of the Imperial Senate in Favour of the Sodalitas Celitica for an Edition of Works of Conrad Celtis, Nuremberg (orig. Quatuor libri amorum secundum quatuor latera Germanie)

Italy,[11] the Netherlands,[12] Portugal,[13] Spain[14] and others, and some overseas nations such as the United States,[15] for instance. The appearance of privileges is certainly a

(1502). Primary Sources on Copyright (1450–1900). eds L. Bently & M. Kretschmer. www.copyrighthistory.org. Accessed on 23 October 2024; etc.

[11] Printing privilege granted to the author Marco Antonio Sabellico to print his 'Decades rerum Venetarum' (1486). Primary Sources on Copyright (1450–1900). eds L. Bently & M. Kretschmer. www.copyrighthistory.org. Accessed on 23 October 2024 (This is the first recorded privilege to an author.); Privilege granted to Benedetto Bordon for 'Triumph of Caesar', Venice (1504). Primary Sources on Copyright (1450–1900). eds L. Bently & M. Kretschmer. www.copyrighthistory.org. Accessed on 23 October 2024.

[12] The Chronicle of Holland, Zealand and Frisia, starting from the time of Adam till the birth of our Lord Jesus, up until the year 1517, Leyden: Jan Severszoon, 1517 (orig. Die Chronyk van Hollandt, Zeelandt ende Vriesland, beghinnende van Adams tyden, tot die geboerte ons Heren Jhesu, voortgaende tot den jare 1517, Leyden: Jan Severszoon, 1517). Brussels (1516). Primary Sources on Copyright (1450–1900). eds L. Bently & M. Kretschmer. www.copyrighthistory.org Accessed on 23 October 2024; Bible: that is The entire Holy Scripture, thoroughly and faithfully translated into Dutch, Delft: Aelbert Hendricksz, 1579 (orig. Biblia: dat is De gantsche Heylighe Schrift, grondelick ende trouwelick verduydtschet, Delft: Aelbert Hendricksz, 1579). The Hague (1579), Primary Sources on Copyright (1450–1900). eds L. Bently & M. Kretschmer. www.copyrighthistory.org. Accessed on 23 October 2024; Simon du Chesne, Squaring of the circle or the manner of finding an equal square in a given circle, Delft: Albert Henry, 1584 (orig. Simon du Chesne, Quadrature du cercle ou manière de trouver un quarre egual au cercle donne, Delft: Albert Henry, 1584). Delft (1584). Primary Sources on Copyright (1450–1900). eds L. Bently & M. Kretschmer. www.copyrighthistory.org. Accessed on 23 October 2024.

[13] The Travels of Marco Polo written by Nicolau Vêneto, printed by Valentim Fernandes, containing a reference to the relevant royal privilege on the front cover (orig. Marco Paulo. Ho liuro de Nycolao Veneto. Ho trallado da carta de huu[m] genoues das ditas terras), Lisbon (1502). Primary Sources on Copyright (1450–1900). eds L. Bently & M. Kretschmer. www.copyrighthistory.org. Accessed on 23 October 2024; Order by Brás Afonso Correia, at the request of Valentim Fernandes, bookmaker (orig. Autos feitos por mandado de Brás Afonso Correia, a requerimento de Valentim Fernandes, livreiro), Lisbon (1503). Primary Sources on Copyright (1450–1900). eds L. Bently & M. Kretschmer. www.copyrighthistory.org. Accessed on 23 October 2024; etc.

[14] Printing Privileges to the Monastery of San Pedro Mártir (Toledo) and Santa María de Prado (Valladolid) (orig. Privilegios de impresión a los Monasterios de San Pedro Mártir (Toledo) y de Santa María de Prado (Valladolid)) (1487), Primary Sources on Copyright (1450–1900). eds L. Bently & M. Kretschmer. www.copyrighthistory.org. Accessed on 23 October 2024; Privilege for printing music for the Indies (org. Privilegio de impresión de libros corales con destino a las Indias), Seville (1559). Primary Sources on Copyright (1450–1900). eds L. Bently & M. Kretschmer. www.copyrighthistory.org. Accessed on 23 October 2024; Don Quixote's Privilege (org. Licencia y privilegio de impresión del Quijote), Madrid (1605), Primary Sources on Copyright (1450–1900). eds L. Bently & M. Kretschmer. www.copyrighthistory.org. Accessed on 23 October 2024; etc.

[15] John Usher's Printing Privilege, Massachusetts (1672). Primary Sources on Copyright (1450–1900). eds L. Bently & M. Kretschmer. www.copyrighthistory.org. Accessed on 23 October 2024; William Bladen's Liberty to print in Maryland (1700). Primary Sources on Copyright (1450–1900). eds L. Bently & M. Kretschmer. www.copyrighthistory.org Accessed on 23 October 2024; North Carolina Printing Privilege to Commissioners (Province) (1746), Primary Sources on Copyright (1450–1900). eds L. Bently & M. Kretschmer. www.copyrighthistory.org. Accessed on 23 October 2024; etc. See also Bracha (2010), pp. 89–114.

notable moment in copyright history; however, none of those privileges, acknowledged authorship, such as creating a property right.[16] As Gieseke states: "(…) The purpose of privileges, however, was the exclusive right to print and publish nothing else; the authorities were not concerned with the relationship between the beneficiary and the author of the work for which the privilege was granted, and the protection of the work itself, as opposed to printed copies, was merely incidental."[17] Thus, instead of protecting authorship, the privilege system was mainly concerned with the business interests of publishing-industry stakeholders and the censorship activities of the authorities. Still, in such a system, authors, as creators of literary and artistic works, received particular recognition and were commonly paid for their work.[18] Also notably, this was the era of the Renaissance and Humanism that elevated 'geniuses'—the poet, the inventor, and the artists—to unprecedented social heights. Although these circumstances were indeed a step forward towards recognising and respecting the authorship and the development of the copyright law system, the authors/creators were still usually perceived "as artisans who crafted their work according to a body of rules inherited from classical rhetoric and poetics"[19]—probably not artisans in the way as they were perceived before the Renaissance, but still not as the authors.[20]

The system of privileges preceded the establishment of a modern copyright system of law, whose foundations can be traced through the philosophical ideas mainly developed in the seventeenth and eighteenth centuries and the events that occurred during the eighteenth century and followed through the nineteenth and the twentieth centuries. The historical background of those times is rich and exciting. From the social and economic aspects, the development of printing technology induced a shift from intensive reading to extensive reading, increasing the demand for creative content. The rise of a middle-class reading public led to a boom in the printing commerce, especially in the eighteenth century.[21] Interests in literature grew

---

[16] De Wolf writes: "In all these grants of monopolies of printing we find no recognition of authorship as creating a property right. Sometimes they were given as a reward of meritorious enterprise to the printer, but oftener as a cheap way of benefiting some courtier or dependent, who was neither printer nor author and who farmed out the grant to somebody else" De Wolf (1925), pp. 2–3.

See also Dock (1974), pp. 162–172; Kostylo (2010), p. 22.

Still, even in those times, several cases can be found within European legislations in which authors claimed their rights concerning control over the publication of their texts, and even succeeded before courts; see Rose (1993), pp. 18–21.

[17] Gieseke (1957), pp. 28–36.

[18] Although, as Dock states, "As soon as a publisher bought the right to print a book, he was considered as sole owner. One did not conceive that the author could claim anything other than the amount promised in the contract"; see Dock (1974), pp. 170–182; see also Patterson (1968a), pp. 374–379.

[19] van Horn Melton (2004), p. 137.

[20] See Kostylo (2010), pp. 39–46; Salokannel (1994), pp. 57–58.

[21] Geller (2000), p. 224; Hesse (2002), pp. 31–32. Consequently, the commercialisation of literature and the demands of the reading public also encouraged a dramatic expansion of piracy. See Hesse (2002), p. 32.

tremendously, and more and more authors appeared, filling in the supply side of the market. Accordingly, the commercial aspirations of authors to receive proper remuneration for the works they created grew, mostly in opposition to the traditional guild monopolies.[22] At the same time, authors started to claim their work as their own creation and not a transmission of God's eternal truths.[23] From the philosophical aspect, the seventeenth and eighteenth centuries brought the Age of Enlightenment (Age of Reason), in which the notion of individual authorship became critical in understanding how works arise.[24] Mainly through the works of individuals such as Locke,[25] Rousseau, Kant, Hegel, Young,[26] d'Héricourt,[27] Diderot,[28] Lessing,[29] and

[22] Thus, in the mid-seventeenth century, Molière protested when a copy of his Les Précieuses ridicules fell into the hands of publishers: "It's a strange thing that one publishes people against their will... Nonetheless, I could not prevent it, and I have suffered the misfortune of having a copy, fleched from my room, fall into the hands of booksellers, who by surprise have obtained the privilege of publishing it" Olagnier (1934), p. 85.

See also Geller (2000), pp. 215–219; Grosheide (2010), p. 90; Kostylo (2010), pp. 30–31.

[23] See Hesse (2002), p. 32; Pfister (2010), pp. 129–130.

[24] See Geller (2000), p. 222; Salokannel (1994), p. 58.

[25] The new ideas of individualism, originality, and aesthetic relativism emerged in England with Locke's Two Treaties of Government from 1690; see Dock (1974), p. 182; Pfister (2010), p. 129.

[26] In regard to Young's Conjectures on Original Composition (1759), Hesse writes: "(...) the poet Edward Young, writing with the assistance of the novelist Samuel Richardson, asserted that the author contributed more than simply his labor to a book - he imprinted its contents with his original personality. According to Young, the labor of an author was thus of a higher order than the labor of an inventor, never mind the labor of a farmer, for the author not only worked upon nature, but produced something from himself, which bore the indelible stamp of a unique personality. While limits might be imposed upon patents for mechanical inventions, products of the mind-bearing the personhood of their author - ought to belong perpetually to their creator. Intellectual property, an invention of the eighteenth century, thus burst into the world claiming to be real property in its purest form" Hesse (2002), p. 33.

[27] The lawyer Louis d'Héricourt argued on behalf of provincial publishers and authors in France that an author creates and his creation belongs to him; he transfers this property to the 'libraire' with all that pertains to it, the main attribute being perpetuity. Thus, he stated: "Having no right on authors' works, the King may not transmit them to anybody without the consent of their legitimate owners... There must be no doubt that privileges which authors and 'libraires' are fore the present obliged to obtain may only be considered as genuine approvals" Louis d'Héricourt's memorandum, Paris (1725–1726).

Primary Sources on Copyright (1450–1900). eds L. Bently & M. Kretschmer. www.copyrighthistory.org. Accessed on 23 October 2024; Quote cited in Dock (1974), pp. 186–188.

[28] Diderot (1970), 5:331 (translation from: Hesse (2002) p. 34): "What form of wealth could belong to a man, if not the work of the mind... if not his own thoughts... the most precious part of himself, that will never perish, that will immortalize him? What comparison could there be between a man, the very substance of a man, his soul, and a field, a tree, a vine, that nature has offered in the beginning equally to all, and which the individual has only appropriated though cultivating it?"

[29] In his essay from 1772, Live and Let Live, Gotthold Lessing writes: "What? The writer is to be blamed for trying to make the offspring of his imagination as profitable as he can? Just because he works with his noblest faculties he isn't supposed to enjoy the satisfaction that the roughest handyman is able to procure? (...) Freely hast thou received, freely thou must give! Thus thought

Fichte,[30] the view emerged that authors have a natural property right in their ideas.[31] Thus, Locke writes: "Though the earth and all inferior creatures be common to all men, yet every man has a 'property' in his own 'person'. This nobody has any right to but himself. The 'labour' of his body and the 'work' of his hands, we may say, are properly his. Whatsoever, then, he removes out of the state that Nature hath provided and left it in, he hath mixed his labour with it, and joined to it something that is his own, and thereby makes it his property. It being by him removed from the common state Nature placed it in, it hath by this labour something annexed to it that excludes the common right of other men. For this 'labour' being the unquestionable property of the labourer, no man but he can have a right to what that is once joined to, at least where there is enough, and as good left in common for others."[32] Defoe writes: "A Book is the Author's Property, 'tis the Child of his Inventions, the Brat of his Brain: if he sells his Property, it then becomes the Right of the Purchaser'."[33] Influenced by the liberation philosophies, the idea of personality emerged, particularly in the domain of copyright law.[34,35] As Saunders writes: "The object of protection was no longer to be just a property (albeit immaterial) but the wholeness and integrity of the human person."[36] The legitimacy of being an individual creator was readily extended to all men, while the concept of originality assumed a new significance as

---

the noble Luther (...) Luther, I answer, is an exception in many things" Lessing (1772) (translation from: Hesse (2002), p. 34).

[30]The philosopher Johann Gottlieb Fichte placed the crucial question in the understanding of copyright – "if creations of the mind were indeed 'property', what exactly was immaterial property?" Within his essay Proof of the Illegality of Reprinting: A Rationale and a Parable, Fichte provided a solution that for an idea to be regarded as piece of property it had to be assigned some distinguishing characteristic that allowed one person, and no other, to claim it as his own. Thus, once published, the ideas in a book belonged to all—but the singular form of their expression remained the sole property of the author. In the essence, by distinguishing between the material and immaterial book, and content and form of ideas, Fichte considers the unique expression of ideas as the matter of 'ownership' of the authors rather than the ideas themselves. Such a concept was critical in establishing the modern copyright law system based on the natural rights of the author; see Hesse (2002), p. 35.

[31]See Hesse (2002), pp. 33–35; von Lewinski (2008), p. 37.

[32]Locke (1690), Book II, Chap. 5, Sec. 27.

[33]Quote cited from Hesse (2002), p. 32.

[34]See Grosheide (2010), p. 93.

[35]The personality theory was mainly developed through the philosophy of Immanuel Kant, the acknowledgement of Otto von Gierke and the critique of Josef Kohler; see Strowel (1993), pp. 98–101.

[36]Saunders further notes: "Rights of personality represent a logic for establishing and protecting rights of authors that is quite different to the Lockean notion of 'man's' natural right as possessor of himself and thus holder of natural property rights to the fruits of his labour. They are also expressive of something more concrete than Kant's depiction of the authorial person among the prolegomena to all actual positive rights and legal obligations" Saunders (1992), p. 115.

an aesthetic criterion.[37] Also importantly, during the late eighteenth and the nineteenth century, the concept of the idea/expression dichotomy was gradually articulated, which allowed distinguishing between the idea (the content) and the expression (the form) of a work of authorship, and also form to be distinguished from the physical carrier which made it possible to communicate the expressed idea to the public.[38] "(…) the work is intangible, the right to it covering the immaterial creation as it is shaped by its author, separate from the ownership of the tangible carrier such as the manuscript, and therefore requiring the acknowledgement of *sui generis* property right."[39] In those surroundings, grounds were set for acknowledging the 'authors' as the owners of their 'work' who can freely dispose of the rights on the work while having inalienable non-economic personal rights that constituted their continuing interest in the treatment of the work.[40] From such developments, it is also possible to trace the beginnings of the specific treatment of copyright as a particular intellectual property right.

Thus, with the development of literature, science and arts, and the ways of exploiting literary and artistic works, "norms of reprinting and copying were contested in the context of political, economic and aesthetic shifts."[41] Most notably in England, France and Germany, the situation was the following—readers wanted cheaper books; governments wanted to increase commerce and have a more educated population within their realms; primarily provincial and foreign publishers without (or a few) privileges were fighting against publishers that held privileges; authors wanted recognition of their rights as absolute and perpetual.[42] Under such circumstances, the need for a legal framework emerged, which resulted in a legislative movement in copyright law during the eighteenth and nineteenth centuries.

---

[37] Pfister (2010), pp. 129–130.

[38] The distinction between the idea and the expression, followed Fichte's concern to locate an incontestable ground for a claim of authorial property, to draw a distinction between a book that can be owned by anybody who acquires it, and the form that the authors give to their ideas, which regardless of being published, remain forever their exclusive property. In addition to that, Kant further contributed in the concept of differentiating between the authorial *ius personalium* and the publisher's personal right to publish once the authorial mandate was obtained. See Grosheide (1986), pp. 221–236; Saunders (1992), pp. 109–115.

[39] See Grosheide (2010), p. 99; Kohler (1880, 1892).

[40] Thus, van Horn Melton writes: "It was not just the quantity of literary producers that made the eighteenth century, relative to previous periods, the age of the author. The modern idea of the author was itself an eighteenth-century creation... And only in the eighteenth century did there emerge the idea of authorship as ownership, or what we today call copyright, with authors considered the proprietors of works that could not be published or sold without their consent... Authors at the same time acquired a new cultural and political identity" van Horn Melton (2004), pp. 123–124; see also Saunders (1992), p. 115.

[41] Kretschmer et al. (2010), p. 6.

[42] See Hesse (2002), pp. 32–33.

The first copyright act is considered to be the British Statute of Anne from 1710.[43,44] Afterwards, France introduced its first copyright legislation in 1791[45] and 1793,[46]

---

[43] An Act for the Encouragement of Learning, by Vesting the Copies of Printed Books in the Authors or Purchasers of such Copies, During the Times therein mentioned, 1710, 8 Anne, c.19 (1710). Primary Sources on Copyright (1450–1900). eds L. Bently & M. Kretschmer. www.copyrighthistory.org. Accessed on 23 October 2024; see Atkinson and Fitzgerald (2014), p. 234; De Wolf (1925), pp. 6–7; Dock (1974), p. 186; Recht (1969), p. 22; van Horn Melton (2004), p. 138.

The Statute of Anne was preceded by the issue of licensing and an attempt to introduce a licensing bill that would provide for censorship without securing literary property; and was followed by a commercial struggle between opposing groups of booksellers, often referred to as 'the battle of booksellers', in which the central issue became the exact nature of authors rights. On the historical setting of the Statute of Anne, see Cornish (2010), pp. 14–2; Rose (1993), pp. 31–36, 67–91.

[44] Some scholars consider that one should be cautious when referring to the Statute of Anne as the first copyright act, due to the following: the Statute of Anne in substance did not bring anything new, it did not use the term 'copyright' or refer to the right to print and reprint books, it was mainly concerned with the regulation of published books and not the protection of authorship. Also, it imposed formalities of registration and deposit of copies as a prerequisite for protection. In that sense, Patterson writes: "(...) At the time the Statute of Anne was enacted, there was only one concept of copyright known to the legislators - the stationer's copyright. Their problem was not to create a new copyright, but to limit the old, in order to destroy the monopoly of the book trade by the booksellers - who, incidentally, were the lobbyists for the legislation."

See Bently (2010), pp. 7–13; Patterson (1968b), pp. 12–13. The historical significance of the Statue of Anne seems questionable, too; see Suarez (2010), pp. 66–68.

[45] This law only covered theatre works of authors. See Report of Le Chapelier on Dramatic Author's property (with the Decree adopted by the National Assembly). Paris (1791). Primary Sources on Copyright (1450–1900). eds L. Bently & M. Kretschmer. www.copyrighthistory.org. Accessed on 23 October 2024; Legislation French law of 13 January 1791, concerning the works of living playwrights, Primary Sources on Copyright (1450–1900). eds L. Bently & M. Kretschmer. www.copyrighthistory.org. Accessed on 23 October 2024; Hesse (2002), p. 126.

[46] Decree of the National Convention, 19 July 1793, regarding the property rights of authors to writings of all kinds, of composers of music, of painters and illustrators (with the report of Lakanal) (orig. Décret de la Convention Nationale du dix-neuf juillet 1793 relatif aux droits de propriété des Auteurs d'écrits en tout genre, des Compositeurs de musique, des Peintres et des Dessinateurs (avec le rapport de Lakanal)), Primary Sources on Copyright (1450–1900). eds L. Bently & M. Kretschmer. www.copyrighthistory.org. Accessed on 23 October 2024.

The enactment of two decrees from 1791 and 1793 was preceded by a quite chaotic period of struggle that included provincial (and some Paris) *libraries*, which held no or a few privileges, Paris *libraries*, which held most of the privileges, authors who were fighting for their position, authority with their own interests. As a result of that situation, the Crown's Edicts of 1777 and 1778 established privileges as legally grounded favours and recognised authors' right to publish and sell their work. However, those types of privileges were still not satisfactory for the parties involved. Later, only after the suppression of privileges, did the authorities decide to finally legalise authors' rights. The two decrees that were ultimately brought were far from being adequate or satisfactory; however, despite their deficiencies, those laws remained in force until the mid-twentieth century; see Decree of the King's Council of State, containing regulations on the duration of book trade privileges, 30 August 1777 (orig. Arrest du Conseil d'Etat du Roi, Portant Règlement sur la durée des Priviléges en Librairie. Du 30 août 1777). Paris (1777). Primary Sources on Copyright (1450–1900). eds L. Bently & M. Kretschmer. www.copyrighthistory.org. Accessed on 23 October 2024; Decree of the King's Council of State, containing regulations on book trade privileges and

and Prussia in 1794.[47] Laws enacted in particular countries were far from being adequate; however, they did provide legislative recognition of authorship and set foundations for developing copyright law systems.

Also, it is noteworthy, particularly in the context of the discussion on the copyright-competition interaction, that already in this early phase of copyright law systems, two main approaches to copyright law started to diverge one from the other. Namely, not everyone agreed with the concept, which mainly influenced continental civil-law legislations, that there is a natural right to a perpetual property in ideas and that legal recognition of that right was simply the statutory confirmation of a universal natural right. Some opponents, such as Condorcet, argued that: "There can be no relationship between property in ideas and [property] in a field, which can serve only one man. [Literary property] is not a property derived from the natural order and defended by social force; it is a property founded in society itself. It is not a true right; it is a privilege."[48] According to such a view of social utilitarianism, "there was no natural property in ideas, and that granting exclusive legal rights to individuals for unique forms of their expression could only be justified because such an arrangement was the best legal mechanism for encouraging the production and transmission of new ideas, a manifest public good."[49] During the eighteenth century, within European countries series of legal battles occurred over which principle should prevail—the natural rights' sanctity of the individual creator or the utilitarian's public interest as the highest aim of the law. Although most of Europe ultimately endorsed the natural rights concept as the foundation of civil law copyright tradition, England shifted towards the utilitarian concept, which would become the foundation of the common law copyright tradition.[50] Although earlier cases, *Tonson v Collins* (1760) and *Millar v Taylor* (1769), led briefly to the recognition of perpetual property rights in the unique expression of ideas, the *Donaldson v Beckett*

---

counterfeitings. 30 July 1778 (orig. Arrêt du Conseil d'Etat du Roi portant réglement sur les privilèges en librairie et les contrefaçons, Du 30 juillet 1778). Paris (1778). Primary Sources on Copyright (1450–1900). eds L. Bently & M. Kretschmer. www.copyrighthistory.org. Accessed on 23 October 2024. See Dock (1974), pp. 186–200; Hesse (1990), pp. 109–137; Pfister (2010), pp. 127–135.

[47] However, the Prussian Statute Book did not define the rights of the authors in their role as partners to an agreement with the publisher. The Baden Code from 1809 determined copyright as a property right of the author, limited to lifetime, for the first time in Germany. Later, Prussia enacted the then most modern copyright legislation in the Law for the Protection of Property in Works of Scholarship and the Arts against Reprinting and Reproduction. Soon followed, the copyright laws of Saxony (1844), Bavaria (1865), North German Confederation (1870). See Vogel (2010), pp. 116–121, 119–120.

There are different opinions in theory on the importance of events that contributed to the recognition of authorship and preceded the copyright legislation. Some believe that the Prussian Civil Code of 1794 recognised the author's right in Article 1294. See Kohler (1907), para. 9 (VI), pp. 68 *et seq.*; Gieseke (1957), p. 79; Bappert (1962), pp. 258 *et seq.*; Recht (1969), p. 43.

[48] Quote cited in Hesse (2002), p. 35; see also van Horn Melton (2004), p. 143.

[49] Hesse (2002), p. 36.

[50] See Grosheide (1994), pp. 203–234, 207; Stewart (1983), pp. 6–8.

(1774) case reversed findings from those judgements and established the concept of a 'limited property right' in the unique expression of ideas through which the utilitarian doctrine of a higher public good trumped the idea of copyright rooted in natural right.[51] On such a development, Patterson comments: "The major consequence of the change of copyright from a publisher's right to an author's right, then, was this: instead of being a limited right in connection with a work for an unlimited period of time, it became an unlimited right for a limited period of time. Unfortunately, the lawmakers passed over the desirable alternative which the Statute of Anne might have been interpreted to provide—a limited right for a limited period of time. Acceptance of this alternative would have had two results: it would have enabled the courts to deal directly with monopoly as a problem of publishers rather than authors; and it would have given the courts an opportunity, which they never had, to develop a body of law in the interest of the author as a creator, to enable him to protect the integrity of his work. Such a body of law, which exists in civil-law countries under the name of moral right, is warranted on its own merits, for any creative endeavor is an extension of one's personality."[52] Following England, the United States (and most of the English-speaking world—the former British colonies and the countries of the British Commonwealth[53])[54] also endorsed the utilitarian approach, which is even incorporated in the Federal Constitution of 1787,[55] and became the basis of the US Copyright Statute (1790).[56] Some argue that the differences between the natural rights and utilitarian-based approaches were not significantly expressed, particularly during this early period. Notably, most European countries went through the same debate, and seminal copyright laws shared similar Enlightenment values. Thus, even in the countries that adopted the civil-law approach, the utilitarian approach certainly left its mark (especially in France), while common-law countries did not remain utterly resistant to the natural rights concept.[57] However, the fact is that this eighteenth and nineteenth-century divergence in fundamental approaches most certainly influenced the further

---

[51] See Hesse (2002), pp. 36–37; Rose (1994), pp. 23–57.

Patterson implies that the departure of common law from the author's right indeed started with the enactment of the Statute of Anne; see Patterson (1968a), pp. 370–371.

[52] Patterson (1968b), p. 18.

[53] See for India: Das (2008), pp. 89–93.

[54] See Goldstein and Hugenholtz (2021), p. 13.

[55] "Congress shall have the power... to promote the progress of Science and useful Arts, by securing for limited Times to Authors and Inventors the exclusive Right to their respective Writings and Discoveries" The Constitution of the United States of America. https://www.senate.gov/civics/resources/pdf/US_Constitution-Senate_Publication_103-21.pdf. Accessed on 23 October 2024, Article 1, Section 8, Clause 8.

[56] US, An Act for the encouragement of learning, by securing the copies of maps, charts, and books, to the authors and proprietors of such copies, during the times therein mentioned, of May 31, 1790, 1 Stat. 124.

[57] See Ginsburg (1990), pp. 991–1031; Geller (1994), pp. 161–164; Goldstein (1989b), pp. 685–686; Strowel (1994), pp. 235–253, 248. With regard to copyright, societies and legislations besides Western Europe and the United States, countries such as China, Russia, Middle Eastern

development of copyright law in continental and Anglo-Saxon legislations. The differences among the systems are still present nowadays, especially regarding the philosophical perception of copyright, the scope of the protection, moral rights, ownership and joint ownership, the role of formalities, limitations and exceptions, transfer/licensing of rights, etc.

Initially, debates over copyright were held on a national level. Namely, during the eighteenth century and the early nineteenth century, copyright was mainly a matter of national concern. The reason for this may be found in the limited intercourse and communication between nations.[58] The interest in international copyright protection grew during the nineteenth century with the industrial revolution; development of cultural industries; increased trade, communication and travel between countries; democratisation of knowledge; the ascent of the bourgeoisie, etc.[59] This development opened the issue of cross-border protection of copyright works, particularly in the states where the same language was spoken, such as the German states. Consequently, in the late first part of the nineteenth century, intra-German treaties were signed among German states, after which followed a series of intra-state treaties concluded between European states and even beyond.[60] The system of bilateral treaties was indeed a step forward in the issue of international copyright protection; however, this system had several weaknesses and was generally unsatisfactory. Thus, dissatisfaction with the bilateral treaties system and recognising the universal character of works steered discussions on the internationalisation of copyright towards the system of multilateral treaties.[61]

In the mid-nineteenth century, the strong initiative was to unify copyright laws on the international level to coordinate the protection of authors and rights holders between nations.[62] Following the three congresses—the Brussels Congress 1858, the Antwerp Congresses 1861 and 1877 and the International Literary and Artistic Congresses 1878—the first copyright multilateral treaty was created. Therein, the central role in the development of copyright internalisation was played by the *Association Littéraire et Artistique International* (ALAI), founded in 1878 by Victor Hugo, its main objective being to promote international recognition of the legal protection of authors for their intellectual work.[63] The Brussels ALAI drafted the document that would eventually become the Berne Convention for the Protection of Literary and

---

countries, African countries and South American countries, had certain tensions between the concept of authors' natural rights and the utilitarian approach, as well; see Hesse (2002), p. 44.

[58] See Geller (2000), pp. 228–235; Ploman and Hamilton (1980), p. 18.

[59] See Ploman and Hamilton (1980), pp. 18–19.

[60] See von Lewinski (2008), pp. 14–16.

[61] See von Lewinski (2008), p. 23; see also Saunders (1992), pp. 170–173.

[62] See Goldstein and Hugenholtz (2021), pp. 9–10.

von Lewinski indicates that already in the mid-eighteenth century, there were advocates for the introduction of the international protection of authors' rights in their works; see von Lewinski (2008), pp. 13–14, 23–32.

[63] See Association Littéraire et Artistique Internationale (ALAI) (n.d.).

Artistic Works (1886)[64]—the oldest multilateral copyright convention.[65] The signing and adoption of the Berne Convention was the turning point in the further development of copyright law around the globe. The Berne Convention established a Union for the protection of the rights of authors in their literary and artistic works. Also, the Berne Convention introduced minimum standards of protection for authors through various measures imposed on Contracting Parties and three basic principles—the principle of national treatment, the principle of automatic protection and the principle of independence of protection. The Berne Convention was revised and complemented numerous times to accommodate new technological developments (Paris 1896, Berlin 1908, Berne 1914, Rome 1928, Brussels 1948, Stockholm 1967, Paris 1971).

Following the Berne Convention, the treaty-based systems of international copyright law continued to develop intensively, especially after the 1950s and the post-WWII politics, internationalism, decolonisation, politics of economic hegemony, and new technological developments—1910 Buenos Aires Convention,[66] 1952 UNESCO's Universal Copyright Convention (UCC),[67] 1961 The Rome Convention for the Protection of Performers, Producers of Phonograms and Broadcasting Organizations,[68] 1971 The Convention for the Protection of Producers of Phonograms Against Unauthorized Duplication of Their Phonograms,[69] 1974 The Convention Relating to the Distribution of Programme-Carrying Signals Transmitted by Satellite,[70] 1994 WTO's Agreement on Trade-Related Aspects of Intellectual Property Rights (the TRIPS Agreement),[71] 1996 WIPO Copyright Treaty,[72] 1996 WIPO

[64] Berne Convention for the Protection of Literary and Artistic Works, Sept. 9, 1886, as revised at Paris on July 24, 1971 and amended in 1979, S. Treaty Doc. No. 99-27 (1986).

[65] See Karnell (2016), p. 413. Goldstein and Hugenholtz state that the Berne Convention is the supreme international copyright treaty; see Goldstein and Hugenholtz (2021), pp. 44–45.

[66] Convention on Literary and Artistic Works Copyright (The Buenos Aires Convention), 11 August 1910. https://www.wipo.int/edocs/lexdocs/treaties/en/bac/trt_bac_001en.pdf. Accessed on 22 October 2024.

[67] Universal Copyright Convention, with Appendix Declaration relating to Articles XVII and Resolution concerning Article XI, 1952. https://www.unesco.org/en/legal-affairs/universal-copyright-convention-appendix-declaration-relating-article-xvii-and-resolution-concerning. Accessed on 22 October 2024.

[68] International Convention for the Protection of Performers, Producers of Phonograms and Broadcasting Organisations (Rome Convention), Rome, October 26, 1961. https://www.wipo.int/edocs/pubdocs/en/wipo_pub_328.pdf. Accessed on 22 October 2024.

[69] Convention for the Protection of Producers of Phonograms Against Unauthorized Duplication of Their Phonograms, 29 October 1971. https://wipolex.wipo.int/en/text/288579. Accessed on 23 October 2024.

[70] Brussels Convention Relating to the Distribution of Programme-Carrying Signals Transmitted by Satellite, 21 May 1974. Accessed on 23 October 2024.

[71] The Agreement on Trade-Related Aspects of Intellectual Property Rights (TRIPS), 1 January 1995. https://www.wto.org/english/docs_e/legal_e/27-trips.pdf. Accessed on 22 October 2024.

[72] The WIPO Copyright Treaty (WCT), 20 December 1996. https://wipolex.wipo.int/en/treaties/textdetails/12740. Accessed on 22 October 2024.

Performances and Phonograms Treaty,[73] 2011 The Anti-Counterfeiting Trade Agreement (ACTA),[74] 2012 The Beijing Treaty on Audiovisual Performances 2013,[75] the Marrakesh VIP Treaty.[76] Nonetheless, despite the convergence of national laws through international treaties, the territorial nature of copyright has remained and prevented the emergence of substantive copyright norms with supranational effects. As coined, and Goldstein and Hughenholtz further elaborate, nowadays, international copyright resembles a 'patchwork' of independent national laws, each with its own rules on the subject matter, ownership of rights and scope, and each exacting specific requirements of foreign works as a condition for protection.[77]

In that sense, in parallel with the internationalisation of copyright during the nineteenth and twentieth centuries, national legislations started enacting modern copyright laws to conform with the development of copyright and its international aspect. Thus, and by not entering into the qualitative analysis of particular laws, Austria enacted its modern copyright act in 1936, Denmark in 1961, Finland in 1961, France in 1957, Germany in 1870, Iceland in 1972, Italy in 1925, Norway in 1961, the Soviet Union in 1925, Sweden in 1960, the United Kingdom in 1911, the United States in 1909, Yugoslavia in 1929, etc.[78] The scope of copyright was rapidly growing following the immense development of industry and technology. However, as Strömholm observes, "it seems fair to state that towards the middle of the 1960s copyright as elaborated by the 19th century jurists had shown its capacity to meet new situations without profoundly modifying the foundations upon which its normal and intellectual identity was based."[79] To keep up with advances in industry and technology, from covering only literature and artistic works, over the years, copyright protection expanded to cover photographs, films, sound recordings, broadcasting, computer programs, databases, etc.[80] In the meantime, the development of copyright also manifested the need for recognition of related rights.[81]

---

[73] The WIPO Performance and Phonogram Treaty (WPPT), 20 December 1996. https://wipolex.wipo.int/en/treaties/textdetails/12743. Accessed on 22 October 2024.

[74] Anti-Counterfeiting Trade Agreement (ACTA) European Parliament resolution of 24 November 2010 on the Anti-Counterfeiting Trade Agreement (ACTA), OJ C 99E, 3.4.2012, pp. 27–29.

Unlike the other treaties, ACTA is not in force and, at the moment, it does not seem likely that it will ever be.

[75] Beijing Treaty on Audiovisual Performances, 24 June 2012. https://www.wipo.int/edocs/mdocs/copyright/en/avp_dc/avp_dc_20.pdf. Accessed on 22 October 2024.

[76] Marrakesh Treaty to Facilitate Access to Published Works for Persons Who Are Blind, Visually Impaired, or Otherwise Print Disabled, 27 June 2013. https://wipolex.wipo.int/en/treaties/textdetails/13169. Accessed on 22 October 2024.

[77] See Geller (1998), pp. 69–90; Goldstein and Hugenholtz (2021), pp. 9–10. On the direct applicability of the international copyright treaties, see Goldstein and Hugenholtz (2021), pp. 25–27.

[78] See Stewart (1983), pp. 311–642.

[79] Strömholm (1976), pp. 1, 29.

[80] See Skone James, Mummery, Rayner James, Garnett, Nimmer, Silman, Skone James (1991), pp. 1–2.

[81] The first organised response to the need for the legal protection of these three categories of related rights was the conclusion of the 1961 Rome Convention; International Convention for the Protection of Performers, Producers of Phonograms and Broadcasting Organisations (Rome Convention),

In the late second half of the twentieth century, the EU had also recognised the importance and economic value of copyright within the EU single market and the need for its partial harmonisation on a regional level. Thus, the EU started developing copyright policies, although the competence for such intervention is questionable and is often accompanied by many struggles among different national copyright legislations and opposing interests.[82] In 1991, the EU initiated its legislative actions towards the harmonisation of copyright. It adopted several legal acts, although even before that initiative, there were the ECJ's judgments dealing with the matter of copyright on the EU level.[83,84] Thus, the EU enacted Directive 91/250/EC on the legal protection of computer programs.[85] Also, in this first phase of harmonisation, the EU legislative actions comprised rental, lending and related rights,[86] satellite broadcasting and cable retransmission,[87] term of protection and related rights,[88] databases,[89] information society[90] and resale

Rome, October 26, 1961. https://www.wipo.int/edocs/pubdocs/en/wipo_pub_328.pdf. Accessed on 22 October 2024.

[82] See Littoz-Monnet (2006), pp. 438–455.

[83] Dreier (2002).

[84] Also, in 1988 the Commission issued the Green Paper on Copyright and the Challenges of Technology issues requiring immediate action, which may be considered as a first step towards the harmonisation of Member States' national copyright law legislations; Green paper on Copyright and the Challenges of Technology issues requiring immediate action, 7 June 1988, COM (88) 172 final.

[85] Council Directive 91/250/EEC of 14 May 1991 on the legal protection of computer programs, OJ L 122, 17.5.1991, pp. 42–46; now: Directive 2009/24/EC of the European Parliament and of the Council of 23 April 2009 on the legal protection of computer programs (Codified version), OJ L 111, 5.5.2009, pp. 16–22.

[86] Council Directive 92/100/EEC of 19 November 1992 on rental right and lending right and on certain rights related to copyright in the field of intellectual property, OJ L 346, 27.11.1992, pp. 61–66; now: Directive 2006/115/EC of the European Parliament and of the Council of 12 December 2006 on rental right and lending right and on certain rights related to copyright in the field of intellectual property (codified version), OJ L 376, 27.12.2006, pp. 28–35.

[87] Council Directive 93/83/EEC of 27 September 1993 on the coordination of certain rules concerning copyright and rights related to copyright applicable to satellite broadcasting and cable retransmission, OJ L 248, 6.10.1993, pp. 15–21.

[88] Council Directive 93/98/EEC of 29 October 1993 harmonising the term of protection of copyright and certain related rights, OJ L 290, 24.11.1993, pp. 9–13; now: Directive 2006/116/EC of the European Parliament and of the Council of 12 December 2006 on the term of protection of copyright and certain related rights (codified version), OJ L 372, 27.12.2006, pp. 12–18 and Directive 2011/77/EU of the European Parliament and of the Council of 27 September 2011 amending Directive 2006/116/EC on the term of protection of copyright and certain related rights, OJ L 265, 11.10.2011, pp. 1–5.

[89] Directive 96/9/EC of the European Parliament and of the Council of 11 March 1996 on the legal protection of databases, OJ L 77, 27.3.1996, pp. 20–28.

[90] Directive 2001/29/EC of the European Parliament and of the Council of 22 May 2001 on the harmonisation of certain aspects of copyright and related rights in the information society, OJ L 167, 22.06.2001, pp. 10–19.

rights.[91] In a second phase, the focus was laid on balancing the need to preserve European cultural heritage and the need to make content accessible online. Other points of focus were: to respect copyright and to reward the authors (with particular focus on the issue of orphan works),[92] out-of-print or out-of-commerce works,[93] dealing with issues of collective societies and cross-border licensing[94] and enabling access to copyright-protected works for certain categories of disabled persons.[95] In the latest phase, the EU was guided by the thesis: "Europe needs a more harmonised copyright regime which provides incentives to create and invest while allowing transmission and consumption of content across borders, building on our rich cultural diversity."[96] Within the Digital Single Market Strategy,[97] as a part of the EU Digital Agenda[98] the EU rendered Regulation 2017/1128 on cross-border portability of online content services in the Single Internal Market[99] and Directive (EU) 2019/790 on copyright and related rights in the Digital Single Market[100] and Directive (EU) 2019/789 laying down rules on the exercise of copyright and related rights applicable to certain online transmissions of

[91] Directive 2001/84/EC of the European Parliament and of the Council of 27 September 2001 on the resale right for the benefit of the author of an original work of art, OJ L 272, 13.10.2001, pp. 32–36.

[92] Directive 2012/28/EU of the European Parliament and of the Council of 25 October 2012 on certain permitted uses of orphan works, OJ L 299, 27.10.2012, pp. 5–12.

[93] Memorandum of Understanding, Key Principles on the Digitisation and Making Available of Out-of-Commerce Works, MEMO/11/619, Brussels, 20.9.2011.

[94] Directive 2014/26/EU of the European Parliament and of the Council of 26 February 2014 on collective management of copyright and related rights and multi-territorial licensing of rights in musical works for online use in the internal market, OJ L 84, 20.3.2014, pp. 72–98.

[95] Directive (EU) 2017/1564 of the European Parliament and of the Council of 13 September 2017 on certain permitted uses of certain works and other subject matter protected by copyright and related rights for the benefit of persons who are blind, visually impaired or otherwise print-disabled and amending Directive 2001/29/EC on the harmonisation of certain aspects of copyright and related rights in the information society, OJ L 242, 20.9.2017, pp. 6–13.

[96] Communication from the Commission to the European Parliament, the Council, the European Economic and Social Committee and the Committee of the Regions, *A Digital Single Market Strategy*, COM(2015) 192 final, p. 7.

[97] Communication from the Commission to the European Parliament, the Council, the European Economic and Social Committee and the Committee of the Regions, *A Digital Single Market Strategy*, COM(2015) 192 final.

[98] European Commission, Digital Single Market: Europe 2020 Strategy, 20.2.2015. https://ec.europa.eu/digital-single-market/en/europe-2020-strategy. Accessed on 23 October 2024. See also Communication from the Commission to the European Parliament, the Council, the European Economic and Social Committee and the Committee of the Regions "Towards a modern, more European copyright framework" COM(2015) 626, final.

[99] Regulation (EU) 2017/1128 of the European Parliament and of the Council of 14 June 2017 on cross-border portability of online content services in the internal market, OJ L 168, 30.6.2017, pp. 1–11.

[100] Directive (EU) 2019/790 of the European Parliament and of the Council of 17 April 2019 on copyright and related rights in the Digital Single Market and amending Directives 96/9/EC and 2001/29/EC, PE/51/2019/REV/1, OJ L 130, 17.5.2019, pp. 92–125.

broadcasting organisations and retransmissions of television and radio programmes.[101] Also, in the harmonisation of copyright law within the EU, it is important to note the fundamental role of the CJEU in interpreting and creating EU copyright law. However, despite the EU's interventions in the field of copyright, every Member State still preserves their own systems of national copyright laws, among which differences are respected.

Nowadays, copyright is facing issues stemming from the ongoing digital revolution. Especially throughout the last decade, the evolution of digital technologies has changed the way work and other protected subject matters are created, produced, distributed and exploited. New uses, actors and business models have emerged. Cross-border uses have also intensified, and new opportunities for consumers to access copyright-protected content have materialised. Throughout history, the development of copyright has always been closely linked to technological developments and occurrences in society. However, legal thoughts do not always promptly follow the requirements of society and industry. Therefore, to adequately address the challenges of the immersive development of digital industries, copyright must further develop and provide new interpretations suitable for new forms of copyright-protected works and their mode of exploitation. Generally, the civil-law systems have fewer problems adapting to newly emerged ways of exploiting copyright. In the natural rights concept of copyright, the author enjoys the right to control the exploitation of the work entirely, so any new ways of use, such as digital uses, are automatically covered by the existing protection. Recognition of such new objects and uses of copyright does not represent an extension of copyright but simply corresponds to the principle that authors enjoy an exclusive right in the material and non-material exploitation of their work.[102] The bigger problem is in the common-law systems requiring legislative interventions to adapt to newly-emerged ways of exploiting copyright. The reason for that is the fact that in those systems, the main idea is that copyright is granted by the state rather than being a natural consequence of creation—so granted exclusive rights are comprehensively listed and precisely defined.[103] However, those systems are not the focus of this research and shall not be addressed aside from particular comparative purposes.

All the above indicate that the economic impact of copyright has become immense. Initially, the establishment of modern copyright has its roots in the development of the printing industry, which triggered the system of privileges. When cheap copies of literary works could be made—copyright gained its economic relevance, and the need to protect the author (and the publisher) from potential infringement of their works emerged. Copyright continued to follow technological

[101] Directive (EU) 2019/789 of the European Parliament and of the Council of 17 April 2019 laying down rules on the exercise of copyright and related rights applicable to certain online transmissions of broadcasting organisations and retransmissions of television and radio programmes, and amending Council Directive 93/83/EEC, PE/7/2019/REV/1, OJ L 130, 17.5.2019, pp. 82–91.

[102] See von Lewinski (2008), pp. 54–55.

[103] von Lewinski (2008), p. 55.

development and gradually spread its focus to other cultural industries such as sound recordings, movies, broadcasting, computer programs, databases, etc., nowadays some of the most profitable industries in the world. With the growth of economic factors, copyright has started to be more intensely associated with national economic and cultural growth. Such development is gradually attracting more and more stakeholders to be involved in copyright industries and drawing the attention of regulatory and supervisory authorities.

That brings us to the point when it should be clearer why, at a certain point in time, copyright law, as substantially a private law, started to draw concerns of competition law, as a public-law discipline. Before further analysing this matter, it is necessary to clarify the nature, purpose and justification of copyright law, and then of competition law.

2.1.2 Nature and Rationale of Copyright Law

Copyright is a national law. There is no uniform worldwide copyright, so authors can only hold a bundle of national, independent rights.[104] Still, despite some variations arising from different legal traditions and national implementations, a handful of universal rules and principles underpin national copyright laws.[105] It is, therefore, possible to discuss a copyright matter from a global or regional perspective.

Lines can sometimes be blurred even between the two main copyright traditions, despite their clear theoretical and some practical differences. Although the civil-law oriented authorship-norms dictate rules to empower authors to control the use by others of their self-expression, while common-law market-place-norms focus on rules to maintain a reliable market in products of the mind—both approaches often lead to much the same result.[106] Thus, on the two different approaches, Geller considers: "The difference between them in theory, however, is greater than it is in practice. Only in certain hard cases do these distinct norms tend to lead to different results, generating tensions (…)."[107] It does not seem unreasonable to agree with such thoughts, particularly when discussing a subject that mainly concerns the economic, corporate aspect of copyright, where differences are less pronounced.[108] Even if copyright is discussed as universally as possible, the fundamental differences between different copyright systems should be respected. As von Lewinski stated on

[104] See von Lewinski (2008), p. 6.

[105] See Goldstein and Hugenholtz (2021), p. 3.

[106] See Geller (1994), pp. 159–160, 170; Goldstein and Hugenholtz (2021), pp. 5–7, 13–14.

[107] Geller (1994), p. 170.

[108] Yet, one must not forget that the differences between common-law and civil-law copyright created many difficulties in the process of internationalisation of copyright, especially from the mid-1980s when the increased economic importance of copyright resulted in more competition and a more aggressive pursuit in achieving particular trade and industry interests of countries and big market players; see von Lewinski (2008), pp. 33–35, 54–55.

the issue of bridging the gap between both systems: "The most 'sustainable' way in dealing with these differences would certainly be to exercise basic respect for the existing differences, which are so closely related to fundamental concepts and cultural views."[109]

This research focuses on a particular copyright matter that has become a significant issue at the regional level of the European Union. Although the research tries to follow what Grosheide named as a 'legal-tradition indifferent point of view',[110] considering the nature and national character of copyright, it is impossible to adopt such an approach fully. Differences between national copyright systems undoubtedly exist, even within the same traditions. However, for the purpose of dealing with the issue of the copyright-competition interaction, it ought to be sufficient to discuss copyright in general from a regional perspective. In the further elaboration, the nature and rationales of copyright will be briefly presented mainly in the spirit of the civil-law tradition. Given that the United Kingdom, as one of the pioneers of the common-law approach, has left the EU, it is now more convenient to discuss a copyright matter that concerns an issue at the EU level.[111] Besides, the rationale of this research is to provide a general solution to the copyright-competition interaction within the EU. When a particular case concerning the copyright-competition interaction occurs, with regard to copyright, the case will certainly be discussed under the rules of the appropriate national copyright law. However, the main copyright principles and rationales on the EU level must be endorsed to avoid possible interesting interpretations of copyright law.

Also, for practical reasons, because there is no adequate alternative in the English language, in the thesis, the notion of 'copyright' is used in its broader sense, primarily in keeping with the meaning of the terminology in civil-law legislation such as *droit d'auteur, Urheberrecht, del diritto di autore, del derecho de autor, auteursrecht, autorsko pravo*, etc., however, still encompassing all subject-matter that can be qualified as copyright under the Berne Convention.[112] The subject of copyright-competition interaction is international, but it is here mainly discussed on the regional level of the EU; hence, it is useful (and probably even necessary) to use joint terminology in such discussions.

Taking into consideration the above technical remarks, in further elaboration, the main principles and rationales of copyright law are discussed to set the grounds for discussing the issue of copyright-competition interaction.

---

[109] von Lewinski (2008), p. 63.

[110] Grosheide (1994), p. 204.

[111] Now, only Ireland and Cyprus belong to the common-law tradition.

[112] Grosheide faces the same terminological issue, see Grosheide (1994), p. 204. For a more detailed discussion on the terminology issue on copyright, see Strowel (1993), pp. 17–27.

Several general grounds or justifications for copyright are a result of its historical development. First, there is a common social justice that the authors should be able to benefit from the fruits of their labour, whereas the royalties can be looked on as a sort of intellectual worker's salary. Second, for the benefit of cultural progress, by copyright protection, the authors will be encouraged to continue creating new works, thus enriching the world of literature, drama, music, information technology and science. Third, from the economic aspect, copyright protection enables that investments in the creation of works (both tangible and intangible) and the exploitation of copyright are more easily paid off, ultimately making the result of a creation more lucrative. Fourth, from the moral aspect, the work is indeed the personal expression of the author's ideas and thoughts; hence, authors should be given the right to freely decide whether, when and how their work may be reproduced or performed in public, as well as to prevent mutilations and changes. Fifth, copyright can also be considered to contribute to national prestige since copyright works ultimately enrich the cultural heritage of a nation.[113]

The theoretical foundations of the civil-law tradition of copyright law lay in the concept of natural-law theory and personality doctrines. In the centre of the civil-law tradition is the author. Works of the mind spring from acts of personal creation, and they are considered to be linked with the creators' personalities and remain with them throughout life and beyond. A work of authorship is, in effect, an extension of the author's personality.[114] In that sense, copyright law originates ex persona and follows a rights approach by linking copyright protection and granting particular legal competence.[115] In other words, products of creativity are the extension of the author—authors' creations naturally belong

[113] See Ploman and Hamilton (1980), p. 24.

[114] Still, even within the civil-law tradition, there is a difference between the monist theory and the dualist theory of copyright. According to the monist theory followed in Germany, moral (or personal) rights are inseparable from economic (property) rights, while according to the dualist theory, followed in France, economic right is alienable and subject to a limited term, and to exemptions and statutory licenses dictated by market realities, but moral right is perpetual and inalienable. See Goldstein and Hugenholtz (2021), pp. 5, 18–19.

[115] According to the common-law approach, copyright originates ex lege and follows a remedy approach, searching for appropriate remedies in individual cases.

to them, and the protection is justified as a matter of right and justice.[116] As Goldstein well said: "(…) authors receive protection for their creations not because they need protection as an inducement for their efforts, but rather because they deserve protection as an inherent natural right attaching to the act of creation."[117,118] In such manner, the French Intellectual Property Code stated: "The author of the work of the mind shall enjoy in that work, by the mere fact of its creation, an exclusive incorporeal property right which shall be enforceable against all persons."[119] Consequently, copyright is an absolute, unrestricted, and essentially individualistic natural right ('sacred right'[120])[121]—a

---

[116] See von Lewinski (2008), p. 38. According to the opposing common-law tradition, copyright is created by the legislator, and is justified because it is necessary to stimulate creation and thereby enhance the general well-being of societies. Copyright is in essence is the right to prevent the copying of physical material, at protecting the copyright owner against reproduction or the use of that material without reproduction. See Stewart (1983), pp. 7–8; von Lewinski (2008), pp. 37–38. Nevertheless, according to the national reports presented by Ginsburg, most copyright regimes combine all the leading rationales of both traditions to some extent; see Ginsburg (2019), pp. 20–26.

[117] Goldstein (1989a), p. 8.

[118] According to the utilitarian approach of the common-law tradition, as adopted in the US, the principles of copyright aim to promote culture and education by encouraging the production of the widest possible array of literary, musical and artistic works, for which economic reward is an incentive. Thus, social benefit holds the central position of copyright. However, the natural rights theory is not utterly rejected and enjoys a certain place even in US copyright law; see ibid., pp. 4, 8–9, 63–64.

[119] France, Intellectual Property Code, Art. L. 111-1.

[120] According to Le Chapelier: "the most sacred, the most legitimate, the most unassailable, and as it were, the most personal of all property, is the work which is the fruit of a writer's thoughts."

See Report of Le Chapelier on Dramatic Author's property (with the Decree adopted by the National Assembly). Paris (1791). Primary Sources on Copyright (1450–1900). eds L. Bently & M. Kretschmer. www.copyrighthistory.org. Accessed on 23 October 2024.

Although that famous declaration is often quoted in support of the author-oriented rationales for copyright, it is almost invariably taken out of context and not used in accordance with its original meaning. Namely, Le Chapelier, indeed made that statement, however, he said it respecting unpublished works. According to him, the main principle is the public domain, to which authors' rights are an exception. Thus, he advocated that the new French Law should put the principle and its exception in the right place, unlike in English copyright law, which sets up a strongly protected right rather than appreciating the principle of the public domain. Anyhow, regardless of its origins, the declaration has found its place among copyright proponents and is also welcome to be used in future endeavours to protect copyright. See Ginsburg (1990), pp. 1006–1007.

[121] See Grosheide (1994) p. 207; Strowel (1994), p. 235.

personality human right recognised on an international,[122] regional[123] and national level.[124,125]

The subject matter of copyright concerns creative works of the human mind. The requirement for a work to be recognised as copyright is that it is an original intellectual production from the literary, scientific or artistic domain having individual character, whatever the mode or form of its expression. The threshold for creativity is low. In the EU, it is sufficient that the work is the "author's own intellectual creation."[126,127] Novelty is not a requirement. In the civil-law legislation, even the fixation of the work is not required, which is in alignment with the

---

[122] See The Universal Declaration of Human Rights, adopted by the United Nations General Assembly of its 183rd meeting, held in Paris on 10 December 1948. https://www.un.org/en/universal-declaration-human-rights/. Accessed on 22 October 2024, Art. 27; International Covenant on Economic, Social and Cultural Rights Adopted and opened for signature, ratification and accession by General Assembly resolution 2200A (XXI) of 16 December 1966 entry into force 3 January 1976, in accordance with Article 27. https://www.ohchr.org/Documents/ProfessionalInterest/cescr.pdf. Accessed on 22 October 2024, Art. 15.

[123] In the EU, copyright, as an intellectual property, is of constitutional value, protected by the EU Charter, the European Convention on Human Rights, the Universal Declaration of the Human Rights and particular Member State's Constitutions. See The Charter of Fundamental Rights of the European Union, OJ C 326, 26.10.2012, pp. 391–407, Art. 17(2); The Convention for the Protection of Human Rights and Fundamental Freedoms, as amended by Protocols Nos. 11 and 14, supplemented by Protocols Nos. 1, 4, 6, 7, 12, 13 and 16. https://www.echr.coe.int/documents/convention_eng.pdf. Accessed on 22 October 2024, Protocol 1, Art 1; The Universal Declaration of Human Rights, adopted by the United Nations General Assembly of its 183rd meeting, held in Paris on 10 December 1948. https://www.un.org/en/universal-declaration-human-rights/. Accessed on 22 October 2024, Art. 27(2).

[124] The Constitution of the Republic of Croatia (Official Gazette no. 56/90, 135/97, 08/98, 113/00, 124/00, 28/01, 41/01, 55/01, 76/10, 85/10, 05/14), Art. 69(4); The Constitution of France. 1958. https://www.conseil-constitutionnel.fr/sites/default/files/as/root/bank_mm/anglais/constiution_anglais_oct2009.pdf. Accessed on 23 October 2024, Art. 34; The Basic Law for the Federal Republic of Germany in the revised version published in the Federal Law Gazette Part III, classification number 100-1, as last amended by Article 1 of the Act of 28 March 2019 (Federal Law Gazette I p. 404). https://www.gesetze-im-internet.de/englisch_gg/englisch_gg.html#p0019. Accessed on 23 October 2024, Art. 1(1), 14, 5; The Constitution of the Portuguese Republic. https://dre.pt/constitution-of-the-portuguese-republic. Accessed on 24 October 2024, Art. 42; The Spanish Constitution. https://www.boe.es/buscar/pdf/1978/BOE-A-1978-40001-consolidado.pdf. Accessed on 23 October 2024, Art. 20(1), 149(1, pt. 9); The Constitution of Sweden. https://www.riksdagen.se/en/how-the-riksdag-works/democracy/the-constitution/. Accessed on 23 October 2024, Art. 16 (commonly, copyright is implicitly protected within the national constitutions, while Sweden is a unique example where copyright is explicitly protected).

[125] See Goldstein and Hugenholtz (2021), pp. 21–24.

[126] Judgment of the Court (Fourth Chamber) of 16 July 2009, *Infopaq International A/S v Danske Dagblades Forening*, C-5/08, EU:C:2009:465, para. 3.

[127] Under the common-law approach, the requirement is "at least some minimal degree of creativity." See US *Feist Publications, Inc. v. Rural Telephone Service Company, Inc.*, 499 U. S. 340, 345 (1991).

personality concept that copyright originates ex persona.[128] It can be said that in the civil-law tradition, originality is based on the individual creativity which is vested in the intellectual effort of an author. In contrast, in the common-law tradition, the criterion of originality primarily refers to the investment of sufficient independent skill and labour,[129] that is, that the work has not been copied from another source.[130] Copyright protection covers all kinds of works such as books, pamphlets and other writings; lectures, addresses, sermons and other works of the exact nature; dramatic or dramatico-musical works; choreographic works and entertainments in dumb show; musical compositions with or without words; cinematographic works to which are assimilated works expressed by a process analogous to cinematography; works of drawing, painting, architecture, sculpture, engraving and lithography; photographic works, to which are assimilated works expressed by a process analogous to photography; works of applied art; illustrations, maps, plans, sketches and three-dimensional works relative to geography, topography, architecture or science. As well, derivative works and compilations, such as collections, translations, adaptations, arrangements of music and other alterations of a literary or artistic work, are also characterised as copyright works without prejudice to the copyright in the original work. There is no exhaustive list of copyright works—any creation of the mind can attract copyright protection as long as it meets the requirements of the Berne Convention and the relevant national law.[131] The rights of performers, pro-

[128] In the common-law regimes, for evidentiary purposes, it is usually required that the work be fixed in a tangible medium to enjoy copyright protection. However, laws are generally open-minded as to the medium of fixation, and, of course, regardless of that requirement, work still exists independently of any particular material object in which it may be concretised. Also, although by the beginning of the twentieth century most of the countries have abandoned other formal prerequisites (e.g. obligation to deposit copies of the work), in some countries, such as the US, registration of works with the Copyright Office is required for judicial enforcement of copyright (for works of U.S. origins) and to award of statutory damages or attorney's fees (for works regardless of country of origin); see Ginsburg (2018), p. 491; Ginsburg (2010), pp. 311–348. In common-law legislation, there is also a *de minimis* requirement for copyright works. The civil-law tradition does not apply quantitative restrictions on copyright.

[129] See Grosheide (1994), p. 209.

[130] See Goldstein (1989a), pp. 62–63; Goldstein (2024a), pp. 2:7–2:24.

[131] Common-law legislation often lists categories of works that can constitute copyrightable subject matter. However, it is not completely clear whether these categories are illustrative or limitative. Namely, could a work of an unlisted category enjoy protection if it fulfils other requirements for copyright protection? See Ginsburg (2018), p. 490.

ducers of phonograms and broadcasting organisations,[132] all in some way contributing to making works available to the public or producing subject matter, are covered by related (or neighbouring) rights, independently of copyright.[133]

The duration of copyright protection begins immediately with the creation of the works, and according to the Berne Convention, the minimum term of the protection is 50 years *post mortem auctoris.*[134] However, in national legislation, it is common for protection to last 70 years *post mortem auctoris.*[135]

Rights stemming from copyright are moral and economic rights. Moral rights are recognised according to the civil-law concept of the personality of the author and are inherent in the property right that arises from the act of creation. They protect the authors' personal and spiritual connection with their work. Moral rights encompass the author's right to be recognised as the creator of the work (right of attribution or 'paternity') and the right to prevent alterations to the work that are deleterious to the honour or reputation of the author (right of integrity).[136] The right to determine whether, when, and how to disclose the work to the public (the right of the first publication or right of divulgation) shares both moral and economic features. Moral rights subsist independently of economic rights, and in the spirit of the civil-law tradition, constitute *ius cogens* and cannot be waived or taken from the author.

Copyright economic rights concern the use of a work. They enable the author to enjoy the benefits of the work economically and to be protected from outside infringement. Authors have an exclusive right to do whatever they want with their

---

[132] Within the EU, the right of database is also protected as a *sui generis* related right, and film producers (as opposed to directors) also enjoy related rights protection; see Directive 96/9/EC of the European Parliament and of the Council of 11 March 1996 on the legal protection of databases OJ L 77, 27.3.1996, pp. 20–28; Judgment of the Court, 9 February 2012, *Martin Luksan v Petrus van der Let*, C-277/10, EU:C:2012:65.

[133] See the International Convention for the Protection of Performers, Producers of Phonograms and Broadcasting Organisations (Rome Convention), Rome, October 26, 1961. https://www.wipo.int/edocs/pubdocs/en/wipo_pub_328.pdf. Accessed on 22 October 2024.

[134] See Article 7 of the Berne Convention for the Protection of Literary and Artistic Works.

[135] See Walter (2010), pp. 515–526.

[136] See Ginsburg (2018), p. 500. Common-law legislations have recently adopted the moral rights of attribution and integrity, however, more sparingly than in civil-law legislations. In the US, there is currently an ongoing revision of the copyright framework regarding moral rights protection. Within its Report from 2019, the US Copyright Office identified three principles concerning moral rights: respecting foundational principles of U.S. law (including the First Amendment, fair use, and limited terms), appreciating the importance creators place on their attribution and integrity interests, and recognising and respecting the diversity among industry sectors and different kinds of works; see United States Copyright Office, Authors, Attribution, and Integrity: Examining Moral Rights in the United States, A Report of Register of Copyright, April 2019. https://www.copyright.gov/policy/moralrights/full-report.pdf. Accessed on 24 October 2024.

work to the exclusion of everyone else. Economic rights mainly encompass the right of reproduction, the right of distribution, the right of public performance/communication to the public, and the right of adaptation. Unlike moral rights, economic rights are transferable. Thus, the author can freely decide whether to use the work individually or establish some economic rights for someone else. In the case of establishing rights originating from the author's copyright, the rightholder enjoys copyright protection in relation to the acquired economic right.

However, although copyright is deemed to be an absolute natural right in the sense of the civil-law tradition, this does not mean that copyright rights are granted in an absolutely unrestricted way. Every national copyright system has embodies limitations to exclusive copyright rights to accommodate various cultural, social, technological, economic and political needs and objects—to 'fine-tune' the rights protected under copyright.[137] Restrictions of copyright protection apply with regard to the protected object,[138] time[139] and particular uses.[140] Concerning the exemption of particular kinds of uses from the author's exclusive rights, two main categories can be distinguished—exceptions and limitations. Exceptions permit the user to engage in the permitted act without having to pay the copyright owner—an author is left without the exclusive right or a statutory right of remuneration.[141] Limitations permit the use but require payment—the author is deprived of the exclusive right, but instead may be guaranteed the right to remuneration. Within limitations, there is also a difference between statutory exemptions, where the law itself permits certain kinds of uses in combination with statutory remuneration rights; and compulsory licenses, where the author has the exclusive right but is compelled by law to make a contract on the utilisation of the work according to equitable terms.[142,143]

Here again, there are significant differences between civil-law and common-law systems resulting from the natural-rights philosophy focused on the author's protection and a utilitarian approach focused on the well-being of society. While civil-law systems leave a relatively narrow scope of limitations and exceptions usually subject to restrictive interpretation,[144] utilitarian common-law systems

[137] See Goldstein and Hugenholtz (2021), pp. 349–350; Hugenholtz (1997).

[138] Works are generally only protected if they fulfil the conditions of protection, such as the criteria of originality. Some works are exempted for public policy reasons, such as official texts.

[139] Copyright rights are usually limited in time, the duration of protection in some systems varies.

[140] See von Lewinski (2008), p. 152.

[141] An example of exceptions is the case of quotations.

[142] Statutory and compulsory licenses are also designated as non-voluntary licenses.

[143] See von Lewinski (2008), pp. 152–153; Hugenholtz and Okediji (2008), pp. 15–16; Okediji (2017), pp. 429–495, 451–456.

[144] See Hugenholtz (2017), pp. 275–280.

leave much more room for limitations and exceptions through the flexible 'fair use' doctrine.[145,146]

To determine when an unauthorised use is lawful, the Stockholm Conference revision of the Berne Convention instituted the so-called 'three-step test' in relation to the reproduction right.[147] 'The three-step test' was later acknowledged by other international treaties—the TRIPS Agreement,[148] WIPO's 'Internet Treaties'[149] and

[145] The 'fair use' doctrine is a copyright limitation characteristic of the common law systems. Although there is no fixed definition of the 'fair use', it can be explained as a privilege for others than the owner of a copyright to use the copyrighted material in a reasonable manner without its consent, notwithstanding the monopoly granted to the owner by the copyright. In the US, it is codified in section 107 of the Copyright Act. Factors to be determined whether the use made of a work in any particular case is fair are the following: "(1) the purpose and character of the use, including whether such use is of a commercial nature or is for non-profit educational purposes; (2) the nature of the copyrighted work; (3) the amount and substantiality of the portion used in relation to the copyrighted work as a whole; and (4) the effect of the use upon the potential market for or value of the copyrighted work."

Thus, the US common law concept of copyright limitations does not require explicit listing of copyright limitations but allows a flexible interpretation through the 'fair use' concept. In comparison to statutory exemptions, which are presumed to be constant, fair use is allowed to limit a use that constantly changes and which one day may be fair, but another day unfair. 'Fair use' can be approached through the private benefit approach and the public benefit approach and its scope is open to situations where social, political or cultural benefits of use outweigh any consequent loses to a copyright holder.

See Goldstein (1989b), pp. 187–243; Goldstein (2024b), pp. 12:1–12:102 Goldstein and Hugenholtz (2021), pp. 350–353; Liu (2019); Samuelson (2017), pp. 12–59; Reichman (2017), pp. 292–314.

[146] Yet, with regard to the exceptions and limitations, there are big differences even among the systems falling under the same copyright tradition. Thus, for instance, with regard to the civil-law system, France and southern countries show a tendency towards fewer limitations and exceptions, while Germany and some of the northern countries show a tendency towards more prescribed limitations and exceptions. In regard to the common law systems, there is a significant difference between the US and the UK. While the US mainly adopted the flexible 'fair use' concept of copyright limitations, the UK has a quite specific and restrictive concept of copyright limitations. Such differences among national systems in relation to the concept of copyright limitations are understandable considering that many limitations have their origins in diverse social and cultural circumstances. As Hugenholtz stated: "We must not say, as they say in the Netherlands, 'shave all sheep over the same comb'."; see von Lewinski (2008), pp. 56–57; Goldstein and Hugenholtz (2021), pp. 349–350; Hugenholtz (1997).

[147] Berne Convention for the Protection of Literary and Artistic Works, Sept. 9, 1886, as revised at Paris on July 24, 1971 and amended in 1979, S. Treaty Doc. No. 99-27 (1986), Article 9, para. 2 (only for reproduction right): "It shall be a matter for legislation in the countries of the Union to permit the reproduction of such works in certain special cases, provided that such reproduction does not conflict with a normal exploitation of the work and does not unreasonably prejudice the legitimate interests of the author."

[148] The Agreement on Trade-Related Aspects of Intellectual Property Rights (TRIPS), Article 13.

[149] The WIPO Copyright Treaty (WCT); Article 16 of The WIPO Performance and Phonogram Treaty (WPPT), Article 10.

the EU InfoSoc Directive.[150,151] The wording of the 'three-step test', as incorporated in Article 13 of the TRIPS Agreement, is the following:

> Members shall confine limitations or exceptions to exclusive rights to certain special cases which do not conflict with a normal exploitation of the work and do not unreasonably prejudice the legitimate interests of the right holder.

Thus, 'the three-step test' generally has a broad scope; some documents, such as the Berne Convention, prescribe it for specific uses (the reproduction right), while others, such as the TRIPS Agreement, allow more general application to practically all the exclusive rights in literary and artistic works. It does not prescribe a template for any preferred system of copyright limitations but permits both the civil-law concept of strictly prescribed limitations and exemptions and the flexible common-law concept of 'fair use'.[152] However, in some national systems, the 'three-step test' constitutes a directly applicable rule of substantive law with respect to the interpretation of limitations. In contrast, in other systems, it represents a norm addressed to the conduct of national legislatures, not individual nationals.[153]

Generally, the concept of copyright limitations that is endorsed in international treaties and is construed more in the spirit of civil-law tradition suggests a closed legal system allowing no limits from outside of copyright law. However, the legal and political situation is somewhat different. Copyright law does not operate in a legal vacuum and interacts with other regimes over which it does not have a natural precedence. Thus, besides those restrictions stemming from copyright law, there are also specific kinds of restrictions in a broader sense regarding the full enjoyment of an author's rights originating outside of copyright law, such as national provisions on censorship, competition law and consumer protection law.[154] Such de facto limitations fall outside the scope of the traditional copyright framework, so copyright law instruments, such as 'the three-step test', do not apply to them.[155] Such outside constraint to copyright represents a complex issue that must be considered in specific situations. Considering that this research discusses the issue of the interaction between copyright and competition law, it will mainly deal with competition law as an outside restriction on the exercise of copyright.

---

[150] Directive 2001/29/EC of the European Parliament and of the Council of 22 May 2001 on the harmonisation of certain aspects of copyright and related rights in the information society, OJ L 167, 22.6.2001, pp. 10–19., Article 5, para. 5.

[151] See Hilthy and Moscon (2021), pp. 60–62.

[152] See Goldstein and Hugenholtz (2021), pp. 354–355; Hugenholtz and Okediji (2008), pp. 19–21.

[153] See Goldstein and Hugenholtz (2021), p. 357. On criticism of the concept of the 'three-step test', see Hugenholtz and Okediji (2008), pp. 17–18.

[154] See von Lewinski (2008), p. 153; Hugenholtz (1997); Goldstein and Hugenholtz (2021), pp. 351–352, 381–382; Guibault (1998).

[155] See Hugenholtz and Okediji (2008), pp. 19, 27.

2.1.3 Copyright as Part of Intellectual Property Rights

The historical meaning and uses of the notion 'intellectual property' can be debated.[156] However, the notion 'intellectual property' is commonly used as an umbrella concept that comprises copyright and industrial property rights (patents, trademarks, design, industrial design, geographical indications). Accordingly, 'intellectual property' does not stand for a body of law, which is often wrongly perceived in the general public and sometimes even in academia. The laws are copyright law, patent law, trademark law, etc., which all have separate historical development, regulation and purpose. Those laws are comprised under the notion of intellectual property only for practical purposes, indicating that they deal with the intangible creations of human intellect.[157]

It seems that an erroneous use of the term 'intellectual property' is especially present in discussions concerning the issue of copyright-competition interaction. Namely, many authors observe this issue as an intellectual property-competition interaction—that is wrong because, in fact, there is no intellectual property law to be considered.[158] If the characteristics of a particular field of law comprised under the notion of intellectual property are not considered, the result is questionable. In the context of the heated issue of interaction of particular intellectual property rights with competition law, general observations on intellectual property cannot provide the bedrock for a fruitful discussion.

However, this does not mean that findings from the interaction of competition law with one particular intellectual property right should not be applied *per analogiam* to the interaction of competition law with other intellectual property rights. Indeed, all intellectual property rights concern intangible creations of human intellect and share certain characteristics that separate them from rights concerning tangible property and traditional ownership. Nonetheless, an analogue analysis of intellectual property rights must be taken with caution while respecting the substance and characteristics of a particular law. It is especially problematic when the two most discussed intellectual property rights, copyright law and patent law, are mixed without proper reconsideration.

Having in mind that this thesis focuses is on the interaction between copyright and competition law, only characteristics of copyright are relevant for the matter discussed as opposed to other intellectual property rights.

---

[156] See Hughes (2012), pp. 1293–1340.

[157] For a presentation on a different view on whether copyright should be observed more as an independent law or more as an integral part of 'intellectual property law', see Grosheide (1994), pp. 223–232.

[158] See, for instance, Lidgard and Atik (2008); OECD (2018); Turner (2015), pp. 3, 8–10.

2.1.4 Concluding Summary

To summarise, from the above brief general overview of copyright law, several things are particularly vital for further discussion on copyright-competition interaction:

- copyright law is a specific private law right with a long and rich tradition, independent of other intellectual property rights
- there are two main legal traditions of copyright, among which differences must be respected and taken into consideration in any comparisons
- within the European Union, every Member State has its own national copyright system of law, while EU legal interventions are directed towards the harmonisation of certain specific aspects of copyright
- copyright is an absolute right with a moral and economic component
- the economic rights of copyright can be commercialised and/or licensed; however, it can also be limited in content for a prescribed list of reasons
- competition law is an external limitation on the exercise of copyright
- currently, there is an ongoing digital evolution that requires further development of copyright law interpretation

2.2 Competition Law

2.2.1 A Brief History of Competition Law

The origin of modern competition law is commonly associated with late nineteenth-century North America. However, anti-competitive practices can be observed throughout history,[159] and an open-minded but cautious view back to the further past might even find traces of competition law in earlier times. Thus, Lord Wilberforce, in his notable work on restrictive trade practices and monopolies, observed laws that dealt with these matters during the pre-competition law history and found some traces of competition law even in ancient[160] and medieval times.[161]

---

[159] Some reports indicate that anti-competitive practices existed even in ancient Egypt and Greece (earlier than 3000 B.C.); see Ewing (2006), pp. 75–76.

[160] For instance, some competition-related-laws from ancient Roman legislation are *Lex Julia de Annona,* Edict of Diocletian from A.D. 301, and the Constitution of Zeno from A.D. 483. See Lord Wilberforce et al. (1966), paras. 108–111.

[161] Thus, in England, some laws dealt with anti-competitive practices even in the tenth century and further throughout the medieval period. In continental parts of Europe, some regulations dealing with anti-competitive practices can be found between the thirteenth and fifteenth centuries in certain Italian municipalities (Viterbo Urbino, Florence), Bohemia, some German towns and France; Lord Wilberforce et al. (1966), paras. 113–117.

However, in the context of the discussion on copyright-competition interaction, times after the invention of the printing press and the occurrence of the privilege and guild system (often intertwined) might be particularly relevant.

Despite the existence of anti-monopoly laws, most of Europe was still facing the issue of monopolisation, which especially surged in the seventeenth century.[162] In England, the Statute of Monopolies was passed in 1623,[163] dealing with the illegal grant of monopolies.[164] However, the Statute also prescribed statutory exceptions, among which were particular privileges and the activities of guilds.[165]

During the eighteenth and nineteenth centuries, monopolistic practices again boomed, and Europe's struggle continued. England, for instance, passed an Act in 1710 to dissolve present monopolies and prevent future monopolies and agreements that restrict competition. However, historical records seem to show that the Act was never intended to succeed. In fact, this matter was not addressed in England's legislation until the mid-twentieth century. Also, during this period, practice showed that the Statute of Edward VI against forestalling, regrating and engrossing was actually having an adverse effect; hence, it was repealed.[166] In France, the *Loi Le Chapelier* of 1791 prohibited members of the same trade from assembling to regulate their common interest (virtually it abolished guilds), while in 1810, Article 419 of the Penal Code prohibited concerted action to manipulate prices above or below that which natural and free competition would have set (that provision stayed in force until 1986, but was amended in 1926).[167]

Although some traces of competition law can indeed be found in these earlier times in Europe, it is widely accepted that modern competition law emerged from the United

[162] See Lord Wilberforce et al. (1966), paras. 125–132.

[163] With regard to the year of the enactment of the Statute of Monopolies, there is some confusion whether the year was 1623 or 1624 (both can be found in relevant literature). The confusion arises because the Parliamentary Session in which it was passed assembled on 12 February 1624 (using modern dating), but at the time this would have been 12 February 1623 (since at that time New Year in England was on Lady Day, 25 March, and it moved to 1 January in 1750). The Act received Royal Assent on 29 May 1624. At that time, all Acts passed within a session commenced on the first day. So legally, the Act was commenced in 1623, but in terms of historical dating, it was commenced and passed in 1624; see The Calendar (New Style) Act 1750, 24 Geo. II c.23 (also known as Chesterfield's Act).

[164] Prior to the 1623 Statute of Laws, in the significant 'case of the monopolies', *Darcy v Allin* (1602), the court ruled that a grant of monopoly for the making of playing cards was illegal and void, thereby establishing that generally the grant of exclusive rights to produce any article was improper; see the case *Darcy v Allin* (1602) 11 Co Rep 84b. Nevertheless, a distinction was drawn between trading within and without the realm. See case *East India Company v Sandys* (1685) St.Tr. 371; see Bohun (1993), pp. 64–65. Fikentscher considers the English Statute of Monopolies as the first modern anti-monopoly law; see Beier et al. (1996), III/A/1.

[165] See Lord Wilberforce et al. (1966), paras. 133–134.

[166] See Lord Wilberforce et al. (1966), paras. 136–139.

[167] OECD (2003a) France, p. 4; Plaisant (1975), pp. 27–30.

States' industrial-nineteenth-century.[168] The US was going through an intensive industrial revolution during the nineteenth century. One of its main results was a dramatic development of the transportation and communication sectors. The railways, telegraph lines and telephone services spread rapidly throughout US territory—forming a large single market. Such circumstances provided a powerful incentive to businesses to exploit economies of scale and economies of scope.[169] Thus, competition increased greatly, and companies were now competing all over the US and beyond. Also, various technological innovations, the formation of more developed capital markets and new managerial methods, and the relaxation of the legal framework encouraged the growth of companies. This development led to low and unstable prices and instability in several sectors, which was often preceded by recurrent economic crises. To maintain their business due to high fixed costs, companies had to reorganise their production and distribution activities, invest in new machinery, enter new markets, etc.—ultimately leading to an even greater decrease in prices and 'price wars' among competitors on the market. Consequently, some companies started forming cartels and trusts to respond to 'price wars' and market instabilities. The formation of cartels and trusts ultimately led to stable prices among the members of cartels and trusts. However, to the detriment of consumers and small produce businesses that used the products of cartelised sectors as inputs. With the formation of cartels and trusts, consumers and producers were squeezed between low sale prices and high input prices. In addition, small businesses often suffered from the unfair business practices of their giant rivals.[170] In a certain way, such developments at that time show much resemblance to today's developments in the digital industry on a global scale. The development of digital technologies provided powerful incentives to businesses to exploit economies of scale and economies of scope, forming large global markets in all kinds of industries. Competition severely increased in the form of start-ups. However, due to low and unstable prices and the instability of many digital sectors, among other things, most of the businesses are not able to grow and survive on their own. Hence, the competition is ultimately concentrated among the Big Tech companies (Google, Apple, Facebook, Amazon and Microsoft) that often hold a dominant position in their relevant markets. Practically, the only significant difference from the developments in the late nineteenth century is that today, intellectual property rights lie beneath such development.

Nevertheless, to fight the situation and survive on the market in the late nineteenth century, small businesses induced the creation of competition law in the United States.[171] The first US competition law, the Sherman Antitrust Act,[172] was enacted

[168] See Colino (2019), p. 3. On an overview of intellectual debates that proceeded (and followed) the creation of modern competition law, see Crane and Hovenkamp (2013).

[169] See Motta (2004), pp. 1–2; Hovenkamp (1991), pp. 131–148, 224.

[170] See Motta (2004), pp. 2–3.

[171] Ewing (2006), p. 85.

[172] An Act to Protect Trade and Commerce Against Unlawful Restraints and Monopolies (The Sherman Antitrust Act of 1890), 26 Stat. 209, 15 U.S.C. §§ 1–38.

in 1890 against the background of rampant cartelisation and monopolisation of the American economy.[173] The Sherman Antitrust Act outlaws every contract, combination, or conspiracy in restraint of trade,[174] and any monopolisation, attempted monopolisation, or conspiracy or combination to monopolise.[175] Also, it prescribes imprisonment and fines for violators. Although the enforcement of the Sherman Antitrust Act started gently during its first decade, it soon the enforcement started to became more severe.[176] However, one of its shortcomings was that it did not encompass mergers. Hence, in 1914, the Clayton Act[177] was introduced to extend the antitrust legislation to cover mergers to reduce competition.[178] The Clayton Act addresses specific practises that the Sherman Act does not clearly prohibit, such as price discrimination,[179] exclusive dealing and tying,[180] and interlocking directorates among competing businesses.[181,182] Also dating from 1914 is the Federal Trade Commission Act[183] that bans unfair methods of competition and unfair or deceptive

[173] See Posner (1976), p. 23; On the debates that preceded the Sherman Act, see Peritz (2000), pp. 9–26.

As Posner observes the framers of the Sherman Act indeed "seem to have been concerned with low-prices harmful to small-business competitors of the trusts and with discriminatory pricing (for example, railroad rebates to Rockefeller's Standard Oil Trust) that placed the trusts' small-business competitors at a disadvantage, as well as with high prices harmful to consumers, but their concern with high prices focused on the wealth-redistributive rather than the allocative effects of monopoly pricing" Posner (2001), p. 34. Lord Wilberforce considers that the Constitution of Zeno might have influenced the US Sherman Act of 1890; see Lord Wilberforce et al. (1966), para. 110.

It is of note that even before the Sherman Act, Canada adopted a similar law in 1889, although its enforcement and significance were much weaker; see An Act for the Prevention and Suppression of Combinations Formed in Restraint of Trade, 1889, 52, Vict. c. 42; see also Ross (1998), pp. 3–4.

[174] Section 1 of The Sherman Antitrust Act of 1890.

[175] Section 2 of The Sherman Antitrust Act of 1890.

[176] See, for instance, the cases: Trans-Missouri Freight Association (1897), Addyston Pipe and Steel (1899), Dr. Miles v. Park & Sons (1911), Standard Oil Company (1911), American Tobacco (1911), Terminal Railroad (1912). Peritz writes that the Supreme Court was struggling with the statute until it adopted the 'rules of reason' in *Standard Oil*; Peritz (2000), pp. 26–27. See Dewey (1990), pp. 6–7; Ewing (2006), pp. 90–92; Kovacic and Shapiro (2000), pp. 44–46; Motta (2004), p. 4; Posner (2001), pp. 35–42; Posner (1976), pp. 24–30; see also Kovacic and Shapiro (2000), pp. 46–49.

[177] An Act to Supplement Existing Laws Against Unlawful Restraints and Monopolies, and for Other Purposes (The Clayton Antitrust Act of 1914), Pub.L. 63–212, 38 Stat. 730, enacted October 15, 1914, codified at 15 U.S.C. §§ 12–27, 29 U.S.C. §§ 52–53.

[178] Section 7 of The Clayton Antitrust Act of 1914. It seems that the Sherman Act not only omitted to comprise mergers, but instead induced the merger boom; see Motta (2004), p. 5.

[179] The Clayton Antitrust Act of 1914, Sec. 2.

[180] The Clayton Antitrust Act of 1914, Sec. 3.

[181] The Clayton Antitrust Act of 1914, Sec. 8.

[182] In its Section 4, The Clayton Act, also, enabled the possibility of recovering treble damages from offenders to victims of unlawful commercial conduct.

[183] The Federal Trade Commission Act of 1914, 15 U.S.C. §§ 41–58.

acts or practices.[184] The Federal Trade Commission Act established the Federal Trade Commission as an independent agency that regulates unfair trade practices and shares with the Department of Justice the responsibility to enforce antitrust laws in the US at the federal level. With some revisions, these are the three core federal antitrust laws still in effect today.[185]

In the US, the period between the two World Wars was not particularly active in enforcing competition laws. Reasons for that can be found in the political, economic and historical context of that time. As of WWI, the coalition between businesses and politics governed the economy, rather than market forces. In the meantime, the Great Depression of 1929 occurred and only reinforced such a situation. Thus, there were not many important antitrust cases under those circumstances, but the focus was on preserving the small businesses, which was also the intention of the Robinson-Patman Act. One of the rare significant cases was *Appalachian Coals v US* (1993), in which the Supreme Court made an exception to the per se prohibition of price-fixing in the context of those times. Later, under different conditions and contexts, in *Socony-Vacum Oil* (1940), the Supreme Court re-established the principle of per se prohibition of price-fixing, after which followed a period of intense antitrust activity again. Some of the notable US cases from that period are *International Salt* (1947), *Alcoa* (1945), *Brown Shoe* (1962), *Philadelphia National Bank* (1963), *Proctor & Gamble* (1967), etc.[186]

At this point, it seems suitable to turn back to Europe. There is a belief that the US significantly influenced European competition law.[187] Thus, Johannes stated at Fordham University in 1978: "in the art of antitrust the Americans are the teachers and the Europeans are the pupils."[188] However, not everyone would agree with such a perception of the relationship between US and European competition law. Some scholars, such as Gerber, believe that the development of European competition law emerged from "ideas developed by European thinkers and decision-makers in response to European conditions, and has spread through Europe along indigenous

[184] The Federal Trade Commission Act of 1914, 15 USC §45. On the conditions that preceded the enactment of the Federal Trade Commission Act, see Winerman (2003), pp. 1–97.

[185] Later, the Robinson-Patman Act of 1936 amended the Clayton Antitrust Act to ban certain discriminatory prices, services, and allowances in dealings between merchants. In 1976, the Hart-Scott-Rodino Antitrust Improvements Act further amended the Clayton Antitrust Act to require companies planning large mergers or acquisitions to notify the government of their plans in advance; The Anti-Price Discrimination Act, Pub. L. No. 74-692, 49 Stat. 1526 (codified at 15 U.S.C. § 13); The Hart–Scott–Rodino Antitrust Improvements Act of 1976, Publ. L. No. 94-435 (codified at 15 U.S.C. § 18).

[186] See Kovacic and Shapiro (2000), pp. 49–52. After criticism from several authors connected to the University of Chicago, the interventionism of the antitrust authorities and courts started to lessen from the 1970s. Some consider case GTE-Sylvania (1977) as the turning point for the shift in the antitrust approach in the US; see Kovacic and Shapiro (2000), pp. 52–55.

[187] See, for instance, Colino (2019), pp. 6–7, 27; Geradin et al. (2012), pp. 14–15.

[188] Johannes (1982), p. 73.

channels rather than through emulation of US antitrust law."[189] Ibáñez Colomo writes that "the factors that have marked the evolution of US antitrust are not prominent in the EU."[190] Anyhow, not entering further into discussion on how strong the influence of US competition law is on the European competition law, the fact is that on the European continent, since its establishment, the European Union had a central role in the development of European competition law (and even beyond on Member States legislation). That is particularly notable in the difference between EU and US copyright-competition cases in the later phase (see *infra* Sect. 5.2.2.2.4). Thus, national legislations followed the EU policy by introducing competition laws into their legal systems. Still, it is noteworthy that some Member States already had competition law ideas and legislation before the establishment of the EU (then the European Community).

Interestingly, some consider Austria as the pioneer of European competition law. Austria did not have the first act on competition law in Europe. However, already in the 1890s, there was an intense debate in Austria on introducing competition law into its legislation. The idea of competition law emerged from the intense and complex social, economic and political situation in Austria during the nineteenth century. Following the 'great depression' in the late 1870s, many cartels started to form in Austria. By the 1880s, cartels had become dominant forces in the economy, controlling production and prices in key industries. Although in the beginning, cartels were not perceived as something harmful, by the 1890s, they were viewed far more critically. Influenced by anti-liberal and social philosophy, an intense discussion on the sanctions against cartels commenced. The outlines of a new solution were first articulated in 1894 at a conference of the *Verein für Sozialpolitik*, which preceded the proposals of a cartel act. Ultimately, due to the specific political circumstances, the proposals did not result in enacting the act on competition law. Nevertheless, there are views that occurrences in Austria significantly influenced the development of competition laws in Europe independently of the US influence, especially with

---

[189] Gerber considers nineteenth-century occurrences in Europe as the foundation of modern competition law—liberalism and political freedom, the battle for economic freedom, industrialisation, the 'Great Depression', managed competition and ultimately re-evaluation of competition and economic freedom; see Gerber (2003), pp. 3, 16–42. Following up on Gerber's unquestionably notable work arguing the authentic and independent development of European competition law, some scholars, such as Leucht and Marquis, took a less unqualified approach to the possible influence of the US on European competition law. In doing so, they particularly took into consideration the fact that the US antitrust was, at that time, already quite advanced with a rich history; that the US had an hegemonic position in the West following the WWII; that there were many Europeans in the US law schools where the US antitrust legislation often served as an object of study; that there was an intense interaction between European and US experts, etc. Having that in mind, the viewpoint that the US had a fairly significant impact on European competition law might seem a more realistic approach (especially for the period of the 1960s and 1970s). In this case, 'significant impact' does not imply copy-paste or negate the special circumstances that further influenced the development of European competition law, especially in a more advanced phase; see Leucht and Marquis (2013), pp. 125–161.

[190] Ibáñez Colomo (2018), p. 4.

regard to Germany.[191] Anyhow, after all the struggle at the *fin de* siècle, in 1951, Austria finally enacted its first competition law (*Kartellgesetz*).[192]

The UK introduced its competition law—the Profiteering Act—as early as 1919. The main concern of the Profiteering Act was to avoid excessive prices after WWI. After the end of the WWII, in 1948, the UK further enacted the Monopolies and Restrictive Practices (Inquiry and Control) Act, motivated by the idea that market competition would help attain full employment. Later, until alignment with EU competition law, the UK competition law system was primarily based upon the Restrictive Trade Practices Act (1956), extended by the Resale Prices Act (1964) and Mergers Act (1965). However, during that period, the impact of competition enforcement was questionable, especially considering the weak powers of the competition authorities.[193]

Germany introduced the Cartel Law in 1923[194] even though the prevailing view at that time was that cartels are something positive—they were perceived as "an instrument to control the instability created by cutthroat competition and price warfare."[195,196] In a notable decision of 1897 on a failed cartel cooperation (the so-called *Saxon Wood Pulp* case[197]), the country's highest court the *Reichsgericht*, declared that cartels not only did not harm the public interest but were generally beneficial. It further aligned its reasoning with the principles of freedom to enter contracts, freedom to enter businesses, and judicial power to invalidate contract terms that contravened the community's moral sense.[198] Nörr comments that "there was no other ruling during the *Reichsgericht*'s seventy years of history which relied as heavily on economics as did the cartel decision."[199] Nevertheless, some consider that events in Austria concerning a discussion on competition law in the late nineteenth century largely influenced the development of competition law in Germany. According to such a viewpoint, the idea of using laws to protect competition

[191] See Gerber (1992), pp. 405–440.

[192] Verordnung des Bundesministeriums für Justiz vom 14. September 1951 zur Durchführung des Kartellgesetzes (KartellG.-DV.), BGBI Nr. 173/1951, Bundesgesetblatt für die Republik Österreich, 3.11.1951., 53. Stück; see Bayer (1952), pp. 656–672; Drahos (2001), pp. 85–87.

[193] See Motta (2004), pp. 11–12.

[194] *Verordnung gegen Missbrauch wirtschaftlicher Machtstellungen, Nov. 2, 1923 (Kartell Verordnung)* REICHSGESETZBLATT 1, 1067. Gerber views this law as the first competition law. Regardless, with the Cartel Act, the first European competition agency was established; see Gerber (2003), p. 7; Kronstein and Leighton (1946), pp. 297–335, 304.

[195] See Motta (2004), pp. 9–10.

[196] Liefmann's comprehensive study on cartels, concerns and trusts from 1932 ending in a conclusion *in favorem* of the cartel and its importance on the market; see Liefmann (1977). Nörr considers the following justification for cartelisation at that time in Germany: the theory of history, collectivism, the period of awareness of power and power politics by the state, and the period of de-legalisation; see Nörr (1995), pp. 5–20, 6–9.

[197] Reichsgericht, decision of 4 February 1897, 38 RGZ 155, 157.

[198] See OECD (2003b) Germany, p. 7.

[199] Nörr (1995), p. 7.

was in keeping with the nineteenth-century industrialisation and depression and 'managed' competition.[200] Besides, the introduction of the Cartel Law was mainly a reaction to the current hyperinflation. The Cartel Law did not explicitly prohibit cartels but required registration with the newly established regulatory agency and placed the so-called external and internal coercion by cartels under control.[201] Also, it did not provide significant effects on the market, especially during the post-Great Depression period and the Nazi regime.[202] Only after 1957 and the enactment of a stricter competition law, which enforced rules against price-fixing agreements and other anti-competitive practices, did Germany genuinely acknowledge and enforce competition law.[203] The shift towards a different approach was encouraged by neo-liberal thinkers who developed a so-called 'ordo-liberal' vision of society, economic freedom and competition.[204]

Besides the countries mentioned above, ideas about competition law spread across Europe even before the establishment of the European Community. Some other countries also enacted competition laws. Thus, in 1925, Sweden enacted the Law on Investigations Relating to Monopolistic Enterprises and Mergers.[205] That law was replaced in 1946 by the Law Relating to the Supervision of Restrictive Practices within Industry and Commerce, and in 1953 by the Restrictive Trade Practices Act, supplemented in 1956 with the Compulsory Notifications Act and General Price Control Act.[206] Norway (although later a non-EU Member State) enacted the Law on Control of Restraints of Competition and Price Abuse (*Trustlov*) in 1926 (repealed in 1953).[207] Poland had laws on unfair competition in 1926 and against cartels in 1933, although not effective until 1945.[208] Yugoslavia introduced a

---

[200] See Gerber (2003), pp. 68–114.

[201] The 'internal coercion' was the coercion within a cartel to discipline its members, while 'external coercion' was applied by the cartel against outsiders; see Beier et al. (1996), III/A/2.

[202] See Kronstein and Leighton (1946). On the opposite point of view, see Gerber (2003), pp. 134–136.

[203] Merger control was initially omitted from the Act Against Restraints of Competition and was introduced in 1973 through an amendment which included merger control, sharpened the provisions for controlling abuse, prohibited resale price maintenance, and permitted more co-operation among smaller firms; see OECD (2003b) Germany, p. 10. That law was still not in direct connection with the EC competition rules; see Drahos (2001), p. 85. In criticism of early EC competition law, Gerber considers Germany as "the only Member State that had paid serious attention to competition" Gerber (1994), pp. 101, 103–104.

[204] See Beier et al. (1996), III/A/2; Drahos (2001), pp. 239–247; Gerber (2003), pp. 7–8.

[205] *Lagen om undersökning angående monopolistika företag och sammanslutningar, Svensk Författningssamling* (SFS) 1925:223.

[206] See Lundberg (1955), pp. 279–283; OECD (2006) Sweden, p. 7.

[207] See Gerber (2003), pp. 156–159.

[208] OECD (2002) Poland, p. 8.

statute that generally proscribed cartels in 1934.[209] Denmark tracks its competition law foundations from 1937.[210] In 1945, France had the *Ordonnance* that regulated pricing. Later, this was supplemented by the Law of 1953, renewed in 1958 and 1967, covering refusal to sell, discriminatory practices, joint sales, imposed prices, and increasing government powers. Also, in 1963, it was extended to cover market-dominant position.[211] The Netherlands introduced competition law in 1958, but it was not explicitly linked with EC competition rules.[212]

Nevertheless, the genuine development of modern competition law in Europe was induced by the establishment of the European Union and introducing competition rules into the establishing treaties. With the development of EU competition law, Member States consequently (and gradually) started introducing or aligning competition laws into their national legislations—especially after the mid-1980s.[213]

Following the post-WWII economic and social situation, the origins of EU competition law can be traced from the series of pro-competitive measures adopted in the 1951 Treaty of Paris,[214] which created the European Coal and Steel Community (ECSC).[215] The purpose of the ECSC was to prohibit trade barriers and discriminatory and other restrictive practices capable of distorting competition among six countries (France, Germany, Italy, Belgium, the Netherlands and Luxembourg). Reasons for introducing competition policy measures within the Treaty of Paris can probably be found, first, in the desire to diminish the danger of German power by making available to other European countries such essential inputs as coal and steel. Second, due to the success of the US economy, which had continuously relied upon antitrust rules, Europe started to appreciate the principle of free compe-

[209] The statute was immediately amended in 1935 and replaced introduced cartel prohibition and discretionary licensing by a system in which the legality of a cartel rested not on the judgment of an official, but upon strict compliance with statutory registration requirements; see Kronstein and Leighton (1946), p. 307.

[210] OECD (1999) Denmark, pp. 9–10.

[211] Plaisant (1975), pp. 30–31.

[212] See Drahos (2001), p. 85.

[213] Gerber (2003), p. 8.

[214] The Treaty establishing the European Coal and Steel Community (The Treaty of Paris), 18 April 1951. https://www.cvce.eu/content/publication/1997/10/13/11a21305-941e-49d7-a171-ed5be548cd58/publishable_en.pdf. Accessed on 22 October 2024.

[215] See Folsom (2014), p. 315. However, the year 1950 can be considered as the 'institutional birth' of European competition law with the Schumann Declaration and the introduction of a new conception of European integration. Namely, among others, the creation of a common market for coal and steel triggered the need to create a public authority to regulate these markets, which were severely distorted by trade barriers, cartels and geographic price discrimination. As a result, the Treaty of Paris creating the European Coal and Steel Community included antitrust provisions that had no real precedents in Europe. However, it should be noted that even before the idea of international competition law had been discussed—at the Havana Conference in 1947, and the notion of common European economic policies had been discussed before 1950 in theoretical terms; see Warlouzet (2010), pp. 1, 7.

tition more.[216] Thus, Article 65 of the Treaty of Paris prohibits agreements and concerted practices between firms or associations and firms, which tend directly or indirectly to prevent, restrict or distort normal competition within the Common Market. Article 66 of the Treaty of Paris deals with the abuse of a dominant position by firms, using such a position to pursue objectives contrary to the Treaty. Also, Article 66 deals with mergers and concentrations between firms in the coal and steel industry. The consent to such a merger could only be given by the High Authority, which granted approval only when the concentration did not give the new entity the power to control prices, restrict production and distribution, distort trade among the Member States, or create an artificially privileged position on the markets.

Following the ECSC, in the creation of the European Community in 1957, the competition was seen as an essential element in creating a common market free from restraints on trade. Hence, competition rules were immediately integrated into the establishing act—the Treaty of Rome[217] (Articles 85–94[218]).[219,220] However, it is noteworthy that merger control was omitted, and did not become the direct object of the EU competition policy until the Merger Regulation in 1989.[221] Following the ECSC's intentions, the objectives of the introduced competition rules were to promote economic progress and the welfare of European citizens.[222]

However, for almost a decade, enforcement of the EC competition rules did not come into practice—not until the Council of Ministers adopted Regulation 17/62[223]

---

[216] See Motta (2004), p. 13.

[217] Treaty establishing the European Economic Community (EEC) (Treaty of Rome), 25 March 1957. https://eur-lex.europa.eu/legal-content/EN/TXT/?uri=CELEX:11957E/TXT. Accessed on 22 October 2024.

[218] Article 85 regulated cartels and restrictive vertical agreements, while Article 86 dealt with undertakings in a dominant position.

[219] Competition rules as integrated within the Treaty of Rome, survived all further major amendments of the main Treaties, although articles were renumbered twice (the Treaty of Amsterdam—Articles 81–89; the Treaty of Lisbon—Articles 101–109)—the Treaty on European Union (Maastricht Treaty), OJ C 191, 29.7.1992, pp. 1–112; Treaty of Amsterdam amending the Treaty on European Union, the Treaties establishing the European Communities and certain related acts, OJ C 340, 10.11.1997, pp. 1–144; Treaty of Nice amending the Treaty on European Union, the Treaties establishing the European Communities and certain related acts, OJ C 80, 10.3.2001, pp. 1–87; Treaty of Lisbon amending the Treaty of European Union and the Treaty establishing the European Community, OJ C 306, 17.12.2007.

[220] Several reasons can be found why competition rules were immediately introduced into the establishing act of the European Economic Community, even though earlier competition law and policy were not high on the agendas of most national governments. Some of the reasons lie in the fact that competition rules had already been included in the ECSC establishing treaty, and that one of the objectives of the EEC was to increase welfare by promoting trade on a market where trade barriers had been eliminated; see Drahos (2001), pp. 51–53.

[221] Council Regulation (EEC) No 4064/89 of 21 December 1989 on the control of concentrations between undertakings, OJ L 395/89, pp. 1–12.

[222] See Motta (2004), p. 14.

[223] EEC Council: Regulation No 17: First Regulation implementing Articles 85 and 86 of the Treaty, OJ 13, 21.2.1962, pp. 204–211.

that established the scheme of enforcement for competition law. The main aim of the adopted Regulation was to ensure that competition would not be distorted on the common market. To do so, the Commission acquired a wide range of powers and obtained a central role in the enforcement of competition law and cooperation with national competition authorities. However, the decisions by the Commission taken under Regulation 17/62 were subject to review by the Court of Justice.[224] Soon after, the Commission's first major decision was taken in 1964 (*Consten and Grundig*[225]—see *infra* Sect. 4.2.1.2), which was later upheld by the Court of Justice in 1966.

However, during this first period of European competition law (up until 2003),[226] there was very little litigation. Until the 1980s and 1990s, the European Community did not have a very significant influence on national competition law systems.[227] Although the (then) ECJ held that Articles 85 and 86 TFEU could produce a direct effect at the national level, the centralisation of competition law enforcement in the hands of the European Commission focused competition law litigation at the EC rather than the national level. In fact, during that time, it was the Commission that prioritised policy and decided on cases relating to anti-competitive practices without any prior agreement from the Member States or the European Parliament.[228] Nevertheless, after the reorientation of competition law within the EU and the alignment of national competition laws with EU competition law, things started to change drastically.[229]

---

[224] Articles 9, 17 of Regulation 17/62.

[225] Judgment of 13 July 1966, *Établissements Consten S.à.R.L. and Grundig-Verkaufs-GmbH v Commission of the European Economic Community*, Joined cases 56 and 58-64, EU:C:1966:41.

[226] According to some scholars, it is possible to divide this period of EU competition law into different stages: the foundations of the European competition policy (1950–1962); the failure of the neofunctionalist dynamic (1962–1985); the subsequent decisive strengthening of this policy (1985–1991); see Warlouzet (2010), p. 2.

[227] See Gerber (2003), p. 180. At the beginning, there were competing visions on how to understand the EU competition rules, whether as a law or more as guidelines for decision-making, how important was the role of the EU competition law, and on the enforceability of Articles 85 and 86; see Gerber (2003), pp. 346–347.

[228] Warlouzet (2010), p. 1.

[229] Prior to the Regulation 1/2003, Dorhos identified the following events as steps towards alignment of national laws with EU competition law: "the establishment of procedural rules in 1962; the *Walt Wilhelm* judgement of 1969, which established that national law can be applied in parallel with EC law but it must not obstruct the effectiveness of the European rules; the early extension of the jurisdiction of the European Commission (CEC) to agreements within the frontiers of one country; more interest in increasing monitoring of regulated sectors and conduct of the state since the 1980s; and subsequently a gradual increase in the significance of decentralisation and subsidiarity since the beginning of the 1990s" Drahos (2001), p. 387; Judgment of 13 February 1969, Walt Wilhelm and others v Bundeskartellamt, C-14/68, EU:C:1969:4; see also Gerber (2003), pp. 369–384. Thus, in 1998, Gerber observes: "In Europe, competition law has achieved practical importance far greater than virtually anywhere else (except the United States). Policy-makers have turned to it in order to achieve goals as diverse as economic growth, political stability and economic integration, and thus

The modernisation of EU competition law began in 1999 when the Commission undertook a review of the EC competition enforcement framework. Following the Commission's review resulting in a white paper,[230] Regulation 1/2003[231] was a significant turning point in the enforcement of EU competition law and launched the second period in applying EU competition law at the national level. This Regulation obliged the Member States to introduce national laws implementing (the then) Articles 81 and 82 TFEU and increased the need for national judges to be familiar with the European Commission's practice, guidance and European courts' case law. The Member States were obliged to create national competition law authorities, alongside sectoral regulators as part of the parallel liberalisation of public sectors such as telecoms, postal services, utilities and transport. The Member States could designate one single national competition authority or allocate competence between several authorities. Litigation at the national level thus focused on judicial review and other forms of public law remedies against decisions taken by the national competition authorities and regulators. In addition to the public-law control of national competition authority decisions, some Member States also developed and refined criminal-law liability for a breach of the national competition-law provisions. However, paradoxically, decentralisation of competition law enforcement did not reduce the Commission's powers. On the contrary, Regulation 1/2003 allowed the Commission to leave 'less important' cases to national authorities to handle while sustaining the power to decide upon cases of greater importance for the single market. Even in cases ruled by NCAs, the Commission gained overall responsibility and necessary legal tools to ensure that all NCAs apply the EU competition rules uniformly, making the Commission the critical enforcer of the EU competition rules.[232] Overall, Regulation 1/2003 strengthened the Commission's powers, which are broader in this area than in any other.[233]

After the adoption of Regulation 1/2003, a more fruitful (and sometimes more problematic) period for competition law on both national and EU levels followed. Throughout its development, EU competition law has undergone various challenges and changing circumstances, which generally stabilised the core principles of EU competition law and enabled somewhat consistent enforcement—ultimately establishing EU competition law as an essential legal discipline and a potent market regulator.

However, nowadays, EU competition law is facing an utterly new set of challenges. We are living in dynamic times of globalisation, innovation and change. In

---

it has become a central tool for structuring economic and political relationships and a major influence on many types of private economic decisions" Gerber (2003), p. 1.

[230] White Paper on Modernisation of the Rules Implementing Articles 85 and 86 of the EC Treaty, COM(1999) 101 final, 28.4.1999, OJ C 132, 12.5.1999, pp. 1–33.

[231] Council Regulation (EC) No 1/2003 of 16 December 2002 on the implementation of the rules on competition laid down in Articles 81 and 82 of the Treaty (Text with EEA relevance), OJ L 1, 4.1.2003, pp. 1–25.

[232] See Regulation 1/2003, Articles 11, 16.

[233] See Warlouzet (2010), p. 1.

these times, the process of digitisation of industry has especially left its mark on how data is generated, stored, processed, exchanged and distributed, that is, how businesses are conducted. New possibilities opened, and business models emerged. In the still-developing digital environment, new issues emerged with the occurrence of digital platforms, digital ecosystems and data economy. Although the core principles and general framework of competition law remain sound in such an environment, theory and practice must consider some new factors to adapt and refine established concepts, doctrines and methodologies in the enforcement of competition law.[234]

2.2.2 *Nature, Character and Objectives of Competition Law*

At the beginning of this section, it seems proper to immediately note that there are some terminological difficulties with regard to competition law, as was the case with 'copyright'. There is no universal definition of competition law, and opinions as to what competition law should achieve very much differ.[235] However, this is not incomprehensible, having in mind that competition law has to adapt to its surroundings—particular forces that influenced the direction of competition policy at particular times. Accordingly, the English term 'competition law' can cause inevitable confusion since not all Member State legislations have exactly the same scope for the terms they use in competition law, which can be directly translated into English. For instance, in Germany, competition law is designated as '*Kartellrecht*',[236] in France as '*droit des ententes*', in Italy as '*diritto della concorrenza*', in the United Kingdom as 'restrictive practices law', in the US as 'antitrust law', etc. In this thesis, the notion 'competition law' is used broadly, in the sense of a law that promotes or seeks to maintain market competition by regulating anti-competitive conduct by companies. Considering that this research discusses the matter of the interaction between competition law and copyright law, competition law should be delimited from the notion of 'unfair competition'. The concept of 'unfair competition' was introduced in the Paris Convention for the Protection of Industrial Property,[237] and it refers to acts of competition contrary to honest practices

[234] On competition law in the digital environment, see Crémer et al. (2019); Zekos (2014), pp. 1–47.

[235] See, for instance, Ezrachi and Stucke (2018), pp. 1–2; Fox (1987), pp. 917–923; Monti (2007), pp. 2–3.

[236] With regard to Germany, Fikentscher comments that *Kartellrecht* is not the proper term to use for competition law since it not only concerns cartels (agreements for a common purpose in restraint of competition) but also other agreements in restraint of competition and restrictive conduct apart from any agreement; see Beier et al. (1996), III/A/1.

[237] Paris Convention for the Protection of Industrial Property of March 20, 1883, as revised at Brussels on December 14, 1900, at Washington on June 2, 1911, at The Hague on November 6, 1925, at London on June 2, 1934, at Lisbon on October 31, 1958, and at Stockholm on July 14, 1967, and as amended on September 28, 1979. https://www.unido.org/sites/default/files/2014-04/Paris_Convention_0.pdf. Accessed on 22 October 2024.

in industrial or commercial matters.[238] Exemplary categories of unfair competition acts are: causing confusion with respect to another's enterprise or its activities; damaging another's goodwill or reputation; misleading the public; discrediting another's enterprise or its activities; unfair competition in respect of secret information.[239]

A similar terminological problem appears with the concept of 'undertaking'. In this thesis, when used, an 'undertaking' is understood in the spirit of EU competition law, particularly following the case *Klaus Höfner and Fritz Elser v Macrotron GmbH* where it was quite clearly explained that an undertaking is a concept that "encompasses every entity engaged in economic activity, regardless of the legal status of the entity and the way in which it is financed."[240,241] Having in mind the above remarks, this thesis focuses on competition rules on prohibited agreements and abuse of dominant position, mainly from the perspective of the European Union.

Generally, modern competition law grew out of the tradition of liberalism, according to which the law and economic freedoms are the fundamental means of organising society and giving it meaning.[242] Thus, competition law ensures that competition is protected from unrestrained market power in a free-market economy. At the essence of competition law and policy is the concept of non-distortion of competition. Under Article 119 TFEU, the EU economic policy is conducted following the principle of an open market economy with free competition. To protect

---

[238] Competition law and unfair competition have different objects of regulation, purpose and objectives—while competition law guarantees competitive freedom, unfair competition law makes sure that market participants follow the rules. Still, sometimes there is an inherent tension between those two laws; see European Parliament, Briefing paper on addressing unfair practices in business-to-business relations in the internal market, IP/A/IMCO/NT/2010-18, PE 457.364, May 2011. https://www.europarl.europa.eu/RegData/etudes/note/join/2011/457364/IPOL-IMCO_NT(2011)45736_EN.pdf. Accessed on 24 October 2024, pp. 15–16. See also Ghidini (2006), pp. 111–114. Protection against unfair competition has also been acknowledged in Article 2 of the TRIPS Agreement.

[239] See WIPO (1996).

[240] Judgment of the Court (Sixth Chamber) of 23 April 1991, *Klaus Höfner and Fritz Elser v Macrotron GmbH*, C-41/90, EU:C:1991:161, para. 21.

[241] "In competition law, the term 'undertaking' must be understood as designating an economic unit for the purpose of the subject-matter of the agreement in question even if in law that economic unit consists of several persons, natural or legal. The requirement of Article 1 (1) of Regulation No 67/67 is therefore fulfilled if one of the parties to the agreement is made up of undertakings having identical interests and controlled by the same natural person, who also participates in the agreement. For in those circumstances competition between the persons participating together, as a single party, in the agreement in question is impossible." Judgment of 12 July 1984, *Hydrotherm Gerätebau GmbH v Compact del Dott. Ing. Mario Andreoli & C. Sas.*, C-170/83, EU:C:1984:271, para. 11.

"(...) the Treaty rules on competition do not apply to activity which, by its nature, its aim and the rules to which it is subject does not belong to the sphere of economic activity or which is connected with the exercise of the powers of a public authority." Judgment of 19 February 2002, *J. C. J. Wouters, J. W. Savelbergh and Price Waterhouse Belastingadviseurs BV v Algemene Raad van de Nederlandse Orde van Advocaten, intervener: Raad van de Balies van de Europese Gemeenschap*, C-309/99, EU:C:2002:98, para. 57. See also Whish and Bailey (2021), pp. 85–103.

[242] See Gerber (2003), p. 1.

that principle, competition law prevents and condemns anti-competitive behaviour on the market. Under TFEU Protocol (27) on the internal market and competition, it is prescribed that the internal market "includes a system ensuring that competition is not distorted."[243] The main task of the competition authorities is to ensure that free competition is not distorted on the internal market and the Member States' national markets.[244] Accordingly, besides the protection of free competition, competition laws also have the function of building and strengthening the internal market by enhancing market integration between the Member States.[245] In the context of the copyright-competition interaction issue, a fundamental understanding of competition law is necessary to understand when and why competition law in some situations interferes with copyright.

When discussing competition law, according to Monti, it is helpful to think about the factors that influence the form of competition law and the decisions that stem from those rules based on the interaction of three components: a political decision about the aims of competition law; an economic theory about how markets behave, how and when they fail, and how market failures may be remedied; and the institution in charge of enforcing competition law.[246] The political aspect of competition law gravitates between two extreme interpretations of competition law as a guardian of economic welfare and as an instrument of public policy. From the first perspective, competition law can be seen solely as promoting economic welfare by ensuring that firms behave in such a way as to minimise costs and maximise the benefits that consumers can obtain from the scarce resources available.[247] From the second perspective, competition law can be seen as a measure to pursue a variety of other public-interest goals—to maximise economic freedom, preserve employment, promote national champions, facilitate restructuring, protect small firms, safeguard cultural values, conserve the environment, etc. Indeed, it is possible to take an

[243] The treaty of Lisbon removed the former Article 3(g) from the Treaty establishing the European Community. This provision provided that the activities of the Community included "a system ensuring that competition in the internal market is not distorted." After Article 3(g) was removed, Protocol (27) on the internal market and competition was introduced; VerLoren van Themaat and Reuder (2018), p. 6.

[244] "There is no doubt that Articles 85 and 86 of the EC Treaty occupy an important position in the system of the Community legal order and serve the general interest which consists in ensuring undistorted competition." Opinion of Advocate General Cosmas of 16 May 2000, *Masterfoods and HV, Case C-344/98*, EU:C:2000:249., para. 105.

See also, for instance, Judgment of 8 October 2008, *Schunk GmbH and Schunk Kohlenstoff-Technik GmbH v Commission of the European Communities*, T-69-04, EU:T:2008:415, para. 39; Judgment of 17 February 2011, *Konkurrensverket v TeliaSonera Sverige AB*, C-52-09, EU:C:2011:83, para. 20.

[245] See Judgment of 1 June 1999., *Eco Swiss China Time Ltd v Benetton International NV*, C-126/87, EU:C:1999:269, para. 36; see also Colino (2019), p. 7. In an article from 1994, Gerber observes that in the prior period, market integration had been the dominant goal of EC competition law; see Gerber (1994), pp. 98, 101–103.

[246] See Monti (2007), p. 4.

[247] In economic terms, the pursuit of productive, dynamic and allocative efficiency; Monti (2007).

intermediate position; however, these two extreme standpoints should serve as a guideline for formulating the desired competition law policy when addressing the political issue of competition law.[248] In addressing the economic issue of competition law on how markets behave, how and when they fail, and how market failures may be remedied, two opposing standpoints can be observed—the structural approach and the self-healing market approach. On the one hand, it is possible to take a structural approach and suggest that the fewer firms there are in a particular industry—the more likely it is that there will be market failures. Thus, a monopoly hinders the achievement of most policy goals that one might design for competition law, whilst a market with many buyers and many sellers operates to guarantee the welfare of consumers. The other standpoint takes a less deterministic line and states that the structure of an industry is insufficient to predict whether firms are acting to promote the aims of competition law; one has to look at the other features of the market to see if there are any pressures that 'discipline' firms. A monopolist in a market where potential entry by others is easy will not raise prices for fear of losing its position of dominance to other competitors. In such a way, the market itself often resolves a possible reduction of competition.[249] Finally, regarding the institutional aspect of competition law, the most common method for enforcing competition law is through a system of administrative control by an agency.[250] The composition and the powers of the competition law institution in charge may be designed to achieve the kinds of goals that competition law seeks to attain. If competition law serves only consumer welfare, then an agency independent of governmental influence is appropriate. However, if competition law is also designed to pursue other public policies, then an agency more responsible to the government might be desirable. Conversely, the professional makeup of the institution may shape the economic and political direction of law enforcement.[251] In practice, clearly, there are many compromises and combinations within and among political, economic and institutional aspects of competition law in creating a specific competition policy. These three different forces may exert different pressures at different times in the history of competition law enforcement, resulting in different outcomes. Although competition law should be observed as a whole, for analytical purposes, it is helpful to consider each of the mentioned aspects independently.[252]

Therefore, it is reasonable to conclude that there is no exhaustive list of competition law objectives. This concept allows competent bodies more flexibility and discretionary powers to adapt their rulings in certain cases to achieve a specific ratio during a particular period. Nevertheless, competition law objectives do exist. They

---

[248] Monti (2007).

[249] Monti (2007).

[250] For example, via the European Commission in the EC, the Office of Fair Trading and the Competition Commission in the UK, the Department of Justice and the Federal Trade Commission in the US.

[251] See Monti (2007), p. 4.

[252] See Monti (2007), pp. 5–6.

developed through practice and legislation based on a particular vision of what competition law is designed to do, and many compromises among lawmakers. Sometimes they are stated more formally in competition laws or enforcement guidelines, and sometimes informally through speeches and presentations.[253] Thus, the development of competition law and policy, doctrine and practice have produced several competition objectives (total surplus, consumer surplus, defence of smaller firms, promoting market integration, economic freedom, fighting inflation, fairness and equity; then social reasons, political reasons, environmental reasons, strategic reasons, etc.).[254] Concerning the EU, there is no one (or more) universally accepted objective(s) of EU competition law.[255] Nevertheless, especially in recent times, consumer welfare and efficiency seem to be widely acknowledged as the two main objectives of the EU competition law,[256] which are commonly addressed in the context of the copyright-competition interaction discussion.

Consumer Welfare

Protection and promotion of consumer welfare are often among the main objectives by which competition policy is driven.[257] To understand the meaning and purpose of consumer welfare, it is essential to identify the 'consumer' in consumer welfare. Keeping in mind the common perception of the term 'consumer' and its economic meaning, it seems evident that this meaning does not correspond with the meaning of 'consumer' in competition policy. According to the OECD glossary:

> Consumer welfare refers to the individual benefits derived from the consumption of goods and services. In theory, individual welfare is defined by an individual's own assessment of

[253] See Lee (2015), p. 3.

[254] See Drahos (2001), pp. 53–56; Geradin et al. (2012), pp. 19–26; Motta (2004), pp. 17–30.

[255] See Colino (2019), pp. 37–39; Korah (1986), pp. 85–109; Whish and Bailey (2021), pp. 19–24.

[256] In somewhat different terms, Colino acknowledges that consumers and trading standards might benefit from the application of competition law but concludes that "competition law aims at protecting competition, not consumers, individual competitors, or trading standards." Such a statement is certainly not wrong, however, in protecting free competition, competition law accordingly also promotes consumer welfare and efficiency, especially within the EU, which often explicitly recognises consumer welfare and efficiency as the main objectives. If encouragement of free competition is to the harm of consumers, individual competitors and trading standards, it is hard to agree that in such cases, competition law interventions are justified; see Colino (2019), pp. 1–2.

[257] In particular literature and case law, there is a distinction between the concepts of consumer welfare and consumer well-being; however, having in mind that they do overlap in their essence, we shall here not further discuss their potential discrepancies; see Ezrachi (2018), pp. 5–6. Different welfare standards are in consideration in competition policies, such as total welfare, social welfare, however, the consumer welfare standard is most often indicated as one of the main objectives of competition law. Judgment of 7 June 2006, *Österreichische Postsparkasse and Bank für Arbeit und Wirtschaft v Commission,* Joined Cases T-213/01 and T-214/01, EU:T:2006:151, para. 115: "...the ultimate purpose of the rules that seek to ensure that competition is not distorted in the internal market is to increase the well-being of consumers... Competition law and competition policy... have an undeniable impact on the specific economic interests of final customers who purchase goods or services."

> his/her satisfaction, given prices and income. Exact measurement of consumer welfare therefore requires information about individual preferences. In practice, applied welfare economics uses the notion of consumer surplus to measure consumer welfare. When measured over all consumers, consumers' surplus is a measure of aggregate consumer welfare. In anti-trust applications, some argue that the goal is to maximise consumers' surplus, while others argue that producer benefits should also be counted.[258]

Namely, the notion of 'consumer welfare' is in practice linked to another term of art in economics—'consumer surplus'.

> Consumers' surplus is a measure of consumer welfare and is defined as the excess of social valuation of product over the price actually paid. It is measured by the area of a triangle below a demand curve and above the observed price.[259]

Despite different interpretations and confusion in terminology in practice, it is widely accepted that the competition law's 'consumer welfare' is a broad term that does not refer only to the ultimate end-user consumer but also to the 'consumers' at the intermediate level, e.g. manufacturers who use a product as an input or distributors of a good or service.[260]

Both the EU and the US competition policies share and use the term 'consumer welfare' in literature and case law.[261] In the US, there is still no clear and consistent understanding of the concept of consumer welfare. There is no consensus—not among academics and not in terms of case law—as to how consumer welfare is to be understood in the US antitrust law, and there are doubts as to the extent the discussion makes any sense in practice.[262]

In the EU, the situation with the interpretation of consumer welfare should be more straightforward since, within its soft law, the EU Commission explicitly identified consumer welfare and allocative efficiency as the goals of Article 101 TFEU.[263] The Guidelines on the application of Article 81(3) of the Treaty provide that the Community competition rules aim to protect competition on the market as a means of enhancing consumer welfare and of ensuring an efficient allocation of resources. Further on, they elaborate that, when an express agreement that restricts competition has pro-competitive effects that outweigh its anti-competitive effects, the net effect of such agreements is to promote the very essence of the competitive process, namely, to win customers by offering better products or

---

[258] OECD (1993), p. 29.

[259] OECD (1993), p. 28.

[260] See EU Communication from the Commission—Notice—Guidelines on the application of Article 81(3) of the Treaty, OJ C 101, 27.4.2004, pp. 97–118, para. 84; EU Communication from the Commission—Guidance on the Commission's enforcement priorities in applying Article 82 of the EC Treaty to abusive exclusionary conduct by dominant undertakings, *OJ C 45, 24.2.2009,* pp. 7–20, para. 19. See Hovenkamp (2019), pp. 114–115.

[261] The term consumer welfare was effectively introduced in antitrust law by Robert Bork in the late 1970s; see Bork (1978), pp. 81–89, 107–115.

[262] Daskalova (2015), pp. 140–142.

[263] See EU Green Paper on Vertical Restraints in EC Competition Policy, COM (96) 721 final, 22 January 1997, p. 52.

better prices than those offered by rivals.[264] The Guidance on the Commission's enforcement priorities in applying Article 82 of the EC Treaty to abusive exclusionary conduct by dominant undertakings indicates that the aim of the Commission's enforcement activity concerning exclusionary conduct is to ensure that dominant undertakings do not impair effective competition by foreclosing their competitors in an anti-competitive way, thus having an adverse impact on consumer welfare, whether in the form of higher price levels than would have otherwise prevailed or in some other form such as limiting quality or reducing consumer choice.[265] Such interpretation of consumer welfare seems to correspond to its original meaning that was first introduced by Bork—total welfare standard based on allocative efficiency consideration.

Therefore, the Commission clearly indicated its standpoint that consumer welfare is positioned as one of the most important objectives that represent the core of competition law. Accordingly, from the wording of the mentioned documents, the consumers are one of the prime beneficiaries of the competition law.

If certain conduct harms consumer welfare, such behaviour is likely to be taken as anti-competitive behaviour. Consumer welfare may be harmed both directly and indirectly, considering that competition provisions cover not only practices that directly cause harm to consumers but also practices that cause consumers harm through their impact on competition.[266] In other words, in its broad principles, the consumer welfare standard only states that actual harm to real people is the reason why competition should be defended.[267] In practice, however, the effects analysis has often focused on identifiable consumer harm, particularly on likely short-run and price-based effects.[268]

---

[264] EU Communication from the Commission—Notice—Guidelines on the application of Article 81(3) of the Treaty, OJ C 101, 27.4.2004, pp. 97–118, paras. 13, 33.

[265] EU Communication from the Commission—Guidance on the Commission's enforcement priorities in applying Article 82 of the EC Treaty to abusive exclusionary conduct by dominant undertakings, OJ C 45, 24.2.2009, pp. 7–20, paras. 1, 19.

[266] See Judgment of 27 March 2012, *Post Danmark A/S v Konkurrencerådet*, C-209/10, EU:C:2012:172, para. 20; Judgment of 17 February 2011, *Konkurrensverket v TeliaSonera Sverige AB*, C-52/09, EU:C:2011:83, para. 24. Further on, in the *GSK* case, the CJEU clarified that to establish harm "it is not necessary that final consumers be deprived of the advantages of effective competition in terms of supply or price" and that "[Article 101 TFEU] aims to protect not only the interests of competitors or of consumers, but also the structure of the market and, in so doing, competition as such." Judgment of 6 October 2009, GlaxoSmithKline Services Unlimited v Commission of the European Communities (C-501/06 P) and Commission of the European Communities v GlaxoSmithKline Services Unlimited (C-513/06 P) and European Association of Euro Pharmaceutical Companies (EAEPC) v Commission of the European Communities (C-515/06 P) and Asociación de exportadores españoles de productos farmacéuticos (Aseprofar) v Commission of the European Communities (C-519/06 P), Joined cases C-501/06 P, C-513/06 P, C-515/06 P and C-519/06 P, EU:C:2009:610, para. 63.

[267] Consumer harm can relate to any type of adverse effects, whether on price, output, choice, quality or innovation.

[268] See Crémer et al. (2019), p. 41.

However, even though consumer welfare is probably the first clearly formulated and even maybe the most critical goal of competition policy, lately, this concept is losing its importance, especially in the EU. Namely, within EU law, increasingly frequently, 'price, quality and choice' are indicated as standards according to which competition policy should be driven. Considering that the EU Commission has in recent times focused on promoting competitiveness and innovation, this does not seem rather strange. In the Staff Working Paper accompanying the Report on Competition Policy, the following objectives were indicated, which are an essential part of the broader general objectives of the Europe 2020 Strategy for smart, sustainable and inclusive growth:

> EU competition policy aims at achieving three main objectives: i) protecting competition on the market as a means of enhancing consumer welfare, ii) supporting growth, jobs and the competitiveness of the EU economy and iii) fostering a competition culture.[269]

Further on, it is explained that competition stimulates entrepreneurship, improves efficiency, and creates the best conditions for innovation, resulting in everyone being better off when markets are competitive—consumers, taxpayers, citizens and businesses.[270]

Such a standpoint of the EU Commission has been affirmed in later soft law.[271] Given this change in its language, it seems that the EU has changed its view on consumer welfare as the ultimate or primary goal of competition policy. Instead, the consumer welfare objective appears to be on equal footing with industrial policy goals, which align with the EU's 2020 agenda and focus on growth and competitiveness.[272] That especially applies to the nowadays extremely actual and present fast-changing digital environment, which is very different from traditional industries. According to the Competition Policy for the Digital Era, European Commission Special Advisers' Report, although the need for the consumer welfare standard in assessing competition cases persists, the practical importance of the consumer welfare standard is reduced in the digital economy.[273]

---

[269] Commission Staff Working Paper Accompanying the Report From the Commission on Competition Policy 2011, COM(2012) 253 final, p. 3.

[270] Ibid.

[271] See EU Commission Staff Working Document Accompanying the document Report From the Commission to the European Parliament, the Council, the European Economic and Social Committee and the Committee of the Regions Report on Competition Policy 2014, COM(2015) 247 final, p. 4; EU Commission Staff Working Document Accompanying the document Report From the Commission to the European Parliament, the Council, the European Economic and Social Committee and the Committee of the Regions Report on Competition Policy 2015, COM(2016) 393 final, p. 4; EU Commission Staff Working Document Accompanying the document Report From the Commission to the European Parliament, the Council, the European Economic and Social Committee and the Committee of the Regions Report on Competition Policy 2017 {COM(2018) 482 final, p. 3.

[272] See EU Communication From the Commission Europe 2020: A strategy for smart, sustainable and inclusive growth, COM(2010) 2020., p. 19.

[273] See Crémer et al. (2019), pp. 40, 41.

Efficiency

There is a wide belief among lawyers and economists that promoting economic efficiency is the fundamental objective of competition.[274] Such a viewpoint is generally in line with the concept of a market-oriented and effects-based 'more economic approach' in modern competition law advocated by the Commission, particularly during the last two decades.[275] However, by looking into relevant literature, case law and soft law, there is no consensus on what exactly should be understood by the notion of 'efficiency'. The importance of efficiency, as part of the economic analysis of competition law, is unquestionable. It is crucial for defining and assessing competition law matters, especially in determining types of conduct that create competition concerns and for the justification of such conduct.[276]

The starting point for understanding efficiency as a competition law objective is to note that there are different types/components of efficiency.[277] There are allocative and productive efficiencies as static efficiencies, and there is dynamic efficiency.[278] The difference between the static and the dynamic concept of efficiencies is the relevant time horizon over which these efficiencies display their effects.[279] Allocative efficiency is achieved when goods and services are produced and distributed to the consumers who value them the most. Allocative efficiency has also been defined technically as marginal cost pricing.[280] Productive efficiency is related to cost minimisation—goods and services will be produced at the lowest possible cost. In other words, allocative efficiency is related to the 'what to produce' and 'for whom to produce' questions, while productive efficiency is related to 'how to produce'.[281] As static efficiencies, allocative and productive efficiencies are one-off gains from improvements in resource allocation, given that no change in

[274] From the US perspective, Posner observes efficiency as 'the ultimate goal of antitrust'. Posner (2001), p. 29; Posner (1976), p. 4.

[275] In the context of EU competition law, the concept 'more economic approach' was initially introduced within the Guidelines on vertical restraints; see Commission notice—Guidelines on Vertical Restraints, OJ C 291, 13.10.2000, pp. 1–44, para. 7.

[276] See OECD, The Role of Efficiency Claims in Antitrust Proceedings 2012, DAF/COMP(2012) 23, 2 May 2013, p. 11; Geradin (2004), p. 2.

[277] See Lee (2015), pp. 7–10; Havyatt (2017).

[278] In addition to allocative, productive and dynamic efficiencies, some authors also define a fourth, broad category, transactional efficiency. In accordance with the principles of 'transaction cost economics', this efficiency allows firms to reduce the transaction costs they incur in dealings with their business partners, and therefore facilitates the achievement of other types of efficiencies; see OECD, The Role of Efficiency Claims in Antitrust Proceedings 2012, DAF/COMP(2012)23, 2 May 2013, p. 14.

[279] OECD, The Role of Efficiency Claims in Antitrust Proceedings 2012, DAF/COMP(2012)23, 2 May 2013, p. 12.

[280] See OECD (2013), pp. 12–13; Geradin (2004), p. 4; Lee (2015), p. 7.

[281] See OECD (2013), p. 13; Geradin (2004), p. 4; Lee (2015), p. 7.

technology occurs.[282] On the other hand, dynamic efficiency results from technical progress. Here, efficiency gains take the form of improvements in production processes and/or new products and/or services. For dynamic efficiency, it is challenging to determine ex-ante whether an innovation activity such as research and development (R&D) will result in actual innovation, especially much more difficult compared to static types of efficiencies.[283]

Generally, competition should promote efficiency by increasing both allocative and productive efficiency and, also, by encouraging innovation. However, in practice, the relationship between those three types is somewhat complex and not so strongly coordinated. An increase in one type of efficiency does not necessarily mean an increase in the other two types of efficiency.[284] Consequently, there is a need for balancing among these three types of efficiencies, where the critical issue is the relative importance given to a particular type of efficiency.

Efficiency in competition law is entwined with different notions of welfare, such as total welfare, social welfare and consumer welfare, in the way that pursuit of efficiency brings or should bring about welfare maximisation and vice versa.[285] The welfare standard in use in a specific competition regime also affects whether certain types of efficiency gains are more readily accepted in practice.[286] In the EU, it seems that by promoting the consumer welfare standard, stress is given to the allocative type of efficiency. As shown earlier, Guidelines on the application of Article 81(3) of the Treaty state that along with consumer welfare, ensuring an efficient allocation of resources is the aim of the Community competition rules.[287] Besides that, the Guidance on the Commission's enforcement priorities in applying Article 82 of the EC Treaty to abusive exclusionary conduct by dominant undertakings states that the Commission strives to ensure that *markets function properly and that consumers benefit from the efficiency and productivity which result from effective competition between undertakings*.[288] Considering that, it seems to a certain extent understandable to acknowledge that EU competition policy emphasises allocative efficiency over other types of efficiency.

There is no consensus among scholars, practitioners and lawmakers on the most appropriate competition law approach. The EU has clearly placed its focus on the promotion of consumer welfare and allocative efficiency. The promotion of

---

[282] See seven flagship initiatives to catalyse progress under each priority theme, EU Communication From the Commission Europe 2020: A strategy for smart, sustainable and inclusive growth, COM (2010) 2020.

[283] See OECD (2013), p. 14; Geradin (2004), p. 4; Lee (2015), p. 8.

[284] See Geradin (2004), p. 4.

[285] Lee (2015), p. 7.

[286] OECD (2013), p. 5.

[287] EU Communication from the Commission—Notice—Guidelines on the application of Article 81(3) of the Treaty, OJ C 101, 27.4.2004, pp. 97–118, paras. 13, 33.

[288] EU Communication from the Commission—Guidance on the Commission's enforcement priorities in applying Article 82 of the EC Treaty to abusive exclusionary conduct by dominant undertakings, OJ C 45, 24.2.2009, pp. 7–20, paras. 5–7.

consumer welfare and allocative efficiency is indeed important, but its benefits are sometimes only short-term. Thus, when creating competition laws and assessing competition cases, it may be advisable to focus more on technological advancements, originality, creativity, and dynamic efficiency to produce long-term healthy competition and a productive environment.[289] Considering the EU's 2020s agendas that are focused on growth, development of new technologies, improvement of competitiveness, digitalisation of markets, etc., such a shift in focus may seem to be effectual—particularly concerning the copyright-based creative industries.

* * *

After analysing the foundations and objectives of competition law, it seems proper to note a further characteristic of competition law—competition law is an interdisciplinary field of law in which economics has a vital role. Without an adequate understanding of economics, it is impossible to approach competition law matters properly. In that sense, Whish and Bailey write: "The analysis of competition issues invariably requires an assessment of market power, and such an assessment cannot be conducted without an understanding of the economic concepts involved."[290] Although it is nowadays commonly accepted that economics has a crucial role in competition law,[291] the economic element is not always adequately addressed in particular competition cases. Economic factors are present in practically every stage of a competition assessment starting from the definition of the relevant market, through the determination of market power, (anti-)competitive effects of particular conduct on the market, application of the theory of harm, and ultimately in the establishment of possible anti-competitive behaviour (as well as in other phases). Without solid economic elements, competition law cases stand on fragile fundamentals that do not fulfil their purpose and objectives. As Colino writes: "Attempts to avoid the 'problem' of economics are likely to result in bad law."[292] That is why competition matters should not be approached one-sidedly only from a legal perspective, but comprehensively—thereby, the economic aspect is always present, while sometimes, depending on a particular case, other disciplines may also be included.

---

[289] See OECD (2013), p. 15.

[290] See Whish and Bailey (2021), p. 2; see also Niels et al. (2023).

[291] However, in the early days of competition law in the EU and the US, the role of economics was not that vigorously emphasised. In the EU the situation has drastically changed from the middle 1990s and now it is widely accepted that competition law enforcement is justified only where a particular conduct could lead to significant harmful effects to the competitive process; and that the extent of any harm is usually related to the degree of market power that a undertaking(s), have or will have on the market; see Geradin et al. (2012), pp. 19, 60; Kovacic and Shapiro (2000), p. 44; Whish and Bailey (2021), p. 2.

[292] Colino considers that economics can be employed in two main ways in relation to competition law: "First, because competition law is aimed in part at remedying market failure, a general macro-economic argument can be made as to the existence of such market failure and the costs imposed by it. Secondly, micro-economic arguments are likely to be relied upon in each individual case to justify intervention or to defend a company's position" Colino (2019), p. 8.

Also, due to the specificity and diversity of competition law, it is impossible to prescribe all situations. Whish and Bailey consider that competition law concerns "cannot be expressed in a codified table of rules capable of precise application in the way, for example, that law on taxation or the relationship of landlord and tenant can."[293] Hence, the open-textured legislative body usually regulates competition law, and, throughout time, the purpose of competition law keeps changing, sometimes even without the need to intervene in the legislative text.[294] The EU also adopted an open-ended approach. Thus, EU competition rules on anti-competitive agreements and abuse of dominant position are virtually based on two provisions worded in broad and vague terms—Article 101 TFEU (anti-competitive agreements) and Article 102 TFEU (abuse of dominant position). There is no definition of a 'restriction of competition' or an 'abuse' of dominant position.[295] However, given the nature and role of the discipline, there are clear advantages of an open-ended approach in regulating competition law (indeed, on condition that there is a sufficient degree of predictability[296]). Keeping in mind the vast and diverse range of practices that might fall under the competition law scrutiny, it is virtually a Herculean task to codify them ex ante. Also, competition law is not intended to be applied in a particular sector but across the board. Due to the interdisciplinary character of competition matters, particularities of a specific industry must be considered due to which competition law must continuously adapt (which is especially difficult in newly developed industries, as is often happening in the present era of digital evolution). In addition to that, open-textured provisions are also advantageous in that they make it possible to refine intervention incrementally to capture theoretical and empirical evidence in the field.[297] Finally, adopting such an approach enabled the EU competition policy to undergo significant changes without the need to amend the wording of the competition rules—particularly Article 101 and 102 TFEU, which have stayed the same since they were incorporated into the Treaty of Rome in 1957.[298]

---

[293] Whish and Bailey (2021), p. 2.

[294] See Monti (2007), pp. 2–3.

[295] Such an approach is also applied within secondary legislation on competition law, while interpretation is provided through particular case law and soft-law documents; see, for instance, Council Regulation (EC) No. 139/2004 of 20 January 2004 on the control of concentrations between undertakings (the EC Merger Regulation), OJ L 24, 29.1.2004, pp. 1–22.

[296] See Monti (2007), p. 15.

[297] See Ibáñez Colomo (2018), pp. 23–24.

[298] Nevertheless, the use of broad and vague provisions also has its downfalls. First, they are, per se, imprecise and not clear without a concrete factual scenario. Then, there is also a high possibility of different interpretations and inconsistency in the application of such norms; see Ibáñez Colomo (2018), pp. 24–25.

2.2.3 A Note on EU Competition Law and Member States' Competition Laws

A brief historical overview of competition law already makes it possible to note that in the EU, there is somewhat of a dualism between the EU competition law and Member States' competition laws. Generally, the division of jurisdiction between the EU and national competition laws can be set so that EU competition law applies when there is an effect on intra-EU trade, while national competition law applies when there is an effect only on the national market.[299] The same can generally be said for the division of competence between the Commission and national competition authorities. However, there are exceptions and the division between EU competition law and Member States' competition laws is not always clear. Nevertheless, it seems that nowadays, that does not represent a problem. First, since the EU competition rules are laid down within the Treaties as primary EU law (or within secondary law in regulations, as in the case of mergers), EU competition law has a direct effect on national legislations without any need for further implementation into national laws.[300] Second, nowadays, Member States have aligned their national competition laws with EU competition law. Thus, even in the cases decided by national competition authorities based on national competition laws, EU competition law interpretations and principles must be followed. Generally, it can be summed up as it follows: EU (competition) law is a source of law in all the Member States of the EU, and takes precedence over national law in the event of conflict; when a national competition authority applies its own competition law to a situation in which Article 101 is relevant, it must also apply Article 101 TFEU, and ought not to reach an inconsistent result; in national cases relating to monopoly abuse, Article 102 TFEU must also be applied, but a stricter standard can be set under national law; EU competition law can only be applied if there is an effect on trade between Member States.[301,302]

Thus, in the context of copyright-competition interaction, this thesis primarily focuses on the interaction between copyright and EU competition law; however, findings from the research are also directly applicable to the interaction between copyright and national competition laws.

---

[299] See Drahos (2001), pp. 215–216.

[300] See Folsom (2014), pp. 78–84, 384–385.

[301] See Colino (2019), pp. 57–71.

[302] See, for instance, Judgment of 16 November 1977, *SA G.B.-INNO-B.M. v Association des détaillants en tabac (ATAB)*, C-13/77, EU:C:1977:185, paras. 30–31; Judgment of 10 January 1985, Association des Centres distributeurs Édouard Leclerc and others v SARL 'Au blé vert' and others, C-229/83, EU:C:1985:1, paras. 14–20; Judgment of 30 January 1985, *Bureau national interprofessionnel du cognac v Guy Clair*, C-123/83, EU:C:1985:33, paras. 23, 25–26; Judgment of 17 November 1993, *Bundesanstalt für den Güterfernverkehr v Gebrüder Reiff GmbH & Co. KG*, C-185/91, EU:C:1993:886, para. 24; Judgment of 17 November 1993, *Criminal proceedings against Ohra Schadeverzekeringen NV*, C-245/91, EU:C:1993:887, paras. 11–14.

2.2.4 Concluding Remarks

To summarise, from the above brief general overview of competition law, several things are particularly vital for the further discussion on copyright-competition interaction:

- competition law in Europe had an independent development, somewhat influenced by the United States tradition
- although some States already had competition laws before, the genuine development of competition law in Europe commenced with the creation of the European Union
- within the European Union, every State has its own national competition laws that substantially follow the European Union competition law
- one of the main objectives of competition law is consumer welfare and efficiency
- competition law is fundamentally regulated by an open-textured legislative body
- currently, there is an ongoing digital evolution that requires further development of competition law interpretation

References

Alford WP (1995) To steal a book is an elegant offense: intellectual property law in Chinese civilization. Stanford University Press, Stanford

Association Littéraire et Artistique Internationale (ALAI) (n.d.) Who we are? https://www.alai.org/en/information/presentation.html. Accessed 22 Oct 2024

Atkinson B, Fitzgerald B (2014) A short history of copyright: the genie of information. Springer, Cham

Bappert W (1962) Wege zum Urheberrecht: Die geschichtliche Entwicklung des Urheberrechtsgedankens. Vittorio Klostermann, Frankfurt am Main

Bayer WF (1952) Das Neue Österreichische Kartellgesetz. Zeitschrift für ausländisches und internationales Privatrecht, 17. Jahrg., H. 4, pp 656–672

Beier FK, Schricker G, Fikentscher W (1996) German industrial property, Copyright and antitrust law, 3rd edn. VCH Verlagsgesellschaft mbH, Weinheim

Bently L (2010) Introduction to Part I: the history of copyright. In: Bently L, Suthersanen U, Torremans P (eds) Global copyright - three hundred years since the Statute of Anne, from 1709 to cyberspace. Edward Elgar, Cheltenham

Bohun J (1993) Protecting prerogative: William III and the East India Trade Debate, 1689-1698. Past Imperfect 2:63–86

Bork RH (1978) The antitrust paradox: a policy at war with itself. Basic Books, Inc., Publishers, New York

Bowker R (1912) Copyright its history and its law being summary of the principles & practices of copyright with special reference to the American Code of 1909 and the British Act of 1911. Houghton Mifflin Company, Boston

Boytha G (1991) Die Historischen Wurzeln der Vielfältigkeit des Schutzes von Rechten an Urheberwerken. In: Dittrich R (ed) Die Notwendigkeit des Uereberrechtsschutzes im Lichte seiner Geschichte. Manzsche Verlags- und Universitätsbuchhandlung, Wien, pp 69–90

Bracha O (2010) Early American printing privileges. The ambivalent origins of authors' copyright in America. In: Deazley R, Kretschmer M, Bently L (eds) Privilege and property: essays on the history of copyright. Open Books Publishers, pp 89–114
Ciceronis MT (1999) Epistulae ad Atticum, XIII. In: Shackleton Bailey DR (ed, trans), Cicero: Letters to Atticus. Loeb Classical Library, vol IV, Harvard University Press, Cambridge, MA
Colino SM (2019) Competition law of the EU and UK, 8th edn. Oxford University Press, Oxford
Cornish W (2010) The Statute of Anne 1709-1710: its historical setting. In: Bently L, Suthersanen U, Torremans P (eds) Global copyright - three hundred years since the Statute of Anne, from 1709 to cyberspace. Edward Elgar, Cheltenham, pp 14–25
Crane DA, Hovenkamp H (2013) The making of competition policy: legal and economic sources. Oxford University Press, New York
Crémer J, de Montjoye Y-A, Schweitzer H (2019) Competition policy for the digital era, European Commission special advisers' report, shaping competition policy in the era of digitization. http://ec.europa.eu/competition/publications/reports/kd0419345enn.pdf. Accessed 22 Oct 2024
Das JK (2008) Intellectual property rights. Kamal Law House, Kolkata
Daskalova V (2015) Consumer welfare in EU competition law. Competition Law Rev 11(1): 131–160
De Wolf RC (1925) Outline of copyright law. John W. Luce & Company, Boston
Dewey D (1990) The antitrust experiment in America. Columbia University Press, New York
Diderot D (1970) Oeuvres Complètes, vol 15. Paris
Dock M-V (1974) The origin and development of the literary property concept (orig. Genèse et évolution de la notion de propriété littéraire). Revue internationale du droit d'auteur, LXXIX, January 1974:126–204
Drahos M (2001) Convergence of competition laws and policies in the European community. Kluwer Law International
Dreier T (2002) The role of the ECJ for the development of copyright in the European Communities. The complete version of a presentation given at the annual International Study Days of the Association littéraire et artistique (ALAI) at Neuchâtel, Switzerland, on 17 Sept 2002. https://www.zar.kit.edu/DATA/~recht/material/ECJ-ALAI/print_version.pdf. Accessed 22 Oct 2024
Dzlatzko (1894) Autor - und Verlagsrecht in Alterhum. Rheinisches Museum für philologie, Neue Folge 49:559–576
Ewing KP (2006) Competition rules for the 21st century: principles from America's experience, 2nd edn. Kluwer Law International, The Hague
Ezrachi A (2018) The goals of EU competition law and the digital economy. Oxford legal studies research paper no. 17/2018, 6 June 2018. https://ssrn.com/abstract=3191766. Accessed 22 Oct 2024
Ezrachi A, Stucke ME (2018) The fight over antitrust's soul. J Eur Competition Law Pract 9(1):1–2
Folsom RH (2014) Principles of European Union. West Academic Publishing, Saint Paul
Fox EM (1987) The battle for the soul of antitrust. Calif Law Rev 75:917–923
Gaius (2024) Institutes, II. http://thelatinlibrary.com/. Accessed 22 Oct 2024
Geller PE (1994) Copyright between marketplace and authorship norms. In: Sherman B, Strowel A (eds) Of authors and origins: essays on copyright law. Clarendon Press, Oxford, pp 159–202
Geller PE (1998) From patchwork to network: strategies for international intellectual property in flux. Duke J Comp Int Law 9:69–90
Geller PE (2000) Copyright history and the future: what's culture got to do with it? J Copyright Soc USA 47:209–264
Geradin D (2004) Efficiency claims in EC competition law and sector-specific regulation. Paper prepared for workshop on comparative competition law: the evolution of European competition law - whose regulation, which regulation? Florence. https://ssrn.com/abstract=617922. Accessed 22 Oct 2024
Geradin D, Layne-Farrar A, Petit N (2012) EU competition law and economics. Oxford University Press, Oxford

Gerber DJ (1992) The origins of European competition law in Fin-de-Siècle Austria. Am J Leg Hist 36(4):405–440
Gerber DJ (1994) The transformation of European community competition law. Harv Int Law J 35(1):97–147
Gerber DJ (2003) Law and competition in twentieth century Europe: protecting Prometheus. Oxford University Press, Oxford (reprint)
Ghidini G (2006) Intellectual property and competition law: the innovation nexus. Edward Elgar, Cheltenham
Gieseke L (1957) Die geschichtliche Entwicklung des deutschen Urheberrechts. Göttinger, rechtswissenschaftliche Studien, vol 22. Verlag Otto Schwartz & Co, Göttingen
Ginsburg JC (1990) A tale of two copyrights: literary property in revolutionary France and America. Tulane Law Rev 64(5):991–1031
Ginsburg JC (2010) The US experience with copyright formalities: a love/hate relationship. Columbia J Law Arts 33(4):311–348
Ginsburg J (2018) Copyright. In: Dreyfuss RC, Pilla J (eds) The Oxford handbook of intellectual property law. Oxford University Press, Oxford, pp 487–516
Ginsburg JC (2019) General report, justifications for author's rights. In: Blomqvist J (ed) Copyright, to be or not to be. Ex Tuto Publishing, Copenhagen, pp 15–26
Godson R (1840) A practical treaties on the law of patents for inventions and of copyright, 2nd edn. Saunders and Benning, Law Booksellers, London
Goldstein P (1989a) Copyright, vol I. Little, Brown and Company, Boston
Goldstein P (1989b) Copyright, vol II. Little, Brown and Company, Boston
Goldstein P (2024a) Goldstein on copyright, vol I. Wolters Kluwer, New York
Goldstein P (2024b) Goldstein on copyright, vol II. Wolters Kluwer, New York
Goldstein P, Hugenholtz PB (2021) International copyright: principles, law and practice, 4th edn. Oxford University Press, Oxford
Grosheide FW (1986) Auteursrecht op maat: beschouwingen over de grondslagen van het auteursrecht in een rechtspolit. Kluwer, Deventer
Grosheide FW (1994) Paradigms in copyright law. In: Sherman B, Strowel A (eds) Of authors and origins: essays on copyright law. Clarendon Press, Oxford, pp 203–234
Grosheide FW (2010) Transition from guild regulation to modern copyright law - a view from the low countries. In: Bently L, Suthersanen U, Torremans P (eds) Global copyright - three hundred years since the Statute of Anne, from 1709 to cyberspace. Edward Elgar, Cheltenham, pp 79–102
Guibault L (1998) Limitations found outside of copyright law, general report. ALAI STUDY DAYS, Cambridge, 14–17 September 1998. The exceptions and limitations to copyright. https://www.ivir.nl/publicaties/download/VUL5BOVT.pdf. Accessed 22 Oct 2024
Hauser A (1962) The social history of art, vol 1. Routledge & K. Paul, London
Havyatt D (2017) The components of efficiency, Network, Australian Competition and Consumer Commission for the Utility Regulators Forum. Issue 62, March 2017. https://www.accc.gov.au/publications/network. Accessed 22 Oct 2024
Hazan J (1970) The origins of copyright law in Ancient Jewish law. Bull Copyright Soc U.S.A. 18(1):23–28
Hesse C (1990) Enlightenment Epistemology and the Laws of Authorship in Revolutionary France, 1777–1793. Representations, Special Issue: Law and the Order of Culture, University of California Press, Spring 1990, pp. 109–137
Hesse C (2002) Intellectual property, 700 B.C., - A.D. 2000. Daedalus – J Am Acad Arts Sci, pp 26–45
Hilthy RM, Moscon V (2021) An international instrument on permitted uses in copyright law. In: Balganesh S, Wee Loon N-L, Sun H (eds) Copyright limitations and exceptions. Cambridge University Press, Cambridge, pp 59–73
Hovenkamp H (1991) Enterprise and American law 1836-1937. Harvard University Press, Cambridge

Hovenkamp HJ (2019) Is antitrust's consumer welfare principle imperiled? J Corp Law 45(1): 101–130

Hugenholtz PB (1997) Fierce creatures. Copyright exemptions: towards extinction? Keynote speech, IFLA/IMPRIMATUR conference, rights, limitations and exceptions: striking a proper balance, Amsterdam, 30–31 October 1997. https://www.ivir.nl/publicaties/download/PBH-FierceCreatures.pdf. Accessed 22 Oct 2024

Hugenholtz PB (2017) Can the EU author's rights accommodate fair use? In: Okediji RL (ed) Copyright law in an age of limitations and exceptions. Cambridge University Press, New York, pp 275–291

Hugenholtz PB, Okediji RL (2008) Conceiving an international instrument on limitations and exceptions to copyright. Institute for Information Law, University of Amsterdam, University of Minnesota, Law School, final report, 6 March 2008. https://www.opensocietyfoundations.org/publications/conceiving-international-instrument-limitations-and-exceptions-copyright. Accessed 22 Oct 2024

Hughes J (2012) A short history of intellectual property in relation to copyright. Cardozo Law Rev 33(4):1293–1340

Ibáñez Colomo P (2018) The shaping of EU competition law. Cambridge University Press, Cambridge

Iustinianus (1998a) Digesta, VI. In: Watson A (ed, trans) The digest of Justinian, vol 1. University of Pennsylvania Press, Philadelphia, pp. 204–205

Iustinianus (1998b) Digesta, XLI. In: Watson A (ed, trans) The digest of Justinian, vol 4. University of Pennsylvania Press, Philadelphia, pp. 4–5

Johannes H (1982) Technology transfer under EEC law—Europe between the divergent opinions of the past and the new administration: a comparative law approach. In: Hawk BE (ed) Annual proceedings of the Fordham Corporate Law Institute Antitrust, Technology Transfers and Joint Ventures in International Trade, Fordham Corporate Law Institute, Matthew Bender, New York, pp 65–94

Karnell GWG (2016) ALAI – initiator and Berne Copyright Convention watch-dog – viewed from a personal and slightly Nordic perspective. In: Karnell GVG, Kur A, Nordell PJ, Westman D, Axhamn J, Carlsson S (eds) Liber Amicorum Jan Rosén. Visby, pp 409–425

Kohler J (1880) Das Autorrecht. eine zivilistische Abhandlung, Jena

Kohler J (1892) Das literarische und artistische Kunstwerk und sein Autorschutz: Eine juridisch-ästhetische Studie. Bensheimer, Mannheim

Kohler J (1907) Urheberrecht an schriftwerken und verlagsrecht, Stuttgart

Korah V (1986) EEC competition policy - legal form or economic efficiency. Curr Leg Probl 39(1): 85–109

Kostylo J (2010) From gunpowder to print: the common origins of copyright and patent. In: Deazley R, Kretschmer M, Bently L (eds) Privilege and property: essays on the history of copyright. Open Books Publishers, pp 21–50

Kovacic EW, Shapiro C (2000) Antitrust policy: a century of economic and legal thinking. J Econ Perspect 14(1):43–60

Kretschmer M, Bently L, Deazley R (2010) Introduction. The history of copyright history: notes from an emerging discipline. In: Deazley R, Kretschmer M, Bently L (eds) Privilege and property: essays on the history of copyright. Open Books Publishers, pp 1–20

Kronstein H, Leighton G (1946) Cartel control: a record of failure. Yale Law J 55(2):297–335

Lee C (2015) The objectives of competition law. ERIA discussion paper series, ERIA-DP-2015-54, August 2015. https://www.researchgate.net/publication/307634289_The_Objectives_of_Competition_Law. Accessed 2 Oct 2024

Lessing GE (1772) Leben und leben lassen. http://www.zeno.org/Literatur/M/Lessing,+Gotthold+Ephraim/%C3%84sthetische+Schriften/Leben+und+leben+lassen. Accessed 22 Oct 2024

Leucht B, Marquis M (2013) American influences on EEC competition law: two paths, how much dependence? In: Patel KK, Schweitzer H (eds) The historical foundations of EU competition law. Oxford University Press, Oxford, pp 125–161

Lidgard HH, Atik J (eds) (2008) The intersection of IPR and competition law: studies of recent developments in European and U.S. law. Chapter I: History and context. Intellecta docysus, Gothenburg

Liefmann R (1977) Cartels, concerns and trusts. Arno Press, New York (reprint)

Littoz-Monnet A (2006) Copyright in the EU: droit d'auteur or right to copy? J Eur Public Policy 13(3):438–455

Liu S (2019) 权利限制与数字技术. Intellectual Property Publishing House, Beijing [English edition: Liu S (2021) Rights Limitations in Digital Age: Reform of Fair Use in Copyright Law (trans: Wang S, Zhang A, Wang H, Wang J). Springer, Singapore]

Locke J (1690) Two treaties of government. https://www.yorku.ca/comninel/courses/3025pdf/Locke.pdf. Accessed 22 Oct 2024

Lord Wilberforce, Campbell A, Elles N (1966) The law of restrictive trade practices and monopolies, 2nd edn. Sweet and Maxwell, London

Lundberg J (1955) Anti-monopoly legislation in Sweden. Ann Public Cooperative Econ 26(4): 279–283

Martialis MV (1976) Epigrammata. In: Heraeus W, Borovskij J (eds) M. Valerii Martialis Epigrammaton libri, Leipzig [trans: Bohn HG (1897) Bohn's classical library: The epigrams of Martial. Bell & Sons, London]

May C, Sell SK (2006) Intellectual property rights: a critical history. Lynne Rienner Publishers, Inc.

Monti G (2007) EC competition law. Cambridge University Press, Cambridge

Motta M (2004) Competition policy: theory and practice. Cambridge University Press, Cambridge

Niels G, Jenkins H, Kavanagh J (2023) Economics for competition lawyers. Oxford University Press, Oxford

Nörr KW (1995) Law and market organization: the historical experience in Germany from 1900 to the law against restraints of competition (1957). J Institutional and Theoretical Economics (JITE) / Zeitschrift für die gesamte Staatswissenschaft 151(1), The New Institutional Economics Market Organization and Market Behavior (Mar 1995), pp. 5–20

OECD (1993) Glossary of industrial organisation economics and competition law. Compiled by Khemani RS, Shapiro DM (eds) http://www.oecd.org/regreform/sectors/2376087.pdf. Accessed 22 Oct 2024

OECD (1999) Denmark - the role of competition policy in regulatory reform. Country Studies

OECD (2002) Poland - the role of competition policy in regulatory reform. Country Studies

OECD (2003a) France - the role of competition policy in regulatory reform. Country Studies

OECD (2003b) Germany - the role of competition policy in regulatory reform. Country Studies

OECD (2006) Sweden - the role of competition policy in regulatory reform. Country Studies

OECD (2013) The role of efficiency claims in antitrust proceedings 2012. DAF/COMP(2012)23, 2 May 2013

OECD (2018) Scoping note on competition and intellectual property rights as a long-term theme for 2019-2020, 6–8 June 2018, OECD Conference Centre, DAF/COMP/WD(2018)4. http://www.oecd.org/officialdocuments/publicdisplaydocumentpdf/?cote=DAF/COMP/WD(2018)4&docLanguage=En. Accessed 22 Oct 2024

Okediji RL (2017) Reframing international copyright limitations and exceptions as development policy. In: Okediji RL (ed) Copyright law in an age of limitations and exceptions. Cambridge University Press, New York, pp 429–495

Olagnier P (1934) Le Droit d'auteur. Tome premier. Librarie générale de droit & de jurisprudence, Paris

Patterson LR (1968a) Copyright and author's rights. Harv Library Bull XVI(4):370–384

Patterson LR (1968b) Copyright in historical perspective. Vanderbilt University Press, Nashville

Peritz RJR (2000) Competition policy in America: history, rhetoric and law. Oxford University Press, Oxford

Pfister L (2010) Author and work in the French print privileges system: some milestones. In: Deazley R, Kretschmer M, Bently L (eds) Privilege and property: essays on the history of copyright. Open Books Publishers, pp 115–136

Plaisant R (1975) French legislation against restrictive trade practices. Tex Int Law J 10(1):26–45
Plinius (1910) Epistulae I. http://www.attalus.org/old/pliny1.html. Accessed 22 Oct 2024 [trans: Firth JB (1910) The Letters of the Younger Pliny, Walter Scott, London, New York]
Ploman EW, Hamilton LC (1980) Copyright: intellectual property in the information age. Routledge & Kegan Paul, London
Posner RA (1976) Antitrust law: an economic perspective. The Chicago University Press, Chicago
Posner RA (2001) Antitrust law, 2nd edn. The University of Chicago Press, Chicago
Prager FD (1944) A history of intellectual property from 1545 to 1787. J Patent Office Soc 26(11): 711–760
Recht P (1969) Le droit d'auteur, une nouvelle forme de propriété: Historie et Théorie, Librairie Générale de Droit et de Jurisprudence. Paris and Editions J. Duculot, Gembloux
Reichman JH (2017) The limits of "limitations and exceptions" in copyright law. In: Okediji RL (ed) Copyright law in an age of limitations and exceptions. Cambridge University Press, New York, pp 292–314
Rintelen M (1958) Urheberrecht und Urhebervertragsrecht nach österreichischem, deutschem und schweizerischem Recht. Springer, Wien
Rose M (1993) Authors and owners. Harvard University Press, Cambridge
Rose M (1994) The author as proprietor: Donaldson v Becket and the genealogy of modern authorship. In: Sherman B, Strowel A (eds) Of authors and origins: essays on copyright law. Clarendon Press, Oxford, pp 23–57
Ross TW (1998) Introduction: the evolution of competition law in Canada. Rev Ind Organ 13(1): 1–23
Salokannel M (1994) Film authorship and the audio-visual environment. In: Sherman B, Strowel A (eds) Of authors and origins: essays on copyright law. Clarendon Press, Oxford, pp 57–78
Samuelson P (2017) Justifications for copyright limitations and exceptions. In: Okediji RL (ed) Copyright law in an age of limitations and exceptions. Cambridge University Press, New York, pp 12–59
Saunders D (1992) Authorship and copyright. Routledge, London
Seneca LA (1935) De Beneficiis, VII, 6. In: Basore JW (ed) L. Annaeus Seneca, Moral essays: vol 3. Heinemann, London [trans: Stewart A L (1887) Annaes Seneca on benefits addressed to aebutius liberalis. George Bell & Sons, London]
Skone James EP, Mummery J, Rayner James JE, Garnett KM, Nimmer D, Silman S, Skone James R (1991) Copinger and Skone James on copyright. Sweet & Maxwell, London
Stewart S (1983) International copyright and neighbouring rights. Butterworths, London
Strömholm S (1967) Le droit moral de l'auteur, en droit allemand, français et Scandinave, avec un aperçu de l'évolution internationale, étude de droit compare. Norstedt & Sönners Förlag, Stockholm
Strömholm S (1976) Copyright - National and international developments: The origins and growth of copyright. In: Beier FK, Schricker G, (eds) International Encyclopedia of Comparative Law: Copyright and Industrial Property. The Hague
Strowel A (1993) Droit d'auteur et copyright: Divergences et convergences - Etude de droit compare. Librarie générale de droit et de jurisprudence, Paris
Strowel A (1994) Droit d'auteur and copyright. In: Sherman B, Strowel A (eds) Of authors and origins: essays on copyright law. Clarendon Press, Oxford, pp 235–253
Suarez MF (2010) To what degree did the Statute of Anne (8 Anne, c.19, [1709]) affect commercial practices of the book trade in eighteen-century England? Some provisional answers about copyright, chiefly from bibliography and book history. In: Bently L, Suthersanen U, Torremans P (eds) Global copyright - three hundred years since the Statute of Anne, from 1709 to cyberspace. Edward Elgar, Cheltenham, pp 54–69
Turner JDC (2015) Intellectual property and EU competition law. 2nd edn. Oxford University Press, Oxford
van Horn Melton J (2004) The rise of the public in enlightenment Europe. Cambridge University Press, Cambridge

VerLoren van Themaat W, Reuder B (eds) (2018) European competition law: a case commentary. Edward Elgar, Cheltenham

Visky K (1987) Geistiges Eigentum der Verfasser im antiken Rom. UFITA

Vogel M (2010) From privilege to modern copyright. In: Bently L, Suthersanen U, Torremans P (eds) Global copyright - three hundred years since the Statute of Anne, from 1709 to cyberspace. Edward Elgar, Cheltenham, pp 116–121

von Lewinski S (2008) International copyright law and policy. Oxford University Press, Oxford

Walter MM (2010) Term directive. In: von Lewinski S, Walter MM (eds) European copyright law: a commentary. Oxford University Press, Oxford, pp 499–677

Warlouzet L (2010) The rise of European Competition Policy, 1950–1991: a cross-disciplinary survey of a contested policy sphere. European University Institute, Florence, The Robert Schuman Centre for Advanced Studies, EUI working papers, RCAS 2010/80

Whish R, Bailey D (2021) Competition law, 10th edn. Oxford University Press, Oxford

Winerman M (2003) The origins of the FTC: concentration, cooperation, control, and competition. Antitrust Law J 71(1):1–97

WIPO (1996) Model provisions on protection against unfair competition. WIPO Publication, No. 832(E), Geneva. https://www.wipo.int/edocs/pubdocs/en/intproperty/832/wipo_pub_832.pdf. Accessed 22 Oct 2024

Zekos G (2014) Economics and law on competition in 21st century globalization. Nova Publishers, New York

Chapter 3
Development, Nature and Field of the Copyright-Competition Interaction Issue

The issue of the interaction between copyright law and competition law emerged gradually, following the development of those laws under their specific circumstances. At a certain point, copyright law and competition law started to interact despite their completely different natures.

After the historical overview of the interaction between copyright law and competition law, this chapter discusses the nature of the relationship between copyright law and competition law in the context of the copyright-competition interaction issues. Within the existing practice, there are different viewpoints on the relationship between the copyright law and competition law. Some experts insist on the conflict relationship, while others advocate complementarity of law, arguing that laws have joint goals. However, such viewpoints do not seem to be in accordance with the fundamental principles of copyright law and competition law.

Copyright law and competition law peacefully co-exist. In the case of their interaction, every conduct must be compliant with the fundamental principles of copyright law and competition law. From the perspective of copyright law, the application of the rules on competition law represents the external limitation in content of exercising copyright law. From the perspective of competition law, the existence of copyright represents a specific situation in which emphasis must be on the effects of copyright instead of allocation and productivity, while the concept of authorship must be considered in the light of consumer welfare.

After defining the relationship between copyright law and competition law, this chapter identifies situations in which the copyright-competition interaction occurs. The focus of this work is on the relationship between copyright and competition rules on prohibited agreements (Article 101 TFEU) and on the relationship between copyright and competition rules on the abuse of dominant position (Article 102 TFEU).

Finally, this chapter provides a discussion on the appropriate methodological approach for dealing with the copyright-competition interaction issue.

D. Gliha, *The Copyright-Competition Interaction within the EU*,
https://doi.org/10.1007/978-3-031-94402-4_3

3.1 Historical Overview of the Copyright-Competition Interaction Issue

Copyright law and competition law have undergone specific historical development, as was presented in the previous chapter. Some may consider that at first glance, there is no direct historical connection between copyright law and competition law, however, the fact is that at a certain point in time, copyright law and competition law started to interact despite their completely different natures. Thus, the issue of the interaction between copyright law and competition law emerged gradually, following the development of those laws under their specific circumstances.

Modern copyright law did not develop before the eighteenth century, and competition law not before the end of the nineteenth century (in Europe, even in the mid-twentieth century). Still, as elaborated earlier (see *supra* Chap. 2 and Sects. 2.1 and 3.1), the roots of copyright law and competition law go back to earlier times. Thus, the first encounters of (pre-)copyright and (pre-)competition can be noted even in times before modern copyright law and competition law developed.

Still, discussing copyright-competition interaction in the ancient era would probably take us be somewhat too far, at least at the current state of the art. For a start, there are as yet no firm enough findings of pre-copyright law and pre-competition law to go further into such a discussion. For the period into which we have a better historical insight, the first signs of interaction between (pre-)copyright and (pre-)competition can already be observed in the privilege and guild system. Namely, privileges were commercial monopolies granting exclusive rights to print and publish particular works. Privileges were mainly of economic and political purpose, granted by state-related authorities (see *supra* Chap. 2, Sect. 2.1). Notably, in the sixteenth and the seventeenth centuries, granted privileges were concentrated within the guilds of publishers—"government-licensed, local organisations of industrial producers."[1,2] Thus, in the guild system, privileges were a form of protection for the craftsman against the risks of the market. In such a way, by granting particular privileges, public authorities directly intervened in competition on the market. Regarding the book trade, Grosheide refers to the privilege system "as a form of public competition law *avant la lettre*," in which the system of gentleman's agreements was established to watch over unfair competition.[3] By observing the function and legal consequences of the guild-system privileges, some elements of (pre-) copyright-competition interaction can be found. 'Copyright' holders (mainly

---

[1] Prak (2006), p. 1.

[2] See Grosheide (2010), pp. 80–87. At that times Europe was generally facing the issue of monopolisation so the organisation of publishers into guild was no exception to that trend; see *supra* Sect. 2.2.1.

[3] Although Grosheide mentions the term 'unfair competition', it seems more likely that his reference concerns what is nowadays perceived as competition law rather than unfair competition (on the distinction between competition law and unfair competition, see *supra* Sect. 2.2.3); Grosheide (2010), pp. 85–86.

publishers) obtained exclusive 'copyright' rights through privileges, while public authorities, by granting privileges, intervened in the market and controlled competition where needed. However, in those times, the objectives of market intervention were indeed different from what they are today and were often driven by religious motives.[4]

Nevertheless, the first concrete copyright-competition interaction concerns emerged in the US during the early development of modern antitrust law. Although the case did not raise direct antitrust issues, the first encounters of copyright law and the US antitrust law can be found in the 1908 *Bobbs-Merrill*[5] decision. In that case, the Court applied the first sale doctrine to prevent resale price maintenance or publisher stipulation of the price at which booksellers must resell books.[6] The Court found that the protection afforded by copyright laws did not extend to controlling the price of a copyrighted work once the copyright holder had sold it. However, it remained open whether the book's sale, plus a separate contractual provision stipulating the resale price, would be enforceable.[7] That question was resolved shortly after in the *Dr. Miles*[8] case, in which the Supreme Court found resale price maintenance by contract to be unlawful under the antitrust laws, and in the process, it rejected an IP defence—namely, that trade secrets protected the medicines whose prices were fixed. Following *Dr. Miles*, the courts have consistently held that the resale price maintenance rule applies categorically, regardless of whether the goods were protected by trade secrets, copyright or other intellectual property rights. Later, the 'misuse' doctrine gradually evolved, first through cases concerning the patent-competition interaction and then later through case law involving other intellectual property rights (including copyright[9]).[10] In essence, the 'misuse' doctrine may be invoked if the copyright owner has violated a specific legal norm in obtaining or enforcing his copyright with consequent injury to the infringer. According to one interpretation, the 'misuse' doctrine is identified with anticompetitive conduct and balances between the policy of preventing piracy of

---

[4]See Grosheide (2010), p. 86.

[5]Bobbs-Merrill Co. v. Straus, 210 U.S. 339 (1908).

[6]Before the *Bobbs-Merrill* case, in *Adams v. Burke* (1873), the court applied the 'first sale' doctrine to preclude a patentee from imposing territorial restrictions on patented goods once the licensee had sold them; *Adams v. Burke,* 84 U.S. 453 (1873).

[7]Hovenkamp (2005), pp. 7–8.

[8]*Dr. Miles Medical Co. v. John D. Park & Sons Co*., 220 U. S. 373, 400-401 (1911).

[9]See, for example, *Lasercomb America v. Reynolds*, 911 F.2d 970, 973, 979 (4th Cir. 1990) (copyright misuse for infringement plaintiff to license database only on condition that licensee not develop a competing database).

[10]Hovenkamp notes that through the early practice, there was an unnecessary differentiation between misuse and antitrust doctrine. 'Misuse' was most generally raised as a defence in an infringement action, while antitrust laws were affirmatively enforced by the government or, occasionally, private plaintiffs; regardless of that, according to Hovenkamp, infringement defendants and courts could just as easily have held that infringement actions could not be based on licensing arrangements that violated the antitrust laws. In the later phase, the courts have given 'misuse' a broader meaning than in relation to antitrust laws; see Hovenkamp (2005), pp. 10, 21–22.

copyrighted matter and the policy of enforcing the antitrust laws.[11] However, some consider that the 'misuse' doctrine might also concern other misconducts and is interchangeable with the unclean hands defence.[12] Although several cases were decided based on the 'misuse' doctrine, particularly in the 1930s and 1940s, only a few of them were successful for the defendants invoking the 'misuse' defence.[13]

The 'misuse' doctrine would eventually be established as the main approach to the copyright-competition interaction issue. However, interestingly, in the phase of US antitrust interventionism in the 1960s and 1970s, the Department of Justice singled out nine licensing practices that would commonly be known as the 'Nine No-Nos'.[14,15] Those practices were considered as per se illegal. Later, already by the early 1980s, the 'Nine No-Nos' fell out of practice, and courts focused back on the rule of reason and the 'misuse' doctrine.[16] In 1995, the Federal Trade Commission and the Department of Justice's Antitrust Division jointly issued the Antitrust Guidelines for the Licensing of Intellectual Property.[17] However, the Guidelines did not have the force of law or bind courts and agencies, but did have a considerable practical value. In an amended version, the Antitrust Guidelines for the Licensing of Intellectual Property[18] are still used nowadays.[19]

Compared to the EU and its Member States, practically from the beginning, the US took a different approach to the copyright-competition interaction issue. Still, considering that the US is a kind of a pioneer of modern competition law and, consequently, of the copyright-competition interaction matter, some influence on

[11] See Goldstein (1989), pp. 177–181; Goldstein (2024b), p. 335.

[12] See Goldstein (1989), pp. 177–178; Goldstein (2024a), pp. 11:38.3–11:51.

[13] Goldstein indicates that only one such case was explicitly decided in favour of the defendants counter copyright holders—*M. Witmark & Sons v. Jensen*. Nevertheless, several later decisions expressly or impliedly validated the defence as the matter of law. The defendants were unsuccessful only because they failed to prove all the elements of the defence; see Goldstein (1989), pp. 178–179. See also M. Witmark & Sons v. Jensen, 80 F. Supp. 843, 850, 79 U.S.P.Q. 6 (D. Minn. 1948), *appeal dismissed*, 177 F.2d 515, 84 U.S.P.Q. 41 (8th Cir. 1949).

[14] The 'Nine No-Nos' referred mainly to the patent-competition case law which was most present especially in the US practice at those times, however, it seems that the 'Nine No-Nos' could also be applied to the cases concerning copyright.

[15] See Gilbert and Shapiro (1997), pp. 284–286.

[16] See American Bar Association (2007), pp. 89–92; Leslie (2011), pp. 41–44. However, interestingly, the copyright 'misuse' defence has not been as widely accepted as the patent 'misuse' defence; see Leslie (2011), pp. 64–65.

[17] 1995 Antitrust Guidelines for the Licensing of Intellectual Property, issued by the U.S. Department of Justice and the Federal Trade Commission, April 6, 1995. https://www.justice.gov/atr/archived-1995-antitrust-guidelines-licensing-intellectual-property. Accessed on 23 October 2024.

[18] 2017 Antitrust Guidelines for the Licensing of Intellectual Property, issued by the U.S. Department of Justice and the Federal Trade Commission, January 12, 2017. https://www.justice.gov/atr/IPguidelines/download. Accessed on 23 October 2024.

[19] On a historical overview of the copyright-competition issue in the US, see American Bar Association (2007), pp. 67–92; Hovenkamp (2005).

Europe indeed exists. That is particularly visible from the development of the exceptional circumstances doctrine compared to the essential facilities doctrine (see *infra* Sect. 5.2.2.2.4). Still, there are fundamental differences between the EU and the US approach to the copyright-competition interaction issue. Those differences were especially notable in dealing with the *Microsoft* case on both sides (see *infra* Sect. 5.2.2.2.3).

Thus, here we will not go into further details of the US approach to the copyright-competition interaction issue, but at this point, it seems proper to turn back to Europe, which is the basic focus of this research.[20]

In discussing copyright-competition interaction from the perspective of the EU, it should first and foremost be noted that although it seems that the CJEU and the EU Commission have the final word in dealing with this specific interdisciplinary issue, the copyright-competition interaction issue in Europe can be viewed as a national as well as an EU matter of law. The CJEU primarily deals with cases that affect cross-border trade; nevertheless, copyright-competition interaction cases may also occur as a completely national issue. Anyhow, having in mind the EU's legal order and competence, this specific matter should always be substantially approached in a harmonised manner—regardless of whether the case is discussed before the EU or national authorities.

In the EU, the copyright-competition interaction issue emerged quite early. The significant case in the EU, *Consten and Grundig*,[21] dealt with the issue of interaction between copyright and a particular intellectual property right (trademark) concerning exclusive licensing. Soon followed the notable *Deutsche Grammophon v Metro*[22] case in which the CJEU[23] discussed the relationship between copyright and competition law through exclusive licensing of copyright and competition rules on prohibited agreements. In the 1990s, the landmark case of *Magill*[24] severely influenced the further understanding of the refusal to license copyright as an abuse of dominant position. *Magill* was followed by the *IMS Health* case and the controversial *Microsoft* case. Besides the cases mentioned, there were also several competition cases concerning collective management organisations.[25]

---

[20] Nevertheless, some parallels with the US approach on the copyright-competition interaction issue will be drawn throughout this thesis.

[21] Judgment of 13 July 1966, *Établissements Consten S.à.R.L. and Grundig-Verkaufs-GmbH v Commission of the European Economic Community*, Joined cases 56 and 58–64, EU:C:1966:41.

[22] Judgment of 8 June 1971, Deutsche Grammophon Gesellschaft mbH v Metro-SB-Großmärkte GmbH & Co. KG, C-78/70, EU:C:1971:59.

[23] Note: At that time the Court was called the European Court of Justice (ECJ), however, for practical reasons in the thesis the abbreviation CJEU designating the current name of the Court is used—the Court of Justice of the European Union. Such a designation does not comprise the case law of the Court of First Instance which will be indicated separately.

[24] Judgment of 6 April 1995, *RTE and ITP v Commission*, Joined Cases C-241/91 P and C-242/91 P, ECLI:EU:C:1995:98.

[25] For instance: Judgment of 30 January 1974, *Belgische Radio en Televisie and société belge des auteurs, compositeurs et éditeurs v SV SABAM and NV Fonior*, Case 127/73, EU:C:1974:6; Judgment of 2 March 1983, *Gesellschaft zur Verwertung von Leistungsschutzrechten mbH (GVL) v Commission of the European Communities*, Case 7/82, EU:C:1983:52; Judgment of 13 July 1989,

The Commission and the CJEU decided several cases concerning the interaction between certain intellectual property rights and competition rules throughout the practice. In their decision-making, the EU institutions were inconsistent in their approach (see *infra* Chaps. 4 and 5). In addition, the reasoning often lacked quality economic analysis and neglected the particularities of the specific intellectual property right concerned. Hence, when discussing the copyright-competition issue in the EU, the case law on the interaction between other intellectual property rights and competition law must be considered. However, in doing so, findings must not be taken over directly without prior consideration of the intellectual property rights involved, but instead carefully *per analogiam*.

Unlike the US, the EU has never issued comprehensive guidelines concerning the interaction between intellectual property rights and competition law. However, to provide more clarity and a more consistent interpretation, the EU addressed the issue within several soft-law documents and some secondary legislation. Thus, the matter of the interaction between intellectual property rights and competition law has been touched upon in documents such as Guidance on its enforcement priorities in applying Article 82 of the EC Treaty to abusive exclusionary conduct by dominant undertakings,[26] Guidelines on Technology Transfer Agreements[27] and the Block Exemption Regulation on Technology Transfer Agreements.[28] Nevertheless, none of these documents deals with the substance of the interaction between intellectual property rights and competition—a problem which has not been settled through case law nor theory.

Nowadays, copyright-competition interaction is a widely recognised issue in the EU. Some of the most notable cases raised before the CJEU concerned the copyright-competition interaction issue (e.g. *Magill, Microsoft*). However, despite several significant rulings and many conducted research and written papers on the copyright-competition interaction issue, no uniform approach has been developed

Ministère public v Jean-Louis Tournier, Case 395/87, EU:C:1989:319; Judgment of 12 April 2013, *International Confederation of Societies of Authors and Composers (CISAC) v European Commission*, T-442/08, EU:T:2013:188, etc.

Such cases mainly concerned the level of fees, the relationship between members and their collecting society and/or the network of relations between collecting societies. However, due to the specificity of collective management organisations that are regulated by copyright law and that are not authors or copyright holders, as successors of authors, such specific copyright-competition interaction cases are not in the focus of this research; Max Planck Institute for Intellectual Property and Competition Law (2013), pp. 10–12, 210–274; Schierholz (2010), pp. 1146–1190.

[26]Communication from the Commission—Guidance on the Commission's enforcement priorities in applying Article 82 of the EC Treaty to abusive exclusionary conduct by dominant undertaking, C 45, 24.2.2009, pp. 7–20.

[27]Communication from the Commission—Guidelines on the application of Article 101 of the Treaty on the Functioning of the European Union to technology transfer agreements, OJ C 89, 28.3.2014, pp. 3–50.

[28]Commission Regulation (EU) No. 316/2014 of 21 March 2014 on the application of Article 101(3) of the Treaty on the Functioning of the European Union to categories of technology transfer agreements, OJ L 93, 28.3.2014, pp. 17–23.

and acknowledged. The problem might be in the fact that commentators often approach this problem too narrowly without prior consideration of the fundamentals of copyright law and competition law. Also, it seems that economic elements have not been adequately taken into consideration.

Still, among the expert public, at the moment, cases concerning the patent-competition interaction issue seem to be discussed more, especially considering standard-essential patents (SEPs) and Fair, Reasonable and Non-Discriminatory (FRAND) terms. However, having in mind the ongoing digital revolution and rapid development of the software industry, it is likely that conducts involving the exercise of copyright will more often be a matter of competition investigations. Besides, there is the upcoming development of artificial intelligence that might open an entirely new dimension of the copyright-competition issue.

Therefore, in these dynamic times of digitalisation and changes in the business and social sector, the time is just right to tackle the issue of copyright-competition interaction and strike a balance between copyright law and competition law without disturbing the substance of these laws.

3.2 The Nature of the Copyright-Competition Issue and the Relationship Between Copyright Law and Competition Law

Copyright-competition interaction is not an independent field of law. It is a specific issue that eventually occurred under the specific economic and social circumstances following the development of copyright law and competition law. It concerns the interaction between two completely independent laws, each with its rationales, framework and consequences.

Copyright law primarily focuses on the author, and possibly on other copyright holders as entitled legal successors of the author's specific rights.[29] Copyright protection arises automatically without formalities and provides certain exclusive rights on the copyright-protected work. By enabling the author and other copyright holders to enjoy and protect the fruits of the author's work freely, copyright law acknowledges private property rights as a reward for labour. Consequently, from a broader perspective, copyright also has a positive effect on promoting science, art and culture, and on providing incentives for further production and investment in creative and original work.[30] On the other hand, competition law has a somewhat

[29] As Ginsburg states with respect to the author as the genuine exploiter of his/her work: "(...) the real economic actors in the copyright system have long been the publishers and other exploiters to whom authors cede their rights," see Ginsburg (2017), p. 60.

[30] Copyright law as an incentive is more stressed in the common law tradition under the utilitarian philosophy. In the civil law systems, where copyright generally enjoys stronger protection, surely copyright law also encourages the further creation of copyright works.

different approach. As a market regulator, competition law is focused mainly on maintaining competition in the market and in consumers in a broader sense affected by the business activities of undertakings. By preventing and sanctioning anti-competitive behaviour, competition policy promotes free undistorted competition, which is one of the cornerstones of the internal market concept.[31]

Several commentators noticed that, especially in the earlier phase of development, under the influence of ordo-liberal philosophy, copyright law and competition law were often considered as conflicting laws.[32] Recently, however, there has been a strong tendency to look on copyright law and competition law as complementarity laws with joint objectives. Although advocates of the complementary approach can be found in the Commission and among many prominent scholars,[33] such an approach has not yet found its way into the practice. Although both viewpoints have their rationales, insisting on such utter approaches does not seem to be the best way to go. Ultimately, they might not produce the desirable outcome, consistent application and legal security.[34] On the one hand, the perception of copyright and competition as conflicting seems to be the offspring of a superficial understanding of copyright law and competition law. On the other side, the complementarity of laws seems to be an artificial construct resulting from an overly extensive interpretation of the objectives of copyright law and competition law (see *infra* Sects. 4.2.3 and 5.2.3).[35]

---

[31] See Daum (2010), p. 54.

[32] See Korah (2006), pp. 1–2; Max Planck Institute for Intellectual Property and Competition Law (2013), p. 37.

On the conflict theory, see also Schmidt (2010), pp. 48–51; see also Anderson (2021), pp. 321–322.

Benabou considers that at the beginning of the copyright-competition interaction in the EU, copyright and competition law regarded each other with mutual neutrality, peacefully coexisting; see Benabou (2009), p. 543.

On the conflict between antitrust and intellectual property rights in the US, see Hovenkamp (2005), pp. 249–276.

[33] For instance, see American Bar Association (2007), p. 86; Apostolopoulos (2007), pp. 237–263; Katz, Veel (2013), pp. 139–184 (regardless of that flaw, the indicated research still enhances the need for the distinction between copyright and other intellectual property rights, see p. 143); Kwok (2011), pp. 261–286; Schmidt (2010), pp. 51–63; Treacy (2024), p. 2.

[34] Other different viewpoints can be found in the literature and practice of the copyright-competition interaction issue (often others refer to intellectual property in general). Thus, Kolstad, for instance, considers that competition law and intellectual property rights have somewhat the same economic objects but are not fully complementary, mostly due to the competition law traditional focus on static efficiency and populistic goals of IP laws—hence there is still a conflict between those two areas of law; see Kolstad (2008), pp. 8–9.

[35] It is reasonable to discuss the complementarity of the objectives of copyright law and competition law in the sense that they may strive towards the same result, but through different means and for different reasons. However, to discuss the complementarity of two laws and argue that they have the same objectives has no justification and is certainly not in line with the rationales of copyright law and competition law.

In fact, copyright law and competition law peacefully coexist. No law is above or below the other one. Each law has its foundations, purpose, rationales and legal effects. Furthermore, copyright law is pure private law, a natural consequence of authorship, while competition law is a form of public law dealing with free and effective competition on the market.[36] In the case of their interaction—when a particular situation occurs that concerns both laws—the laws are *in pari materia.* Thus, the approach to the field of interaction must be comprehensive and based upon the existing principles of copyright law and competition law.[37] In that manner, the copyright-competition interaction issue can be settled without disrupting the substance of copyright law and competition law in doing so.

To properly define the relationship between copyright law and competition law, and consequently, set the grounds for discussion on copyright-competition interaction, it is proper to find a place for competition law in copyright law and vice versa. As discussed above (see *supra* Sect. 2.1.2), copyright is considered an absolute property right. Nonetheless, the exercise of exclusive copyright rights can be restricted for a specified list of reasons. The reasons for competition law (anti-competitive behaviours) are not covered by the limitations and exceptions stemming from the traditional copyright framework. However, the fact is that in specific situations, competition law restricts the exercise of copyright. Such a restriction is, in essence, a de facto limitation of the exercise of certain copyright rights.[38] In that sense, Anderman and Schmidt perceive the status of competition rules with regard to copyright law in the following way: "(...) the new competition rules are a development of an existing 'second tier' of regulation to the exercise of IPRs, an 'external' system of regulation that applies to anti-competitive conduct not prevented by the 'internal' system of regulation offered by IP legislation." Thus, "the limits of permitted exercise of IPRs are drawn not only by the laws of IP but also by reference to the rules of competition law."[39] From the wording of their thought, it seems that Anderman and Schmidt's perception is mainly in line with the perception of van Lewinski who deems that competition law is a limitation of the author's right in a broader sense originating outside of copyright law.[40] Indeed, such a perception of

[36] See Anderman and Schmidt (2019), pp. 4–5.

[37] Differently, Benabou deems that the peaceful coexistence of copyright law and competition law stands only when there is no element of inter-relationship between copyright and competition; see Benabou (2009), pp. 543–544.

[38] From the comparative perspective, the situation is somewhat different in the US common law system. Such a system has a flexible approach to the copyright limitations that are observed mainly through the 'fair use' doctrine. Accordingly, in such a system, competition law as a restriction to the exercise of copyright is observed differently from the systems which have closed lists of exceptions and limitations. Thus, in the US common law system, the copyright-competition interaction issue is discussed through the 'fair use' and 'misuse' doctrines; see Goldstein and Hugenholtz (2021), pp. 349–351, 382–383.

[39] Anderman and Schmidt (2019), p. 319; see also Rahnasto (2003), pp. 42–49.

[40] See von Lewinski (2008), p. 153. In that sense, see also Goldstein and Hugenholtz (2021), pp. 381–382; Benabou (2005), pp. 649–650.

the status of competition law regarding copyright law seems to be the proper one—the only one that is fundamentally sustainable. Within international copyright law, some legal basis for allowing such external limitation to the exercise of copyright might be found within Articles 8 and 40 of the TRIPS Agreement. Thus, Article 8, para. 2 of the TRIPS agreement states:

> Appropriate measures, provided they are consistent with the provisions of this agreement may be needed to prevent the abuse of intellectual property rights by right-holders or the resort to practices which unreasonably restrain trade or adversely affect the international transfer of technology.

Further on, Article 40, paras. 1 and 2 of the TRIPS Agreement state:

> 1. Members agree that some licensing practices or conditions pertaining to intellectual property rights which restrain competition may have adverse effects on trade and may impede the transfer and dissemination of technology.
> 2. Nothing in this Agreement shall prevent Members from specifying in their legislation licensing practices or conditions that may in particular cases constitute an abuse of intellectual property rights having an adverse effect on competition in the relevant market. (…)[41]

Anyhow, it is vital not to confuse external limitations on the exercise of copyright with copyright exceptions and limitations. Dreier, for instance, provides a somewhat different viewpoint. He considers that competition law is (or at least should be) recognised within the list of copyright exceptions and limitations.[42] Thus, he deems that European copyright law already regulates competition to some point[43] and should further craft "appropriately fine-tuned exceptions and limitations," taking care of the interests of competition in general.[44] Although such a viewpoint is surely interesting, it does not seem convincing and deviates from the fundamental understanding of copyright limitations and exceptions.

From the competition law perspective, there are two main perceptions of copyright. One is to treat copyright as any other private property right. The other is to acknowledge the specific intellectual component of copyright and allow some

---

[41] Some scholars consider that Articles 8 and 40 of the TRIPS Agreement provide basis for allowing competition law to limit the exercise of copyright law; see Malbon et al. (2014), pp. 596–612; Subramanian (2010), pp. 997–1023; Ullrich (2005), pp. 726–757; Firth (2021), pp. 67–68.

Interestingly, in *Microsoft*, in support of its decision, the CFI cited Article 40(2) of the TRIPS Agreement to reject Microsoft's argumentation with regard to the substantive application of Articles 13 and 31(k) of the TRIPS Agreement; see Judgment of 17 September 2007, *Microsoft v Commission*, T-201/04, EU:T:2007:289, para. 1192.

[42] See Dreier (2010), pp. 232–254.

[43] For instance, Dreier considers that "by granting exclusive right to some market participants and not to others, already regulate competition." He also notes the private copying exception and allowing the free use of works of architecture or sculpture designed to be located permanently in public as examples of limitations and exceptions concerned with market failure. However, in doing so, he fails to show where indeed competition, in the sense of competition law, comes into play; see Dreier (2010), pp. 235, 243.

[44] See Dreier (2010), pp. 237–238, 242–244. In that sense, see also Firth (2021), pp. 52–53.

limited special concessions.[45] In the context of copyright-competition interaction, it seems proper to endorse the latter approach and recognise the specific status of copyright in competition law matters. If copyright were taken as any other private property right, then there would not be any copyright-competition interaction issue. Every competition law intervention involving the exercise of some copyright right would just be conducted in a standard way without any concessions (see *infra* Sects. 4.2.5 and 5.2.5). However, the fact is that the specific status of copyright in competition matters has been recognised in practice and theory (see *infra* Chaps. 4 and 5). Despite having a general framework provided for all kinds of conduct that might fall under the scrutiny of competition assessment, competition law ought to be flexible and easily adjustable to particular situations due to its open-ended approach. Thus, Ginsburg, Geradin and Klovers state: "IP rights are not subject to special competition rules or principles in the EU."[46] Indeed, competition law does not need to be amended to acknowledge the particularities of copyright. However, in the application of competition law, the specific method of assessment should be applied to acknowledge the particularities of copyright (see *infra* Sects. 4.3 and 5.3). Generally, competition law allows necessary adjustments of the method of assessment, appropriate for the given situation.[47] In that sense, the presence of copyright should be comprehended as a specific situation in which the focus should mainly be on the effects of copyright instead of allocation and productivity, while the concept of authorship should be taken into consideration in the light of consumer welfare.[48] With such an understanding, the open-ended approach of competition law seems to be well enough suited to acknowledge the specificity of copyright matters without any further legislative actions, respectively allowing it to be calibrated *pro tanto*.

Therefore, the copyright-competition interaction issue should be discussed within the existing rules and principles of copyright law and competition law. On the one hand, it should be observed as an outside restriction on the exercise of copyright. On the other hand, it should be perceived as a specific situation that must be approached based on fundamental competition law principles through a tailored method of evaluation. Thus, having all things considered, to settle the copyright-competition interaction issue, there is no need for the disruption of the substance of copyright law or competition law with extensive and artificial interpretations.

After the relationship between copyright law and competition law is settled, the next thing that should be discussed concerns economics. In the assessment of situations concerning copyright-competition interaction, economic factors play a vital role. Copyright produces specific economic effects in comparison to classical private property rights. That is also one of the reasons we established above that copyright deserves a special status in competition assessments. To take into account

[45] See Anderman and Schmidt (2019), p. 319.

[46] See Ginsburg et al. (2019), p. 110.

[47] See Benabou (2005), pp. 650–654.

[48] Namely, unlike in standard competition law assessment, the interest of end-users should not prevail when in direct conflict with the author's interests.

the specific economic effects of copyright, in the context of competition law and (anti-)competitive effects on a market, there is (or should be) a generally stronger emphasis on dynamic efficiency than on allocative or productive efficiency. This is in line with the market-oriented and effects-based 'more economic approach' in the context of the creative industry and innovation-based markets. Several commentators have endorsed such an understanding. Somewhat in that sense, Mackenrodt, for instance, writes that: "Intellectual property law relies on exclusion to promote dynamic efficiency. IPR exclude static competition by imitation to provide an incentive for innovative activity and stimulate dynamic competition by substitution."[49] Kolstad considers that: "If economic analysis can establish dynamic efficiency as a common goal for IP law and competition law, the common theoretical framework could form the basis for an analysis of conduct based on IPRs under Articles 81 and 82."[50] By taking into account the issue with ex post assessment of welfare effects of (not) applying competition law to intellectual property rights cases, Drexl goes a step further and argues for a process-oriented concept of 'dynamic competition'. He explains that competition law should actually aim to protect the competitive process that enhances innovation (or, in the case of copyright, creativity and originality) instead of dynamic efficiency. Therefore, "the emphasis of the analysis would have to be on the given market situation and factors that induce firms to be innovative."[51] Indeed, competition law should observe copyright from a more dynamic perspective rather than a static one. However, in doing so, we must not forget that economic incentive is not the main goal of copyright (at least not in the spirit of the civil-law tradition). Despite that, copyright may have an encouraging effect on dynamic competition,[52] on which the competition assessment should focus.[53] Having that in mind, by paraphrasing Drexl, when the exercise of copyright comes under the focus of competition law, it seems reasonable to conclude that the emphasis of the competition assessment should be on protecting the competitive process that stimulates further creation.

Finally, in relation to the assessment of competitive processes and effects on the market and even beyond, it is crucial to make a distinction between different

---

[49] Mackenrodt (2008), p. 84.

[50] Kolstad (2008), p. 6.

[51] Drexl (2008), pp. 39–40.

[52] In literature, the notion of 'dynamic competition' can be found in a somewhat different meaning than the one used in this discussion. Thus, some consider that dynamic competition stands for the introduction of new technologies that displace existing markets and is interchangeable with the notion of 'competition for the market'. The result of such 'dynamic competition' is a "monopoly position that is likely to persist for some time, until a new monopolist comes up that overturns the position of the previous incumbent," see Graef et al. (2014), p. 3.

[53] According to the report of the Max Planck Institute for Intellectual Property and Competition Law (now: Max Planck Institute for Innovation and Competition), from a competition law perspective, it is possible to also apply the concept of dynamic efficiency and dynamic competition to cultural goods protected by copyright law; Max Planck Institute for Intellectual Property and Competition Law (2013), p. 39.

intellectual property rights. Every intellectual property right has its own rationales and economics appropriate for the intangible property concerned (see *supra* Sect. 2.1.3). Thus, copyright is a subjective right of absolute character that has characteristics of both property and non-property rights.[54] Accordingly, the economic effect on the market is not the same whether the particular situation concerns copyright, patent, trademark or some other intellectual property right. Still, one of the most common mistakes in approaching the issue of interaction between particular intellectual property rights and competition law lies exactly here. Namely, sometimes even with a solid economic argumentation, experts often do not distinguish between different intellectual property rights, and most commonly, for instance, consider innovation as the characteristic of all intellectual property rights.[55] Such an omission cannot provide a solid bedrock for further assessment. Hence, for a proper understanding of processes on the market and the (anti-)competitive effects of a particular conduct involving the exercise of copyright, it is crucial not to mix intellectual property rights. Otherwise, from both a legal and economic perspective, the result can only be deficient.

Besides that, when discussing the copyright-competition interaction issue, in addition to the overall effect of copyright on the market, the presence of copyright and its specific economics also affect practically every other stage of the competition assessment, starting from the very definition of a relevant market. Hence, in any copyright-competition interaction analysis, it is vital to start with the fundamentals and, above all, define the intellectual property right in the matter. If a case concerns copyright, it is not sufficient just to note that the exercise of copyright is present in a particular case. It is necessary to establish further the specific object of copyright and define the exercise of the exclusive right that is under the competition assessment. All these factors have an impact and must be appropriately taken into consideration so that competition assessment can adapt to the needs of a particular situation.[56]

3.3 The Field of the Copyright-Competition Interaction

One of the main practical questions of the copyright-competition interaction issue is what it covers.

Throughout the years, there were many discussions on how to perceive the relationship between copyright and competition law, including the question of whether rights stemming from copyright may even be a matter for competition

[54] See Henneberg (2001), pp. 5–7; Gliha (1998), p. 376.

[55] See, for instance, Kolstad (2008), pp. 4, 7; Mackenrodt (2008); OECD (2018) Scoping Note; Treacy (2024); Turner (2015), pp. 3–5; Wildgen (2008), pp. 55–56; Zevgolis (2018), pp. 22, 31. Such a (wrongful) approach can also be found in some legal documents, such as the 2004 and 2014 versions of the Guidelines on Technology Transfer Agreements; the US Antitrust Guidelines for the Licensing of Intellectual Property.

[56] See Anderman and Schmidt (2019), p. 10.

intervention. Within the practice, several different approaches can be recognised on how to approach the copyright-competition issue. In the beginning, the abstract distinction between the existence and exercise of copyright was developed to try to protect the existence of copyright, although, in practice, it turned out somewhat differently. Later, the approach that advocated full competition intervention regardless of the presence of copyright within a particular conduct seemed to become more popular. Anyhow, regardless of the prevailing approach, the fact is that the copyright-competition interaction issue occurs in practice and is widely acknowledged and discussed as a legal and economic issue.

Generally, the copyright-competition interaction issue occurs when a certain conduct involving the exercise of a copyright right falls under the scrutiny of competition rules. Accordingly, regarding the copyright-competition interaction issue, it is mainly a matter of the economic component of copyright. According to Goldstein and Hugenholtz, the predominant forces that have shaped copyright law are economic rather than ideological.[57] In that sense, here we are mainly discussing the corporate aspect of copyright rather than the individual aspect; when and why particular economic uses of copyright can be limited for the reasons of protecting competition in a relevant market. Considering the ratio and economic character of competition law, moral copyright rights are intact and, due to their nature, obviously cannot be the subjects of the copyright-competition interaction issue.

Several kinds of conduct have been recognised throughout practice as a matter of the copyright-competition interaction (although not necessarily always explicitly). Some of those conducts are exclusive field of use licensing, exclusive territorial licensing, unilateral refusal to license, parallel trade, tying, price-fixing, collective societies, mergers and acquisitions, etc. Practically any economic activity on the market involving an exercise of economic copyright rights might fall under the scrutiny of competition rules. Thus, copyright law might interact with competition rules on prohibited agreements, abuse of dominant position and mergers and acquisitions. Nevertheless, an intervention of competition law on the exercise of copyright may come only exceptionally under specific circumstances.

The research focuses on the interaction between the exercise of copyright and competition rules on prohibited agreements (Article 101 TFEU) and abuse of dominant position (Article 102 TFEU). The most common situations that are a matter of interest are licensing practices and refusal to license.

[57] See Goldstein and Hugenholtz (2021), p. 7.

3.4 Methodological Approach to the Copyright-Competition Interaction Issue: Rule-Based v. Standard-Based Approach

There is a debate on what kind of methodological approach is appropriate for dealing with cases concerning the copyright-competition interaction issue. The two common approaches are the rule-based approach[58] and the standard-based approach. The rule-based approach entails ex ante setting of a structured test of liability. The standard-based approach consists of a flexible resolution of each case on the grounds of open-ended, multi-factor, and *post hoc* considerations such as reasonableness, consumer welfare, competition on the merits, efficiency, fairness, equity, etc.[59] Sullivan considers: "Standards allow the decision maker to take into account all relevant factors or the totality of the circumstances," whereas a rule "binds a decision maker to respond in a determinate way to the presence of delimited triggering facts."[60] Generally, on the pros and cons of each approach, and based on an overview of the most relevant findings, Kerber elaborates the following: "Rules are more costly to enact than standards, because they require more fixed set-up costs in finding and formulating them. However, the adjudication and enforcement costs under standards are deemed as higher than under rules. Therefore, rules might be more appropriate if the frequency of the behaviour is high, whereas standards might otherwise incur less cost. Since it is assumed that rules convey more clearly what the content of the law is and that legal advice about the application of rules is less costly than about the application of a standard, individuals tend to be better informed about the law under rules than under standards. Therefore, it can also be expected that their compliance with the law is higher under rules. If the effects of a behaviour vary widely, a standard might be more appropriate; otherwise, rules might be preferable. This is connected with the advantages of a standard for solving the problems of over- and under-inclusiveness, because a standard might be better able to differentiate between the beneficial and harmful behaviour. Another important dimension is the extent of flexibility. If the law is promulgated in the form of standards, then it is much easier to adapt the content of the law to new circumstances and problems, leading to a higher degree of flexibility than under rules."[61]

Thus, there is no universal rule about which approach is better. Some fields of law (such as tax law) naturally incline towards rules, while for others (such as constitutional law), standards seem more appropriate.[62]

[58] According to Posner, a rule "singles out one or a few facts and makes them legally determinative," Posner (2001), p. 39.

[59] See Petit (2017), p. 101.

[60] Sullivan (1992), pp. 22–123.

[61] Kerber (2008), p. 492.

[62] See Crane (2007), p. 52.

When discussing competition law, the debate on the rule-based approach and the standard-based approach has some roots in the US antitrust's debate on '*per se* rules v. rule of reason'—which emerged immediately with the development of antitrust law.[63] As elaborated before, the EU competition law is indeed somewhat different from the US antitrust law, although some mutual influences can be found in both systems (see Chap. 2 and Sect. 3.1). Generally, there are numerous material differences between the two systems, and the EU competition law does not have the concept of *per se* rules and the rule of reason in the way the US antitrust law does.[64] However, especially in the context of Article 101 TFEU, there is a distinction between the restriction of competition by object and effect. Colomo considers that the division between 'by object' and 'by effect' in essence mirrors the divide between rules and standards.[65] Recently, by taking into consideration an open-ended character of competition law in the light of many newly developed industries and overall dynamic business surroundings, there is a greater tendency towards the rule of reasons over the *per se* rules (in the EU, there is a tendency towards a comprehensive legal and economic assessment and effect on a market).[66] The reason for that can be found in the fact that the rule of reason approach allows for a much more differentiated analysis of the circumstances and effects in a particular case. In the EU, there is a similar tendency. Keeping in mind that the EU competition law has never adopted the concept of the US antitrust's rule of reason,[67] it would be more correct to consider this as a tendency towards a more reasonably comprehensive approach. Such a shift is aligned with the 'more economic approach' within the EU competition policy.[68]

In that context, the discussion on the rule-based v. standard-based approach can be considered as a discussion on finding the optimal complexity of legal rules and the extent of considering specific criteria and circumstances, finding a balance

---

[63] *Per se* prohibition means that a business behaviour is forbidden per se, i.e. without considering the specific circumstances of a case, a rule of reason approach allows for a much more differentiated analysis of the circumstances and effects in that particular case; see Kerber (2008), p. 489.

[64] Discussions of the rule of reason in EU competition law are often very imprecise and misplaced. EU competition law surely has not copied the US antitrust concept of the rule of reason; therefore, it is only possible to discuss the rule of reason in relation to whether the judgements and decisions are good and reasonable. In this sense, the focus within the EU competition law context of the 'rule of reason' is on assessing market effects; see Whish and Bailey (2021), pp. 142–143; Vogel (2020), p. 135.

[65] See Ibáñez Colomo (2018), p. 85.

Therein, the big difference as opposed to the US antitrust *per se* rules is certainly that in EU competition law restrictions by object allow the possibility of justification; see Whish and Bailey (2021), pp. 127–128.

[66] See Schmidt (2010), pp. 8–9.

[67] See, for instance, Judgment of 18 September 2001, *Métropole télévision (M6), Suez-Lyonnaise des eaux, France Télécom and Télévision française 1 SA (TF1) v Commission of the European Communities*, T-112/99, EU:T:2001:215, paras. 72–76.

[68] See Kerber (2008), pp. 489–490.

between accuracy and administrability.[69] Here, the main question is whether the copyright-competition interaction should be approached with more emphasis on a structured test of liability or more on the basis of open-ended standards.

Cases concerning the copyright-competition interaction issue are usually highly complex and require a comprehensive approach comprising copyright law, competition law and economics. In the previous practice, it seems that the CJEU preferred the rule-based approach in cases dealing with the exercise of copyright and competition rules on prohibited agreements. Article 101 TFEU in itself imposes a structured process.[70] However, in the lack of a unitary and comprehensive approach, the CJEU seems to be turning to standards in some situations. Although the use of standards provides more flexibility, which may especially be helpful for fields where in-depth case-by-case analysis is required, it turns out that the CJEU was using standards for justification rather than for quality decision-making (see *infra* Sect. 4. 2.1). Still, up until now, such cases can generally be characterised by inconsistent approaches and legal insecurity.

There is undoubtedly a need for a structured and well-founded approach to maintaining legal security and a unitary approach in cases concerning copyright-competition interaction. As Crane states, "One strong advantage of rules over standards is predictability, which matters most when one is trying to incentivize appropriate behavior."[71] Thus, to make advancements in this field and protect both copyright holders and healthy competition on the market, there is an evident need for a rulebook.[72] However, due to the diversity of cases that may occur and the necessity for an economic component, it is also vital to maintain a certain dose of flexibility. Many criteria and information must be taken into account for the assessment of the legality of behaviour.[73] Thus, the use of particular standards is desirable if the standards are well-defined to serve their purpose. In that sense, standards should be "viewed more as the delegation of authority to administrative or judicial bodies for refining and changing the rule-like application of the law, and less as an alternative to the rule-character of the law."[74] In other words, for dealing with the copyright-competition interaction issue, within the boundaries of a structured approach, standards should be used for refining and adapting fundamental principles and rules to the specific circumstances of particular cases—to sufficiently articulate a

---

[69] By analysing the relevant literature, such an explanation of rules v. standards does not seem to be completely conventional, however, it might be appropriate in the development of understanding of the copyright-competition interaction issue; see Kaplow (1992), pp. 557–629; Kaplow (1995), pp. 150–163; Kaplow (2000), pp. 502–528; Kerber (2008), pp. 492–493; Parisi et al. (2004), pp. 131–148; Schäfer (2006), pp. 113–134.

[70] See Petit (2017), pp. 109, 112–115.

[71] Crane (2007), p. 85.

[72] On argumentation *pro* rule-based approach, see Petit (2017), pp. 116–117.

[73] See Kaplow's definition of the complexity of legal rules; Kaplow (1992, 1995).

[74] Kerber (2008), p. 496.

theory of harm.[75] Colomo writes that: "A legal test is expected to meet the conflicting demands of administrability and accuracy."[76] Therefore, there must be a balanced mixture of rules and standards to answer the specific needs of the complex copyright-competition interaction issue, and so, maintain consistency and legal security. A suggestion for the denomination of such an approach is the 'structured rule of reasonableness'.

References

American Bar Association (2007) Intellectual property and antitrust handbook. ABA Publishing, Chicago

Anderman S, Schmidt H (2019) EU competition law and intellectual property rights: the regulation of innovation, 3rd edn. Oxford University Press, Oxford

Anderson M (2021) International report. In: Kobel P, Kilpatrick B, Kobel P, Këllezi P (eds) Competition law analysis of price and non-price discrimination & abusive IP based legal proceedings. Springer, Cham, pp 317–333

Apostolopoulos H (2007) Refusal-to-deal cases of IP rights in the aftermarket of US and EU law: convergence of both law systems through speaking the same language of law and economics. DePaul Bus Commercial Law J 5(2):237–263

Benabou V-L (2005) Neutral or harmful effects of competition law on copyright or Liaisons Dangereuses (Dangerous Love Affairs) on the Carte du Tendre. In: Exploring the sources of copyright. ALAI Congress, Paris, 18–21 September 2005, pp 648–663

Benabou VL (2009) European competition law and copyright: where do we stand? Where do we go? In: Derclaye E (ed) Research handbook on the future of EU copyright. Edward Elgar, Cheltenham, pp 543–566

Colino SM (2019) Competition law of the EU and UK, 8th edn. Oxford University Press, Oxford

Crane DA (2007) Rules versus standards in antitrust adjudication. Wash Lee Law Rev 64(1): 50–110

Daum F (2010) Copyright, competition law, and free movement of goods. In: von Lewinski S, Walter MM (eds) European copyright law: a commentary. Oxford University Press, Oxford, pp 50–70

Dreier T (2010) Regulating competition by limitations and exceptions. In: Torremans P (ed) Copyright law: a handbook of contemporary research. Edward Elgar, pp 232–254

Drexl J (2008) Is there a 'more economic approach' to intellectual property and competition law? In: Drexl J (ed) Research handbook on intellectual property and competition law. Max Planck Institute for Innovation and Competition, Munich, pp 27–53

Firth A (2021) The essential facilities principle and other issues of competition. In: Stamatoudi I, Torremans P (eds) EU copyright law: a commentary, 2nd edn. Edward Elgar, Cheltenham, pp 44–73

Gilbert R, Shapiro C (1997) Antitrust issues in the licensing of intellectual property: the nine no-no's meet the nineties. In: Baily MN, Reiss PC, Winston C (eds) Brookings papers on economic activity: microeconomics. Brooking Institution, Washington D.C., pp 283–336

[75] According to the theory of harm, harm must first be articulated, then tested and supported by robust evidence of the effects alleged; Colino (2019), pp. 9–10; Whish and Bailey (2021), p. 34.

[76] Therein, an administrable test is one that can be readily applied in cases other than the one from which it stems. An accurate legal test is said to be one that captures faithfully the rationale and assumptions on which it is based; see Ibáñez Colomo (2018), p. 29.

Ginsburg JC (2017) The role of the author in copyright. In: Okediji RL (ed) Copyright law in an age of limitations and exceptions. Cambridge University Press, New York, pp 60–84

Ginsburg DH, Geradin D, Klovers K (2019) Antitrust and intellectual property in the United States and the European Union. In: Muscolo G, Tavassi M (eds) The interplay between competition law and intellectual property. Wolters Kluwer, Alphen aan den Rijn, pp 99–119

Gliha I (1998) Hrvatski autorskopravni poredak: neke Novosti. In: Žuvela M (ed) 13. savjetovanje Aktualnosti hrvatskog zakonodavstva i pravne prakse. Opatija, 4–6 Nov 1998, Organizator, Zagreb, pp 365–402

Goldstein P (1989) Copyright, vol II. Little, Brown and Company, Boston

Goldstein P (2024a) Goldstein on copyright, vol II. Wolters Kluwer, New York

Goldstein P (2024b) International intellectual property law: cases and materials, 6th edn. Foundation Press, Eagan

Goldstein P, Hugenholtz PB (2021) International copyright: principles, law and practice, 4th edn. Oxford University Press, Oxford

Graef I, Wahyuningtyas SY, Valcke P (2014) How Google and others upset competition analysis: disruptive innovation and European competition law. Conference paper, 25th European Regional Conference of the International Telecommunications Society (ITS): "Disruptive Innovation in the ICT Industries: Challenges for European Policy and Business," Brussels, Belgium, 22–25 June 2014, International Telecommunications Society (ITS), Calgary

Grosheide FW (2010) Transition from guild regulation to modern copyright law - a view from the low countries. In: Bently L, Suthersanen U, Torremans P (eds) Global copyright - three hundred years since the Statute of Anne, from 1709 to cyberspace. Edward Elgar, Cheltenham, UK, pp 79–102

Henneberg I (2001) Autorsko pravo. Informator, Zagreb

Hovenkamp HJ (2005) IP and antitrust policy: a brief historical overview. All Faculty Scholarship, at Penn Law, 1916. https://scholarship.law.upenn.edu/faculty_scholarship/1916. Accessed 22 Oct 2024

Ibáñez Colomo P (2018) The shaping of EU competition law. Cambridge University Press, Cambridge

Kaplow L (1992) Rules versus standards: an economic analysis. Duke Law J 42:557–629

Kaplow L (1995) A model of the optimal complexity of legal rules. J Law Econ Organ 11(1): 150–163

Kaplow L (2000) General characteristics of rules. In: Encyclopedia of law and economics, pp 502–528

Katz A, Veel P-E (2013) Beyond refusal to deal: a cross-atlantic view of copyright, competition and innovation policies. Antitrust Law J 79(1):139–184

Kerber W (2008) Rules vs. standards or standards as delegation of authority for making (optimally differentiated) rules. In: Eger T, Bigus J, Ott C, von Wangenheim G (eds) Internationalisierung des Rechts und seine ökonomische Analyse. Gabler, Wiesbaden, pp 489–498

Kolstad O (2008) Competition law and intellectual property right - outline of an economics-based approach. In: Research handbook on intellectual property and competition law. Max Planck Institute for Innovation and Competition, Munich, pp 3–26

Korah V (2006) Intellectual property rights and the EC competition rules. Hart Publishing, Oxford

Kwok KHF (2011) A new approach to resolving refusal to license intellectual property disputes. World Competition 34(2):261–286

Leslie CR (2011) Antitrust law and intellectual property rights. Oxford University Press, Oxford

Mackenrodt M-O (2008) Assessing the effects of intellectual property rights in network standards. In: Drexl J (ed) Research handbook on intellectual property and competition law. Max Planck Institute for Innovation and Competition, Munich, pp 80–103

Malbon J, Lawson C, Davison M (2014) The WTO agreement on trade-related aspects of intellectual property rights: a commentary. Edward Elgar, Cheltenham

Max Planck Institute for Intellectual Property and Competition Law, Munich (2013) Report: copyright, competition and development. December 2013. https://www.ip.mpg.de/fileadmin/

ipmpg/content/forschung_aktuell/02_copyright_competition/report_copyright-competition-development_december-2013.pdf. Accessed 22 Oct 2024
OECD (2018) Scoping note on competition and intellectual property rights as a long-term theme for 2019–2020, 6–8 June 2018, OECD Conference Centre, DAF/COMP/WD(2018)4. http://www.oecd.org/officialdocuments/publicdisplaydocumentpdf/?cote=DAF/COMP/WD(2018)4&docLanguage=En. Accessed 22 Oct 2024
Parisi F, Fon VN, Ghei N (2004) The value of waiting in lawmaking. Eur J Law Econ 18:131–148
Petit N (2017) The antitrust and intellectual property intersection in European Union law. In: Blair RD, Sokol DD (eds) Handbook of antitrust, intellectual property and high tech. Cambridge University Press, Cambridge, pp 92–11
Posner RA (2001) Antitrust law, 2nd edn. The University of Chicago Press, Chicago
Prak M (2006) Craft guilds in North-Western Europe (England, France, Low Countries). In: The return of the guilds, Utrecht University, Utrecht, 5–7 October 2006
Rahnasto I (2003) Intellectual property rights, external effects and antitrust law. Oxford University Press, Oxford
Schäfer HB (2006) Rules versus standards in rich and poor countries: precise legal norms as substitutes for human capital in low-income countries. Supreme Court Econ Rev 14:113–134
Schierholz A (2010) Collective rights management in Europe. In: von Lewinski S, Walter MM (eds) European copyright law: a commentary. Oxford University Press, Oxford, pp 1146–1190
Schmidt C (2010) Refusal to license intellectual property rights as abuse of dominance, political economics competition and regulation, vol 11. Peter Lang GmbH Internationaler Verlag der Wissenschaften, Frankfurt am Main
Subramanian S (2010) EU obligation to the TRIPS Agreement: EU Microsoft decision. Eur J Int Law 21(4):997–1023
Sullivan KM (1992) The justice of rules and standards. Harv Law Rev 106:22–123
Treacy P (2024) EU competition law and intellectual property rights. Edward Elgar, Cheltenham
Turner JDC (2015) Intellectual property and EU competition law, 2nd edn. Oxford University Press, Oxford
Ullrich H (2005) Expansionist intellectual property protection and reductionist competition rules: a TRIPS perspective. In: Maskus KE, Reichman JH (eds) International public goods and transfer of technology under a globalized intellectual property regime. Cambridge University Press, Cambridge, pp 726–757
Vogel L (2020) European competition law, 3rd edn. LawLex, Paris
von Lewinski S (2008) International copyright law and policy. Oxford University Press, Oxford
Whish R, Bailey D (2021) Competition law, 10th edn. Oxford University Press, Oxford
Wildgen PA (2008) Law and economics perspective. In: Lidgard HH, Atik J (eds) The intersection of IPR and competition law: studies of recent developments in European and U.S. law, Chapter I: History and context. Intellecta docysus, Gothenburg, pp 50–59
Zevgolis NE (2018) The interaction between intellectual property law and competition law in the EU: necessity of convergent interpretation with the principles established by the relevant case law. In: Bharadwaj A, Devaiah VH, Gupta I (eds) Multi-dimensional approaches towards new technology: insights on innovation, patents and competition. Springer Open, pp 21–42

Part II
The Copyright-Competition Interaction Issue: Special Part

Chapter 4
The Exercise of Copyright Under the Prism of Article 101 TFEU

One of the most common copyright-competition interaction issue is exercise of copyright falling under the scope of the competition rules on prohibited agreements. This chapter provides a critical analysis of the relevant case law and doctrine.

This research identified several different approaches to the copyright-competition interaction issue: the inherency theory, the exceptional circumstances doctrine, the theory of complementarity, the theory of absolutism and standard competition law approach in copyright matters. Each approach has a certain rationale for being discussed in the context of this subject. However, none of the indicated approaches is entirely appropriate to providing a coherent and sustainable grounds for dealing with the copyright-competition interaction issue. In the application of those approaches many problems occur, often coming from disrespecting the fundamentals of copyright law and competition law. Commonly, copyright is not distinguished from other intellectual property right with a consequence of mixing legal and economic characteristics and effects of particular intellectual property rights. Thus, sometimes characteristics of patents are being attributed to other intellectual property rights, not considering particularities of those other rights. That is especially problematic for copyright as a non-industrial property right with an emphasised non-economic aspect. Besides, the indicated approaches commonly neglect economic components present in the copyright-competition interaction issue. Despite the existing tendency in the EU of the "more economic approach" with an emphasis on dynamic efficiency, it seems that economic analysis is often superficially performed.

Considering the flaws of the identified approaches, on the grounds of the conducted analysis, this chapter provides a new approach to the copyright-competition interaction issue for the cases of the exercise of copyright under the competition rules on prohibited agreements that respects the fundamental principles of copyright law and competition law.

D. Gliha, *The Copyright-Competition Interaction within the EU*,
https://doi.org/10.1007/978-3-031-94402-4_4

4.1 Introduction

The authors are free to dispose of the copyright rights they acquire on a particular copyright-protected work as the creators of the work. They may decide to exercise the copyright rights they hold on a particular work fully; that is common, particularly for authors who derive the primary income from their creative activities. They may decide just to enjoy the work they created without having any commercial intentions, or for whatever reason, they may completely ignore the work they produced and never exercise any right stemming from copyright. Authors can do practically whatever they want with their work, which is one of the beauties of the concept of authorship. If they decide to exploit the copyright economically, they consequently enter some market.[1] Here again, authors can exercise economic rights stemming from the copyright they hold on their own, or they can decide to license some or all economic rights to someone else, who can again license those rights further, depending on a particular arrangement.[2] Of course, copyright work can also be created as part of the employment relationship. In that case, characteristic of civil law systems, the employer will acquire the right to use copyright based on the employment agreement (if so agreed).[3] However, that does not diminish the author's rights. Quite the opposite, entering into an employment agreement represents the author's will to license economic rights to the employer.[4] Thus, nowadays, the real economic actors are usually not the authors themselves but publishers and other exploiters who obtained economic rights derived from the author's copyright.[5]

In the EU, the competition rules on prohibited agreements are contained in Article 101 TFEU, prescribing, in para. 1, the general prohibition rule:

> The following shall be prohibited as incompatible with the internal market: all agreements between undertakings, decisions by associations of undertakings and concerted practices which may affect trade between Member States and which have as their object or effect the prevention, restriction or distortion of competition within the internal market.

---

[1] Authors are commonly recognised as competitors on the market, as are undertakings, from the EU competition perspective.

[2] Since the copyright-competition interaction issue concerns not only the author but any copyright holder, moreover, some companies are more likely to be involved in this issue—in the further text, the notion of 'copyright holder' is used to designate the one disposing of some economic right stemming from a particular copyright.

[3] See Gliha (2006), pp. 775–820.

[4] Unlike in the civil law systems, where the author's moral rights are generally inalienable, in the legal systems following the common law tradition, there is no obstacle to vesting copyright not only in those natural persons who create a work but also in others, including legal persons that make investments in context with the works. Thus, according to the 'work for hire' doctrine, the employer is considered the legal author of a work created by an employee within the employment relationship. Within those two systems, there are some variations among particular national legislations. See Goldstein, Hugenholtz (2021), pp. 228–232, 236–237; von Lewinski (2008), pp. 47–50.

[5] See Ginsburg (2017), pp. 60–84.

Article 101 TFEU is not concerned with individual behaviour but with specific coordination of independent undertakings, leading to a distortion of competition. Hence, the activation of Article 101 TFEU necessarily implies the existence of an agreement; however, an agreement in the competition law sense is interpreted quite extensively (see *infra* Sect. 4.3.2.1). Competition rules on prohibited agreements require more than one independent undertaking to be involved in the conduct.

Thus, when an agreement involving the exercise of economic copyright rights potentially produces anti-competitive effects on the relevant market, the copyright-competition interaction issue emerges. Concerning copyright, such agreements, naturally, form some kind of licensing arrangement. However, it is not straightforward what should be considered an anti-competitive agreement that distorts competition and, consequently, should be sanctioned under the competition rules on prohibited agreements. In order to settle this issue, it is necessary to reconsider the fundamentals to provide a proper approach and ultimately a method of assessment.

4.2 Theoretical Foundations and Different Approaches to the Issue of the Exercise of Copyright and Competition Rules on Prohibited Agreements

The interaction between intellectual property rights and competition rules on prohibited agreements immediately occurred in the EU, with the first significant case raised before the CJEU—*Consten and Grundig*. That case concerned trademarks. However, implications from that case are undoubtedly relevant for copyright-competition case law, especially considering that differences between intellectual property rights are seldom taken adequately into consideration in relation to competition law.

In dealing with the matter of the interaction between copyright and competition rules on prohibited agreements, particularly in the beginning, the CJEU mainly relied upon the so-called inherency theory. Following the inherency theory, the rationales for dealing with the copyright-competition interaction issue are built upon the copyright exercise v. existence dichotomy and the use of particular standards. This approach was heavily criticised for several reasons discussed below, and also, it commonly mixed competition rules on prohibited agreements with EU rules on the free movement of goods.

Besides the inherency theory, through their practice, the Commission and the CJEU relied upon several other doctrines, sometimes acknowledging a unique approach to the copyright-competition interaction issue, while at other times approaching it through standard competition law assessment.

Also, several soft law documents have different approaches to the issue of the exercise of copyright under the competition rules on prohibited. Recently, it seems that the complementarity approach is advocated the most.

Taking into consideration theory and practice mainly in the EU, with regard to the exercise of copyright under the competition rules on prohibited agreements, this research identified several main approaches to the copyright-competition interaction issue:

1. The inherency theory
2. The exceptional circumstances doctrine
3. The complementarity theory
4. The theory of absolutism
5. The standard competition law approach in copyright matters

Some approaches were extensively applied in practice, while others were considered more on a theoretical level. Nevertheless, regardless of the level of application of a particular approach, it seems that neither theory nor practice has produced an adequate comprehensive approach dealing with the issue of exercising copyright under the competition rules on prohibited agreements. Moreover, throughout the history of this issue, practice and theory have shown to be anything but harmonised and comprehensive. Due to the specificity of the issue, not many cases have emerged before the competent bodies. However, the ones that did occur were mainly significant. Thus, it is of the utmost importance to find a proper, comprehensive and uniform approach that would be universally accepted in dealing with the cases concerning the exercise of copyright under the scrutiny of Article 101 TFEU. An approach that respects the principles and rationales of copyright law and competition law, without mixing the characteristics of copyright with other intellectual property rights, and that acknowledges the specific economics related to the issue in the matter.

However, that does not mean that findings from cases concerning the exercise of other intellectual property rights and competition rules on prohibited agreements cannot be considered. Every right has its particularities, and interference with competition law should not always be approached in the same manner for copyright, patents, trademarks, industrial design, etc.—which is often neglected in theory and practice. However, due to certain similar principles and in lack of more diverse practice, such cases can also contribute to the overall understanding of the copyright-competition interaction; but when analysed, differences among individual intellectual property rights must be taken into consideration. Thus, the *Consten and Grundig* case, for instance, is commonly analysed within the copyright-competition interaction matter as the first case concerning the interaction of an intellectual property right and competition law. Nevertheless, one must remember that this case concerned trademark and not copyright and hence should be applied only *per analogiam*. The differences among different intellectual property rights especially come to the fore in more complex cases where it is necessary to have a clearly defined subject matter and an in-depth economic analysis.

4.2.1 *The Inherency Theory*

4.2.1.1 General

One of the earliest theoretical foundations of copyright-competition interaction was the inherency concept. The inherency theory can be seen as a traditional and normative approach. Generally, it observes intellectual property rights as exemptions from competition law. According to the inherency theory, competition law application is allowed only if conduct involving the exercise of a particular intellectual property right that restrains competition is outside the substance of that intellectual property right.[6] In the case of copyright, that in practice means that competition law may interfere with copyright only when the exercise of a particular copyright right goes beyond what was granted by copyright law. Otherwise, the competition authorities should refrain from the exclusivity of copyright.

Although the inherency theory did not exert much influence on the later development of copyright-competition interaction case law,[7] it has undoubtedly left some important theoretical foundations. Regarding the interaction of the exercise of copyright with the competition rules on prohibited agreements, the most significant case that should be observed is *Deutsche Grammophon v Metro* (copyright). However, in the lack of more diverse practice, cases concerning other intellectual property rights, such as *Consten and Grundig* (trademark), *Parke Davis* (patents), *Nancy Kean Gifts* (designs) and *Windsurfing* (patents), should also be noted for a deeper understanding of the inherency concept and its influence on the issue of intersection between the exercise of copyright and competition rules on prohibited agreements.

[6] See Drexl (2008), p. 35.

The so-called 'Content Theory' rationalises things in a similar way. In situations where the exercise remains within the scope of the substance of the intellectual property right, there is no need for competition examination in the first place. If the exercise exceeds the scope, it is treated—from a competition law perspective—as any other restriction of competition. Later on, the modified version of the 'Content Theory', 'the Four-Fields Theory', acknowledged that also acts that remain within the scope of the substance of an intellectual property right could infringe competition. Thus, it identified four fields: first, the exercise remains within the substance of the intellectual property right, and is harmless from the competition law perspective; second, the exercise remains within the substance of intellectual property right, but constitutes an infringement of competition law; third, the exercise exceeds the substance of the intellectual property right, but does not constitutes infringement of competition law; fourth, the exercise exceeds the substance of the intellectual property right, and constitutes an infringement of competition law. See Fikentscher et al. (1995), pp. 757–765; Fikentscher (1995), p. 152; Fikentscher (1996), pp. 540–541; Daum (2010), p. 58.

[7] See Petit (2017), p. 94.

4.2.1.2 Inherency-Related Case Law

4.2.1.2.1 Deutsche Grammophon v Metro[8]

Deutsche Grammophon v Metro is commonly considered to be the first case concerning the copyright-competition interaction issue in the EU.

In the *Deutsche Grammophon v Metro* case, Deutsche Grammophon Gessellschaft GmbH sold records in both Germany and France. Due to market conditions, a French subsidiary of Deutsche Grammophon, Polydor, charged lower prices than those in Germany for the same records. Metro-SB-Großmärkte GmbH & Co. KG bought the records in France for resale in Germany at a price below the price Deutsche Grammophon charged, which provoked Deutsche Grammophon to invoke its copyright on the records involved to stop this practice of Metro. Thus, the dispute occurred, and during the procedure before national courts, the Appeal Court, Hanseatisches Oberlandesgericht, decided to stay the national proceedings to ask the CJEU to provide interpretation on whether the exercise of copyright by Deutsche Grammophon was contrary to Article 85 (101) TFEU.

However, the CJEU found that the dispute in the matter, in fact, concerned the issue of interference between copyright and provisions on the free movement of products instead of copyright-competition interaction. In effect, the CJEU ultimately grounded its decision on the basis of provisions on the free movement of products and ruled in favour of Metro, concluding that Deutsche Grammophon had exhausted its distribution right in the records by consenting to put them on the market in France. Therefore, Deutsche Grammophon could not oppose the import of records to Germany by Metro.

Regarding the competition law, the CJEU found no elements indicating that the matter concerned the prohibited agreement in Article 85 [101] TFEU, stating that "the exercise of the right does not exhibit those elements of the contract or concerted practice referred to in Article 85 (1)..."[9,10] Nevertheless, the CJEU gave certain remarks on how to approach situations in which copyright intersects with competition law, which still makes this case relevant in the context of the copyright-competition interaction issue. The CJEU stated that:

> The exercise of the exclusive right referred to in the question might fall under the prohibition set out by this provision each time it manifests itself as the subject, the means or the result of an agreement which, by preventing imports from other Member States of products lawfully

[8] Judgment of 8 June 1971, *Deutsche Grammophon Gesellschaft mbH v Metro-SB-Großmärkte GmbH* & Co. KG, C-78/70, EU:C:1971:59.

[9] Judgment of 8 June 1971, *Deutsche Grammophon Gesellschaft mbH v Metro-SB-Großmärkte GmbH & Co. KG*, C-78/70, EU:C:1971:59, para. 7.

[10] Further on, CJEU also noted that there were no elements of potential abuse of dominant position of Deutsche Grammophon since it did not hold a dominant position just by holding a right related to copyright, and also there were no indications of abuse (Judgment of 8 June 1971, *Deutsche Grammophon Gesellschaft mbH v Metro-SB-Großmärkte GmbH & Co. KG*, C-78/70, EU: C:1971:59, paras. 16–19).

> distributed there, has as its effect the partitioning of the market.[11] (...) It is thus in the light of those provisions, especially of Articles 36, 85 and 86, that an appraisal should be made as to how far the exercise of a national right related to copyright may impede the marketing of products from another Member State.[12]

In the following paragraph, the CJEU argued that:

> (...) the Treaty does not affect the existence of rights recognized by the legislation of a Member State with regard to industrial and commercial property, the exercise of such rights may nevertheless fall within the prohibitions laid down by the Treaty.

The case of *Deutsche Grammophon v Metro* certainly is one of the cornerstone cases in the EU where the CJEU gave several seminal interpretations: the exhaustion doctrine was first applied; it was the first time the CJEU discussed the relationship of free movement of goods and copyright, as well as competition law and copyright.

Without entering into a discussion on the correctness of the CJEU's interpretation in *Deutsche Grammophon v Metro,* it seems that indeed there was no agreement between the parties which would fall under the scrutiny of Article 85 [101] TFEU in a dispute between Deutsche Grammophon and Metro. Namely, to activate Article 101 TFEU, one of the main requirements is that there is an agreement (in a broad sense), decision or concerted practice involved that could disrupt free competition. That was not the case in *Deutsche Grammophon v* Metro. Nevertheless, the case indicated that in the EU, there is potential confusion between the rules on the free movement of goods and competition law in cases connected with the exercise of copyright. Namely, although the CJEU did note the distinction between the competition rule on prohibited agreements and the rules on the free movement of goods,[13] the wording of the judgment suggests that those two sets of rules overlap, particularly in relation to the application of the justification in Article 36 TFEU.[14] However, the competition rules on prohibited agreements and the rules on the free movement of goods have different legal bases and rationales; hence, they ought not to be mixed. The rules on the free movement of goods do not apply to competition matters, although both issues can indeed be separately raised in the same case. Still, the confusion between those rules was to be even more present in some of the later case law[15] (on the relationship between the competition rules and the rules on the free movement of goods, see *infra* Sect. 4.2.1.4).

---

[11] Judgment of 8 June 1971, *Deutsche Grammophon Gesellschaft mbH v Metro-SB-Großmärkte GmbH & Co. KG*, C-78/70, EU:C:1971:59, para. 6.

[12] Judgment of 8 June 1971, *Deutsche Grammophon Gesellschaft mbH v Metro-SB-Großmärkte GmbH & Co. KG*, C-78/70, EU:C:1971:59, para. 11.

[13] Judgment of 8 June 1971, *Deutsche Grammophon Gesellschaft mbH v Metro-SB-Großmärkte GmbH & Co. KG*, C-78/70, EU:C:1971:59, para. 7.

[14] Judgment of 8 June 1971, *Deutsche Grammophon Gesellschaft mbH v Metro-SB-Großmärkte GmbH & Co. KG*, C-78/70, EU:C:1971:59, paras. 10–11.

[15] See, for instance, Judgment of 29 February 1968, *Parke, Davis and Co. v Probel, Reese, Beintema-Interpharm and Centrafarm*, C-24/67, EU:C:1968:11, pp. 71–72; Judgment of 18 February 1971, *Sirena S.r.l. v Eda S.r.l. and others*, C-40/70, EU:C:1971:18, para. 5; Judgment of 10 July 1991, *RTE v Commission*, T-69/89, EU:T:1991:39, paras. 67–71; Judgment of 10 July

Besides, the more significant issue stemming from *Deutsche Grammophon v Metro* is the fact that the CJEU based its reasoning on the distinction between the existence and the exercise of copyright. Although such a distinction has a theoretical significance, its practical value is doubtful when applied to particular cases. When stating that the existence of copyright is not affected by the Treaty provisions, while its exercise might be, no guidelines were provided on how to distinguish this dichotomy in practice. Furthermore, the explanation that the exercise may infringe competition rules when it manifests itself as the subject, the means or the result of an agreement which may have as its effect the partitioning of the market—still, seems quite general and abstract (see *infra* Sect. 4.2.1.3).

4.2.1.2.2 Consten and Grundig[16]

Prior to *Deutsche Grammophon v Metro*, the first case in general in the EU dealing with the issue of interaction between some intellectual property rights and competition law was the well-known *Consten and Grundig* case. *Consten and Grundig* did not involve copyright but trademark. Although the approach throughout this thesis is to keep a clear line between different rights comprised under the notion of intellectual property rights, various forms of intellectual property indeed have certain similarities that place them under the similar principles and conceptual rules (see *supra* Sect. 2.1.3; Sect. 3.2). Thus, as the first such case, *Consten and Grundig* set the ground for further developing cases concerning the intersection of competition law with particular intellectual property rights.

Consten and Grundig concerned a dispute over an exclusive distributorship agreement between Établissements Consten S.à.R.L. and Grundig-Verkaufs-GmbH, having effect on the territory of France, after a third party bought Grundig's products in Germany and began distributing "grey imports" into France. Ultimately, the CJEU upheld the Commission's standpoint that such an exclusive distributorship agreement was unlawful, although it annulled the part of the Commission's decision that declared that the whole agreement constitutes an infringement of Article 85 [101] TFEU, instead of only specific provisions.

From the reasoning of the judgment, it is interesting to extract the part of the decision dealing with the relationship between trademark and competition law. Namely, the CJEU concluded that the agreement by which Grundig, as the trademark holder by virtue of international registration, authorised Consten to register it in France in its own name tends to restrict competition and infringe Article 85 [101] TFEU. According to the CJEU, such an arrangement would not constitute an

---

1991, *BBC v Commission*, T-70/89, EU:T:1991:40, paras. 54–58; Judgment of 10 July 1991, *ITP v Commission*, EU:T:1991:41, paras. 52–56.

[16] Judgment of 13 July 1966, *Établissements Consten S.à.R.L. and Grundig-Verkaufs-GmbH v Commission of the European Economic Community*, Joined cases 56 and 58-64, EU:C:1966:41.

infringement if Consten could continue to use the trademark to achieve the same object as pursued by the agreement, which has been held to be unlawful.

In further explanation, the CJEU first excluded the possibility of applying Article 36 TFEU and then referred to Article 222 [345] TFEU, stating that the "Treaty shall in no way prejudice the rules in the Member States governing the system of property ownership."[17] Namely, the CJEU held that the injunction concerning the registered trademark in the matter "to refrain from using rights under national trademark law to set an obstacle in the way of parallel imports does not affect the grant of those rights but only limits their exercise to the extent necessary to give effect to the prohibition under Article 85(1) TFEU."[18] To further elaborate, the CJEU then stated that the Community (the EU) body of rules on competition, because of its nature and its function, does not allow "the improper use of rights under any national trademark-law in order to frustrate the Community's law on cartels."[19] What standard "the improper use" is—no further explanation was provided.

Consten and Grundig is undoubtedly one of the most critical cases of the CJEU's history. Through its reasoning, the case provided several seminal substantive interpretations and laid the groundwork for further dealing with cartels and competition law in general. However, regarding the relationship between intellectual property (trademark) law and competition law, the CJEU left several issues wide open. Namely, in the absence of any prior interpretations of this specific matter, the CJEU based its reasoning on the distinction between the existence and exercise of copyright while supporting its reasoning through inherency concepts. Through its argumentation, the CJEU did not provide criteria when and why particular intellectual property rights can infringe rules on prohibited agreements under Article 101 TFEU. The CJEU only mentioned the standard "the improper use" without further elaborating on what would constitute the improper use of a particular intellectual property right. Also, the distinction between the existence and exercise of copyright, used in this context, seems somewhat unclear. The CJEU discusses the limitation of the exercise of an intellectual property right to the extent necessary to give effect to the prohibition under Article 85 [101] TFEU. It is indisputable that competition rules should not interfere with the substance of the right; however, how far that limitation may go remains unclear. Thus, *Consten and Grundig* can be acknowledged as the case that commenced the discussion on the relationship between individual intellectual property rights and competition law in the

---

[17] Judgment of 13 July 1966, *Établissements Consten S.à.R.L. and Grundig-Verkaufs-GmbH v Commission of the European Economic Community*, Joined cases 56 and 58-64, EU:C:1966: 41, p. 345.

[18] Judgment of 13 July 1966, *Établissements Consten S.à.R.L. and Grundig-Verkaufs-GmbH v Commission of the European Economic Community*, Joined cases 56 and 58-64, EU:C:1966: 41, p. 345.

[19] Judgment of 13 July 1966, *Établissements Consten S.à.R.L. and Grundig-Verkaufs-GmbH v Commission of the European Economic Community*, Joined cases 56 and 58-64, EU:C:1966: 41, p. 346.

EU. However, it also left legal uncertainty that has not been resolved even after more than 50 years.

In that case, the focus was, indeed, on the exclusive distributorship agreement in general and not solely on the registered trademark, which was only part of the provisions forming absolute territorial protection.[20] Thus, although the reasoning lacks comprehensive argumentation on the relationship between trademark and competition law, taking everything into account, the judgment seems somewhat plausible. Also, it should be borne in mind that *Consten and Grundig* was the first case before the CJEU dealing not only with the matter of the interaction between a particular intellectual property right and competition law, but also with exclusive distributorship agreements in general.

4.2.1.2.3 Parke Davis[21]

In *Parke Davis,* the case concerned a dispute between the holder of Dutch patents related to a pharmaceutical process and companies that imported related pharmaceutical products from Italy, where such patents could not be granted. In the case, the CJEU provided the following interpretation: "first, that the existence of the rights granted by a Member State to the holder of a patent is not affected by the prohibitions contained in Articles 85(1) [101(1)] and 86 [102] of the Treaty; secondly, that the exercise of such rights cannot of itself fall either under Article 85(1) [101(1)], in the absence of any agreement, decision or concerted practice prohibited by that provision, or under Article 86 in the absence of any abuse of dominant position; finally, that a higher sale price for the patented product as compared with that of the unpatented product coming from another Member State does not necessarily constitute an abuse."[22] Here, the CJEU did not further discuss what kind of exercise of intellectual property might infringe competition rules on prohibited agreements. However, it made it clear that before going into further evaluation, it must be determined whether there is an agreement, decision or concerted practice involved. Otherwise, there is no room for the activation of Article 101 TFEU.[23]

---

[20] Judgment of 13 July 1966, *Établissements Consten S.à.R.L. and Grundig-Verkaufs-GmbH v Commission of the European Economic Community*, Joined cases 56 and 58-64, EU:C:1966:41, pp. 344–345.

[21] Judgment of 29 February 1968, *Parke, Davis and Co. v Probel, Reese, Beintema-Interpharm and Centrafarm*, C-24/67, EU:C:1968:11.

[22] Judgment of 29 February 1968, Parke, *Davis and Co. v Probel, Reese, Beintema-Interpharm and Centrafarm*, C-24/67, EU:C:1968:11, pp. 72–73.

[23] In *Parke Davis*, the CJEU also made several interesting remarks relating to the relationship between rules on free movement of goods and competition rules in view of intellectual property rights by comparing the fields through Article 36 TFEU. Namely, the CJEU concluded that since prohibitions and restrictions on imports may be justified under Article 36 TFEU, for similar reasons, the exercise of the rights arising from particular intellectual property rights does not, of itself, constitute an infringement of the rules on competition laid down by the Treaty. See Judgment of

4.2.1.2.4 Sirena v EDA[24]

In *Sirena v EDA,* Sirena was the holder of trademarks on Italian territory assigned to it by the US company Mark Allen. Novimpex, the defendant, imported goods under those trademarks to Italy from a German licensee of Mark Allen—which initiated the dispute. In this case, the CJEU acknowledged that the issue of the intellectual property rights-competition interaction is not expressly regulated within the EU and that the national character of rules on individual intellectual property rights is likely to create obstacles, both to the free movement of goods and the EU competition rules.[25] As in earlier cases, in dealing with such a situation, the CJEU used an analogy with Article 36 TFEU (free movement of goods), concluding that the principle is equally applicable to the questions of competition. In that sense, the CJEU again noted that "the rights recognized by a Member State on the subject of industrial and commercial property are not affected, so far as their existence is concerned, by Articles 85 [101] and 86 [102] of the Treaty, their exercise may still fall under the prohibitions imposed by those provisions."[26] The CJEU further concluded that "the exercise of trademark might fall within the ambit of the prohibitions contained in the Treaty each time it manifests itself as the subject, the means or the result of a restrictive practice."[27] Preventing the import of products bearing a legally acquired trademark from a different Member State infringes Article 85 [101] TFEU.[28] The CJEU provided further explanation stating that before restrictive practices can come under Article 85(1) [101(1)], they must affect trade between Member States to an appreciable extent, and restrict competition within the market. Also, the CJEU acknowledged that the public interest protected by a trademark is lower than that protected by other rights comprised under the notion of intellectual property.[29] As can be seen, generally, in *Sirena v EDA* the CJEU followed formulations and terminology from similar prior case law. The elaboration

---

29 February 1968, *Parke, Davis and Co. v Probel, Reese, Beintema-Interpharm and Centrafarm*, C-24/67, EU:C:1968:11, p. 71.

[24] Judgment of 18 February 1971, *Sirena S.r.l. v Eda S.r.l. and others*, C-40/70, EU:C:1971:18.

[25] Judgment of 18 February 1971, *Sirena S.r.l. v Eda S.r.l. and others*, C-40/70, EU:C:1971:18, para. 4.

[26] Judgment of 18 February 1971, *Sirena S.r.l. v Eda S.r.l. and others*, C-40/70, EU:C:1971:18, para. 5. In addition to its reasoning the CJEU also referred to Regulation 67/67 stating that intellectual property rights should not be exercised in an abusive manner to create absolute territorial protection (Regulation No. 67/67/EEC of the Commission of 22 March 1967 on the application of Article 85 (3) of the Treaty to certain categories of exclusive dealing agreements, OJ 57, 25.3.1967, pp. 849–852.). See Judgment of 18 February 1971, *Sirena S.r.l. v Eda S.r.l. and others*, C-40/70, EU:C:1971:18, para. 6.

[27] Judgment of 18 February 1971, *Sirena S.r.l. v Eda S.r.l. and others*, C-40/70, EU:C:1971:18, para. 9.

[28] Judgment of 18 February 1971, *Sirena S.r.l. v Eda S.r.l. and others*, C-40/70, EU:C:1971:18, para. 11.

[29] Judgment of 18 February 1971, *Sirena S.r.l. v Eda S.r.l. and others*, C-40/70, EU:C:1971:18, para. 7.

in *Sirena v EDA* does seem more evident; however, criticism on vagueness and practical applicability of the interpretation of exercise of intellectual property rights with rules on competition remains. Nevertheless, the CJEU made a step further by recognizing that competition law may not interact in the same manner with all individual intellectual property rights.

4.2.1.2.5 EMI v CBS[30]

In the *EMI v CBS* case, EMI records Ltd., the holder of the trademark 'Columbia' on the territories of the EU Member States, brought actions for infringements of the trademark against subsidiaries of 'Columbia' trademark holder in the USA, CBS Inc. This case is especially interesting in comparison to *Sirena v EDA* since it dealt with a similar issue, except it involved imports from a third country into the EU Member States. In *EMI v CBS* the CJEU generally followed the classical inherency interpretation that "the exercise of that right might fall within the ambit of the prohibitions contained in the Treaty if it were to manifest itself as the subject, the means, or the consequence of a restrictive practice."[31] However, the CJEU noted that "the mere exercise of the national trade-mark rights" cannot infringe the competition rules on prohibited agreements,[32] and, ultimately, provided a ruling in favour of EMI records Ltd., as the holder of the trademark on the territories of the EU Member States. The reasoning in *EMI v CBS* is somewhat different from the one provided in *Sirena v EDA*, but this might be explained by the fact that one case concerned trade between Member States while the other concerned trade from a third country to the EU.[33]

4.2.1.2.6 Tepea v Commission[34]

Tepea v Commission discussed an oral exclusive distribution agreement between two undertakings, including the grant of the exclusive right to use trademarks registered in the Netherlands. Unlike in certain other cases that touched upon the

---

[30] Judgment of 15 June 1976, *EMI Records Limited v CBS Grammofon A/S*, C-86/75, EU:C:1976:86.

[31] Judgment of 15 June 1976, *EMI Records Limited v CBS Grammofon A/S*, C-86/75, EU:C:1976:86, para. 24.

[32] See Judgment of 15 June 1976, *EMI Records Limited v CBS Grammofon A/S*, C-86/75, EU:C:1976:86, paras. 24–29.

[33] Petit considers that in establishing a liability of an undertaking under Article 101 TFEU, the interpretation provided in *EMI v CBS* actually reversed the interpretation from *Sirena v EDA* by insisting on a proof of an additional agreement or concerted practice and stating that "the mere exercise of the national trade-mark rights" cannot infringe the competition rules on prohibited agreements; see Petit (2017), pp. 95–96.

[34] Judgment of 20 June 1978, *Tepea BV v Commission of the European Communities*, C-28-77, EU:C:1978:133.

issue of interference between individual intellectual property rights and competition rules on prohibited agreements, in this case, the existence of an agreement was truly determined, which is a prerequisite for determining the infringement of Article 85 [101] TFEU. Through its reasoning, the CJEU found that:

> The skillful use of trade-mark law has in this way strengthened the territorial protection given by the exclusive distribution agreement, the existence of which is admitted, the combined effect of these two techniques securing absolute and permanent protection.[35]

However, the CJEU also made a further remark, "that such an agreement does not fall within the prohibition contained in Article 85 if it affects trade between Member States only to an extent which is not appreciable."[36] Nevertheless, in this case, the CJEU did find that the agreements between Theal and Watts, which by preventing parallel imports secured for Theal absolute territorial protection which was made still more effective by the prohibition on exports imposed by Watts, had as their main object and effect the prevention of competition in the protected area within the Common Market.[37] As such, the CJEU determined the infringement of Article 85 [101] TFEU. In *Tepea v Commission*, the CJEU did not find its reasoning on the existence v. exercise dichotomy, unlike in most of the other similar cases that may be seen as influenced by the inherency theory. Herein, the CJEU viewed a trademark as a means of obtaining absolute territorial protection and used several standards such as "the skilful use of trademark," "extent which is not appreciable," etc.

4.2.1.2.7 Maize Seed[38]

The so-called *Maize Seed* case discussed the exclusive licensing between Mr. Eisele and INRA of plant breeders' rights concerning the granting of exclusive propagating and selling rights over those seeds for the territory of Germany, as well as an understanding between Mr. Eisele and Louis David KG preventing the undertaking from importing and selling INRA's seed into Germany. The CJEU concluded that plant breeders' rights are not different in nature from other intellectual property rights.[39] Hence, the CJEU referred to cases *EMI v CBS* and *Tepea* and considered that the following understanding is relevant for that case: "The exercise of that right

[35] Judgment of 20 June 1978, *Tepea BV v Commission of the European Communities*, C-28-77, EU: C:1978:133, para. 44.

[36] Judgment of 20 June 1978, *Tepea BV v Commission of the European Communities*, C-28-77, EU: C:1978:133, para. 47.

[37] Judgment of 20 June 1978, *Tepea BV v Commission of the European Communities*, C-28-77, EU: C:1978:133, paras. 53, 57.

[38] Judgment of 8 June 1982, L.*C. Nungesser KG and Kurt Eisele v Commission of the European Communities*, Case 258/78, ECLI:EU:C:1982:211.

[39] Judgment of 8 June 1982, L.C. *Nungesser KG and Kurt Eisele v Commission* of the European Communities, Case 258/78, ECLI:EU:C:1982:211, paras. 35, 41.

might fall within the ambit of the prohibitions contained in the Treaty if it were to manifest itself as the subject, the means or the consequence of an agreement."[40] "(…) where an agreement granting exclusive rights to utilize an industrial or commercial property right in a certain territory, in conjunction with an agreement appointing the licensee sole distributor for that territory, has the effect of ensuring absolute territorial protection for the licensee by preventing parallel imports."[41] Following those understandings, the CJEU distinguished two set of circumstances in the case. First, an "open exclusive license or assignment and the exclusivity of the license relates solely to the contractual relationship between the owner of the right and the licensee, whereby the owner merely undertakes not to grant other licenses in respect of the same territory and not to compete himself with the licensee on that territory." Second, an "exclusive license or assignment with absolute territorial protection, under which the parties to the contract propose, as regards the products and the territory in question, to eliminate all competition from third parties, such as parallel importers or licensees for other territories."[42] Although the Commission considered that both situations are contrary to Article 101 TFEU, the CJEU concluded that the grant of an open exclusive license generally does not affect the position of third parties such as parallel importers and licensees for other territories and in itself is not contrary to the competition rules on prohibited agreements.[43] However, regarding absolute territorial protection, the CJEU considered that it manifestly goes beyond what is indispensable for improving production or distribution or promoting technical progress.[44]

4.2.1.2.8 Coditel II[45]

Coditel II was concerned with the preliminary ruling on the issue of whether the exclusive copyright license to exhibit films granting absolute territorial protection to the licensee is contrary to Article 101 TFEU. The CJEU held that "the mere fact that the owner of the copyright in a film has granted to a sole licensee the exclusive right to exhibit that film in the territory of a Member State and, consequently, to prohibit, during a specified period, its showing by others, is not sufficient to justify the finding

[40] Judgment of 8 June 1982, L.*C. Nungesser KG and Kurt Eisele v Commission of the European Communities*, Case 258/78, ECLI:EU:C:1982:211, para. 29.

[41] Judgment of 8 June 1982, L.*C. Nungesser KG and Kurt Eisele v Commission of the European Communities*, Case 258/78, ECLI:EU:C:1982:211, para. 30.

[42] Judgment of 8 June 1982, L.*C. Nungesser KG and Kurt Eisele v Commission of the European Communities*, Case 258/78, ECLI:EU:C:1982:211, para. 53.

[43] Judgment of 8 June 1982, L.*C. Nungesser KG and Kurt Eisele v Commission of the European Communities*, Case 258/78, ECLI:EU:C:1982:211, para. 58.

[44] Judgment of 8 June 1982, L.*C. Nungesser KG and Kurt Eisele v Commission of the European Communities*, Case 258/78, ECLI:EU:C:1982:211, para. 77.

[45] Judgment of 6 October 1982, *Coditel SA, Compagnie générale pour la diffusion de la télévision, and others v Ciné-Vog Films SA and others*, Case 262/81, ECLI:EU:C:1982:334.

that such a contract must be regarded as the purpose, the means or the result of an agreement, decision or concerted practice prohibited by the Treaty."[46] Although the CJEU did not find infringement of Article 101 TFEU, it explained when such exercise of copyright rights might be contrary to the competition rules on prohibited agreements. Namely, the CJEU held that that would be the case where "where there are economic or legal circumstances the effect of which is to restrict film distribution to an appreciable degree or to distort competition on the cinematographic market, regard being had to the specific characteristics of that market."[47] Moreover, the CJEU noted that "it is for national courts, where appropriate, to make such inquiries and in particular to establish whether or not the exercise of the exclusive right to exhibit a cinematographic film creates barriers which are artificial and unjustifiable in terms of the needs of the cinematographic industry, or the possibility of charging fees which exceed a fair return on investment, or an exclusivity the duration of which is disproportionate to those requirements, and whether or not, from a general point of view, such exercise within a given geographic area is such as to prevent, restrict or distort competition within the common market."[48] With such reasoning, the CJEU also applied the inherency concept and, thereby, acknowledged the particularities of a specific object of copyright.

4.2.1.2.9 Keurkoop v Nancy Kean Gifts[49]

Keurkoop v Nancy Kean Gifts was a dispute over the import of ladies' handbags protected by an industrial design. The CJEU primarily analysed the case through the rules on the free movement of goods. However, the CJEU provided certain remarks with regard to Article 85 (101) TFEU. The CJEU stated the following:

> Although a right to a design, as a legal entity, does not as such fall within the class of agreements or concerted practices envisaged by Article 85 (1) TFEU, the exercise of that right may be subject to the prohibitions contained in the treaty when it is the purpose, the means or the result of an agreement, decision or concerted practice.[50]

In the further text, the CJEU also provided an example of an exercise that could infringe Article 85 (101) TFEU: "the situation where persons simultaneously or successively file the same design in various member states in order to divide up the

[46] Judgment of 6 October 1982, *Coditel SA, Compagnie générale pour la diffusion de la télévision, and others v Ciné-Vog Films SA and others*, Case 262/81, ECLI:EU:C:1982:334, para. 15.

[47] Judgment of 6 October 1982, *Coditel SA, Compagnie générale pour la diffusion de la télévision, and others v Ciné-Vog Films SA and others*, Case 262/81, ECLI:EU:C:1982:334, para. 17.

[48] Judgment of 6 October 1982, *Coditel SA, Compagnie générale pour la diffusion de la télévision, and others v Ciné-Vog Films SA and others*, Case 262/81, ECLI:EU:C:1982:334, paraa. 19, 20.

[49] Judgment of 14 September 1982, *Keurkoop BV v Nancy Kean Gifts BV*, C-144/81, EU:C:1982: 289.

[50] Judgment of 14 September 1982, *Keurkoop BV v Nancy Kean Gifts BV*, C-144/81, EU:C:1982: 289, para. 27.

markets within the community among themselves."[51] However, aside from the example provided, the CJEU did not provide any further interpretation but instructed national courts to ascertain in each case the possibility of whether an exercise of an exclusive right may lead to infringement of competition rules on prohibited agreements.

4.2.1.2.10 Windsurfing[52]

There was also another inherency coloured case, *Windsurfing*, in which the CJEU determined that as contrary to Article 85 [101] TFEU, several clauses of licensing agreements between Windsurfing, which was the holder of patents over several parts of a sailboard, and sailboard manufacturers. In general, the licensing agreements contained clauses requiring prior approval by Windsurfing of the boards used by licensees, as well as non-challenging clauses. In a discussion on inherency-related cases, it is especially interesting to highlight the following finding of the CJEU:

> It must be stated that such a clause clearly does not fall within the specific subject-matter of the patent, which cannot be interpreted as also affording protection against actions brought in order to challenge the patent's validity, in view of the fact that it is in the public interest to eliminate any obstacle to economic activity which may arise where a patent was granted in error.[53]

In *Windsurfing*, the CJEU did not ground its decision on the distinction between existence and exercise of an intellectual property right. The CJEU acknowledged that in competition proceedings, the Commission is not entitled to determine the scope of the patent; however, it is competent to exercise its powers when the scope of the patent is relevant for determining whether there has been an infringement of Article 85 or 86 TFEU.[54] Furthermore, the CJEU noted that in its review, it "must be limited only to determining whether in the light of the legal position existing in the State in which a patent was granted, the Commission had made a reasonable assessment of the scope of the patent."[55] When considering that the Court based its reasoning on the issue of whether conduct falls within the specific subject matter of the patent, it seems somewhat confusing how the competition authority may determine that a patent was granted in error. Regardless of that, the concept of specific subject matter as used in *Windsurfing* does not seem like a proper approach

---

[51] Judgment of 14 September 1982, *Keurkoop BV v Nancy Kean Gifts BV*, C-144/81, EU:C:1982:289, para. 28.

[52] Judgment of 25 February 1986, Windsurfing International Inc. v Commission of the European Communities, C-193/83, EU:C:1986:75.

[53] Judgment of 25 February 1986, *Windsurfing International Inc. v Commission of the European Communities*, C-193/83, EU:C:1986:75, para. 92.

[54] Judgment of 25 February 1986, *Windsurfing International Inc. v Commission of the European Communities*, C-193/83, EU:C:1986:75, paras. 23–26.

[55] Judgment of 25 February 1986, *Windsurfing International Inc. v Commission of the European Communities*, C-193/83, EU:C:1986:75, para. 28.

in dealing with such cases. From the wording of the case, it seems unclear what kind of conduct concerning intellectual property could infringe the competition rules.

4.2.1.3 Concluding Remarks on the Inherency Theory Given the Relationship Between the Exercise of Copyright and the Competition Rules on Prohibited Agreements

The inherency theory is mainly based on the 'existence v. exercise' dichotomy and standards such as 'specific subject-matter', 'essential function', etc., as can be seen from the previous selection of cases.

The common feature of most inherency-coloured cases is that they acknowledge the very existence of individual intellectual property rights as immune from competition intervention, while their exercise might fall under the scrutiny of competition law. To try to define the limits of competition intervention in the exercise of intellectual property rights, the CJEU used several leitmotiv formulations as cited in the above case law. The guiding phrase of such an approach seems to be the following: "the exercise of copyright might fall within the ambit of the rules on competition each time it manifests itself as the subject, the means or the result of a restrictive practice."

Although the use of the dichotomy between the existence and exercise of intellectual property rights in relation to competition law might seem plausible in theory, it turned out to be questionable in practice.[56] The distinction was primarily developed by reference to the EU rules on the free movement of goods (Article 36 TFEU), and the CJEU never thoroughly explained the extension of the distinction

[56] Hay and Oldekop note the following on the existence v exercise dichotomy:

> The distinction between the 'existence' and the 'exercise' of industrial property of course cannot serve as a practical test to identify those aspects of industrial property not affected by the Treaty aspects of its use which are subject to the Treaty prohibitions (…) Hay and Oldekop (1977), p. 123 in connection with p. 128.

Lianos and Dreyfus state:

> The distinction between 'exercise' and 'existence' may be subject to criticism as it is difficult to distinguish between the core of the IP right, its scope, and its exercise, unless the distinction reflects a decision over a list of legitimate activities that can fall within the scope of IP right, similar to the approach followed in the US with regard to the scope of the IP rights. Lianos and Dreyfuss (2013), p. 53.

Tritton writes:

> On closer examination, this doctrine is seen to be rather empty and valueless. Tritton (1994), pp. 422–428, p. 423.

Some scholars noted that since the judgement in *Coditel II*, the existence v the exercise dichotomy has not featured as an important element of the CJEU's reasoning in cases involving intellectual property rights. However, considering that *Keurkoop v Nancy Kean Gifts* and *Windsurfing* came later, evidently, there was still some inherency-based case law even after *Coditel II*. See Czapracka (2009), p. 96; Keeling (2003), p. 55.

to the rules on competition.[57] The problem with this concept is to distinguish what constitutes existence and what constitutes exercise, which is especially problematic when it comes to copyright. It lacks clear meaning in relation to something as intangible as copyright.[58] Thus, already in 1975, in its Fourth Report on Competition Policy, the Commission indicated that it was facing a problem with the clarity of the discussed dichotomy.[59] In that sense, several commentators have criticised this dichotomy as inapplicable, artificial, vague and useless. Ramalho argues that copyright is only valuable if a right holder can use it, or in other words, that intellectual property rights exist to be exercised.[60] Korah further considers: "In legal theory, it is impossible to draw the line between existence and exercise, except at the extremes. The existence of a right comprises all the ways in which it may be exercised. In ruling that an important difference rests on a distinction, which cannot be drawn by logical analysis, the ECJ created a very flexible instrument for it to develop the law and reduce the possibilities of dividing the Common Market through the use of national or regional intellectual property rights."[61]

It is certainly questionable to clearly distinguish the existence from the exercise of copyright clearly. Nevertheless, it is still possible to consider using that distinction for setting up theoretical grounds for further interpretation of the interaction between copyright law and competition law. Namely, it is important to note that copyright law acknowledges a bundle of economic rights to the author, but the author is not obliged to exercise those rights. With that in mind, regarding the copyright-competition interaction issue in relation to prohibited agreements, the existence of copyright may be perceived as an expression of the peaceful coexistence of copyright law and competition law. Competition law respects the existence of copyright, and copyright per se does not interfere with the competition law objectives. An exercise of those economic copyright rights, which a holder of copyright is entitled to, cannot in itself constitute a breach of competition law. Only under specific

57 See Skone James, Mummery, Rayner James, Garnett, Nimmer, Silman, Skone James (1991), pp. 425–426.

58 See Keeling (2003), p. 55.

59 The Commission, Fourth Report on Competition Policy (Addendum to the 'Eighth General Report on the Activities of the Communities'), Brussels - Luxembourg, April 1975. https://ec.europa.eu/competition/publications/annual_report/ar_1974_en.pdf. Accessed on 24 October 2024, p. 20.

> On a legal plane, the Commission faces the problems of definition exposed by the Court of Justice in its distinction between the existence of nationally protected industrial property rights, which is not to be affected by Community law, and the exercise of these rights, which can be subject to the Treaty rules.

60 See Ramalho (2016), pp. 67–70.

61 Korah (2006), pp. 3–4. In her earlier paper, Korah also writes that the existence v exercise dichotomy is a 'metaphysical distinction'. Korah (2002), p. 805. See also Czapracka stating:

> Indeed, the value of an IP right depends on the ability to exercise it: if an IP right cannot be exercised, the fact that its existence is unaffected is of little consolation to the right holder. Czapracka (2009), pp. 95–96.

exceptional circumstances, if an exercise of copyright exceeds normal exploitation, may competition law constrain such exercise (see *infra* Sect. 4.3.1).[62] To that end, as Keeling noted: "Perhaps the one useful element in the existence/exercise dichotomy is that it serves as a reminder that, whatever limitations Community law imposes on the exercise of an intellectual property right, it must not destroy the substance of the right. The nucleus of the exclusive right recognized by national law must remain intact. The judicial and legislative organs of the Community law must not curtail the exercise of the right to such an extent as to produce a confiscatory effect."[63]

In the inherency-coloured cases, in attempts to define situations in which competition intervention into the exercise of copyright is justified, the CJEU used certain standards such as 'specific subject-matter',[64] 'essential function',[65] 'improper use',[66] 'degenerate into an abuse',[67] 'skilful use',[68] 'an extent which is

---

[62] In this part, the author intentionally avoids using the term exceptional circumstances to avoid confusion with the exceptional circumstances doctrine features.

[63] Keeling (2003), p. 56.

[64] The closest the CJEU came to defining the specific subject-matter of copyright was in *Warner Bros and Metronome v Christiansen* and *Phil Collins* (see Keeling (2003), pp. 66–67):

> The two essential rights of the author, namely the exclusive right of performance and the exclusive right of reproduction, are not called in question by the rules of the Treaty.

Judgment of 17 May 1988, *Warner Brothers Inc. and Metronome Video ApS v Erik Viuff Christiansen*, C-158/86, EU:C:1988:242, para. 13.

> The specific subject-matter of those rights, as governed by national legislation, is to ensure the protection of the moral and economic rights of their holders. The protection of moral rights enables authors and performers, in particular, to object to any distortion, mutilation or other modification of a work which would be prejudicial to their honour or reputation. Copyright and related rights are also economic in nature, in that they confer the right to exploit commercially the marketing of the protected work, particularly in the form of licences granted in return for payment of royalties.

Judgment of 20 October 1993, *Phil Collins v Imtrat Handelsgesellschaft mbH and Patricia Im- und Export Verwaltungsgesellschaft mbH and Leif Emanuel Kraul v EMI Electrola GmbH*, Joined Cases C-92/92 and 263/92, EU:C:1993:847, para. 20.See also Vogel (2020), pp. 304–305.

[65] The CJEU's meaning of the essential function of copyright may be seen from the *Coditel I* and *Coditel II* case, where the Court held that "the fact that the right of a copyright owner and his assigns to require fees for any showing of a film is part of the essential function of copyright in this type of literary and artistic work." Judgment of the Court of 18 March 1980, *SA Compagnie générale pour la diffusion de la télévision, Coditel, and others v Ciné Vog Films and others*, C-62/79, EU:C:1980:84, para. 14. See also Judgment of the Court of 6 October 1982, *Coditel SA, Compagnie générale pour la diffusion de la télévision, and others v Ciné-Vog Films SA and others*, C-262/81, EU:C:1982:334, para. 12. See also Vogel (2020), p. 305.

[66] Judgment of 13 July 1966, *Établissements Consten S.à.R.L. and Grundig-Verkaufs-GmbH v Commission of the European Economic Community*, Joined cases 56 and 58-64, EU:C:1966:41, para. 346.

[67] Judgment of 29 February 1968, *Parke, Davis and Co. v Probel, Reese, Beintema-Interpharm and Centrafarm*, C-24/67, EU:C:1968:11, p. 72.

[68] Judgment of 20 June 1978, *Tepea BV v Commission of the European Communities*, C-28-77, EU:C:1978:133, para. 44.

not appreciable'.[69] However, the problem with the use of such standards is that in particular cases, they were left undefined and used chiefly for philosophical and rhetorical purposes—to dispel concerns of competition activism in particular intellectual property right cases, and Member States' concerns over the division of competence between the EU and the Member States.[70] In other words, the CJEU often arbitrarily modified such standards from case to case to fit the particular problem under consideration and justify its interpretation. Remarkably, that was the case concerning the specific subject matter.[71] Anyhow, by an overview of the above-cited inherency-based case law, it seems that such an approach often worked counter to and not for particular intellectual property rights holders. Instead of exoneration from competition liability, in most discussed cases where the inherency theory was applied, liability for infringement of competition rules was affirmed. In the cases concerning copyright, such a result is probably even more disturbing.

The use of such concepts serves (or can serve) well in rationalising and understanding the copyright-competition intersection in general. However, in specific situations, the use of inherency-coloured concepts seems too abstract and inappropriate for a decision-making process. In that manner, Petit states that "the rationalization of the early case-law on the antitrust-IP intersection as inherency spirited resembles to a legal fable."[72] Also, the inherency theory takes copyright (as well as other intellectual property rights) for granted without explaining its economic rationale. The view behind such a standpoint is that competition law enforcers should largely refrain from interfering with the exclusivity of the property right, even if the specific right creates market dominance—such interference would generally harm the incentive structure of innovation, originality and creativity.[73] Without a proper economic component in copyright-competition interaction issues, it is hardly possible to comprehensively evaluate a particular situation.

For those reasons, the inherency theory has not left a significant mark on the later development of cases concerning the exercise of copyright and competition rules on prohibited agreements; however, its importance should not be overlooked. In attempts to rationalise the copyright-competition intersection, inherency-influenced interpretations have provided seminal theoretical foundations in approaching this specific field of law, especially for cases concerning the exercise of copyright under Article 101 TFEU.

---

[69] Judgment of 20 June 1978, *Tepea BV v Commission of the European Communities*, C-28-77, EU:C:1978:133, para. 47. See also Judgment of 25 November 1971, *Béguelin Import Co. v S.A.G.L. Import Export*, C-22/71, EU:C:1971:113, para. 16.

[70] See Petit (2017), pp. 96–97.

[71] See Daum (2010), pp. 61–62; Ławniczak (2008), pp. 65–66.

From time to time, such undefined reasoning can be the CJEU's *modus operandi* in other types of cases as well.

[72] Petit (2017), p. 96.

[73] Drexl (2008), p. 35.

4.2.1.4 The Relationship Between the Competition Rules and the Rules on the Free Movement of Goods in Relation to Copyright

Throughout practice, it seems that in the EU, cases that involved inherency concepts were often intertwined with the EU rules on the free movement of goods. Thus, for further discussion on this topic and in relation to copyright, it may be helpful to distinguish the EU rules on the free movement of goods and EU competition rules.

In the case law influenced by the inherency theory, the CJEU often referred to Articles 30 and 36 TFEU concerning the free movement of goods.[74] The starting point for such reference was the interpretation that rules on the free movement of goods and competition rules on prohibited agreements pursue the same objective—the unity of the internal market and the abolition of obstacles to trade between the Member States[75]—and, hence, have the same meaning.

Indeed, the rules on the free movement of goods and the competition rules on prohibited agreements may coincide in certain aspects, particularly in relation to the establishment of the internal market; nevertheless, they have different legal bases and rationales, and, hence, must not be mixed. Thus, some agreements may be compatible with the rules on the free movement of goods but fall under the scope of competition rules on prohibited agreements, and vice versa.[76] Namely, on the one hand, the rules on the free movement of goods are "the specific and natural instrument for maintaining the unity of the Common Market with regards to the circulation of goods."[77] They contain obligations for the Member States not to apply measures that might impede the free flow of goods within the EU.[78] On the other hand, competition rules aim to protect free competition on the market and concern

---

[74] See, for instance, Judgment of 29 February 1968, *Parke, Davis and Co. v Probel, Reese, Beintema-Interpharm and Centrafarm*, C-24/67, EU:C:1968:11, pp. 71–72; Judgment of 18 February 1971, *Sirena S.r.l. v Eda S.r.l. and others*, C-40/70, EU:C:1971:18, para. 5; Judgment of 10 July 1991, *RTE v Commission*, T-69/89, EU:T:1991:39, paras. 67–71; Judgment of 10 July 1991, *BBC v Commission*, T-70/89, EU:T:1991:40, paras. 54–58; Judgment of 10 July 1991, *ITP v Commission*, EU:T:1991:41, paras. 52–56.

[75] See Skone James et al. (1991), p. 445.

[76] See, for instance, Judgment of 15 June 1976, *EMI Records Limited v CBS United Kingdom Limited*, C-51/75, EU:C:1976:85, paras. 28, 38.

[77] Hay and Oldekop (1977), pp. 131–132.The purpose of rules on the free movement of goods, alongside with the other fundamental freedoms, is to achieve the fundamental aim of the TFEU, "to fuse together the economics of the Member State and to create an integrated market in which the factors of production, as well as the fruits of production, can move freely, without let or hindrance, thus achieving, over a period of time, a better allocation of resources and greater all-round prosperity." Keeling (2003), p. 5.

[78] Also, the rules on the free movement of goods generally do not provide for a *de minimis* rule, unlike the competition rules on prohibited agreements. However, it is noteworthy that some scholars are reconsidering the transfer of the *de minimis* rule from the EU competition law to the field of the internal market freedoms, thereby acknowledging that undoubtedly "the rule is not identical in both fields, as its purpose is not the same." See Hojnik (2013), pp. 25–45.

anti-competitive measures for private entities.[79] Accordingly, the rules on the free movement of goods, particularly Article 36 TFEU, do not apply to competition cases.[80] In the TFEU, no justification whatsoever can be found for applying the provisions on the free movement of goods to competition law, or vice versa—both sets of rules seem clear enough for independent application. However, that does not mean that the competition rules and the rules on the free movement of goods cannot supplement each other, i.e. competition law may serve to maintain free movement of goods.[81]

Nevertheless, the interaction between copyright law and competition law is an entirely separate issue from the issue of the free movement of goods and copyright.[82] There is no need or justification for an analogy between those two issues. In relation to competition, copyright does not need any justification to be freely exercised. Quite the opposite, the intervention of competition law into the exercise of copyright can be seen only as an exemption (see discussion *supra* Sect. 3.3).

Although it may seem obvious, it should be noted that a clear line must be drawn between cases concerning the intersection of copyright with competition rules and those concerning copyright and the rules on the free movement of goods.

4.2.2 The Exceptional Circumstances Doctrine

The exceptional circumstances doctrine is one of the leading theoretical foundations of the copyright-competition intersection. According to this doctrine, copyright, as an intellectual property right, enjoys a special regime in competition evaluations. In *AstraZeneca v Commission*[83] the CJEU stated that the situation in the matter, where the undertaking in dominant position defended its statutory right to free deregistration of marketing authorisations over capsules, "is in no way an exceptional case and does not justify a derogation from Article 82 EC, unlike a situation in which the unfettered exercise of an exclusive right awarded for the realisation of an

[79] See Hay and Oldekop (1977), p. 138.

[80] Judgment of 13 July 1966, *Établissements Consten S.à.R.L. and Grundig-Verkaufs-GmbH v Commission of the European Economic Community*, Joined cases 56 and 58-64, EU:C:1966:41, p. 345. See Skone James et al. (1991), pp. 424–426, 445–446. See also Myrick (1992), pp. 298, 304.

[81] In a comprehensive analysis of the CJEU's case law on the rules on free movement and competition, Mortelmans observes that some convergence between those two sets of rules can be found in the practice of the CJEU (such as in *Consten and Grundig*, for instance). However, he notes that there are clear differences between competition rules and rules on free movement, and full convergence is surely not desirable. See Moretalmans (2001), pp. 613–649.

[82] See Rognstad (2008), pp. 429–431.

[83] Judgment of 6 December 2012, *AstraZeneca AB and AstraZeneca plc v European Commission*, C-457/10 P, EU:C:2012:770.

investment or creation is limited."[84] The case obviously dealt with an abuse of dominance matter. However, by such a formulation, the CJEU clearly confirmed the general, special status of particular intellectual property rights as opposed to other non-IPR property rights.[85]

In cases involving copyright, competition liability is set at a level higher than in other 'regular' (non-IPR) cases.[86] The exercise of copyright is generally deemed presumptively lawful regarding competition rules, save in exceptional circumstances. Therefore, it can be seen that under this theory, the exercise of copyright and other intellectual property rights is set as an exception from competition law provisions where infringement exists only as an exception from an exception.

The emergence of the exceptional circumstances doctrine is commonly associated with the *Magill*[87] case concerning the refusal to license copyright.[88] This doctrine

---

[84] Judgment of 6 December 2012, *AstraZeneca AB and AstraZeneca plc v European Commission*, C-457/10 P, EU:C:2012:770, para. 150.

[85] See Petit (2017), pp. 101–102.

[86] However, following the *Oscar Bronner v Mediaprint* case, there is a viewpoint that the presence of the 'exceptional circumstances' is required for all refusals to deal with cases, whether or not they include the exercise of certain IPRs (Judgment of 26 November 1998, *Oscar Bronner GmbH & Co. KG v Mediaprint Zeitungs und Zeitschriftenverlag GmbH & Co. KG, Mediaprint Zeitungsvertriebsgesellschaft mbH & Co. KG and Mediaprint Anzeigengesellschaft mbH & Co. KG*, C-7-97, EU:C:1998:569, paras. 39–40). Furthermore, the 'exceptional circumstances' concept was used in non-IPR cases arguing: "As access to the Court is a fundamental right and a general principle ensuring the rule of law, it is only in wholly exceptional circumstances that the fact that legal proceedings are brought is capable of constituting an abuse of a dominant position within the meaning of Article 86 of the Treaty." (Judgment of 17 July 1998, *ITT Promedia NV v Commission of the European Communities*, T-111/96, EU:T:1998:183 para. 60). In some of the IPR cases dealing with an abuse of dominant position, the exceptional circumstances doctrine was not applied, as expected, but the case was evaluated as a conventional exploitative abuse case, referring to non-IP precedents in support of its reasoning (Judgment of 16 July 2009, *Der Grüne Punkt - Duales System Deutschland GmbH v Commission of the European Communities*, C-385/07 P, EU:C:2009:456). See Petit (2017), pp. 102–103.

[87] Judgment of 6 April 1995, *RTE and ITP v Commission*, Joined Cases C-241/91 P and C-242/91 P, ECLI:EU:C:1995:98.

[88] Nonetheless, the notion of the exceptional circumstances is mentioned in earlier case law, not necessarily connected to the intellectual property rights. See, for instance, Judgment of 13 February 1979, *Hoffmann-La Roche & Co. AG v Commission of the European Communities*, C-85-76, ECLI:EU:C:1979:36, para. 90:

> Obligations of this kind to obtain supplies exclusively from a particular undertaking, whether or not they are in consideration of rebates or of the granting of fidelity rebates intended to give the purchaser an incentive to obtain his supplies exclusively from the undertaking in a dominant position, are incompatible with the objective of undistorted competition within the Common Market, because — unless there are exceptional circumstances which may make an agreement between undertakings in the context of Article 85 and in particular of paragraph (3) of that article, permissible — they are not based on an economic transaction which justifies this burden or benefit but are designed to deprive the purchaser of or restrict his possible choices of sources of supply and to deny other producers access to the market.

has heavily influenced the understanding of copyright-competition interaction; however, it was mainly applied in cases under Article 102 TFEU—refusal to license cases[89] and IP remedy cases.[90] Practically no cases concerning the exercise of copyright under Article 101 TFEU were influenced by the exceptional circumstances doctrine.[91] Several reasons can be found for that. First, the exceptional circumstances test was developed primarily through and for the cases concerning potential abuse of dominant position. Considering differences between competition evaluation under Article 101 and Article 102, the exceptional circumstances test may indeed be tailor-made only for abuse of dominance situations and, therefore, not suitable for prohibited agreements cases. Second, an explanation may be found in the fact that with the development of the doctrine of exhaustion in copyright and other IPR cases, the Commission's concerns about market partitioning were lessened. Also, following the *Nungesser*[92] case, vertical exclusive IP licenses were generally considered pro-competitive. The abolition of the notification of licensing agreements to the Commission[93] may also have dried up the number of IP Article 101 TFEU cases in this aspect.[94]

Still, the wording of cases such as *AstraZeneca v Commiss*ion[95] implicitly infers that the concept of the exceptional circumstances doctrine generally applies to cases of interaction between intellectual property and competition and not solely to abuse of dominant position (Article 102 TFEU).

The exceptional circumstances doctrine will further be discussed in the chapter on the refusal to license copyright as an abuse of dominant position (see *infra*

[89] See Judgment of 6 April 1995, *RTE and ITP v Commission*, Joined Cases C-241/91 P and C-242/91 P, ECLI:EU:C:1995:98; Judgment of 29 April 2004, *IMS Health*, C-418/01, EU:C:2004:257; Judgment of 17 September 2007, *Microsoft v Commission*, T-201/04, EU:T:2007:289.

[90] See Judgment of 13 September 2012, *Protégé International Ltd v European Commission*, T-119/09, EU:T:2012:421, para. 48.

[91] Some may see it in the reasoning of the patent law case *Lundbeck*, the Commission implicitly rejected the applicability of the theory of exceptionalism under Article 101 TFEU. The General court confirmed the EC's viewpoint, and later, the CJEU dismissed the Lundbeck A/S's and Lundbeck Ltd's appeal (The Commission, case AT.39226, *Lundbeck*, C(2013) 3803 final, 19.6.2013; Judgment of 8 September 2016, *Lundbeck v Commission*, Case T-472/13, ECLI:EU:T:2016:449; Judgement of 25 March 2021, Case C-591/16 P, *Lundbeck v. Commission*, ECLI:EU:C:2021:243). See also Petit (2017), p. 103).

[92] Judgment of 8 June 1982, L.*C. Nungesser KG and Kurt Eisele v Commission of the European Communities*, Case 258/78, ECLI:EU:C:1982:211.

[93] Council Regulation (EC) No. 1/2003 of 16 December 2002 on the implementation of the rules on competition laid down in Articles 81 and 82 of the Treaty, OJ L 1, 4.1.2003, pp. 1–25, para. 3.

[94] See Anderman and Schmidt (2019), pp. 109–110; Petit (2017), p. 103.

[95] In para. 150 which it was stated that the statutory right to deregistration "is in no way an exceptional case and does not justify a derogation from Article 82 EC, unlike a situation in which the unfettered exercise of an exclusive right awarded for the realisation of an investment or creation is limited"—the CJEU does not circumscribe the special competition regime for IPR only for an abuse dominant position situation, but rather for the exercise of IPR in general. Judgment of 6 December 2012, *AstraZeneca AB and AstraZeneca plc v European Commission*, C-457/10 P, EU:C:2012:770, para. 150.

Sect. 5.2.2). Nevertheless, the concept of the exception from exception may also be applied to cases concerning the exercise of copyright under competition rules on prohibited agreements. Namely, the understanding that copyright (and other IPRs) should have special treatment under competition rules seems a rightful and appropriate approach that satisfies both the complementary and opposing interests of copyright law and competition law. That does not imply that copyright should entirely be exempt from competition interventions, but rather that competition liability in the exercise of an individual right arising from copyright should indeed be an exemption. For now, it can be left aside, whether such a situation should be addressed as the 'exceptional circumstances', 'special circumstances' or something else. The essential thing is that in cases concerning the copyright-competition intersection situation, the concept and particularities of copyright (and other IPRs) are not neglected and that quality economic analysis is included in the comprehensive evaluation.

Maybe the concept of 'exceptional circumstances', as developed in the refusal to license cases, is not the appropriate solution for cases concerning the exercise of copyright under Article 101 TFEU. However, that is far from concluding that nothing at all from this theoretical foundation should be applied to cases concerning the exercise of copyright and competition rules on prohibited agreements—quite the opposite (see *infra* Sect. 5.2).

4.2.3 The Theory of Complementarity

The complementarity concept of the interaction between copyright law and competition law was introduced in practice in 2004 in a soft law document—Guidelines on Technology Transfer Agreements,[96] although the roots of this theory can be traced to earlier academic literature.[97] In the EU, the theory of complementarity seems to have been introduced as an alternative to the exceptional circumstance doctrine, which was at the time the main fundamental of the refusal to license cases within the issue of interaction between intellectual property rights and competition law.[98]

The complementarity concept introduced in para. 7 of the general principles of the 2004 Guidelines on Technology Transfer Agreements was reproduced verbatim

[96] Commission Notice — Guidelines on the application of Article 81 of the EC Treaty to technology transfer agreements, OJ C 101, 27.4.2004, pp. 2–42.

[97] The complementarity theory foundations can be traced back to the works of Bowman before it was endorsed by academia. See Bowman (1973).

[98] Petit argues that the complementarity theory "seems to pair with an implicit rejection of the theory of exceptionalism." Petit (2017), p. 106. However, in the 2004 IMS Health case, the CJEU consolidated the *Magill* exceptional circumstances concept. Later on in 2007, in *Microsoft*, the CJEU provided its new interpretation of exceptional circumstances. Thus, it seems more plausible to say that this actually was the golden period of the exceptional circumstances doctrine (from *Magill* (1995) to *Microsoft* (2007)), and that the complementarity concept was introduced as an alternative rather than as an instant substitute. Also, the 2004 Guidelines on Technology Transfer Agreements still used refer to exceptional circumstances when discussing the existence of a hardcore restriction (Guidelines on Technology Transfer Agreements (2004), paras. 18, 75).

in para. 7 of the general principles of the revised 2014 Guidelines on Technology Transfer Agreements:[99]

> The fact that intellectual property laws grant exclusive rights of exploitation does not imply that intellectual property rights are immune from competition law intervention. Article 101 of the Treaty is in particular applicable to agreements whereby the holder licenses another undertaking to exploit his intellectual property rights. Nor does it imply that there is an inherent conflict between intellectual property rights and the Community competition rules. Indeed, both bodies of law share the same basic objective of promoting consumer welfare and an efficient allocation of resources. (...) Therefore, both intellectual property rights and competition are necessary to promote innovation and ensure a competitive exploitation thereof.

In comparison, interestingly, the US Antitrust Guidelines for the Licensing of Intellectual Property seem to stand on the same grounds:

> The intellectual property laws and the antitrust laws share the common purpose of promoting innovation and enhancing consumer welfare. The intellectual property laws provide incentives for innovation and its dissemination and commercialization by establishing enforceable property rights for the creators of new and useful products, more efficient processes, and original works of expression. In the absence of intellectual property rights, imitators could more rapidly exploit the efforts of innovators and investors without providing compensation. Rapid imitation would reduce the commercial value of innovation and erode incentives to invest, ultimately to the detriment of consumers. The antitrust laws promote innovation and consumer welfare by prohibiting certain actions that may harm competition with respect to either existing or new ways of serving consumers.[100]

The core idea behind the theory of complementarity is that copyright law (as well as other intellectual property rights) and competition law share specific, common, basic goals of consumer welfare and efficiency. According to Drexl's interpretation of this approach, from the economic point of view, with regard to efficiency, copyright and competition law should strive jointly towards enhancing dynamic competition on the market. Thus, competition law must keep markets open and maintain competitive pressure on copyright holders to compete with better products, respectively, in the case of copyright, to invest in originality and creativity.[101] Without competitive pressure, there are no guarantees that the author and potential copyright holder would reinvest monopoly profits. However, in a competitive scenario, a competitor can hope to win monopoly profits by further investments. In other words, according to this approach, intervention under competition law is directed towards safeguarding the competitive pressure needed to maintain of the overall inventive structure for innovation.[102]

---

[99]Communication from the Commission — Guidelines on the application of Article 101 of the Treaty on the Functioning of the European Union to technology transfer agreements, OJ C 89, 28.3.2014, pp. 3–50.

[100]US Antitrust Guidelines for the Licensing of Intellectual Property, issued by the U.S. Department of Justice and the Federal Trade Commission, January 12, 2017. https://www.justice.gov/atr/IPguidelines/download. Accessed on 23 October 2024, sect. 1.0.

[101]See Drexl (2008), p. 36.

[102]Drexl (2008), pp. 44–45.

What does the complementarity concept mean for copyright-competition interaction? Unlike the inherency theory and the exceptional circumstances doctrine that generally defer to the interests of copyright, the theory of complementarity clearly allows ex post competition intervention into the field of copyright. However, the foundation of this theory is that copyright and competition complement each other, rather than collide. Such a concept restricts the intensive intervention of competition law in the field of copyright. It ultimately may even favour copyright holders as opposed to the inherency theory and the exceptional circumstances doctrine, which, from the above examples, were shown to be often working counter to copyright (and other intellectual property rights) holders in practice.

Thus, within the framework of the complementarity theory, the so-called 'balancing approach' was introduced as the standard for determining a potential violation of Article 101 TFEU. How far competition law can intervene in copyright depends on the variables integrated into the equation—factors included in weighing between the private interest of safeguarding copyright holders and the public interest of protecting undistorted competition. In relation to the non-challenge clauses, the following balancing test was introduced in the 2014 Guidelines on Technology Transfer Agreements:

> The public interest of strengthening the incentive of the licensor to license out by not being forced to continue dealing with a licensee that challenges the very subject matter of the licence agreement has to be balanced against the public interest to eliminate any obstacle to economic activity which may arise where an intellectual property right was granted in error. In balancing those interests it should be taken into account whether the licensee fulfils all the obligations under the agreement at the time of the challenge, in particular the obligation to pay the agreed royalties.[103]

Although this balancing test is undoubtedly inspired by the complementarity concept, it is noteworthy that it refers to the inherency-coloured case *Windsurfing* case ('intellectual property granted in error').

In practice, the complementarity concept has not gained popularity within the CJEU case law. One non-competition case worth mentioning that acknowledged the complementarity concept to some degree is *Scarlett Extended*.[104] In that case, the CJEU provided interpretation on balancing between the interests of IP owners and the freedom of third parties to conduct their own business, and stated:

> The protection of the right to intellectual property is indeed enshrined in Article 17(2) of the Charter of Fundamental Rights of the European Union ('the Charter'). There is, however, nothing whatsoever in the wording of that provision or in the Court's case-law to suggest that that right is inviolable and must for that reason be absolutely protected. (...) the

[103] Communication from the Commission — Guidelines on the application of Article 101 of the Treaty on the Functioning of the European Union to technology transfer agreements, OJ C 89, 28.3.2014, pp. 3–50, para. 138.

[104] Judgment of 24 November 2011, *Scarlet Extended SA v Société belge des auteurs, compositeurs et éditeurs SCRL (SABAM)*, C-70/10, EU:C:2011:771.

protection of the fundamental right to property, which includes the rights linked to intellectual property, must be balanced against the protection of other fundamental rights.[105]

Indeed, competition law objectives go far beyond the freedom of third parties to conduct their own business; however, the findings from *Scarlett Extended* might also be helpful for the interpretation of the copyright-competition interaction issue.

Interestingly, the theory of complementarity was not introduced into the Block Exemption Regulation on Technology Transfer Agreements.[106]

Nevertheless, the complementarity theory evidently found its proponents within the academic society and has been widely present among scholars in recent discussions on copyright-competition interaction. Some of them view applying the complementarity concept to the copyright(IPRs)-competition intersection as the more economic approach.[107] The theory focuses on the protection of effective competition and the economic interests of consumers; it also allows analysis of the effects of specific conduct connected with a particular intellectual property right.[108] Thus, Drexl writes that "the Commission would be well advised to extend its concept of complementary goals of IP law and competition law from the field of technology transfer agreements to the area of abuse of dominance and merger control."[109]

However, the biggest problem with the theory of complementarity is that, with a few exceptions, its advocates (the Commission included) tend to ignore the particularities of an individual intellectual property right. Generally, they argue that innovation and consumer welfare are the joint objectives of intellectual property rights and competition law, without reconsidering whether innovation in particular is even an objective of an intellectual property right in a specific matter.[110] It seems that the characteristics of patent law are often automatically attributed to other intellectual property rights as well, without taking into consideration their rationales, ultimately leading to the wrong result. Concerning copyright, it is possible to discuss creativity and originality in the context of dynamic efficiency, but surely this is not the case with innovation. Even if we put aside the issue of innovation as a goal of copyright and replace it with originality and/or creativity, a more conventional understanding of copyright law would rather consider copyright as a fundamental right with the goal of an acknowledging a property right as a reward for labour

[105] Judgment of 24 November 2011, *Scarlet Extended SA v Société belge des auteurs, compositeurs et éditeurs SCRL (SABAM)*, C-70/10, EU:C:2011:771, paras. 43–44. See also Judgment of 16 February 2012, *Belgische Vereniging van Auteurs, Componisten en Uitgevers CVBA (SABAM) v Netlog NV*, C-360/10, para. 41.

[106] Commission Regulation (EU) No. 316/2014 of 21 March 2014 on the application of Article 101(3) of the Treaty on the Functioning of the European Union to categories of technology transfer agreements, OJ L 93, 28.3.2014, pp. 17–23.

[107] Almunia (2013); Choi and Heinemann (2016), p. 406; Drexl (2008), pp. 43, 53; Ghidini (2006), pp. 5–7; Heinemann (2002), pp. 1, 25–27.

[108] Drexl (2008), p. 45.

[109] Drexl (2008), p. 53.

[110] See, for instance, Schmidt (2010), pp. 53–69.

(or even as an incentive according to the common law tradition[111]). Thus, copyright might have an encouraging effect on dynamic competition (i.e. to create further works), but would not see competition with other works as the goal (see *supra* Sect. 2.1.2).

Besides being conceptually questionable, the differences between individual intellectual property rights come to the fore in concrete analysis. It also seems problematic that in the context of the complementarity approach, the objectives of intellectual property rights and competition law are observed as the same. There is no valid justification for such an approach, considering the rationales of copyright law and competition law.

However, with the proper reconsideration of the individual intellectual property rights in a matter, the complementarity theory would seem less problematic and potentially even welcome in a certain way. The perception of the objectives of competition law and effects of copyright law as complementary—not in a conflict—may even contribute to discussion on the copyright-competition interaction issue through a better understanding of the relationship between copyright law and competition law.

Stressing the need for balancing interests seems reasonable and useful for a comprehensive approach to the copyright-competition interaction issue. However, identifying the parameters for weighing the interests of copyright and the interests of competition law is still left open. The 'balance of interests' ought not to be confused with balancing within copyright (rights vs. exceptions on the basis of fundamental rights). Also, due to the concept that competition law can potentially intervene directly in practically any exercise of copyright, caution should be used that the theory of complementarity does not serve as a theoretical foundation for diminishing copyright and the position of copyright holders. Such an approach would contravene the fundamental values of copyright, and as such, would not be acceptable.

Therefore, if certain concepts from the complementarity theory are endorsed, adequate parameters are necessary for determining the anti-competitive effects of conduct involving the exercise of copyright rights.

4.2.4 The Theory of Absolutism

The so-called 'theory of absolutism' can be seen as one of the radical approaches to copyright-competition interaction. In its narrow and grammatical interpretation, this 'theory' considers copyright, as well as other rights contained under the notion of intellectual property rights, "as statutory-crafted islands in a sea of competition and grants IPR owners' absolute freedom to exploit their rights without any risk of antitrust liability."[112] Generally, it is reasonable to conclude that this approach is

---

[111] See Goldstein (1989), pp. 4–9.

[112] Petit (2017), p. 92; Käseberg (2012), pp. 25–26.

rooted in the extensive interpretation of the civil law tradition, according to which copyright is an absolute, unrestricted and essentially individualistic right. Although the concept of absolutism indeed lies in the essence of the civil law tradition (see *supra* Chap. 2), in the context of the copyright-competition interaction issue, we mainly discuss the factual outside limitations on the exercise of economic copyright rights. Hence, even from the philosophical point of view, there can be no justification for every conduct involving the exercise of copyright to be completely immune from any competition intervention, nor does this stem from the concept of the absolutism of copyright (see *supra* Sect. 2.1.2).[113] In that sense, it seems reasonable to agree with Dreier, who writes: "(…) copyright is not completely shielded from control by competition law, competition law only comes in late, operates on a posteriori control and is a heavy instrument based on rather cumbersome enforcement mechanisms."[114] Ginsburg, Geradin and Klovers consider: "IP rights are not subject to special competition rules or principles in the EU. As in U.S. antitrust law, the same principles that would apply to other forms of property - apply to IP rights, and IP rights do not immunize their holder from the application of competition rules." [115] Also, the Guidelines on the application of Article 101 TFEU to technology transfer agreements (TT Guidelines) state: "The fact that intellectual property laws grant exclusive rights of exploitation does not imply that intellectual property rights are immune from competition law intervention."[116]

From the economic point of view, this approach may also be seen as an extreme interpretation of the neo-Schumpeterian concept: "never interfere with intellectual property rights as you cannot measure the costs of such intervention."[117] According to the Schumpeterian concept of 'creative destruction', what really drives competition is "competition from the new commodity, the new technology, the new source of supply, the new organization."[118] Thus, regarding the relationship between intellectual property rights and competition, Schumpeter advocates a cautious approach where competition policy should not indiscriminately ban all restrictive behaviour without considering the virtues of creative destruction.[119] Based primarily on the view that monopoly power is necessary to enhance innovation and dynamic efficiency, some economists and lawyers take this approach to argue that competition law should entirely refrain from any intervention into the field of intellectual property rights. According to the proponents of such an approach, interfering with an

---

[113] See Anderman and Schmidt (2019), p. 5.

[114] Dreier (2010), p. 242.

[115] Before that statement, they state that in the US system, it is also acknowledged that the ownership of copyright does not provide immunity from otherwise unlawful competition conspiracy. See Ginsburg et al. (2019), pp. 105, 110.

[116] Communication from the Commission — Guidelines on the application of Article 101 of the Treaty on the Functioning of the European Union to technology transfer agreements, OJ C 89, 28.3.2014, pp. 3–50, para. 7.

[117] Drexl (2008), p. 43.

[118] Schumpeter (2003), p. 84.

[119] Schumpeter (2003), pp. 89–91.

intellectual property right has greater costs (in dynamic efficiency) than the costs (in allocative efficiency and price competition) of non-interfering.[120]

It is reasonable to conclude that, due to their specific nature, intellectual property rights, particularly copyright, also have specific economics (see *supra* Sect. 3.2). From the market perspective, each intellectual property right is in some way focused on dynamic efficiency. Thus, short-term losses in allocative efficiency and price competition, which are, from a competition perspective, hardly accepted for tangible property, may, in the case of intellectual property rights, be beneficial for long-term dynamic competition. That does not mean, however, that it is always, without any exception, justified to keep competition law out of the exercise of copyright and other intellectual property rights.

Practice and theory have recognised the issue of copyright-competition interaction, where competition law indeed may, in certain situations, interfere with the exercise of particular rights stemming from copyright. For licensing, that means, in essence, that a specific arrangement in a licensing agreement may fall under the scrutiny of competition law regardless of whether it involves the exercise of a certain right arising from copyright.

Therefore, literally taken, within the context of copyright-competition intersection, "the theory of absolutism" can in its extensive interpretation immediately be rejected since it is unrealistic and hardly justified, even from a purely copyright perspective. The fact is that interaction between the exercise of copyright and competition rules is a common occurrence. In the normal exploitation of copyright, competition law cannot (or should not) sanction the holder. That stems from the nature and exclusivity of copyright, which is considered to be an absolute right, but not in the sense of its utterly unrestricted exercise. However, the conceptual absolutism of copyright does not isolate it from the legal system as such. Even copyright law prescribes certain limitations and exceptions to the exercise of copyright (see *supra* Sect. 2.1.2). In the context of copyright-competition interaction, in certain specific/exceptional situations, violations of competition rules may occur when certain conduct involving copyright produces anti-competitive effects on a relevant market. Under what conditions the exercise of copyright constitutes an infringement of competition law is debatable and will be further discussed within this thesis. Nevertheless, it should be noted that potential competition law interventions into particular instances of the exercise of copyright do not undermine the value and 'sanctity' of copyright, if appropriately conducted.

Taken literally, "the theory of absolutism" in its extensive interpretation is certainly not a solution to the copyright-competition interaction issue. For this reason, it was not applied in any of the related cases or legal documents. Still, the idea of the absoluteness and significance of copyright is surely a helpful thought in the discussion of an appropriate approach to the issue of copyright-competition

[120] See criticism of such interpretation in Drexl (2008), pp. 41–43.

interaction. In existing practice, the importance of copyright was often neglected, which ultimately led to individuals' questionable decisions.[121]

4.2.5 The Standard Competition Law Approach in Copyright Matters

There is a debate about whether an exercise of copyright (as well as of other intellectual property rights) should even enjoy a special status as opposed to other conduct that may fall under the scrutiny of competition law. Not all scholars and competition law enforcers deem that copyright should have stronger protection than other forms of property.[122] For instance, from the comparative perspective, according to the US Guidelines for the Licensing of Intellectual Property:

> The Agencies apply the same general antitrust principles to conduct involving intellectual property that they apply to conduct involving any other form of property.[123]

Although this approach is not often explicitly discussed in research papers on the copyright-competition interaction, it ought to be mentioned for a deeper and more comprehensive understanding of this specific matter.

The essence of this approach is that copyright and other intellectual property rights cannot be placed above other forms of property rights. Competition rules are created primarily to regulate anti-competitive behaviour on a relevant market. Thus, the competition authorities intervene only when there is a certain distortion on the market. If a specific exercise of rights stemming from copyright distorts competition, competition law should interfere as a corrector. Interestingly, in *Football Association Premier League,*[124] the CJEU recognized the existence of broadcasting right in the case and, by referring to *Coditel II*, acknowledged that the mere fact that the right holder granted an exclusive copyright right to a sole licensee during a specified period is not sufficient to justify the finding that such an agreement has an anti-competitive object. However, in the further assessment of the anti-competitiveness

---

[121] From the earlier cited case law (see *supra* Sect. 4.3), the importance of particular intellectual property rights was surely neglected in most of the analysed decisions. In practically none of the decisions did the competent authorities adequately assess the particular intellectual property in the matter, and appropriately apply the fundamental principles of a particular intellectual property right in the case under the scrutiny of the competition rules on prohibited agreements.

[122] "Many argue that intellectual property rights should be treated the same as other property. Identical treatment would appear to imply that intellectual property should not be given special status (..)" Lewis and Yao (1995), p. 603.

[123] US Antitrust Guidelines for the Licensing of Intellectual Property, issued by the U.S. Department of Justice and the Federal Trade Commission, January 12, 2017. https://www.justice.gov/atr/IPguidelines/download. Accessed on 23 October 2024, sect. 2.1.

[124] Judgment of 4 October 2011, *Football Association Premier League Ltd and Others v QC Leisure and Others Karen Murphy v Media Protection Services Ltd*, Joined cases C-403/08 and C-429/08, EU:C:2011:631.

of the agreement in the matter, the CJEU did not actually apply any copyright-specific approach but decided that the agreements were contrary to Article 101(1) TFEU without any specific considerations concerning the presence of copyright (in a broader sense). Hence, this case may be considered as an example of the standard competition law approach in the context of copyright-competition interaction matters.[125]

An approach that, in essence, does not acknowledge the specificities of copyright or of other intellectual property rights is not the appropriate way forward. Due to its specific economics, some instances of the exercise of copyright and other intellectual rights may provide long-term positive effects for competition in view of dynamic efficiency, despite having adverse short-term effects on allocative efficiency and competition price. Also, there are uncertainties concerning the value of intellectual property rights, especially copyright, and how it can best be used on the market.[126] Although it is not necessary to constitutionally set copyright and other forms of intellectual property above the ownership of tangible property,[127] the nature of intellectual property rights, and especially copyright, should be taken into

[125] See Judgment of 4 October 2011, *Football Association Premier League Ltd and Others v QC Leisure and Others Karen Murphy v Media Protection Services Ltd*, Joined cases C-403/08 and C-429/08, EU:C:2011:631, paras. 134–146.

[126] See Lewis and Yao (1995), pp. 605–606.

[127] In the EU, copyright, as an intellectual property, is of constitutional value, protected by the EU Charter, the European Convention on Human Rights, the Universal Declaration of the Human Rights and particular Member State Constitutions; see The Charter of Fundamental Rights of the European Union, OJ C 326, 26.10.2012, pp. 391–407, Art. 17(2); The Convention for the Protection of Human Rights and Fundamental Freedoms, as amended by Protocols Nos. 11 and 14, supplemented by Protocols Nos. 1, 4, 6, 7, 12, 13 and 16. https://www.echr.coe.int/documents/convention_eng.pdf. Accessed on 22 October 2024, Protocol 1, Art. 1; The Universal Declaration of Human Rights, adopted by the United Nations General Assembly of its 183rd meeting, held in Paris on 10 December 1948. https://www.un.org/en/universal-declaration-human-rights/. Accessed on 22 October 2024, Art. 27(2).

In relation to the constitutional order of the Member States, see, for instance, The Constitution of the Republic of Croatia (Official Gazette no. 56/90, 135/97, 08/98, 113/00, 124/00, 28/01, 41/01, 55/01, 76/10, 85/10, 05/14), Art. 69(4); The Constitution of France. 1958. https://www.conseil-constitutionnel.fr/sites/default/files/as/root/bank_mm/anglais/constiution_anglais_oct2009.pdf. Accessed on 23 October 2024, Art. 34. The Basic Law for the Federal Republic of Germany in the revised version published in the Federal Law Gazette Part III, classification number 100-1, as last amended by Article 1 of the Act of 28 March 2019 (Federal Law Gazette I p. 404). https://www.gesetze-im-internet.de/englisch_gg/englisch_gg.html#p0019. Accessed on 23 October 2024, Arts. 1(1), 14, 5; The Constitution of the Portuguese Republic. https://dre.pt/constitution-of-the-portuguese-republic. Accessed on 24 October 2024, Art. 42; The Spanish Constitution. https://www.boe.es/buscar/pdf/1978/BOE-A-1978-40001-consolidado.pdf. Accessed on 23 October 2024, Art. 20(1), 149(1, pt. 9); The Constitution of Sweden. https://www.riksdagen.se/en/how-the-riksdag-works/democracy/the-constitution/. Accessed on 23 October 2024, Art. 16 (commonly, copyright is implicitly protected within the national constitutions, while Sweden is one of the unique examples where copyright is explicitly protected). The situation is somewhat different in the US where the Constitution gives Congress the authority to create copyright rights without the requirement to do so. Nevertheless, once copyright is awarded, it gains constitutional value. The Constitution of the United States of America. https://www.senate.gov/civics/resources/pdf/US_

consideration.[128] Even the US Guidelines for the Licensing of Intellectual Property, which in general advocate standard anti-competitive analysis, emphasise that the characteristics of intellectual property rights must, in any case, be taken into consideration.[129]

Although the argumentation for this approach may have some foundations, practice and theory have acknowledged the specific status of copyright in view of competition law. Surely, the main principles of competition law apply in any competition assessment; however, it should be reconsidered whether the classical method of competition evaluation is appropriate in acknowledging the specific characteristics of copyright in cases involving the exercise of copyright under the scrutiny of Article 101 TFEU. In essence, to deal with the interaction between copyright and competition, there is no need to refine competition law; but there is a need to adapt to a specific situation, which should fundamentally not be an issue, having in mind the open-ended settings of competition law.

4.3 The More Traditional Approach to the Copyright-Competition Interaction Issue—the Exercise of Copyright and the Competition Rules on Prohibited Agreements

4.3.1 Introduction: Theoretical Foundation

Currently, the copyright-competition issue has still not moved from the phase where, conveniently described by Temple Lang, "the law has developed piecemeal without any explicit framework or general principle, and the Court has never explained the principles comprehensively."[130]

As shown above, practically every theory has its merits and flaws. The inherency theory was based on a solid theoretical foundation, based on the existence v exercise dichotomy, and concepts such as specific-subject matter, essential function. However, applied in practice, the use of such concepts and standards seems questionable. Although the application of this theory ought to have protected the copyright and its holders, in practice, it seemed to work more as a means to justify competition intervention than to strengthen copyright protection. The exceptional circumstances

Constitution-Senate_Publication_103-21.pdf. Accessed on 23 October 2024, Article 1, Section 8, Clause 8.

[128] On differences between particular intellectual property rights and tangible property rights, see also Lamping (2015), pp. 138–139; Lianos and Dreyfuss (2013), pp. 48–50; Schmidt (2010), p. 86.

[129] In that sense, Lewis and Yao state: "(…) the characteristics of intellectual property could mean that it, on average, should be treated more leniently by the antitrust officials. We believe that this is likely to be the case." Lewis and Yao (1995), pp. 604–605.

[130] Temple Lang (2010), p. 411.

doctrine left a significant mark in cases concerning refusal to license, but was neglected entirely in cases involving the exercise of copyright under the scrutiny of Article 101 TFEU. The complementarity theory included some additional economic components and gained a number of proponents in academia and regulatory bodies. Nevertheless, its application in practice did not take hold. Also, this theory lacked concrete parameters in dealing with real-life cases and often unfoundedly forced the complementarity of laws through a questionable interpretation of the objectives of competition law and copyright law. Even the utter approaches, such as the theory of absolutism and the standard competition law approaches, have a value in the discussion on the exercise of copyright and the competition rules on prohibited agreements.[131] Nevertheless, both practice and theory have shown that the exercise of copyright is not unconditionally immune from competition intervention, as well as that the enforcement of competition law must respect specific characteristics of copyright.

Although some of these approaches, in theory, stand more on the side of copyright law, while others are more on the side of competition law, in practice, all of them may be used to argue either side. For instance, the complementarity theory may provide stronger protection for copyright holders than the inherency theory, although it should, in theory, be the reverse.

In any case, there is still no consensus on the appropriate approach in dealing with cases concerning the exercise of copyright and competition rules on prohibited agreements. All the approaches that emerged obviously have some substantial flaws.

It is all about proper balancing.

It is necessary to find a comprehensive approach that is fundamentally grounded and economically sustainable to strike a balance between the rationales of copyright law and competition law. The issue is not so novel any more, and it can be firmly stated that in some specific situations, it is justified for competition law to intervene in a particular exercise of economic copyright rights.

We established before that the most fundamentally sustainable interpretation of the relationship between copyright law and competition law is that, in general, the two laws peacefully coexist. In the case of their interaction, from the perspective of copyright law, competition law represents an outside factual limitation to the exercise of copyright, while, at the same time, competition law acknowledges particularities of copyright during competition law assessment (see *supra* Sect. 3.3). Hence, it remains to define the situations of copyright-competition interaction and formulate the appropriate method of assessment, particularly for cases concerning the competition rules on prohibited agreements.

Copyright-competition interaction does not concern the 'normal' exploitation of copyright. It encompasses the exercise of copyright directed towards distorting

[131] In relation to patents, Kaplow also discusses the appropriateness of the two utter approaches—the regime that deems an intellectual property right holder's practice to be illegal if it violates any aspect of competition law, and the regime that assumes that competition law cannot restrict intellectual property right holders because they have an absolute privilege—and suggests an alternative intermediate approach of the ratio test. See Kaplow (1984), pp. 1818–1839.

competition by the conclusion of a prohibited agreement in this case. Here, the bar is set higher than for the exercise of other property rights affected by the competition rules on prohibited agreements. Anderman and Schmidt seem to agree with such a viewpoint and further add that competition law interferes only in extreme cases where copyright is used as an "instrument of abuse" or as a means of restricting competition.[132]

It is vital to have an appropriate method of assessment to identify such conducts—a test that acknowledges the particularities of the copyright-competition interaction situation and remains within the fundamental rules and principles of copyright law and competition law. The proposal for such a test is presented below (see *infra* Sect. 4.3.2).

However, developing a specific test is not, per se, sufficient to ensure appropriate and convincing results in dealing with this matter. Dealing with cases of copyright-competition interaction requires an evaluator with appropriate knowledge in copyright law and competition law. Without a proper understanding of those laws, it is hardly possible to properly acknowledge the meaning and effects of copyright in the matter, to define a market or to determine (anti-)competitive effects of the conduct. Also, in-depth economic analysis is required to comprehensively approach the copyright-competition interaction issue. Lawyers are usually badly placed to assess the lawfulness of a given behaviour in a system that requires them to look at the likely effects of that behaviour on the market.[133] As Drexl indicates: "The price to be paid for economic precision is a loss of legal certainty."[134] Therefore, aside from proper legal knowledge, it is also crucial to have appropriate evaluators with a substantial understanding of economics in dealing with the copyright-competition interaction issue. Only in that way is it possible to form a comprehensive approach that would satisfy all the involved interests and ultimately provide legal certainty and predictability for all stakeholders.

4.3.2 The Method of Assessing Cases Concerning the Exercise of Copyright and Competition Rules on Prohibited Agreements

For cases concerning the exercise of copyright under the scrutiny of Article 101 TFEU, a specific approach is required to acknowledge the particularities characteristic of copyright-competition interaction situations (see *supra* Sect. 3.2). To do so, the method of assessment must be well structured and defined, theoretically founded and practically applicable.

---

[132] See Anderman and Schmidt (2019), pp. 5–6.

[133] See Drexl (2008), p. 31.

[134] Drexl (2008), p. 31.

Although every phase of the assessment is essential and must be processed with great care, the core of the assessment is the anti-competitiveness test. The anti-competitiveness test should ultimately show whether there is such an exceptional situation that justifies the enforcement of competition law on the conduct involving the exercise of economic copyright rights. Since there is as yet no such appropriate test, this research suggests a test that is deemed to be tailor-made for dealing with cases concerning the exercise of copyright and competition rules on prohibited agreements. The suggestion for the name of this test is the copyright-competition test of reasonableness (see *infra* Sect. 4.3.2.5). For such a test to be functional, it must be well-balanced between accuracy and administrability—accurate in the sense that it can be readily applied in cases other than the one from which it initially stems; administrable in the sense that it captures faithfully the rationale and assumptions on which it is based.[135]

Therefore, the suggested method of assessment, appropriate for the cases concerning the exercise of copyright under Article 101 TFEU, is divided into the following stages that will be explained in detail in further elaboration:

1. Existence of the agreement
2. Analysis of the copyrights involved in the conduct
3. Definition of the relevant market
4. Market share
5. Anti-competitive behaviour
6. Exoneration

4.3.2.1 Determining the Existence of an Agreement

In EU legislation, competition rules on prohibited agreements are contained in the very structured Article 101 TFEU, stating:

> The following shall be prohibited as incompatible with the internal market: all agreements between undertakings, decisions by associations of undertakings and concerted practices which may affect trade between Member States and which have as their object or effect the prevention, restriction or distortion of competition within the internal market (...).

The provision's wording automatically implies that for the activation of Article 101 TFEU, there must be a particular agreement between two or more parties, or a decision by an association, or a concerted practice (jointly referred to as an agreement).[136]

---

[135] See Ibáñez Colomo (2018), p. 29.

[136] In the wording of the provision, three forms of prohibited collusions are noted. However, the distinction between agreement and concerted practices is blurred. The notion concerted practice comprises all "coordination between undertakings which, without having reached the stage where an agreement, properly so-called has been concluded, knowingly substitutes practical cooperation between them for the risk of competition," see Judgment of the Court of 14 July 1972, *Imperial Chemical Industries Ltd. v Commission of the European Communities*, C-48/69, EU:C:1972:70,

What is considered to be an agreement (agreement, decision or concerted practice) within the meaning of Article 101 TFEU is extensively interpreted. Different kinds of informal arrangements may fall within the scope of the 'agreement'. Aside from legal contracts, which are undoubtedly agreements, competition law would also consider as agreements: 'gentlemen's agreement'[137] and simple understanding[138] regardless that neither is binding; a 'protocol' which reflects genuine concurrence of will;[139] connected agreements might be treated as a single one;[140] contractual terms and conditions in a standard-form contract;[141] an agreement which has expired by effluxion of time but the effects of which continue to be felt;[142] the constitution of a trade association;[143] regulations governing the operation of an association;[144] an agreement entered into by a trade association might be

para. 64. Decisions of associations comprise, "for example, conduct by which the members of a trade association co-ordinate their conduct, whether engaged in through resolutions of the association, recommendations, the operation of certification schemes or through the association's constitution itself," see Keeling (2003), p. 307.

In French the term *entente* covers all the three notions of prohibited collusions in Article 101/1 TFEU. English does not have such a term; however, it is common to refer all three forms of collusion as agreements. Hence, throughout this thesis the word agreement is used to loosely cover all the three categories (see also Keeling (2003), p. 307).

[137] Judgment of 15 July 1970, *ACF Chemiefarma NV v Commission of the European Communities*, Case 41/69, EU:C:1970:71, paras. 106–116.

[138] Judgment of 10 December 1985, *Stichting Sigarettenindustrie and others v Commission of the European Communities*, Joined cases 240, 241, 242, 261, 262, 268 and 269/82, EU:C:1985:488 (an 'understanding' between trade associations held to be an agreement); 82/853/EEC: Commission Decision of 7 December 1982 relating to a proceeding under Article 85 of the EEC Treaty (IV/30.070 - National Panasonic), OJ L 354, 16.12.1982, pp. 28–35 (there was no formal agreement between Panasonic and its dealers, but the Commission still held that there actually was an agreement as opposed to a concerted practice between them); 91/532/EEC: Commission Decision of 5 June 1991 relating to a proceeding under Article 85 of the EEC Treaty (Case No. IV/32.879 - Viho/Toshiba), OJ L 287, 17.10.1991, pp. 39–43 (the Commission found in an understanding between Toshiba's subsidiary and certain distributors that an export prohibition should apply, regardless that the standard distribution agreements had been amended to remove an export prohibition clause).

[139] 94/210/EC: Commission Decision of 29 March 1994 relating to a proceeding pursuant to Articles 85 and 86 of the EC Treaty (IV/33.941 - HOV SVZ/MCN, OJ L 104, 23.4.1994, pp. 34–57.

[140] 87/3/EEC: Commission Decision of 4 December 1986 in proceedings under Article 85 of the EEC Treaty (IV/31.055 - ENI/Montedison), OJ L 5, 7.1.1987, pp. 13–22.

[141] 79/68/EEC: Commission Decision of 12 December 1978 relating to a proceeding under Article 85 of the EEC Treaty (IV/29.430 - Kawasaki), OJ L 16, 23.1.1979, pp. 9–16; Judgment of 11 January 1990, *Sandoz prodotti farmaceutici SpA v Commission of the European Communities*, C-277/87, EU:C:1990:6.

[142] Judgment of 17 December 1991, *SA Hercules Chemicals NV v Commission of the European Communities*, T-7/89, EU:T:1991:75, para. 257; Judgment of the Court of 15 June 1976, EMI Records Limited v CBS United Kingdom Limited, C-51/75, EU:C:1976:85, p. 267.

[143] 84/191/EEC: Commission Decision of 30 March 1984 relating to a proceeding under Article 85 of the EEC Treaty (IV/30.804 - Nuovo CEGAM), OJ L 99, 11.4.1984, pp. 29–37.

[144] See 89/44/EEC: Commission Decision of 12 December 1988 relating to a proceeding under Article 85 of the EEC Treaty (IV/27.393 and IV/27.394, Publishers Association - Net Book

construed as an agreement on the part of its members;[145] 'incohate understandings and conditional or partial agreement' during a bargaining process;[146] guidelines issued by one person that are adhered to by another;[147] circular warnings sent by an manufacturer to its dealers may be considered as part of the general agreement;[148] exchange of correspondence;[149] exchange of information between competitors where it reduces 'strategic uncertainty' in the market;[150] the fact that formal agreement has not been reached on all matters does not preclude the finding of an agreement,[151] etc. The list is surely open-ended and left for further interpretation, depending on a specific situation and arrangement. Also, the fact that another party forced the one party into an agreement does not affect the existence of an

---

Agreements), OJ L 22, 26.1.1989, pp. 12–35, upheld by Judgment of 9 July 1992, *Publishers Association v Commission of the European Communities*, T-66/89, EU:T:1992:84, partially annulled by the Judgment of 17 January 1995, *The Publishers Association v Commission of the European Communities*, C-360/92, EU:C:1995:6.

[145] See Judgment of the Court of 29 October 1980, *Heintz van Landewyck SARL and others v Commission of the European Communities*, Joined cases 209 to 215 and 218/78, EU:C:1980:248.

[146] 1999/60/EC: Commission Decision of 21 October 1998 relating to a proceeding under Article 85 of the EC Treaty (Case No. IV/35.691/E-4: - Pre-Insulated Pipe Cartel) (Notified under number C(1998) 3117), OJ L 24, 30.1.1999, pp. 1–70.

[147] See 2000/146/EC: Commission Decision of 14 December 1999 relating to a proceeding pursuant to Article 15(1)(b) of Council Regulation No. 17 (Case No. IV/34.237/F3 - Anheuser-Busch Incorporated - Scottish & Newcastle) (notified under document number C(1999) 4499), OJ L 49, 22.2.2000, pp. 37–44, para. 26.

[148] See 2001/711/EC: Commission Decision of 29 June 2001 relating to a proceeding under Article 81 of the EC Treaty (Case COMP/F-2/36.693 — Volkswagen) (notified under document number C (2001) 1698), OJ L 262, 2.10.2001, pp. 14–37; although the Commission finding of an agreement was later rejected by the GC and the CJEU - Judgment of 3 December 2003, *Volkswagen AG v Commission of the European Communities*, T-208/01, EU:T:2003:326, paras. 30–68; Judgment of 13 July 2006, *Commission of the European Communities v Volkswagen AG*, C-75/04 P, EU: C:2006:460, para. 54.

[149] See 2003/675/EC: Commission decision of 30 October 2002 relating to a proceeding pursuant to Article 81 of the EC Treaty and Article 53 of the EEA Agreement (COMP/35.587 PO Video Games, COMP/35.706 PO Nintendo Distribution and COMP/36.321 Omega — Nintendo) (notified under document number C(2002) 4072), OJ L 255, 8.10.2003, pp. 33–100, para. 196; Judgment of 30 April 2009, CD-Contact Data GmbH v Commission of the European Communities, T-18/03, EU:T:2009:132, paras. 52–69; Judgment of 10 February 2011, *Activision Blizzard Germany GmbH v European Commission*, C-260/09 P, EU:C:2011:62.

[150] See Communication from the Commission — Guidelines on the applicability of Article 101 of the Treaty on the Functioning of the European Union to horizontal co-operation agreements, OJ C 11, 14.1.2011, pp. 1–72, para. 61 (Communication from the Commission – Guidelines on the applicability of Article 101 of the Treaty on the Functioning of the European Union to horizontal co-operation agreements, C/2023/4752, OJ C 259, 21.7.2023, pp. 1–125, para. 280).

[151] See 1999/60/EC: Commission Decision of 21 October 1998 relating to a proceeding under Article 85 of the EC Treaty (Case No. IV/35.691/E-4: - Pre-Insulated Pipe Cartel) (Notified under number C(1998) 3117), L 24, 30.1.1999, pp. 1–70, para. 134.

agreement,[152] nor the fact that the natural person who agreed on behalf of an undertaking did not have the proper authority to do so.[153, 154]

Within the case law previously referred to the interaction between intellectual property rights and competition law, some examples of agreements that fell under the scrutiny of Article 101 TFEU (or were at least considered as possible agreements under Article 101 TFEU) were the following: the agreement on authorising a party to register a trademark in anoother country;[155] the agreement on the sale, the assignment and transfer of all rights, titles and interests in the trademark;[156] the agreement on the transfer of the trademark;[157] the oral exclusive distribution agreement including the grant of the exclusive right to use the trademarks on the territory of a Member State;[158] the assignment of plant breeders' rights over certain varieties of hybrid maize seeds and the granting of exclusive propagating and selling rights over those seeds for the territory of a Member State;[159] the settlement reached to prevent that undertaking from importing and selling seeds in a Member State;[160] the exclusive copyright license to exhibit films within the territory of a Member State for a specified period;[161] the simultaneous or successive filing of the same design in various Member States by undertakings in order to divide up the markets within the EU among themselves;[162] the patent licensing agreements;[163] the exclusive

[152] See Judgment of 2 February 2012, *Denki Kagaku Kogyo Kabushiki Kaisha and Denka Chemicals GmbH v European Commission*, T-83/08, EU:T:2012:48, paras. 47, 61–62.

[153] Judgment of the Court of 8 July 2008, *BPB plc v Commission of the European Communities*, T-53/03, EU:T:2008:254, para. 25.

[154] See Whish and Bailey (2021), pp. 103–120.

[155] Judgment of 13 July 1966, *Établissements Consten S.à.R.L. and Grundig-Verkaufs-GmbH v Commission of the European Economic Community*, Joined cases 56 and 58-64, EU:C:1966: 41, p. 345.

[156] Judgment of 18 February 1971, *Sirena S.r.l. v Eda S.r.l. and others*, C-40/70, EU:C:1971:18, para. 2.

[157] Judgment of 15 June 1976, *EMI Records Limited v CBS Grammofon A/S*, C-86/75, EU:C:1976: 86, paras. 2–4.

[158] Judgment of 20 June 1978, *Tepea BV v Commission of the European Communities*, C-28-77, EU:C:1978:133, paras. 1, 40.

[159] Judgment of 8 June 1982, L.C. *Nungesser KG and Kurt Eisele v Commission* of the European Communities, Case 258/78, ECLI:EU:C:1982:211, para. 3.

[160] Judgment of 8 June 1982, L.C. *Nungesser KG and Kurt Eisele v Commission* of the European Communities, Case 258/78, ECLI:EU:C:1982:211, para. 3.

[161] Judgment of 6 October 1982, *Coditel SA, Compagnie générale pour la diffusion de la télévision, and others v Ciné-Vog Films SA and others*, Case 262/81, ECLI:EU:C:1982:334, para. 9.

[162] Judgment of 14 September 1982, *Keurkoop BV v Nancy Kean Gifts BV*, C-144/81, EU:C:1982: 289, para. 28.

[163] Judgment of 25 February 1986, Windsurfing International Inc. v Commission of the European Communities, C-193/83, EU:C:1986:75, para. 9.

copyright license agreement to broadcast.[164] As we can see from the above examples, there were several variations of intellectual property rights 'agreements' under Article 101 TFEU. When it comes to copyright, in practice, most likely such 'agreement' would constitute a copyright licensing agreement, involving the exercise of an economic copyright right.

However, a copyright right per se cannot constitute an 'agreement'. Thus, the CJEU has on several occasions noted that particular intellectual property, such as a legal right, does not in itself possess the elements of a contract or concerted practice referred to in Article 101(1) TFEU.[165]

All things considered, determining the existence of an agreement should indeed be the first step in any competition assessment of prohibited agreements.[166] This is a standard competition law requirement that needs to be satisfied in the evaluation of potential anti-competitive behaviour. The cases on copyright-competition interaction are no exception to that rule. Consequently, if there is no agreement between parties, or a decision by association, or concerted practice involving the exercise of copyright (no agreement in a broader sense encompassing all three indicated categories)—there should be no room for further competition concerns.[167]

[164] Judgment of 4 October 2011, *Football Association Premier League Ltd and Others v QC Leisure and Others Karen Murphy v Media Protection Services Ltd*, Joined cases C-403/08 and C-429/08, EU:C:2011:631, para. 137.

[165] See, for instance, Judgment of 29 February 1968, *Parke, Davis and Co. v Probel, Reese, Beintema-Interpharm and Centrafarm*, C-24/67, EU:C:1968:11, p. 71; Judgment of 18 February 1971, *Sirena S.r.l. v Eda S.r.l. and others*, C-40/70, EU:C:1971:18, para. 9; Judgment of 14 September 1982, *Keurkoop BV v Nancy Kean Gifts BV*, C-144/81, EU:C:1982:289, para. 27; Judgment of 15 June 1976, *EMI Records Limited v CBS Grammofon A/S*, C-86/75, EU:C:1976:86, para. 24.

[166] Naturally, during and even before the phase of determining the existence of an agreement, the question may also arise whether the subject(s) under investigation even fall within the definition of an 'undertaking', which is the subject of competition law. If not, competition rules certainly do not apply, regardless of the existence of an agreement.

[167] However, that does not prevent the Court from further analysing the conduct in the matter in search of other potential violations of EU law. For instance, in *Deutsche Grammophon v Metro* the CJEU noted that "the exercise of the right does not exhibit those elements of contract or concerted practice," concluded that it is necessary to consider compatibility of the conduct in the matter with other provisions of the Treaty, and discussed the situation in relation to the free movement of goods (Judgment of 8 June 1971, *Deutsche Grammophon Gesellschaft mbH v Metro-SB-Großmärkte GmbH & Co. KG*, C-78/70, EU:C:1971:59, para. 7). Also, where a parent company and its subsidiary, which actually constitute one economic unit (regardless of their separate legal personalities) enter into an agreement, there is no competition which could be restricted and, hence, no room for the application of Article 101 TFEU. See Judgment of 25 November 1971, *Béguelin Import Co. v S.A.G.L. Import Export*, C-22/71, EU:C:1971:113, paras. 7–9; Judgment of the Court of 31 October 1974, *Centrafarm BV and Adriaan de Peijper v Sterling Drug Inc.*, C-15/74, EU:C:1974:114, para. 41; Judgment of 31 October 1974, *Centrafarm BV and Adriaan de Peijper v Winthrop BV*, C-16/74, EU:C:1974:115, para. 32.

4.3.2.2 Analysis of the Copyright Right Involved Within the Conduct

After it has been established that the case in the matter involves an agreement, a decision or a concerted practice, the next necessary step is to analyse if the conduct in the matter involves an exercise of some copyright right. If the conduct does not involve an exercise of copyright, then the case does not concern a copyright-competition interaction matter; ergo, there is no need for a specific approach in the competition assessment. Otherwise, the presence of copyright affects almost all the further stages of competition evaluation and, hence, must be appropriately taken into consideration. Thus, the analysis of copyright represents a necessary preliminary phase in the assessment of copyright-competition interaction matters.

As indicated before, one of the main flaws of the existing case law on the copyright-competition interaction issue is particularly the lack of copyright analysis. Very few cases (if any) pay sufficient attention to the fact that competition evaluation deals with a specific copyright right. In most of the cases raised before the CJEU, there is almost no discussion on whether the conduct in the matter even concerns the use of copyright, the object of the copyright concerned, the exercise of which copyright right is questionable, consequences of a particular copyright right and its effects on the market, specific economics of the copyright etc. Usually, the Court merely acknowledges the involvement of copyright and moves on with the competition assessment without paying additional attention to an analysis of the copyright right involved. For instance, in *Deutsche Grammophon,* the Court just noted that the case concerned the exclusive right of distributing the copyright-protected articles of the manufacturer of sound recordings. No further analysis was provided.[168]

The situation is even worse if the court does not even acknowledge the particular intellectual property right concerned, but just refers to intellectual property rights in general without any further explanation. That is even more problematic than not having a proper analysis of the copyright in the matter. The importance of distinguishing individual intellectual property rights was already discussed before (see *supra* Sect. 3.2). Each particular type of intellectual property rights has its own particularities, purpose and legal consequences. Some general principles related to one intellectual property right may apply *per analogiam* to another intellectual property right. However, the differences between particular intellectual property

[168] Judgment of 8 June 1971, *Deutsche Grammophon Gesellschaft mbH v Metro-SB-Großmärkte GmbH & Co. KG*, C-78/70, EU:C:1971:59, para. 4.In relation to other intellectual property rights discussed in the context of copyright-competition interaction, see also for instance Judgment of 13 July 1966, *Établissements Consten S.à.R.L. and Grundig-Verkaufs-GmbH v Commission of the European Economic Community*, Joined cases 56 and 58-64, EU:C:1966:41; Judgment of 29 February 1968, *Parke, Davis and Co. v Probel, Reese, Beintema-Interpharm and Centrafarm*, C-24/67, EU:C:1968:11; Judgment of 18 February 1971, *Sirena S.r.l. v Eda S.r.l. and others*, C-40/70, EU:C:1971:18; Judgment of 15 June 1976, *EMI Records Limited v CBS Grammofon A/S*, C-86/75, EU:C:1976:86; Judgment of 29 February 1968.

rights are significant, especially in the case of copyright as a non-industrial property right. In view of competition law, copyright must be observed separately from the other intellectual property rights. Whether a certain conduct represents anti-competitive behaviour depends on the preliminary issue concerning the effects of the actual intellectual property right on the market. Copyright has particular rationales and produces specific effects on the market. For instance, it is often confused in both practice and theory that innovation is not related to copyright but to patents. When the exercise of copyright is involved in the assessment, then originality and creativity are characteristics of copyright, and they should be the guiding factors in identifying the effects on the market.[169]

However, even within copyright, there are significant differences that must be acknowledged. Copyright covers a whole array of different objects that fall under the protection of copyright law, ranging from literature, over sound recordings, movies and audiovisual and visual arts, to the most complex source codes. It is an open list of works that can be recognised as copyrights under copyright law, while ways of exploitation change over time. Thus, in the view of the copyright-competition interaction issue, it is necessary not only to acknowledge the existence of copyright law but also to recognise the object of copyright in the matter, its content, purpose and economic effects. A good example of distinguishing different objects of copyright is *Coditel II*. In that case, the CJEU acknowledged the specificities of a film as a copyright-protected work (in particular the producer's right) in relation to other objects of copyright such as books or records. While literary and artistic objects of copyright such as books and records, are placed at the disposal of the public inseparably from the circulation of the material form of the works, the work of a film is made available to the public by screenings that may be infinitely repeated and the commercial exploitation of which comes under the movement of services, no matter whether the means whereby it is shown to the public be the cinema or television.[170] The means of making a work available to the public and ways of commercial exploitation are surely relevant for further decision-making in the case, such as the definition of a relevant market and the determination of the copyright effects on the market. Another positive example is the *Football Association Premier League*. In that case, the Court acknowledged and even analysed the relevant copyright framework, in particular in relation to the broadcasting right and

[169] See Max Planck Institute for Intellectual Property and Competition Law (2013), p. 39.

[170] See Judgment of 6 October 1982, *Coditel SA, Compagnie générale pour la diffusion de la télévision, and others v Ciné-Vog Films SA and others*, Case 262/81, ECLI:EU:C:1982:334, para. 11. However, on such distinction with respect to the EU's fundamental freedoms Korah considers: "(…) the distinction between the mechanical rights, subject to rules for the free movement of goods, and performing rights, subject to the rules for the provision of services, was commercially artificial, although they are governed by different parts of the EC Treaty." See Korah (2006), p. 13.

communication to the public.[171] It also discussed in detail the relevant circumstances of the exercise of copyright in the matter.[172]

Thus, only when competition assessment involves an appropriate analysis of the exercise of copyright is decision-making capable of producing a convincing and comprehensive result. Unfortunately, this part of the assessment was mainly neglected in the cases and literature discussing the copyright-competition interaction matter. In general, this criticism is aimed at all the identified theoretical approaches related to copyright-competition interaction (see *supra* Sect. 4.2).

Some consider that in cases concerning competition law, the courts have no authority to second-guess the legitimacy of copyright and other intellectual property rights under national law.[173,174] That is certainly true; however, here, that is not even expected of the courts. At first sight, it may sound a bit contradictory when the CJEU is allegedly supposed to refrain from dealing with copyright matters while it directly interferes in the exercise of rights stemming from copyright. However, in the case of copyright-competition interaction, the Commission and the CJEU, as well as the national authorities, when competent, should also consider copyright in the assessment of potential anti-competitive behaviour. To do so, it is vital to properly consider the applicable copyright law with all its rules and principles instead of avoiding it. In the cases of copyright-competition interaction, analysis and the application of copyright law are completely aligned with the open-ended approach of competition law and the vast powers given to competition authorities. The only issue is to appropriately the reasoning to a specific situation appropriately.

Therefore, there must be an in-depth analysis of the copyright in the matter. This analysis does not have to be extensive, but it should, by all means, be present. Avoiding discussion of the copyright element may have a severe negative impact on the correctness of the assessment, particularly in the definition of the relevant market and the determination of the effects of conduct on the market. For those reasons, in dealing with such complex cases, experts with a fundamental understanding of copyright, competition law and economics should be involved in the decision-making process.[175]

---

[171] See Judgment of 4 October 2011, *Football Association Premier League Ltd and Others v QC Leisure and Others Karen Murphy v Media Protection Services Ltd*, Joined cases C-403/08 and C-429/08, EU:C:2011:631, paras. 1–29.

[172] See Judgment of 4 October 2011, *Football Association Premier League Ltd and Others v QC Leisure and Others Karen Murphy v Media Protection Services Ltd*, Joined cases C-403/08 and C-429/08, EU:C:2011:631, paras. 35–38.

However, this case somewhat deviates from other discussed case law, considering that only a small portion of the case actually discussed the copyright-competition issue (paras. 134–146).

[173] Unlike in the cases concerning the free movement of goods and services.

[174] See Myrick (1992), p. 304.

[175] On the issue of the legal approaches used by the CJEU and the legal background of the judges in relation to matters concerning copyright law, see Favale (2021), pp. 1078–1080; Anderson (2021), p. 333. See also European Commission, Study on judges' training needs in the field of European competition law, Final report, January 2016. https://op.europa.eu/en/publication-detail/-/

4.3.2.3 Definition of the Relevant Market

Defining the relevant market is an essential aspect of any competition law analysis.[176] Sometimes it may even play a crucial role in the evaluation of a particular case. However, adequately defining the relevant market is often a highly complex matter to resolve. Fligstein and Mara-Drita state that "markets are social constructions that reflect the unique interactions of their firms and nations."[177] The issue of market definition will not be discussed in detail here, but only certain particularities relevant to the cases concerning the exercise of copyright under Article 101 TFEU will be addressed.

In 1997, the Commission issued the Notice on the definition of relevant market.[178] The Commission's Notice on the definition of relevant market serves as a primary guideline in defining the relevant market in competition matters.[179] The document summary notes: "In the event of a suspected infringement of the competition rules, the first element to be considered is the relevant market."[180] However, for cases concerning the exercise of copyright under Article 101 TFEU that might not be the best way to go; for the reasons stated above, the first step should be to determine the existence of the agreement. For that step, there is no need to define the

---

publication/bfe6ccba-9a94-11e6-9bca-01aa75ed71a1/language-en. Accessed on 24 October 2024; Brison (2005), pp. 596–605.

[176] According to the Commission:

> Market definition is a tool to identify and define the boundaries of competition between firms. It serves to establish the framework within which competition policy is applied by the Commission. The main purpose of market definition is to identify in a systematic way the competitive constraints that the undertakings involved face. The objective of defining a market in both its product and geographic dimension is to identify those actual competitors of the undertakings involved that are capable of constraining those undertakings' behaviour and of preventing them from behaving independently of effective competitive pressure. It is from this perspective that the market definition makes it possible inter alia to calculate market shares that would convey meaningful information regarding market power for the purposes of assessing dominance or for the purposes of applying Article 85.

Commission Notice on the definition of relevant market for the purposes of Community competition law, OJ C 372, 9.12.1997, pp. 5–13, para. 2.

[177] Fligstein and Mara-Drita (1996), p. 25.

[178] Commission Notice on the definition of relevant market for the purposes of Community competition law, OJ C 372, 9.12.1997, pp. 5–13

[179] Although, as stated in the Notice on the definition of relevant market, "the Commission's interpretation of 'relevant market' is without prejudice to the interpretation which may be given by the." CJEU; Commission Notice on the definition of relevant market for the purposes of Community competition law, OJ C 372, 9.12.1997, pp. 5–13, para. 6.

[180] Definition of relevant market, Summary, Document 31997Y1209(01), 20.4.2011.
According to Kostecka-Jurczyk:

> Determination of the relevant market is both the first and the most significant step in antitrust proceedings, because an entrepreneur's market position is always determined in relation to the relevant market. See Kostecka-Jurczyk (2012), p. 129.

relevant market. If there is no agreement, decision or concerted practice, there is no room whatsoever for applying Article 101 TFEU. Second, it is crucial to have an analysis of the copyright in the matter before entering the stage of defining the relevant market. In competition cases, the existence of copyright per se has a number of consequences. In the case of copyright, different objects of copyright produce different economic effects and, consequently, affect the relevant market. Regarding the definition of the relevant market, the copyright element affects both the product and the geographical dimension; hence, it must be included in the assessment. If the analysis of copyright is not included in the definition of the relevant market, such a definition would probably not be accurate. Unfortunately, it seems that in cases concerning the exercise of copyright, the element of copyright was often neglected.

In that sense, the existence of copyright might make things more difficult for a proper definition of the relevant market. In its 2013 report, the Max Planck Institute identified several major reasons for that:

> First, where cultural content is concerned, highly subjective consumer preferences are largely unreliable and weak indicators for assessing demand side substitutability. Second, in media markets in particular, dynamic technological developments make it very difficult to decide which technological distribution networks can be regarded as substitutable. Third, many copyright related cases require enforcers to take into account the phenomenon of 'two-sided markets'. For instance, in the newspaper industry, the readers' market has to be clearly distinguished from the market of advertising. Enforcers therefore often have to assess effects on two or even more markets after having engaged in a most difficult and extensive definition of the relevant markets.[181,182]

A good example of how complex it is to define the relevant market in the copyright-competition interaction situations can be found in a comparative South African merger case. In the *Primedia*[183] case, South African competition authorities faced unreliable econometric evidence and inconclusive evidence from the demographics of audience and advertiser profiles, so they had to rely on the opinion of the undertakings under the assessment.[184] Besides that, the competition authority also struggled to find degrees of closeness between the relevant firms in

---

[181] Also, "This feature generally plays an important role in competition cases relating to intermediaries and, in particular, in media markets in which services are provided to the audience for free. Such free of charge TV or radio operators have to attract both audience and advertising customers. Since only the latter pay for the service, the relevant market is that for advertising. But firms only pay for advertising to the extent that their commercials actually reach the audience. Therefore, the definition of the relevant advertising market correlates with the audience outreach of the specific operator." Max Planck Institute for Intellectual Property and Competition Law (2013), pp. 73–74.

[182] Max Planck Institute for Intellectual Property and Competition Law (2013), pp. 7, 73–74.

[183] The Competition Appeal Court, Primedia Limited, Capricorn Capital Partners (Pty) Ltd, New Africa Investments Limited v The Competition Commission, Decision of 9 May 2008, Case 39/AM/MAY06. https://www.comptrib.co.za/other-court-judgments. Accessed on 22 October 2024.

[184] *Primedia Limited, Capricorn Capital Partners (Pty) Ltd, New Africa Investments Limited v The Competition Commission*, para. 41.

defining the market for differentiated products.[185] They overcame the problem by drawing such concentric circles around the target firm and the acquiring firm. Ultimately, the South African Competition Appeal Court stated that the case did not admit to forensic precision.[186] It also considered that the applied method of assessing the relevant market was an imperfect tool[187] and further emphasised the complexity of the situation.[188]

The copyright factor must not be neglected in the definition of the relevant market, although sometimes that might further complicate things. The specific nature and characteristics of copyright in the relevant surroundings must nevertheless be taken into consideration. Furthermore, the relevant market should be assessed in a dynamic context rather than a static one, which can be particularly complex in relation to the product dimension.

Several competition law regimes have introduced additional guidelines to try to tackle the issue of defining the relevant market when copyright and other intellectual property rights are part of the assessment. Thus, the EU has introduced additional guidelines on the application of Article 101 TFEU to technology transfer agreements (TT Guidelines).[189] Paragraph 21 of the TT Guidelines describes the relevant product market:

> The relevant product market comprises the contract products (incorporating the licensed technology) and products which are regarded by the buyers as inter changeable with or substitutable for the contract products, by reason of the products' characteristics, their prices and their intended use. Contract products can be part of a final and/or an intermediate product market.

Further, para. 22 clarifies the relevant technology market:

> The relevant technology markets consist of the licensed technology rights and its substitutes, that is to say, other technologies which are regarded by the licensees as inter changeable with or substitutable for the licensed technology rights, by reason of the technologies' characteristics, their royalties and their intended use. Starting from the technology which is marketed by the licensor, it is necessary to identify those other technologies to which licensees could switch in response to a small but permanent increase in relative prices, that is to say, to the royalties. An alternative approach is to look at the market for products incorporating the licensed technology rights.

[185] *Primedia Limited, Capricorn Capital Partners (Pty) Ltd, New Africa Investments Limited v The Competition Commission,* para. 42.

[186] *Primedia Limited, Capricorn Capital Partners (Pty) Ltd, New Africa Investments Limited v The Competition Commission,* para. 44.

[187] *Primedia Limited, Capricorn Capital Partners (Pty) Ltd, New Africa Investments Limited v The Competition Commission,* paras. 42, 44.

[188] *Primedia Limited, Capricorn Capital Partners (Pty) Ltd, New Africa Investments Limited v The Competition Commission,* para. 41.

[189] Communication from the Commission — Guidelines on the application of Article 101 of the Treaty on the Functioning of the European Union to technology transfer agreements, OJ C 89, 28.3.2014, pp. 3–50.

It is also interesting to observe some comparative solutions relevant for guidance in cases concerning the exercise of copyright and competition rules on prohibited agreements. For instance, within the US Guidelines for the Licensing of Intellectual Property in connection with licensing of intellectual property rights, three different types of markets are distinguished—goods markets, technology markets and research and development markets. Goods markets comprise markets for final or intermediate goods made using the intellectual property or upstream markets for goods that are used as inputs, along with the intellectual property rights, in the production of goods.[190] Technology markets consist of the intellectual property that is licensed and its close substitutes—that is, the technologies or goods that are close enough substitutes to constrain significantly the exercise of market power with respect to the intellectual property that is licensed.[191] Research and development markets consist of the assets comprising research and development related to the identification of a commercialisable product, or directed to particular new or improved goods or processes, and the close substitutes for that research and development.[192] For each type of market, additional guidelines are provided on when and how to assess and approach a particular market.

Unfortunately, it seems that in practice, a low level of market analysis is a joint feature of the copyright-competition interaction cases.[193] Considering the importance of this step, it must be conducted properly. Inadequate assessment of the relevant market may have further consequences in the evaluation of the case and, ultimately, on decision-making. Moreover, the copyright factor must be appropriately taken into account in an in-depth economic assessment of the relevant market.

Once the relevant market has been defined, market shares can be assigned to the various sources of competition on the market and used as an indication of the relative strength of the market players. This factor is also essential in cases concerning the exercise of copyright for the determination of a potential safe harbour for minor agreements (*de minimis notice*).

4.3.2.4 Market Share

At first sight, in the cases dealt with under Article 101 TFEU, market shares do not play an important role. Generally, an agreement between two or more independent undertakings is required, where the market power of the undertakings does not matter (so much), unlike in the abuse of dominance cases. Still, to conduct a proper, comprehensive assessment of the potential anti-competitive conduct on the matter, it

[190] US Antitrust Guidelines for the Licensing of Intellectual Property, issued by the U.S. Department of Justice and the Federal Trade Commission, January 12, 2017. https://www.justice.gov/atr/IPguidelines/download. Accessed on 23 October 2024, sect. 3.2.1.

[191] Ibid., sect. 3.2.2.

[192] Ibid., sect. 3.2.3.

[193] See Benabou (2009), pp. 555–556.

is nevertheless required to calculate the market shares of the undertakings under the assessment.[194] That is especially the case for situations concerning the copyright-competition interaction issue, since here, a usual requirement is a comprehensive evaluation of the anti-competitive effect of conduct involving an exercise of copy-right rights. Namely, competition law looks more lenient on undertakings with small market shares.

There may be no threshold of market power requirement for the activation of Article 101 TFEU, but there is a so-called *de minimis* doctrine in which the size of market shares plays an important role. Within EU competition law, the *de minimis* doctrine was first formulated in *Völk v. Vervaecke*[195] and was later acknowledged in further practice[196] and by the Commission. According to the *de minimis* doctrine, agreements that do not to an appreciable extent impact inter-state trade or competition fall outside the scope of Article 101 TFEU. On the issue of appreciability, to provide guidance, the Commission issued a Notice on Agreements of Minor Importance.[197] According to the Notice, the *de minimis* doctrine does not apply to object

---

[194] According to the *De Minimis* Notice, the market shares are to be calculated on the basis of sales value data or, where appropriate, purchase value data. If value data are not available, estimates based on other reliable market information, including volume data, may be used. See Communication from the Commission — Notice on agreements of minor importance which do not appreciably restrict competition under Article 101(1) of the Treaty on the Functioning of the European Union (*De Minimis* Notice), OJ C 291, 30.8.2014, pp. 1–4, para. 12.

[195] Judgment of 9 July 1969, *Franz Völk v S.P.R.L. Ets J. Vervaecke*, C-5/69, EU:C:1969:35.:

> An exclusive dealing agreement, even with absolute territorial protection, may, having regard to the weak position of the persons concerned on the market in the products in question, escape the prohibition laid down in Article 85(I).

[196] See Judgment of 28 May 1998, *John Deere Ltd v Commission of the European Communities*, C-7/95 P, EU:C:1998:256, para. 77; Judgment of 21 January 1999, Carlo Bagnasco and Others v Banca Popolare di Novara soc. coop. arl. (BNP) (C-215/96) and Cassa di Risparmio di Genova e Imperia SpA (Carige) (C-216/96), Joined cases C-215/96 and C-216/96, EU:C:1999:12, para. 34; Judgment of 23 November 2006, *Asnef-Equifax, Servicios de Información sobre Solvencia y Crédito, SL v Asociación de Usuarios de Servicios Bancarios (Ausbanc)*, C-238/05, EU:C:2006:734, para. 50; Judgment of the Court of 24 October 1995, *Bayerische Motorenwerke AG v ALD Auto-Leasing D GmbH*, C-70/93, EU:C:1995:344, para. 18; Judgment of 28 April 1998, *Javico International and Javico AG v Yves Saint Laurent Parfums SA (YSLP)*, C-306/96, EU:C:1998:173, para. 12; Judgment of 2 April 2009, *Pedro IV Servicios SL v Total España SA*, C260/07, EU:C:2009:215, para. 68.

According to *Völk v. Vervaecke*, if an agreement does not have an appreciable impact either on inter-state trade or on competition, it does not fall under the prohibition of competition rules on prohibited agreements. Differently, in the case of *Expedia Inc. v Autorité de la concurrence*, the CJEU abandoned the test of double appreciability for object restrictions and considered that an agreement must not have appreciable impact on both inter-state trade and competition to avoid the prohibition of Article 101(1) TFEU; See Judgment of 13 December 2012, *Expedia Inc. v Autorité de la concurrence and Others*, C-226/22, EU:C:2012:795, paras. 16, 17, 37.

[197] Communication from the Commission — Notice on agreements of minor importance which do not appreciably restrict competition under Article 101(1) of the Treaty on the Functioning of the European Union (*De Minimis* Notice), OJ C 291, 30.8.2014, pp. 1–4. The Commission initially introduced the *de minimis* notice in 2001. See Commission Notice on agreements of minor

restrictions.[198] When it does apply, market share thresholds are used for determining when a restriction of competition is not appreciable. Although the Notice provides a kind of safe harbour for the agreements falling below the threshold, it does not in any way bring about danger for agreements with a market share above the threshold.[199] Thus, the Notice covers only the appreciability of the effect on competition. The concept of appreciable effect on trade between Member States, which also may cause the agreement to be considered as of minor importance, is covered by the Commission's Guidelines on the effect on trade contained in [Articles 101 and 102 TFEU].[200]

The main provision of the Notice is set out in para. 8, stating:

> The Commission holds the view that agreements between undertakings which may affect trade between Member States and which may have as their effect the prevention, restriction or distortion of competition within the internal market, do not appreciably restrict competition within the meaning of Article 101(1) of the Treaty:
>
> (a) if the aggregate market share held by the parties to the agreement does not exceed 10 % on any of the relevant markets affected by the agreement, where the agreement is made between undertakings which are actual or potential competitors on any of those markets (agreements between competitors); or
> (b) if the market share held by each of the parties to the agreement does not exceed 15 % on any of the relevant markets affected by the agreement, where the agreement is made between undertakings which are not actual or potential competitors on any of those markets (agreements between non-competitors).

Thus, if a market share of the parties to the horizontal agreement does not exceed 10%, respectively 15% for the vertical agreement, such agreement will fall outside the prohibition set out in Article 101(1) TFEU.[201] In relation to the effect on trade between the Member States, it is required that the aggregate market share of the parties on any relevant market within the Community affected by the agreement does not exceed 5% and, in the case of horizontal agreements, 40 million euro of the

---

importance which do not appreciably restrict competition under Article 81(1) of the Treaty establishing the European Community (de minimis), OJ C 368, 22.12.2001, pp. 13–15.

[198] See para. 1 of *De Minimis* Notice.

[199] See Whish and Bailey (2021), p. 149.

[200] See Commission Notice — Guidelines on the effect on trade concept contained in Articles 81 and 82 of the Treaty, C 101, 27.4.2004, pp. 81–96.

[201] However, one should note that an agreement that does not infringe Article 101 TFEU may still infringe the law of some Member State. Namely, the De Minimis Notice has no binding effect on national competition authorities and national courts, and they are therefore not obliged to apply it. See Antitrust: Commission adopts revised safe harbours for minor agreements ('De Minimis Notice') and provides guidance on 'by object' restrictions of competition - European Commission, Frequently asked questions, MEMO, 25 June 2014. https://ec.europa.eu/commission/presscorner/detail/en/MEMO_14_440. Accessed on 24 October 2024.

aggregate annual Community turnover of the undertakings concerned in products covered by the agreement in cases of horizontal agreements.[202]

This general concept of EU competition law is also relevant for cases concerning copyright-competition interaction. Only the cases of major importance will fall under the scrutiny of the competition rules on prohibited agreements, which is wholly in keeping with the concept that the use of copyright may be limited by competition rules only exceptionally. The agreements of minor importance, which involve the exercise of copyright, are not considered problematic in the view of Article 101 TFEU. Hence, in such a case, there is no need for a further custom-made assessment of anti-competitive behaviour as required in the other copyright-competition cases not covered by this safe harbour.

Still, it ought to be noted that the De Minimis Notice has no binding effect on national competition authorities and national courts, and they are therefore not obliged to apply it.[203] Thus, an agreement that would not infringe Article 101 TFEU may still infringe the competition law of some Member State. Even in such cases, at this stage of evaluation, it seems useful, if not necessary, to follow the structured analysis of the copyright-competition interaction assessment and calculate the market shares of the undertakings concerned. First, it may be relevant in the exemption stage, particularly if some block exemptions apply.[204] Second, although the size of market shares is not a prerequisite in relation to competition rules on prohibited agreements, they may still be an element in evaluating whether particular conduct under investigation distorts competition by producing anti-competitive effects.

All things considered, after the relevant market has been adequately defined and before the analysis of anti-competitive behaviour, the next step ought to be the calculation of market shares of the undertakings under the competition investigation. If the *de minimis* doctrine applies, it should first be determined whether the agreement is appreciable enough to fall under the competition rules on prohibited agreements.

---

[202] Commission Notice — Guidelines on the effect on trade concept contained in Articles 81 and 82 of the Treaty, C 101, 27.4.2004, pp. 81–96, para. 52.

[203] See Antitrust: Commission adopts revised safe harbours for minor agreements ('De Minimis Notice') and provides guidance on 'by object' restrictions of competition - European Commission, Frequently asked questions, MEMO, 25 June 2014. https://ec.europa.eu/commission/presscorner/detail/en/MEMO_14_440. Accessed on 24 October 2024.

[204] Concerning the relationship between the De Minimis Notice and block-exemptions, para. 14 of De Minimis Notice notes:

> The safe harbour created by the market share thresholds set out in points 8, 9, 10 and 11 is particularly relevant for categories of agreements not covered by any Commission block exemption regulation. The safe harbour is also relevant for agreements covered by a Commission block exemption regulation to the extent that those agreements contain a so-called excluded restriction, that is a restriction not listed as a hardcore restriction but nonetheless not covered by the Commission block exemption regulation.

Otherwise, market shares need to be considered to provide a full understanding of the effect of the relevant agreement with respect to (anti-)competitiveness, and with respect to potential exemptions.

4.3.2.5 Anti-competitive Behaviour

The crucial question in discussions on the matter of copyright-competition interaction is— what kind of exercise of copyright can be considered as anti-competitive in the light of the competition rules on prohibited agreements?

The general provision in Article 101(1) TFEU prescribes that the following are anti-competitive:

> (…) agreements between undertakings, decisions by associations of undertakings and concerted practices which may affect trade between Member States and which have as their object or effect the prevention, restriction or distortion of competition within the internal market, and in particular those which:
>
> (a) directly or indirectly fix purchase or selling prices or any other trading conditions;
> (b) limit or control production, markets, technical development, or investment;
> (c) share markets or sources of supply;
> (d) apply dissimilar conditions to equivalent transactions with other trading parties, thereby placing them at a competitive disadvantage;
> (e) make the conclusion of contracts subject to acceptance by the other parties of supplementary obligations which, by their nature or according to commercial usage, have no connection with the subject of such contracts.

Thus, for an agreement to fall under the prohibition set out in Article 101(1), there are two general requirements:

(1) that the agreement affects trade between Member States;
(2) that the agreement has as its object or effect the prevention, restriction or distortion of competition within the internal market.

The first requirement is just a general jurisdictional test whose aim is to make the boundary between the respective areas covered by the EU competition law and national competition law. Thus, even if the agreement does not affect the trade between the Member States, it still may fall under the prohibition set out in Article 101(1) TFEU.[205] As Keeling stated, the aim of the competition rules on prohibited agreements "is not to increase the volume of trade between the Member States but to ensure that competition in the common market is not distorted."[206]

The second requirement is more in line with the essence of the prohibition in Article 101(1) TFEU. Thus, the focus on the issue of anti-competitive behaviour is—

[205] See Judgment of 13 July 1966, *Établissements Consten S.à.R.L. and Grundig-Verkaufs-GmbH v Commission of the European Economic Community*, Joined cases 56 and 58-64, EU:C:1966:41, pp. 341–342.
[206] Keeling (2003), p. 308.

what kind of agreement restricts competition? It should also be noted that the terms 'prevention', 'restriction' and 'distortion' do not have substantially different meanings. For the sake of simplicity, it is common in both practice and theory to use only one of those terms when discussing the prevention/restriction/distortion of competition.[207]

In the case law, when dealing with the copyright-competition interaction cases under Article 101 TFEU, the CJEU often used the formulation that the exercise of a particular intellectual property right might fall within the ambit of the prohibitions of the competition rules on prohibited agreements if it were to manifest itself as the subject, the means, or the consequence of the restrictive practice.[208] In the cases influenced by the exceptional circumstances doctrine, the guiding phrase sounds more as if the copyright might infringe competition rules on prohibited agreements in the exceptional circumstances (which are still left undefined for the cases concerning Article 101 TFEU). Under the complementarity theory, the case law has not yet been developed to formulate any guiding formulation in relation to what conduct involving the use of copyright constitutes an infringement of the competition rules on prohibited agreements. Considering the concept of complementarity, one can imagine that such a guiding phrase would be formulated somehow, as there is a violation of Article 101 TFEU if the interest of undistorted competition prevailed over the interests of safeguarding copyright holders.

What does that mean in essence? None of these formulations, or the general provision prescribed in Article 101 TFEU, provides us with the answer to what indeed is the examining principle in observing a particular exercise of copyright as potentially anti-competitive conduct, infringing the competition rules on prohibited agreements.

To sort out the situation, it is necessary to consider and articulate the theory of harm—the concept that implicitly lies behind any competition concern but is often neglected in discussions on anti-competitive behaviour. Recently, there has been an increasing focus on the European competition authorities[209] and academia[210] on the need to articulate the theory of harm behind anti-competitive conduct. Zenger and Walker consider that "the requirement to present a theory of harm imposes a logically consistent approach to the assessment of anti-competitive behaviour. If the theory of harm is made explicit by competition authorities, then this makes it

---

[207] See Keeling (2003), pp. 307–308.

[208] See, for instance, *EMI v CBS* where the Court further elaborated that the exercise of intellectual property rights in matters must not "manifest itself as the result of the agreement of concerted practices which have as their object or effect the isolation or partitioning of the common market." Judgment of 15 June 1976, *EMI Records Limited v CBS Grammofon A/S*, C-86/75, EU:C:1976:86, para. 24 *et* 35.

[209] Through the Guidelines on the application of [101(3)], the Commission set out a commitment to prove a theory of harm and balance pro- and anti-competitive effects. See Communication from the Commission — Notice — Guidelines on the application of Article 81(3) of the Treaty, OJ C 101, 27.4.2004, pp. 97–118, para. 11.

[210] See Colino (2019), pp. 9–10; Whish and Bailey (2021), p. 34.

much harder for internally inconsistent or speculative competition concerns to survive the process of assessment."[211] A well-developed theory of harm should have the following characteristics:

- it should articulate how competition and, ultimately, consumers will be harmed relative to an appropriately defined counterfactual;
- it should be internally logically consistent;
- it should be consistent with the incentives that the various parties face; and
- it should be consistent with (or at least not inconsistent with) the available empirical evidence.[212] Thus, particularly in the assessment of copyright-competition interaction cases, which generally call for an effects-based approach,[213] a theory of harm must be clearly articulated in the reasoning of the case.

The critical element of the anti-competitiveness of the agreement is that it has as its "object or effect the prevention, restriction or distortion of competition within the internal market." For an agreement to be considered anti-competitive, it must involve conduct that strongly deviates from the 'normal use' of copyright.[214] However, as we know, copyright is generally deemed to be an absolute right whose exercise may only be limited in content in prescribed situations, listed in the closed list of exceptions and limitations. Exceptionally, outside the copyright framework, there are additional limitations to the exercise of copyright-competition law is one of them (see *supra* Sect. 2.1; Sect. 3.2). However, restrictions on the exercise of copyright by means of competition law must be interpreted as the utmost restrictions. Thus, the situations in which competition rules on prohibited agreements can indeed limit the use of copyright must be genuinely exceptional. Otherwise, competition law interferes with the substance of copyright law and, consequently, diminishes the rights of authors and other rights holders.

There is still no clarity on how to identify such extreme commercial conduct that deviates from the 'normal' exercise of copyright and constitutes an anti-competitive agreement. For this, a specific, accurate and administrable test is required. The test deemed to have such characteristics is suggested below. The test of reasonableness

---

[211] Zenger and Walker (2012), p. 185.

[212] See Zenger and Walker (2012), p. 185.

[213] Although, due to its specificity, it should in any case be avoided for the copyright-competition cases to be assessed as a restriction by object. It should be noted that the theory of harm is even present in the object assessments; however, in such cases, it is presumed that the theory of harm is known from the outset. Nevertheless, especially in the context of the theory of harm object category should not be extensively applied because the presumed theory of harm can be flawed due to a lack of a realistic anti-competitive intent and effect. See Zenger and Walker (2012), pp. 195–202.

[214] For instance, to describe the situation when exercise of intellectual property rights violates competition rules on prohibited agreement, Ginsburg, Geradin and Klovers use the formulation "coordinating with other entities to restrain trade unreasonably." See Ginsburg et al. (2019), p. 99.

focuses on the copyright effects and competition law objectives in a dynamic context (see *supra* Sect. 3.2). The test is designed as a means of identifying exceptional circumstances in which agreements involving the exercise of copyright indeed represent a restriction of competition, with competition liability being the appropriate sanction. The rationale of the test is to preserve the substance of copyright and enhance creative processes on the market to the benefit of authors, rights holders and end-users. In other words, it should question whether the assessed exercise of copyright has an object or is already producing long-term negative effects on originality and creativity, on competition in the relevant market, to the harm of consumers.

The test of reasonableness is constituted in the following way:

(1) First, it is required to establish whether the particular agreement's object or effect, involving the use of some copyright right, represents a distortion of dynamic competition on the relevant market. If so, the conduct negatively affects the competitive process that enhances creativity and originality.
(2) Second, as a consequence of the first criterion, it is required to determine whether the creation of new creative and original works or the emergence of new creative industries or innovation-based markets were significantly limited. In the context of this criterion, it might even be considered to broaden it to innovations. Namely, copyright works might also provide incentives for or enable the creation of some innovations. For instance, copyright-protected software might contribute to the creation of a utility patent, or a documentary movie might have a positive effect on the development of a scientific field. Such innovations might not fall into the category of copyright-protected works, but, for instance, patents. Still, they can raise the overall value of the intellectual property on the market, to the benefit of the consumers. In other words, it may be beneficial for the overall competition in the context of competition law objectives.
(3) Third, it is required to establish whether the conduct in the matter produces long-term harm to the consumers as the end-users of copyright-protected work. In this regard, the focus is on the present and potential future consequences on the interests of users. It should be established whether consumers have, for instance, been deprived of some creative content or burdened by unreasonably higher costs of some service.
(4) Fourth, it is required to establish whether the situation represents a special case that is not in conflict with the 'normal' exploitation of the copyright-protected work and does not unreasonably prejudice the legitimate interests of authors or right-holders. This criterion is derived from the copyright three-step test. It was already explained that, generally, copyright is an absolute property right, and authors can do whatever they want with copyright. Copyright limitations and exceptions are prescribed explicitly, while external restrictions, such as competition law, must be genuinely exceptional. Considering that outside restrictions

are not part of the copyright framework, maybe it would be appropriate to consider such limitations as those that fall outside the 'normal' exploitation of copyright[215] and do not unreasonably prejudice the legitimate interests of authors or right-holders.[216] However, copyright rules do not directly apply to such limitations. Thus, it is widely accepted that the three-step test does not generally apply, either (see *supra* Sect. 2.1). Regardless, in the context of copyright-competition interaction, this research advocates that the content of the three-step test is appropriate as part of the anti-competitiveness test for copyright-competition interactions.[217] In that sense, the copyright interpretation of the three-step test should apply *per analogiam*. Therefore, as the final criterion, this requirement should consider whether the potential establishment of competition liability would contravene the guaranteed copyright protection.

Only if the above four requirements are satisfied can the agreement under assessment be considered to produce an anti-competitive effect. Still, even if the four conditions are satisfied, it is still possible for a particular conduct to be exempted from the prohibition of competition rules on prohibited agreements in the next stage of the assessment (see *infra* Sect. 4.3.2.6).

The four conditions are obviously not in line with prior practice and theory. However, considering that the copyright-competition interaction issue is still unresolved, we suggest the application of those conditions as the appropriate solution to settling the issue of exercising copyright under the competition rules on prohibited agreements. The test of reasonableness strives to acknowledge the fundamentals of copyright law and competition law, and still provide a solution to this interdisciplinary issue. A hypothetical application of the test will be presented below (see *infra* Sect. 4.3.2.7). Nevertheless, the actual value of the suggested test can only be demonstrated if applied in practice.

---

[215] It is widely accepted that the reading of the part of the three-step test—"no conflict with normal exploitation of a work"—is essentially economic. In the context of the copyright-competition interaction, the matter is exclusively of an economic nature. See Goldstein and Hugenholtz (2021), p. 356; Hugenholtz and Okediji (2008), p. 23. In relation to the copyright three-step test, Ginsburg and Treppoz consider that "exceptions and limitations would be presumed not to conflict with normal exploitation if they are confined to a scope that does not enter into economic competition with non-exempted uses." See Ginsburg and Treppoz (2015), p. 464.

[216] Considering "the unreasonable prejudice of legitimate interests of authors and other right holders," Ginsburg and Treppoz explain that the condition implies several steps. First, to define the interests of the right holders at stake and which attributes make them legitimate; second, to develop an interpretation of the term 'prejudice' and what amount of it reaches a level that should be considered 'unreasonable'; see Ginsburg and Treppoz (2015), p. 467.

[217] Although this research does not follow Dreier's perception of copyright limitations and exceptions in the context of competition law, Dreier's research provides support for applying the content of the three-step test to the copyright-competition interaction cases; see Dreier (2010), p. 244.

4.3.2.6 Exemptions to the Prohibited Agreements in the Light of Exercise of Copyright

Article 101(1) TFEU prescribes the prohibition of agreements that distort competition, while Article 101(2) TFEU prescribes the consequence of such agreements—void agreement. However, even if an agreement is considered as anti-competitive contrary to Article 101(1) TFEU, there is still a possibility to avoid the prohibition. In Article 101(3) TFEU, EU competition law provides a defence for undertakings against the finding of an infringement of Article 101(1) TFEU:

> 3. The provisions of paragraph 1 may, however, be declared inapplicable in the case of:
> - any agreement or category of agreements between undertakings,
> - any decision or category of decisions by associations of undertakings,
> - any concerted practice or category of concerted practices,
>
> which contributes to improving the production or distribution of goods or to promoting technical or economic progress, while allowing consumers a fair share of the resulting benefit, and which does not:
>
> (a) impose on the undertakings concerned restrictions which are not indispensable to the attainment of these objectives;
> (b) afford such undertakings the possibility of eliminating competition in respect of a substantial part of the products in question.

In other words, an agreement that falls within the prohibition of Article 101(1) TFEU might still be exempted.[218] Article 101(3) can be applied in individual cases or to categories of agreements and concerted practices by way of block exemption regulation.[219]

The general conditions for an agreement to enjoy the benefits of Article 101(3) TFEU are the following:

- must contribute to improving the production or distribution of goods or to promoting technical or economic progress;[220]

---

[218] Guidelines on the application of Article [101(3)] lay down analytical framework for the application of Article 101(3) (Communication from the Commission — Notice — Guidelines on the application of Article 81(3) of the Treaty, OJ C 101, 27.4.2004, pp. 97–118).

[219] See Communication from the Commission — Notice — Guidelines on the application of Article 81(3) of the Treaty, OJ C 101, 27.4.2004, pp. 97–118, para. 2.

[220] Benefits produced by an agreement must be something of objective value to the EU as a whole and not a private benefit to the parties themselves. Advantages of the agreement must outweigh the detriments it might produce. If the agreement produces effects on more than one market, objective benefits in each of the markets must be taken into account. In that sense, this condition can still be observed through a narrower or broader perspective, whether only improvements in economic efficiency should be taken into consideration or also non-competition considerations which go beyond the enhancement of economic efficiency; see Whish and Bailey (2021), pp. 163–171. See also, for instance, Judgment of 13 July 1966, *Établissements Consten S.à.R.L. and Grundig-Verkaufs-GmbH v Commission of the European Economic Community*, Joined cases 56 and 58/64, EU:C:1966:41, p. 350; Judgment of the Court of 15 July 1994, *Matra Hachette SA v Commission of the European Communities*, T-17/93, EU:T:1994:89, paras. 109–110; Judgment

- must not impose on the undertakings concerned restrictions which are not indispensable to the attainment of these objectives;[221]
- must allow consumers a fair share of the resulting benefit;[222] and
- must not afford such undertakings the possibility of eliminating competition in respect of a substantial part of the products in question.[223]

---

of 6 October 2009, *GlaxoSmithKline Services Unlimited v Commission of the European Communities (C-501/06 P) and Commission of the European Communities v GlaxoSmithKline Services Unlimited (C-513/06 P) and European Association of Euro Pharmaceutical Companies (EAEPC) v Commission of the European Communities (C-515/06 P) and Asociación de exportadores españoles de productos farmacéuticos (Aseprofar) v Commission of the European Communities (C-519/06 P),* Joined cases C-501/06 P, C-513/06 P, C-515/06 P and C-519/06 P, EU:C:2009:610, paras. 92–95.

[221] In essence, the indispensability criterion goes before the question of fair share for consumers since the latter would not arise if the restricions are not indispensable; see Communication from the Commission — Notice — Guidelines on the application of Article 81(3) of the Treaty, OJ C 101, 27.4.2004, pp. 97–118, para. 39. See also, for instance, Judgment of 25 October 1977, *Metro SB-Großmärkte GmbH & Co. KG v Commission of the European Communities*, C-26/76, EU:C:1977:167, paras. 44–45; Judgment of the Court of 15 July 1994, *Matra Hachette SA v Commission of the European Communities*, T-17/93, EU:T:1994:89, para. 138; Judgment of 28 February 2002, *Compagnie générale maritime and Others v Commission of the European Communities,* T-86/95, EU:T:2002:50, para. 381.

According to the para. 73 of the Guidelines on the application of Article 81(3) of the Treaty, the indispensability condition implies a two-fold test: first, whether the restrictive agreement itself is reasonably necessary to achieve the efficiencies; and second, whether the individual restrictions of competition flowing from the agreement are reasonably necessary for the attainment of the efficiencies. In doing so, the efficiencies must be specific to the agreement, and parties must demonstrate both the nature of any restriction and that its intensity is reasonably necessary to produce the claimed efficiencies. A restriction is indispensable if its absence would eliminate or significantly reduce the efficiencies that follow from the agreement or make it significantly less likely that they will materialise. Also, a restriction may be indispensable only for a certain period—once the time expires, it will cease to be so. See Whish and Bailey (2021), p. 172.

[222] This condition is a sort of 'pass-on' requirement. The undertakings concerned must show that a fair share of the benefits that result from an agreement will accrue to consumers if the exemption from para. 3 Article 1 TFEU applies. The concept of consumers covers all direct or indirect users of the product involved in all the relevant markets concerned; see Whish and Bailey (2021), pp. 172–173. See also, for instance, Judgment of 25 October 1977, *Metro SB-Großmärkte GmbH & Co. KG v Commission of the European Communities*, C-26/76, EU:C:1977:167, paras. 46-48; Judgment of 17 January 1995, *The Publishers Association v Commission of the European Communities*, C-360/92 P, EU:C:1995:6, para. 29; Judgment of 23 November 2006, *Asnef-Equifax, Servicios de Información sobre Solvencia y Crédito, SL v Asociación de Usuarios de Servicios Bancarios (Ausbanc),* C-238/05, EU:C:2006:734, para. 72.

[223] The fourth condition in para. 105 of the Guidelines on the application of Article 81(3) of the Treaty states that, ultimately, protection of rivalry and the competitive process are given priority over potentially pro-competitive efficiency gains which could result from restrictive agreements. It further explains that Article 101(3) TFEU recognises the fact that rivalry between undertakings is an essential driver of economic efficiency, including dynamic efficiencies in the shape of innovation. In other words, the ultimate aim of Article 101 is to protect the competitive process. See Communication from the Commission — Notice — Guidelines on the application of Article 81(3) of the Treaty, OJ C 101, 27.4.2004, pp. 97–118, paras. 105, 107–116. See also, for instance, Judgment of 14 May 1975, *Kali und Salz AG and Kali-Chemie AG v Commission of the European Communities*,

To activate the exemption under Article 101(3) TFEU, all four conditions must be satisfied cumulatively in an individual case. That was stressed on several occasions through case law[224] and soft law.[225] However, no limitations are prescribed for the content of the agreement. Practically any type of agreement that restricts competition may enjoy the benefit of Article 101(3) TFEU,[226] in the light of the circumstances specific to each particular case.[227]

Thus, in the Commission's decision *Film purchases by German television stations*,[228] the Commission investigated exclusive film licensing agreements concluded between MHM/UA, a major US film production and distribution company, and ARD, an association of public broadcasting organisations in Germany. The Commission considered that, in regard to the criteria established in *Coditel II*, the exclusive agreements restricted competition.[229] However, after several amendments of the agreements, the Commission concluded that the conditions in Article 101(3) TFEU were eventually satisfied and that the conduct of the undertakings was exempted from the prohibition under Article 101(1) TFEU.[230] Later on, the

---

Joined cases 19 and 20/74, EU:C:1975:58, paras. 6–7; Judgment of the Court of 8 June 1982, *L.C. Nungesser KG and Kurt Eisele v Commission of the European Communities*, C-258/78, EU:C:1982:211, para. 75; Judgment of the Court of 28 February 2002, *Atlantic Container Line AB and Others v Commission of the European Communities*, T-395/94, EU:T:2002:49, paras. 300 and 330.

[224] See, for instance, Judgment of 17 January 1984, *Vereniging ter Bevordering van het Vlaamse Boekwezen, VBVB, and Vereniging ter Bevordering van de Belangen des Boekhandels, VBBB, v Commission of the European Communities*, Joined cases 43/82 and 63/82, EU:C:1984:9, para. 61; Judgment of 23 November 2006, *Asnef-Equifax, Servicios de Información sobre Solvencia y Crédito, SL v Asociación de Usuarios de Servicios Bancarios (Ausbanc)*, C-238/05, EU:C:2006:734; Judgment of 7 February 2013, Protimonopolný úrad Slovenskej republiky v Slovenská sporiteľňa a.s, C-68/12, U:C:2013:71.

[225] See Communication from the Commission — Notice — Guidelines on the application of Article 81(3) of the Treaty, OJ C 101, 27.4.2004, pp. 97–118, para. 42.

[226] See Whish and Bailey (2021), pp. 161–163.

[227] See Communication from the Commission — Notice — Guidelines on the application of Article 81(3) of the Treaty, OJ C 101, 27.4.2004, pp. 97–118, para. 6.:

> The standards set forth in the present guidelines must be applied in light of the circumstances specific to each case. This excludes a mechanical application. Each case must be assessed on its own facts and the guidelines must be applied reasonably and flexibly.

[228] 89/536/EEC: Commission Decision of 15 September 1989 relating to a proceeding under Article 85 of the EEC Treaty (IV/31.734 - Film purchases by German television stations), OJ L 284, 3.10.1989, pp. 36–44.

[229] 89/536/EEC: Commission Decision of 15 September 1989 relating to a proceeding under Article 85 of the EEC Treaty (IV/31.734 - Film purchases by German television stations), OJ L 284, 3.10.1989, pp. 36–44, pp. 41–42.

[230] 89/536/EEC: Commission Decision of 15 September 1989 relating to a proceeding under Article 85 of the EEC Treaty (IV/31.734 - Film purchases by German television stations), OJ L 284, 3.10.1989, pp. 36–44, pp. 43–44.

Commission discussed the application of Article 101(3) in another case concerning the film and TV industry and licensing of work protected by artistic copyright—*Telenor/Canal+/Canal Digital*.[231] Telenor applied for a negative clearance under Article 101(1) TFEU or, alternatively, for exemption under Article 101(3) TFEU in respect of three agreements entered into, inter alia, with Groupe Canal+ SA and its subsidiary Canal+ Television AB for conducting pay-TV operations in Nordic regions via the direct-to-home satellite platform of Canal Digital AS. The notified arrangement consisted of sale-purchase, distribution and supply agreements, including pay-TV channel exclusivity, pay-TV channel non-compete and PPV/NVOD channel exclusivity and non-compete.[232] In this case, the Commission again considered that the agreements restricted competition.[233] However, after further amendments, the Commission concluded that the conditions in Article 101(3) were satisfied[234] and found that the agreements were exempted from the prohibition of Article 101(1) TFEU.[235]

The concept of exemption under Article 101(3) TFEU is different from, for instance, the one within the US antitrust law that deals with such 'exemptions' through the rule of reason doctrine. Still, in a way, it can be considered that Article 101(3) TFEU in itself contains what is in the US antitrust law perceived as the rule of reason concept.[236]

[231] Notice published pursuant to Article 19(3) of Council Regulation No. 17 concerning an application for negative clearance or exemption under Article 81(3) of the EC Treaty (Case COMP/C2/38.287 — Telenor/Canal+/Canal Digital), OJ C 149, 26.6.2003, pp. 16–17.

[232] Notice published pursuant to Article 19(3) of Council Regulation No. 17 concerning an application for negative clearance or exemption under Article 81(3) of the EC Treaty (Case COMP/C2/38.287 — Telenor/Canal+/Canal Digital), OJ C 149, 26.6.2003, pp. 16–17.The agreement falls outside the block exemptions for vertical agreements because the licenses were not ancillary to a vertical agreement; see Whish and Bailey (2021), p. 823.

[233] Notice published pursuant to Article 19(3) of Council Regulation No. 17 concerning an application for negative clearance or exemption under Article 81(3) of the EC Treaty (Case COMP/C2/38.287 — Telenor/Canal+/Canal Digital), OJ C 149, 26.6.2003, p. 16–17, p. 17.

[234] In regard to the PPV/NVOD channel exclusivity, the Commission concluded that it does not even restrict Article 101(1) TFEU and granted a negative clearance.

[235] See The Commission, case COMP/C.2-38.287 ñ Telenor / Canal+ / Canal Digital, C(2003) 5192 final, 29.12.2003, p. 78. Unlike in the mentioned case, interestingly in the *Football Association Premier League* case, to determine that the agreement does not enjoy exemption from Article 101(3) TFEU, the CJEU did not discuss the conditions contained in Article 101(3) TFEU, but only referred to reasoning on the (non) justification of restriction of the free movement of services due to intellectual property rights (Article 31 and 36 TFEU). See Judgment of 4 October 2011, Football Association Premier League Ltd and Others v QC Leisure and Others, Karen Murphy v Media Protection Services Ltd, Joined cases C-403/08 and C-429/08, EU:C:2011:631, para. 145.

[236] See Whish and Bailey (2021), pp. 142–143.

Generally, the Article 101(3) TFEU exemption is surely available for a conduct involving an exercise of copyright. In relation to the assessment of copyright-competition interaction, the conditions for the activation of Article 101(3) TFEU are partially already included in the test suggested above (see *supra* Sect. 4.3.2.5). However, the conditions in Article 101(3) TFEU still stay substantially different, and conduct involving the exercise of copyright that is considered to be contrary to Article 101(1) TFEU might qualify for the exemption in Article 101(3) TFEU.

In addition, and according to the general exemption rule under Article 101(3) TFEU, EU competition law allows another way of avoiding the prohibition under Article 101(1) TFEU—through the so-called 'block-exemptions' specifically prescribed for some particular situations.[237] In essence, the concept of block exemptions provides a safe harbour for specific categories of agreements that satisfy the requirements of a particular block exemption. Such block-exemption makes them valid without specific authorisation.[238] The current block exemptions do not prescribe the clauses that may individually benefit from block exemption, but there are often prescribed 'hardcore restrictions' that must not be included if an agreement is to enjoy the benefit of block exemption. Also, most block exemptions require a certain market threshold to be satisfied.

In the context of copyright-competition interaction, the relevant block-exemptions are mainly general: the block-exemption on vertical supply and distribution agreements (Regulation (EU) No. 2022/720)[239] and, particularly, the block-exemption on technology transfer agreements (Regulation (EU) No. 316/2014)[240] in relation to software copyright.

Regulation 2022/720 provides block-exemption from Article 101(1) TFEU to vertical agreements in which: the market shares of the supplier and buyer do not exceed 30% of the relevant market;[241] do not contain any of the listed 'hardcore'

---

[237] It is mainly the Commission that adopts block exemptions, acting under powers conferred upon it by regulations of the Council.

[238] In Regulation 1/2003, the EU abolished the system of individual exemptions, but the concept of block exemptions nevertheless remained. See Communication from the Commission — Notice — Guidelines on the application of Article 81(3) of the Treaty, OJ C 101, 27.4.2004, pp. 97–118, para. 2.

[239] Commission Regulation (EU) 2022/720 of 10 May 2022 on the application of Article 101(3) of the Treaty on the Functioning of the European Union to categories of vertical agreements and concerted practices (Text with EEA relevance), C/2022/3015, OJ L 134, 11.5.2022, pp. 4–13.

[240] Commission Regulation (EU) No. 316/2014 of 21 March 2014 on the application of Article 101(3) of the Treaty on the Functioning of the European Union to categories of technology transfer agreements Text with EEA relevance, OJ L 93, 28.3.2014, pp. 17–23.

[241] Article 3 of Regulation (EU) No. 2022/720.

restrictions;[242] and exclude particular restrictions.[243] The idea behind this block-exemption is that such agreements may, for instance, help a manufacturer to enter a new market, or avoid the situation whereby one distributor 'free rides' on the promotional efforts of another distributor, or allow a supplier to depreciate an investment made for a particular client. In that manner, the block-exemption on vertical supply and distribution agreements also applies to agreements involving licensing or use of copyright.[244] Although the case law is not entirely developed in that regard, it can be imagined that, for instance, a franchise agreement involving the license of copyright might fall within this block exemption.[245]

[242] Article 4 of Regulation (EU) No. 2022/720:

1. Suppliers are not allowed to fix the (minimum) price at which distributors can resell their products (resale price maintenance);
2. Partitioning by territory or by customer is prohibited. Distributors must remain free to decide where and to whom they sell. The regulation contains exceptions to this rule, which, for instance, enable companies to operate an exclusive distribution system or a selective distribution system, or neither an exclusive distribution system nor a selective distribution system;
3. Selected distributors, while being prohibited to sell to unauthorised distributors, cannot be restricted in the end-users to whom they may sell;
4. Selected distributors must remain free to sell or purchase the contract goods to or from other selected distributors within the network;
5. Prevention of the effective use of the internet by the buyers or its customer to sell the contract goods and services is prohibited, without prejudice to the possibility of imposing on the buyer other restrictions of online sales or restrictions of online advertising that do not have the object of preventing the use of an entire online advertising

   Channel;

6. An agreement between a manufacturer of spare parts and a buyer which incorporates these parts into its own products may not prevent or restrict sales by the manufacturer of these spare parts to end-users, independent repairers or service providers.

[243] Article 5 of Regulation (EU) No. 330/2010:

- obligations not to compete during the contract;
- obligations not to compete after termination of the contract;
- the exclusion of specific brands in a selective distribution system.

[244] Article 3 para. 3 of Regulation (EU) No. 330/2010:

> The exemption provided for in paragraph 1 shall apply to vertical agreements containing provisions which relate to the assignment to the buyer or use by the buyer of intellectual property rights, provided that those provisions do not constitute the primary object of such agreements and are directly related to the use, sale or resale of goods or services by the buyer or its customers. The exemption applies on condition that, in relation to the contract goods or services, those provisions do not contain restrictions of competition having the same object as vertical restraints which are not exempted under this Regulation.

[245] See analogy in Max Planck Institute for Intellectual Property and Competition Law (2013), p. 27.

Regulation (EU) No. 316/2014 exempts particular licensing agreements ('technology transfer agreements'[246]) between undertakings that have limited market power (i.e. market share of under 20% for agreements between competitors and 30% for agreements between non-competitors), and that fulfil certain conditions.[247] These are deemed to have no anti-competitive effects or, if they do, the positive effects outweigh the negative ones and thus do not contravene EU competition rules. As is generally typical of block exemptions, Regulation 316/2014 also prescribes 'hardcore restrictions'[248] and 'excluded restrictions'.[249] Regulation 316/2014 explicitly prescribes what kinds of rights are considered to be 'technology rights'. In relation to the copyright-competition interaction issue, software copyrights are covered by this specific block exemption.[250] Thus, a licensing agreement of software copyright entered into between two undertakings for the production of contract products by the licensee and/or its sub-contractor(s) would be exempted from the scrutiny of Article 101(1) TFEU.

Overall, certainly, copyright per se is not a sufficient reason for an anti-competitive prohibited agreement to be justified. A specific method of evaluation that acknowledges the particularities of copyright should be applied during the whole assessment. However, EU competition law provided Article 101(3) TFEU and block-exemption that indeed represent an objective justification that may exempt particular conduct from the consequences of Article 101(2) TFEU, even though it falls under the prohibition of Article 101(1) TFEU.

---

[246] According to Article 1 para. 1 Point (c) of Regulation 316/2014, 'technology transfer agreement' means:

(i) a technology rights licensing agreement entered into between two undertakings for the purpose of the production of contract products by the licensee and/or its sub-contractor (s),
(ii) (an assignment of technology rights between two undertakings for the purpose of the production of contract products where part of the risk associated with the exploitation of the technology remains with the assignor."

[247] Article 3 of Regulation 316/2014.

[248] Article 4 of Regulation (EU) 316/2014.

[249] Article 5 of Regulation (EU) 316/2014.

[250] Article 1, para. 1, Point (b) Subpoint (vii) of Regulation (EU) 316/2014.
Other types of copyright are not covered by Regulation (EU) 316/2014, and, consequently, do not enjoy the benefit of this particular block-exemption.

4.3.2.7 Algorithm of the Suggested Copyright-Competition Interaction Assessment Method for the Cases Concerning the Exercise of Copyright Under the Competition Rules on Prohibited Agreements (Fig. 4.1)

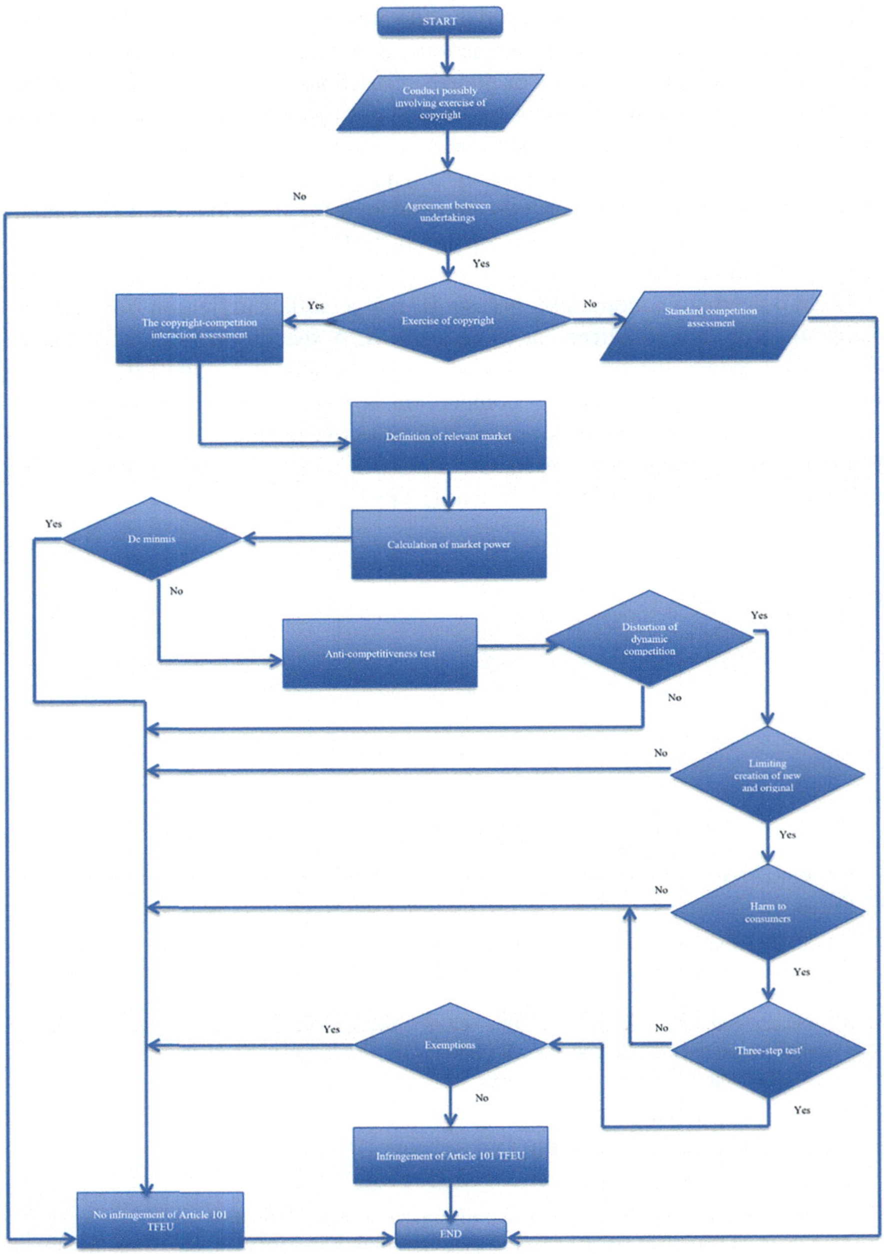

Fig. 4.1 Algorithm of the suggested copyright-competition interaction method of assessment for the cases concerning the exercise of copyright under the competition rules on prohibited agreements

4.3.3 Case Study—the Application of the Structured Test of Reasonableness on a Hypothetical Case Concerning the Exercise of Copyright Under the Competition Rules on Prohibited Agreements

This research intends to design an appropriate method of assessment for cases concerning the exercise of copyright under the competition rules on prohibited agreements. Since the method has obviously not been tested in practice, provided below is a simplified hypothetical situation to illustrate how the method should be applied. The factsheet is to some extent inspired by the US case *United States v. Paramount Pictures, Inc.*[251] and the 1994 Monopolies & Mergers Commission (MMC) report on the supply of films in the UK.[252]

- ***Factsheet:***

  Movie Company GmbH. is a German film studio holding exclusive copyright rights for the movie 'Alf'. Films International Sarl. is a competing French film studio holding exclusive copyright rights for the movie 'The Foggy Day'. Both films covered the inspirational story of an individual forced to confront the spiritual crisis of his out-of-balance life, and the subsequent wisdom that he gains on a life-changing odyssey that enables him to create a life of passion, purpose and peace. Each film had a very high budget and was expected to become a blockbuster. Besides, the theatrical release of both films was supposed to happen at the same time.

  Considering that the films 'Alf' and 'The Foggy Day' targeted the same audience, they are the so-called twin movies, the director of Movie Company GmbH. and the director of Films International Sarl. met at an informal meeting. As part of their conversation, they considered that it would be mutually beneficial if the films had the same ticket prices in the cinemas. Hence, they agreed that they would endeavour to maintain the same fees for the distribution of the films in cinemas to ensure the highest possible gross box office for both films. After their release, the films were shown worldwide, including in all the EU Member States. However, the films were not shown in cinemas that would not agree to the aligned pricing policies of the Movie Company GmbH. and Films International Sarl.

  A group of small independent film studios realised that after the release of 'Alf' and 'The Foggy Day', viewership of their competing movies had significantly fallen while 'Alf' and 'The Foggy Day' were fully booked. Hence, they filed a complaint to the EU Commission claiming that companies Movie Company

---

[251] See The Supreme Court of the United States, *United States v. Paramount Pictures, Inc. et al.* 334 U.S. 131, 68 S. Ct. 915; 92 L. Ed. 1260; 1948 U.S. LEXIS 2850; 77 U.S.P.Q. (BNA) 243; 1948 Trade Cas. (CCH), 62, 244.

[252] See OECD (1995), pp. 43–47.

GmbH. and Film International Sarl. had concluded an agreement violating competition rules on prohibited agreements.

• *Test:*

(1.) Agreement

The first thing in any competition assessment concerning the competition rules on prohibited agreements (Article 101 TEU) is to establish whether there is an agreement between the undertakings under the investigation.

In the described case, the representatives of the undertakings had an informal oral agreement to engage in conduct that resulted in potentially anti-competitive behaviour. Considering that competition law has a very loose interpretation of arrangement, there is no obstacle to establishing such an arrangement as an agreement. Nonetheless, it is usually more difficult to establish an oral agreement than when there is a written trace of the agreement.

(2.) Analysis of Copyright

After establishing that there indeed was an agreement between the undertakings, the next step is to establish if the conduct concerns the exercise of copyright. This step is crucial, considering that it will direct the entire further assessment. If the case involves the exercise of copyright, the specific method should apply throughout the whole assessment to acknowledge the particularities of the copyright involved.

Thus, it is necessary to define the conduct under investigation and analyse whether it includes the exercise of copyright. In the described case, in essence, the undertakings had agreed to fix the prices of the cinema tickets to view two competing movies. Movies are the object of copyright protection, and generally, the holder of copyright rights on a movie can do practically whatever he wants with the movie. Hence, competition intervention definitely interferes with the rights holders' exclusive right to freely determine compensation for the public performance license.

In the assessment, it is necessary to evaluate the applicable copyright framework (preferably by citing the relevant provisions of copyright law). Besides the general copyright framework, for the needs of further assessment, it should be further required to analyse the specific object of copyright and its particularities. Considering that in this case the objects of copyright are movies, the particularities of movies should be concisely described in the context of copyright law.

(3.) Definition of the Relevant Market

The establishment of copyright is particularly vital for the stage of defining the relevant market. The exercise of copyright provides specific economic effects due to the exclusivity of the rights and affects both the product and the geographical dimension of the market.

In the described case, the object of the investigation is the film market, i.e. the distribution of movies in cinemas. Therefore, it is necessary to establish if the relevant market comprises the film distribution or the film exhibition market. In doing so, it should also be questioned if the relevant market differs from film distribution in other means other than in cinema. Considering that in the described case the films are the objects of copyright and of competition investigation, it deals with highly subjective consumer preferences that are largely unreliable and weak indicators for assessing demand side substitutability.

After the product dimension of the market has been defined, it is next necessary to determine the geographical dimension of the relevant markets. In other words, it is necessary to define the area in which the undertakings concerned are involved in the supply and demand of products or services, in which the conditions of competition are sufficiently homogeneous and which can be distinguished from neighbouring areas because the conditions of competition are appreciably different in those areas. In the particular case, some indicators of the extent of the geographical dimension of the market are the following—if the films were shown in cinemas worldwide or only in particular territories; if such pricing policy was universal or it operated only on particular national or regional levels; can particular national markets be distinguished one from another due to the preferences of consumers. Considering that both undertakings holding rights on the films were residents of different EU Member States and that the movies were shown worldwide, it is likely that the geographical dimension would comprise more national territories, possibly even the whole region. In this respect, differences between national copyright systems might also have an influence.

(4.) Market Shares

After the market structure has been defined, it is possible to calculate market shares. Market shares are not a prerequisite for the application of Article 101 TFEU; it is sufficient that there is an agreement between undertakings. Still, considering that copyright-competition interaction is an effects-based assessment, the assessment of the market power of the undertakings is required to comprehensively evaluate the anti-competitive effect of the conduct under the investigation.

The case concerns two undertakings functioning in the film industry market. However, the evaluation of market power does not solely depend on the overall business activities of the undertakings, but largely depends on the definition of the relevant market and what share of the defined market can be attributed to the undertakings involved. In that sense, market structure will be largely affected if the markets cover more or less national territories, more or less genres of films, etc.

Considering that the film market shows a tendency towards business concentration, it is likely that the undertakings would have a significant market share, although that depends on the circumstances of the particular case.

However, if the market shares of the undertakings are significantly low, there is a possibility that under the *de minimis* doctrine, the conduct would fall outside the scope of Article 101 TFEU (nonetheless, if the case is decided before national authorities, the *de minimis* doctrine might not be applicable). Besides, the market power will also affect the possibility of exemption in a later phase of the assessment.

(5.) Anti-competitiveness Test

The anti-competitiveness test is the core of the competition assessment. In accordance with the test of reasonableness suggested in this work to establish anti-competitive conduct, the first step is to evaluate whether the particular agreement's object or effect, involving the use of some copyright right, represents a distortion of dynamic competition on the relevant market. The two undertakings indeed concluded an agreement involving the exercise of copyright on two films. The effect of the agreement was the alignment of ticket prices for showing the films in cinemas. Considering that the undertakings are two renowned film studios holding rights to blockbuster movies, there is a significant chance that the conduct of the undertaking would negatively affect the competitive process on the market. Namely, the alignment of prices by blockbuster movie holders might have a negative effect on the viewership of films coming from smaller film studios.

If the first condition has been established, next it is necessary to establish if the consequence of the conduct is a significant limitation on creating new, creative and original works. In the context of the case, it would be required to establish that the negative effect on the viewership of films coming from smaller film studios results in the reduction of the films created by those studios.

Besides the previous conditions, to establish the anti-competitiveness of a conduct, the conduct must also produce long-term harm to consumers as the end-users of films protected by copyright. In that sense, it would be necessary to determine that, as a result of the conduct, consumers would have to pay higher ticket prices for cinemas or have fewer films available to watch.

Finally, to secure that potential competition law intervention would only represent an outside constraint on the exercise of copyright under investigation, it would be required to analyse if the potential intervention conflicts with the 'normal' exploitation of copyright and does not unreasonably prejudice the legitimate interests of authors or rights holders. In other words, it must be established that prohibiting agreements void would not affect copyright protection on the films.

If all four conditions are satisfied, then it is justified to establish a violation of competition rules on prohibited agreements.

(6.) Potential Exemptions

Of course, even if the conduct represents a violation of Article 101(1) TFEU, there is still a chance to exempt the conduct

However, considering that the conduct in the case involves films, it is unlikely that such conduct would even satisfy the first condition of Article 101(3) TFEU – "contributes to improving the production or distribution of goods or to promoting technical or economic progress." Also, it is not very likely that the conduct would fall under the scope of any of the available block exemptions.

4.3.4 Conclusion

The copyright-competition interaction issue in relation to the competition rules on prohibited agreements is indeed far from being settled. Besides the substantial issues on the general relationship between copyright law and competition law, in both practice and academia, copyright is often not distinguished from other intellectual property rights. Consequently, copyright particularities and specific economics are not being adequately taken into consideration. Sometimes, competition rules are still not distinguished from the rules on the free movement of goods, which was especially confusing in the earlier case law. Besides, the importance of articulating the theory of harm is neglected. There is no structured method of assessing the copyright-competition interaction cases. All of that and more lead to inconsistent practice, confusing reasoning and general insecurity for everyone.

In the present times, such a situation is clearly not acceptable. With the emergence of new copyright-protected objects on the one hand, and the increase of dynamic competition on the other hand, it is likely that the copyright-competition interaction cases will occur more often. Hence, the need for change is imminent. This chapter provides a solution on how to approach and settle the situations of the interaction between the exercise of copyright and competition rules on prohibited agreements. In any case, one must have in mind that the exercise of copyright only exceptionally infringes competition rules on prohibited agreements, particularly given the vast number of exonerations provided by competition rules on prohibited agreements and the specific approach required for assessing the exercise of copyright from the perspective of competition law.

References

Almunia J (2013) Speech - Intellectual property and competition policy. In: 8th IP Summit 2013, December 9, 2013, Paris. https://ec.europa.eu/commission/presscorner/detail/en/SPEECH_13_1042. Accessed 22 Oct 2024

Anderman S, Schmidt H (2019) EU competition law and intellectual property rights: the regulation of innovation, 3rd edn. Oxford University Press, Oxford

Anderson (2021) International Report. In: Kobel P, Kilpatrick B, Kobel P, Këllezi P (eds) Competition law analysis of price and non-price discrimination & abusive IP based legal proceedings. Springer, Cham, pp 317–333

Benabou VL (2009) European Competition Law and Copyright: where do we stand? Where do we go? In: Derclaye E (ed) Research handbook on the future of EU copyright. Edward Elgar Publishing, Cheltenham, pp 543–566

Bowman WS (1973) Patent and antitrust law: a legal and economic appraisal. University of Chicago Press, Chicago

Brison F (2005) Application of the essential facilities theory to intellectual property: comparative analysis - a European approach. In: Exploring the sources of copyright. ALAI Congress, Paris, 18–21 Sept 2005, pp 596–605

Choi YS, Heinemann A (2016) Restrictions of competition law in licensing agreements: the worldwide convergence of competition laws and policies in the field of intellectual property. Eur Bus Org Law Rev 17(3):405–422

Colino SM (2019) Competition law of the EU and UK, 8th edn. Oxford University Press, Oxford

Czapracka K (2009) Intellectual property and the limits of antitrust: a comparative study of US and EU approaches. Edward Elgar Publishing Ltd, Cheltenham, UK

Daum F (2010) Copyright, competition law, and free movement of goods. In: von Lewinski S, Walter MM (eds) European copyright law: a commentary. Oxford University Press, Oxford, pp 50–70

Dreier T (2010) Regulating competition by limitations and exceptions. In: Torremans P (ed) Copyright law: a handbook of contemporary research. Edward Elgar Publishing, pp 232–254

Drexl J (2008) Is there a 'more economic approach' to intellectual property and competition law? In: Drexl J (ed) Research handbook on intellectual property and competition law. Max Planck Institute for Innovation and Competition, Munich, pp 27–53

Favale M (2021) The role of the Court of Justice in the development of EU copyright law: an empirical experience. In: Stamatoudi I, Torremans P (eds) EU copyright law: a commentary, 2nd edn. Edward Elgar Publishing, Cheltenham, pp 1073–1086

Fikentscher W (1995) Urhebervertragsrecht und Kartellreht. In: Beier FK, Götting H-P, Lehmann M, Moufang R (eds) Urhebervertragsrecht: Festgabe für Gerhard Schricker zum 60. Verlag C.H. Beck, Geburtstag, pp 149–192

Fikentscher W (1996) The draft international antitrust code (DIAC) in the context of international technological integration - the institutional and jurisdictional architecture. Chicago-Kent Law Rev 72(2):533–543

Fikentscher W, Heinemann A, Kunz-Hallstein HP (1995) Das Kartellrecht des Immaterialgüterschutzes im Draft International Antitrust Code. GRUR International, pp 757–765

Fligstein N, Mara-Drita I (1996) How to make a market: reflections on the attempt to create a single market in the European Union. Am J Sociol 102(1):1–33

Ghidini G (2006) Intellectual property and competition law: the innovation nexus. Edward Elgar Publishing, Cheltenham UK, Northampton, MA, USA

Ginsburg DH, Geradin D, Klovers K (2019) Antitrust and intellectual property in the United States and the European Union. In: Muscolo G, Tavassi M (eds) The interplay between competition law and intellectual property. Wolters Kluwer, Alphen aan den Rijn, pp 99–119

Ginsburg JC (2017) The role of the author in copyright. In: Okediji RL (ed) Copyright law in an age of limitations and exceptions. Cambridge University Press, New York, pp 60–84

Ginsburg JC, Treppoz, E (2015) international copyright law: U.S. and EU perspectives - text and cases. Edward Elgar Publishing, Cheltenham

Gliha I (2006) Pravo na autorskim djelima nastalim u radnom odnosu i po narudžbi. In: Parać Z, Petrović S, Miladin P, Markovinović H, Hrabar D (eds) Liber Amicorum Jakša Barbić. Pravni faukultet u Zagrebu, Zagreb, pp 775–820

Goldstein P (1989) Copyright, vol I. Little, Brown and Company, Boston

Goldstein P, Hugenholtz PB (2021) International copyright: principles, law and practice, 4th edn. Oxford University Press, Oxford

Hay P, Oldekop D (1977) EMI/CBS and the rest of the world: trademark rights and the European communities. Am J Comp Law 25(1):120–151

Heinemann A (2002) Immaterialgüterschutz in der Wettbewerbsordnung. Mohr-Siebeck, Tübingen

Hojnik J (2013) De Minimis rule within the EU internal market freedoms: towards a more mature and legitimate market? Eur J Legal Stud 6(1):25–45

Hugenholtz PB, Okediji RL (2008) Conceiving an international instrument on limitations and exceptions to copyright. Institute for Information Law, University of Amsterdam, University of Minnesota, Law School, final report, 6 March 2008. https://www.opensocietyfoundations.org/publications/conceiving-international-instrument-limitations-and-exceptions-copyright. Accessed 22 Oct 2024

Ibáñez Colomo P (2018) The shaping of EU competition law. Cambridge University Press, Cambridge

Kaplow L (1984) The patent-antitrust intersection: a reappraisal. Harv Law Rev 97:1813–1897

Käseberg T (2012) Intellectual property, antitrust and cumulative innovation in the EU and the US, Hart studies in competition law. Hart Publishing

Keeling DT (2003) Intellectual property rights in EU law volume I - free movement and competition law. Oxford University Press, Oxford

Korah V (2002) The interface between intellectual property and antitrust: the european experience. Antitrust Law J 69(3):801–839

Korah V (2006) Intellectual property rights and the EC competition rules. Hart Publishing, Oxford and Portland

Kostecka-Jurczyk D (2012) Determination of the relevant market as a criterion of assessment of concertation effects in the practice of antitrust authorities. Wroclaw Rev Law Adm Econ 2(2): 129–138

Lamping M (2015) Refusal to licence as an abuse of market dominance: from commercial solvents to microsoft. In: Hilty RM, Liu K-C (eds) Compulsory licensing: practical experiences and ways forward. Springer, Heidelberg, pp 121–145

Ławniczak N (2008) A European perspective. In: Lidgard HH, Atik J (eds) The intersection of IPR and competition law: studies of recent developments in European and U.S. law. Chapter II: IPR, Parallel Trade and Competition. Intellecta docysus, Gothenburg, pp 62–76

Lewis TR, Yao DA (1995) Some reflections on the antitrust treatment of intellectual property. Antitrust Law J 63(2):603–619

Lianos I, Dreyfuss RC (2013) New challenges in the intersection of intellectual property rights with competition law: a view from Europe and the United States. UCL Centre for Law, Economics and Society, CLES 4/2013, April 2013. https://www.ucl.ac.uk/cles/sites/cles/files/cles-4-2013 new.pdf. Accessed 22 Oct 2024

Max Planck Institute for Intellectual Property and Competition Law, Munich (2013) Report: Copyright, Competition and Development. December 2013. https://www.ip.mpg.de/fileadmin/ipmpg/content/forschung_aktuell/02_copyright_competition/report_copyright-competition-development_december-2013.pdf. Accessed 22 Oct 2024

Moretalmans K (2001) Towards convergence in the application of the rules on free movement and on competition? Common Mark Law Rev 38(3):613–649

Myrick RE (1992) Will intellectual property on technology still be viable in a unitary market. Eur Intell Prop Rev 14(9):298–304

OECD (1995) Competition policy and film distribution. Policy Roundtables

Petit N (2017) The antitrust and intellectual property intersection in European Union law. In: Blair RD, Sokol DD (eds) Handbook of antitrust, intellectual property and high tech. Cambridge University Press, Cambridge, pp 92–11

Ramalho A (2016) The competence of the European Union in copyright lawmaking: a normative perspective of EU powers for copyright harmonization. Springer, Cham

Rognstad OA (2008) The exhaustion/competition interface in EC law - is there room for holistic approach? In: Drexl J (ed) Research handbook on intellectual property and competition law. Max Planck Institute for Innovation and Competition, Munich, pp 427–450

Schmidt C (2010) Refusal to license intellectual property rights as abuse of dominance, political economics competition and regulation, vol 11. Peter Lang GmbH Internationaler Verlag der Wissenschaften, Frankfurt am Main

Schumpeter JR (2003) Capitalism, socialism and democracy. Routledge, London

Skone James EP, Mummery J, Rayner James JE, Garnett KM, Nimmer D, Silman S, Skone James R (1991) Copinger and Skone James on Copyright. Sweet & Maxwell, London

Temple Lang J (2010) European competition law and intellectual property rights—a new analysis, ERA Forum 11(3): 411–437 https://doi.org/10.1007/s12027-010-0157-9. Accessed 22 Oct 2024

Tritton G (1994) Articles 30 and 36 and intellectual property: is the jurisprudence of the ECJ now of an ideal standard? Eur Intell Prop Rev 16(10):422–428

Vogel L (2020) European competition law, 3rd edn. LawLex, Bruylant

von Lewinski S (2008) International copyright law and policy. Oxford University Press, Oxford

Whish R, Bailey D (2021) Competition law, 10th edn. Oxford University Press, Oxford

Zenger H, Walker M (2012) Theories of harm in European competition law: a progress report. In: Bourgeois J, Waelbroeck D (eds) Ten years of effects-based approach in EU competition law: state of play and perspectives. GCLC Annual Conference Series, Bruylant, pp 185–209

Chapter 5
The Interaction Between Copyright and Competition Rules on Abuse of Dominance

The other common copyright-competition interaction issue is refusal to license copyright falling under the scope of the competition rules on abuse of a dominant position. This chapter provides a critical analysis of the relevant case law and doctrine.

This research identified several different approaches to the copyright-competition interaction issue: the inherency theory, the exceptional circumstances doctrine, the theory of complementarity, the theory of absolutism and the standard competition law approach in copyright matters. Each approach has a certain rationale for being discussed in the context of this subject. However, none of the indicated approaches entirely provides a coherent and sustainable foundation for dealing with the copyright-competition interaction issue. In the application of those approaches, many problems occur, often stemming from the failure to respect the fundamentals of copyright law and competition law. Commonly, copyright is not distinguished from other intellectual property rights, leading to a conflation of the legal and economic characteristics as well as the effects of particular intellectual property rights. Thus, sometimes, the characteristics of patents are being attributed to other intellectual property rights, disregarding the particularities of those other rights. This is especially problematic for copyright, which, as a non-industrial property right, has a distinct non-economic aspect. Additionally, the indicated approaches commonly overlook the economic components present in copyright-competition interaction issues. Despite the EU's prevailing tendency toward a 'more economic approach' with an emphasis on dynamic efficiency, it seems that economic analysis is often superficially performed.

Considering the flaws of the identified approaches based on the conducted analysis, this chapter provides a new approach to the copyright-competition interaction issue in cases of refusal to license copyright under competition rules on abuse of a dominant position while respecting the fundamental principles of copyright law and competition law.

D. Gliha, *The Copyright-Competition Interaction within the EU*,
https://doi.org/10.1007/978-3-031-94402-4_5

5.1 Introduction

Copyright holders are free to exercise their rights over individual copyright-protected work—whether as authors or successive rights holders. Sometimes copyright holders manage to capitalise on the copyright they hold to develop a business of immense market power. In some cases, such a position can be obtained through a successful competition process, while in others, which seems to be more often the case in recent dynamic times, it can be achieved by having creative and original business models to create whole new markets, in which they have a competitive head start as pioneers.

Competition law is highly cautious of undertakings holding a dominant position. Paragraph 1, Article 102, of the Treaty on the Functioning of the European Union (TFEU) lays down:

> Any abuse by one or more undertakings of a dominant position within the internal market or in a substantial part of it shall be prohibited as incompatible with the internal market in so far as it may affect trade between Member States.

Thus, competition law requires the special responsibility of undertakings holding a dominant position to act in accordance with competition rules in the market. Unlike in Article 101 TFEU, in Article 102 TFEU, there is no requirement for an agreement or a second player. The focus is on the individual undertaking with an extremely high market share having a dominant position in a relevant market. Also, there is no general exemption rule, as provided in Paragraph 3, Article 101, TFEU, nor are there block exemptions, so the possibility of justification for anti-competitive behaviour is hugely narrowed.

Concerning the copyright-competition interaction issue, individual authors and most other copyright holders are generally safe from the scrutiny of Article 102 TFEU. The scrutiny of competition rules on abuse of dominance is reserved only for strong market players. Hence, there are not many cases involving abuse of dominance, particularly those concerning copyright-competition interaction. Nevertheless, the cases that do arise are often very significant. The best examples are probably *Magill* and *Microsoft*. However, in the current dynamic times of originality, creativity and innovation, one can imagine that more and more such cases may arise, particularly in today's era of platforms and digital models, where it has become common for new markets to emerge daily, bringing more undertakings into the position of dominance within their respective sectors.

5.2 Theoretical Foundations and Different Approaches to the Issue of Refusal to License Copyright as an Abuse of a Dominant Position

In the context of abuse of dominance and Article 102 TFEU, one of the main issues of the copyright-competition interaction is the refusal to license copyright. Not many cases have been brought before EU competent bodies concerning this specific issue, although those that were adjudicated drew significant attention. The most remarkable development in this particular field came during the 1990s and 2000s with the *Magill*, *IMS Health* and *Microsoft* cases. Mainly during the first decade of the 2000s, there were intense discussions on this matter in the academic society. However, discussions have gradually lessened, and still, no adequate solutions have been provided on how to approach this specific issue.

From existing case law and academic research, several approaches can be identified. Through soft law, the Commission has also contributed to the overall understanding of the issue of refusal to license and competition rules. Taking all into consideration, it seems that the exceptional circumstances doctrine has left the most significant mark in practice and theory, although other approaches were also present in theory and practice. This research identified the following approaches in relation to the issue of refusal to license as an abuse of dominance:

1. The inherency theory
2. The exceptional circumstances doctrine
3. The complementarity theory
4. The theory of absolutism
5. The standard competition law approach in copyright matters

All of the recognised approaches seem to be too abstract and not comprehensive; the copyright element was often neglected, while economic factors were not adequately included. Thus, to properly address the specific issue of interaction between the exercise of copyright and competition rules on dominance, it is necessary to discuss this issue further. Prior findings within this field should serve as a basis for further development. However, for a comprehensive approach, the focus should primarily be on the particularities of copyright and on economic analysis. A balance must be struck between the effects of copyright and the objectives of competition law.

5.2.1 The Inherency Theory

Unlike in cases dealing with the exercise of economic copyright rights under Article 101 TFEU (see *supra*, Sect. 4.2.1), the influence of the inherency theory was not as present in cases concerning the refusal to license copyright under Article 102 TFEU. The two main inherency-related cases dealing with refusal to license—*CICRA v Renault*[1] and *Volvo v Veng*[2]—concerned design rights. However, since most of the reasoning in the two cases refers to intellectual property (exclusive rights) in general, their findings apply to cases involving other intellectual property rights (IPRs).

[1]Judgment of 5 October 1988, *Consorzio italiano della componentistica di ricambio per autoveicoli and Maxicar v Régie nationale des usines Renault*, C-53/87, EU:C:1988:472.

[2]Judgment of 5 October 1988, *AB Volvo v Erik Veng (UK) Ltd*, C-238/87, EU:C:1988:477.

Hence, they are worth discussing in the context of refusal to license copyright as an abuse of a dominant position.

Both cases involved similar matters, though with some minor factual differences. In *CICRA v Renault*, Renault refused to allow independent repairers to manufacture and market spare parts protected by design rights. In *Volvo v Veng*, Volvo refused to allow the unauthorised import of automobile spare parts, also protected by design rights. The Court of Justice of the European Union (CJEU) decided both cases in a uniform way on the same day.

In the mentioned cases, the CJEU produced several seminal findings. Firstly, the Court found that 'the determination of the conditions and procedures under which protection of designs and models is granted is a matter for national rules. It is thus for the national legislature to determine which products are to benefit from protection, even where they form part of a unit which is already protected as such.'[3] Secondly, 'the right of the proprietor of a protected design to prevent third parties from manufacturing and selling or importing, without its consent, products incorporating the design constitutes the very subject-matter of his exclusive right. It follows that an obligation imposed upon the proprietor of a protected design to grant to third parties, even in return for a reasonable royalty, a license for the supply of products incorporating the design would lead to the proprietor thereof being deprived of the substance of his exclusive right, and that a refusal to grant such a license cannot in itself constitute an abuse of a dominant position.'[4] Thirdly, the 'mere fact of securing the benefit of an exclusive right granted by law, the effect of which is to enable the manufacture and sale of protected products by unauthorised third parties to be prevented, cannot be regarded as an abusive method of eliminating competition'.[5] Fourthly, the CJEU gave an example where the exercise of the exclusive right 'may be prohibited by Article 86 if it involves/gives rise, on the part of an undertaking holding a dominant position, certain abusive conduct such as the arbitrary refusal to supply spare parts to independent repairers, the fixing of prices for spare parts at an unfair level or a decision no longer to produce spare parts for a particular model even though many cars of that model are still in circulation, provided that such conduct is liable to affect trade between Member States'.[6]

From the discussed cases, it can be noted that the CJEU applied the existence v. exercise dichotomy. In essence, the CJEU stated that the mere fact of obtaining an

[3] Judgment of 5 October 1988, *AB Volvo v Erik Veng (UK) Ltd*, C-238/87, EU:C:1988:477, para. 7.

[4] Judgment of 5 October 1988, *AB Volvo v Erik Veng (UK) Ltd*, C-238/87, EU:C:1988:477, para. 8.

[5] Judgment of 5 October 1988, *Consorzio italiano della componentistica di ricambio per autoveicoli and Maxicar v Régie nationale des usines Renault*, C-53/87, EU:C:1988:472, para. 15; Judgment of 5 October 1988, *AB Volvo v Erik Veng (UK) Ltd*, C-238/87, EU:C:1988:477, para. 9.

[6] Judgment of 5 October 1988, *Consorzio italiano della componentistica di ricambio per autoveicoli and Maxicar v Régie nationale des usines Renault*, C-53/87, EU:C:1988:472, para. 16. In *Volvo v Veng*, the CJEU explicitly noted that no abusive conduct can be found in the present case. Judgment of 5 October 1988, *AB Volvo v Erik Veng (UK) Ltd*, C-238/87, EU:C:1988:477, para. 10.

intellectual property right does not constitute an abuse of a dominant position within the meaning of Article 102 TFEU.[7] However, the exercise of an intellectual property right may be prohibited if it involves certain abusive conduct. In addition to that, the CJEU also used some inherency standards to support its argumentation, such as the specific subject matter of individual intellectual property rights.[8]

Criticism of the inherency concepts has already been presented in the previous chapter concerning the exercise of copyright under Article 101 TFEU (see *supra*, Sect. 4.2.1), and it is also applicable to the issue of refusal to license copyright under Article 102 TFEU. Although the inherency-influenced reasoning is too abstract and has little practical value, in *CICRA v Renault* and *Volvo v Veng*, the CJEU kept it simple, which ultimately led to plausible preliminary rulings. However, regardless of the fact that the CJEU even provided examples of when an exercise of a particular intellectual property right can cause an abuse of a dominant position, the practical value of such an interpretation is highly doubtful. For that reason, it is not surprising that the CJEU eventually gave up using inherency concepts in cases concerning the refusal to license as an abuse of a dominant position.

The Court of First Instance (CFI) also used the inherency theory to uphold the Commission's decisions in the *Magill* cases. The cases concerned the conduct of British and Irish television broadcasters holding copyright rights over their weekly schedule, which prevented a third party from creating a novel, comprehensive television magazine covering all channels.[9] In all three cases, the CFI based its reasoning on an analogy with the rules governing the free movement of goods and the standard of the essential function of copyright.[10]

However, this reasoning of the CFI was rejected in the later phase. In his Opinion, Advocate General (AG) Gulmann firmly criticised the CFI's reasoning,[11] although he ultimately adhered to the core principles of the inherency theory. AG Gulmann

---

[7] See also Judgment of 23 May 1978, *Hoffmann-La Roche & Co. AG v Centrafarm Vertriebsgesellschaft Pharmazeutischer Erzeugnisse mbH*, C-102/77, EU:C:1978:108, para. 16.

[8] Also, in *Hoffmann-La Roche v Centrafarm*, the Court held that the exercise of intellectual property rights, in accordance with Article 36 TFEU, was not in itself contrary to competition rules on abuse of dominance unless used as 'an instrument for the abuse' of a dominant position. Judgment of 23 May 1978, *Hoffmann-La Roche & Co. AG v Centrafarm Vertriebsgesellschaft Pharmazeutischer Erzeugnisse mbH*, C-102/77, EU:C:1978:108, para. 16.

[9] Judgment of 10 July 1991, *RTE v Commission*, T-69/89, EU:T:1991:39; Judgment of 10 July 1991, *BBC v Commission*, T-70/89, EU:T:1991:40; Judgment of 10 July 1991, *ITP v Commission*, EU:T:1991:41. The Commission found the broadcaster's conduct as an abuse of dominant position and an infringement of Article 102 TFEU.

[10] Judgment of 10 July 1991, *RTE v Commission*, T-69/89, EU:T:1991:39, paras. 67–75; Judgment of 10 July 1991, *BBC v Commission*, T-70/89, EU:T:1991:40, paras. 54–63; Judgment of 10 July 1991, *ITP v Commission*, EU:T:1991:41, paras. 52–60.

[11] Opinion of Advocate General Gulmann of 1 June 1994, *RTE and ITP v Commission*, Joined Cases C-241/91 P and C-242/91 P, EU:C:1994:210.

emphasised the importance of the specific subject matter of copyright, thus acknowledging the subject-specific matter as an expression of the reasoning that for each intellectual property right, it is possible to identify a number of core rights that the holder of that right enjoys under national law.[12] He criticised the use of the existence v. exercise dichotomy, arguing that this dichotomy has no independent significance for resolving specific questions of delimitation and is basically an expression of the same conceptual approach.[13] According to AG Gulmann, the specific subject matter of copyright must be taken as a starting point when considering cases on refusal to license as an abuse of a dominant position.[14] However, he further indicated that the Court's application of the specific subject matter to the free movement of goods and undistorted competition, where the definition of the specific subject matter is absolute, is a misconception. Namely, he argued that the Court wrongly implied that any exercise of rights falling within the specific subject matter enjoys immunity from the Treaty provisions. According to AG Gulman, such interpretation raises problems with an explanation of field of interference of copyright with competition law rules.[15] If the definition of a specific subject matter is not absolute, it may reasonably be assumed that Article 102 TFEU can also affect the rights that, in principle, fall within the specific subject matter if those rights are exercised under special circumstances. Thus, AG Gulmann observes the restrictions imposed pursuant to Article 102 TFEU as exceptions from interference with the specific subject matter of the intellectual property right in question and not as specifying the scope of the specific subject matter.[16] Interestingly, already in his Opinion, AG Gulmann noted special circumstances that substantially correspond to the exceptional circumstances

---

[12] See Opinion of Advocate General Gulmann of 1 June 1994, *RTE and ITP v Commission*, Joined Cases C-241/91 P and C-242/91 P, EU:C:1994:210, para. 28.

According to AG Gulmann, the specific subject matter of copyright in practice and doctrine is synonymously referred to also as the actual substance of copyright, the essential rights of the copyright proprietor. See *Opinion of Advocate General Gulmann of 1 June 1994, RTE and ITP v Commission*, Joined Cases C-241/91 P and C-242/91 P, EU:C:1994:210, para. 32.

[13] See Opinion of Advocate General Gulmann of 1 June 1994, *RTE and ITP v Commission*, Joined Cases C-241/91 P and C-242/91 P, EU:C:1994:210, para. 31.

[14] See Opinion of Advocate General Gulmann of 1 June 1994, *RTE and ITP v Commission*, Joined Cases C-241/91 P and C-242/91 P, EU:C:1994:210, para. 32.

[15] See Opinion of Advocate General Gulmann of 1 June 1994, *RTE and ITP v Commission*, Joined Cases C-241/91 P and C-242/91 P, EU:C:1994:210, paras. 45, 46, 51.

However, in introductory remarks, AG Gulmann acknowledges that, in general, 'copyright laws give copyright owners the right to restrict competition'; Opinion of Advocate General Gulmann of 1 June 1994, *RTE and ITP v Commission*, Joined Cases C-241/91 P and C-242/91 P, EU:C:1994:210, para. 11.

[16] See Opinion of Advocate General Gulmann of 1 June 1994, *RTE and ITP v Commission*, Joined Cases C-241/91 P and C-242/91 P, EU:C:1994:210, paras. 51, 53.

AG Gulmann also elaborated that including competition law in the definition of the essential function of copyright aims was wrong, considering that such a definition would imply that competition rule aims outweigh copyright. See CJEU, Opinion of Advocate General Gulmann of 1 June 1994, *RTE and ITP v Commission*, Joined Cases C-241/91 P and C-242/91 P, EU:C:1994:210, paras. 67, 70.

concept described in later case law. Such exceptional circumstances were considered to be a guiding standard in determining abusive behaviour—circumstances 'in connection with a refusal to license that it can no longer be regarded as a refusal to license in itself'.[17]

Nevertheless, on appeal, the CJEU refused to follow AG Gulmann's approach and reviewed the cases through the lens of specific subject matter and the essential function of copyright. Still, the CJEU (briefly) acknowledged the specific (exceptional) circumstances concept as the basis for determining potential abuse of a dominant position. Had the CJEU decided to rely on the inherency-related specific subject matter concept, as advised by AG Gulmann, it is likely that ultimately no abuse would have been determined.[18] Many commentators see the CJEU's decision in *Magill* as the definite end of the inherency theory, at least in cases concerning the exercise of a particular intellectual property right in interaction with competition rules.[19]

5.2.2 *The Exceptional Circumstances Doctrine*

5.2.2.1 General

The exceptional circumstances doctrine seems to have emerged as a reaction to the inherency theory. As already indicated above, the development of the exceptional circumstances doctrine began with AG Gulmann's opinion in *Magill* and was later embraced by the CJEU in its decision in *Magill*.[20] Subsequently, the CJEU further advanced the exceptional circumstances doctrine, primarily through the cases of *IMS Health*[21] and *Microsoft*.[22]

The exceptional circumstances doctrine has heavily influenced the copyright-competition issue, in particular with regard to the exercise of copyright under Article 102 TFEU. As was already noted before (see *supra, Ch 4, Section II.2*), the exceptional circumstances doctrine applies a specific criteria for evaluating copyright-related conduct under competition law. Unlike the standard competition assessment applied to non-IPR cases, this doctrine permits competition liability only exceptionally—as an exception of an exception. Thus, only in exceptional circumstances can conduct involving the exercise of economic copyright rights

---

[17] See Opinion of Advocate General Gulmann of 1 June 1994, *RTE and ITP v Commission*, Joined Cases C-241/91 P and C-242/91 P, EU:C:1994:210, paras. 40, 80–87.

[18] See also Czapracka (2009), p. 81.

[19] See Petit (2017), p. 98.

[20] Judgment of 6 April 1995, *RTE and ITP v Commission*, Joined Cases C-241/91 P and C-242/91 P, ECLI:EU:C:1995:98.

[21] Judgment of 29 April 2004, *IMS Health*, C-418/01, EU:C:2004:257.

[22] Judgment of 17 September 2007, *Microsoft v Commission*, T-201/04, EU:T:2007:289.

infringe competition rules on abuse of dominance. Otherwise, the exercise of copyright is deemed presumptively lawful from the perspective of competition law.

The CJEU discussed what the exceptional circumstance are through its case law, mainly when dealing with cases related to refusal to license under Article 102 TFEU.

5.2.2.2 Case Law Related to Exceptional Circumstances

5.2.2.2.1 *Magill*: Commencement of the Exceptional Circumstances Doctrine

Magill is the cornerstone case for the exceptional circumstances doctrine. After the CJEU rejected the inherency-related reasoning from the CFI decision and AG Gulmann's Opinion, this meant the end of the inherency-related concepts and the beginning of the exceptional circumstances doctrine as the leading approach to copyright-competition interaction matters. Interestingly, through different stages of the procedure, *Magill* also showed how three different approaches applied to the same factsheet could produce different results.

In his Opinion, AG Gulmann identified the existence of special circumstances as the critical question when determining whether Article 102 could even be applied to cases involving refusal to license copyright.[23] Although the CJEU did not follow the approach advocated by AG Gulmann, it did use the concept of special circumstances, though under the concept of exceptional circumstances. The CJEU noted that '(...) the exercise of an exclusive right by the proprietor may, in exceptional circumstances, involve abusive conduct'.[24] However, the issue with the CJEU's interpretation in *Magill* was the lack of convincing and comprehensive

---

[23] For instance, AG Gulmann states:

> The question is whether there may exist such special circumstances in connection with a refusal to license that it can no longer be regarded as a refusal to license in itself. If Article 86 can apply where the dominant undertaking has done no more than refuse to grant licences, but where there were special circumstances in connection with the refusal to license, the position will be that the infringement of Article 86 can be terminated only by granting licences.

Opinion of Advocate General Gulmann of 1 June 1994, *RTE and ITP v Commission*, Joined Cases C-241/91 P and C-242/91 P, EU:C:1994:210, para. 40:

'(...) Article 86 can also affect rights which are in principle within the specific subject-matter if those rights are exercised in special circumstances.' *Ibid.*, para. 51.

'It follows that both in Article 86 analysis and in Articles 30 and 36 analysis the Court must further specify whether rights which are in principle within the specific subject-matter are exercised in such special circumstances that they create unacceptable hindrances to undistorted competition or the free movement of goods.' *Ibid.*, para. 62.

'The key question in these cases is, of course, when there exist such special circumstances.' *Ibid.*, para. 63.

[24] Judgment of 6 April 1995, *RTE and ITP v Commission*, Joined Cases C-241/91 P and C-242/91 P, ECLI:EU:C:1995:98, para. 50.

argumentation. The Court merely stated that the undertakings in a dominant position prevented the appearance of a new product—the product which the intellectual property owner does not offer and for which there is a potential demand;[25] that there was no justification for such a refusal;[26] and that the undertakings reserved the secondary market to themselves by excluding all competition on that market.[27] Thus, the CJEU plainly identified the conditions establishing the exceptional circumstances situation, however without providing any further explanation.

With such flawed reasoning, it seems that the CJEU indeed took a formalistic approach by completely neglecting a discussion on the issue of the specific subject matter of copyright and the determination of exceptional circumstances. Also, it did not perform any quality economic analysis, which is needed for a proper and comprehensive evaluation of competition. Instead of meticulously elaborating on the new approach introduced for refusal to license cases, with its superficial reasoning in its judgment in *Magill*, the CJEU opened even more issues than there had ever been before.[28]

5.2.2.2.2 *IMS Health*: Development of the Exceptional Circumstances Doctrine

Almost a decade after *Magill*, the CJEU had another opportunity, through the *IMS Health* case, to settle the unresolved issues left after its first attempt to implement the exceptional circumstances concept as the basis for dealing with cases concerning refusal to license copyright under Article 102 TFEU. The key issues that were left open after *Magill* were whether the conditions should be cumulatively satisfied to constitute an exceptional circumstances situation and whether the list of conditions is exhaustive or non-exhaustive. Also, the gist of the particular conditions was left undefined since they had merely been noted without any further elaboration.

However, before going further into the *IMS Health* case, it should be noted that the CJEU, in the meantime, also decided the *Bronner*[29] case on the basis of the exceptional circumstances doctrine. The *Bronner* case concerned the refusal of a newspaper publisher in a dominant position to include a newspaper publisher with a

---

[25] Judgment of 6 April 1995, *RTE and ITP v Commission*, Joined Cases C-241/91 P and C-242/91 P, ECLI:EU:C:1995:98, para. 54.

[26] Judgment of 6 April 1995, *RTE and ITP v Commission*, Joined Cases C-241/91 P and C-242/91 P, ECLI:EU:C:1995:98, para. 55.

[27] Judgment of 6 April 1995, *RTE and ITP v Commission*, Joined Cases C-241/91 P and C-242/91 P, ECLI:EU:C:1995:98, para. 56.

[28] See Czapracka (2009), pp. 79–80.

[29] Judgment of 26 November 1998, *Oscar Bronner GmbH & Co. KG v Mediaprint Zeitungs- und Zeitschriftenverlag GmbH & Co. KG, Mediaprint Zeitungsvertriebsgesellschaft mbH & Co. KG and Mediaprint Anzeigengesellschaft mbH & Co. KG*, C-7/97, EU:C:1998:569.

smaller share in the market in its home-delivery scheme service in return for a reasonable remuneration. The case did not directly involve any intellectual property right, which, for some commentators, supports the view that the exceptional circumstances doctrine is not IPR specific.[30] Nevertheless, in *Bronner*, the CJEU built its reasoning on the findings from *Magill*[31] and further discussed the exceptional circumstances doctrine.[32] The case is significant since in *IMS Health*, the CJEU often referred to *Bronner* and undoubtedly formed its reasoning on the basis of that case.[33]

It is also noteworthy that, in the meantime, the CFI also endorsed the exceptional circumstances doctrine in *Micro Leader Business*.[34] However, in that case, the CFI did not go into fully assessing what the exceptional circumstances are but merely noted:

> It is clear from the case-law that whilst, as a rule, the enforcement of copyright by its holder, as in the case of the prohibition on importing certain products from outside the Community into a Member State of the Community, is not in itself a breach of Article 86 of the Treaty, such enforcement may, in exceptional circumstances, involve abusive conduct.[35]

---

[30] However, through its reasoning, the CJEU questions the possibility of the direct applicability of case law on the exercise of intellectual property rights to the exercise of any property rights whatsoever. Moreover, in his Opinion, AG Jacobs notes the specificity of competition cases when dealing with intellectual property rights. See Judgment of 26 November 1998, *Oscar Bronner GmbH & Co. KG v Mediaprint Zeitungs- und Zeitschriftenverlag GmbH & Co. KG, Mediaprint Zeitungsvertriebsgesellschaft mbH & Co. KG and Mediaprint Anzeigengesellschaft mbH & Co. KG*, C-7/97, EU:C:1998:569, para. 41; Opinion of Advocate General Jacobs of 28 May 1998, *Bronner*, C-7/97, EU:C:1998:264, paras. 62–64.

[31] Judgment of 26 November 1998, *Oscar Bronner GmbH & Co. KG v Mediaprint Zeitungs- und Zeitschriftenverlag GmbH & Co. KG, Mediaprint Zeitungsvertriebsgesellschaft mbH & Co. KG and Mediaprint Anzeigengesellschaft mbH & Co. KG*, C-7/97, EU:C:1998:569, paras. 40–41.

[32] In *Bronner*, the CJEU concluded that for the indispensability criteria, 'it is not enough to argue that it is not economically viable by reason of the small circulation of the daily newspaper or newspaper to be distributed. For such access to be capable of being regarded as indispensable, it would be necessary at the very least to establish (…) that it is not economically viable to create a second home delivery scheme for the distribution of daily newspapers with a circulation comparable to that of the daily newspapers distributed by the existing scheme.' Therefore, the CJEU did not find an abuse of dominant position in the case. Judgment of 26 November 1998, *Oscar Bronner GmbH & Co. KG v Mediaprint Zeitungs- und Zeitschriftenverlag GmbH & Co. KG, Mediaprint Zeitungsvertriebsgesellschaft mbH & Co. KG and Mediaprint Anzeigengesellschaft mbH & Co. KG*, C-7/97, EU:C:1998:569, paras. 45–47.

Notably, the CJEU based its reasoning mostly on the indispensability criterion, without discussing the new product criterion.

[33] See, for instance, Judgment of 29 April 2004, *IMS Health*, C-418/01, EU:C:2004:257, paras. 28, 37, 40 and 41.

[34] Judgment of 16 December 1999, *Micro Leader Business v Commission of the European Communities*, T-198/98, EU:T:1999:341.

[35] Judgment of 16 December 1999, *Micro Leader Business v Commission of the European Communities*, T-198/98, EU:T:1999:341, para. 56.

In the case in question, concerning the Microsoft's attempt to restrict the Canadian wholesaler Micro Leader Business from exporting copyright-protected computer software marketed in Canada to France, the CFI annulled the Commission's decision (rejecting the Micro Leader Business's complaint) due to a lack of assessment.

IMS Health involved a refusal to license rights to a copyright-protected database structure, a system presenting regional pharmaceutical sales data in Germany. In its reasoning, the CJEU clearly acknowledged the exceptional circumstances doctrine established in *Magill* and stated: '(...) exercise of an exclusive right by the owner may, in exceptional circumstance, involve abusive conduct'.[36] To constitute exceptional circumstances, the CJEU concluded that the refusal by an undertaking holding a copyright must concern a product or service indispensable for carrying on a particular business, that the refusal is preventing the emergence of a new product for which there is a potential consumer demand, that it is unjustified and that the refusal must be such as to exclude any competition in a secondary market.[37] The significance of *IMS Health* was that the conditions establishing the exceptional circumstances were elaborated in detail.

Firstly, with regard to the condition concerning indispensability, the CJEU explained that 'it must be determined whether there are products or services which constitute alternative solutions, even if they are less advantageous, and whether there are technical, legal or economic obstacles capable of making it impossible or at least unreasonably difficult for any undertaking seeking to operate in the market to create, possibly in cooperation with other operators, the alternative products or services'.[38]

---

[36] Judgment of 29 April 2004, *IMS Health*, C-418/01, EU:C:2004:257, para. 35.

[37] Judgment of 29 April 2004, *IMS Health*, C-418/01, EU:C:2004:257, para. 38. In *IMS Health*, the CJEU mentions three conditions required to constitute exceptional circumstances. The first condition—indispensability of the protected product or service for carrying on a particular business—is discussed under a separate question and, in the following text, is already included when mentioning refusal: '(...) in order for the refusal by an undertaking which owns a copyright to give access to a product or service indispensable for carrying on a particular business to be treated as abusive, it is sufficient that three cumulative conditions be satisfied, namely, that that refusal is preventing the emergence of a new product for which there is a potential consumer demand, that it is unjustified and such as to exclude any competition on a secondary market'. However, in essence, the indispensability requirement is also one of the exceptional circumstances conditions; hence, there are indeed four and not three conditions.

[38] Judgment of 29 April 2004, *IMS Health*, C-418/01, EU:C:2004:257, para. 28. As cited from the *Bronner* case, such economic obstacles may exist if, at very least, 'the creation of those products or services is not economically viable for production on a scale comparable to that of the undertaking which controls the existing product or service'. Judgment of 29 April 2004, *IMS Health*, C-418/01, EU:C:2004:257, para. 28.

In relation to technical obstacles, the CJEU mentioned that a high level of participation by the pharmaceutical laboratories in the improvement of the copyright-protected 1860 brick structure has created a dependency by users in regard to that structure. Hence, it was likely that those laboratories would have to make exceptional organisational and financial efforts in order to acquire the studies on the regional sales of pharmaceutical products presented on the basis of a structure other than the copyright-protected 1860 brick structure. Consequently, the supplier of the alternative structure might be obliged to offer terms which are such as to rule out any economic viability of business on a scale comparable to that of the undertaking which controls the protected structure. Judgment of 29 April 2004, *IMS Health*, C-418/01, EU:C:2004:257, para. 29; Opinion of Advocate General Tizzano of 2 October 2003, *IMS Health*, C-418/01, EU:C:2003:537, paras. 83–84.

Secondly, with regard to the emergence of a new product, the Court noted that the interest in the protection of free competition may only prevail over the interest in the protection of intellectual property rights and the economic freedom of its owner where refusal to grant a licence prevents the development of a secondary market, to the detriment of consumers.[39] The product protected by an intellectual property right must be indispensable for operating in the secondary market, and the undertaking that requested the licence must intend to produce and offer new products or services not offered by the owner of the intellectual property right and for which there is potential consumer demand.[40]

Thirdly, the Court just noted that justification must be observed through objective considerations.[41] What those objective considerations are, or might be, was not further elaborated.

Fourthly, concerning the likelihood of excluding all competition, the Court relied on the findings from the *Bronner*[42] case and further explained that it is relevant to distinguish between an upstream market, constituted by the product or service, and a secondary downstream market, on which the product or service in question is used for the production of another product or the supply of another service.[43] It is sufficient that a potential market or even a hypothetical market can be identified; however, there must be interconnection between the upstream and downstream markets.[44] 'Such is the case where the products or services are indispensable in order to carry on a particular business and where there is an actual demand for them on the part of undertakings which seek to carry on the business for which they are

[39] Especially from AG Tizzano's opinion, it seems that, according to that view, consumer harm is a key factor in balancing between intellectual property rights and competition rules. See Opinion of Advocate General Tizzano of 2 October 2003, *IMS Health*, C-418/01, EU:C:2003:537, para. 62.

[40] Judgment of 29 April 2004, *IMS Health*, C-418/01, EU:C:2004:257, paras. 48–49. In relation to the new product criterion from *IMS Health*, Hull and Strowel raise concern that, according to such an interpretation, a dominant undertaking might be required to license copyright in its own market as long as the competitor is able to show that it intends to introduce a new product. See Hull and Strowel (2005), p. 687.

[41] Judgment of 29 April 2004, *IMS Health*, C-418/01, EU:C:2004:257, para. 51.

[42] Although the case did not directly involve intellectual property rights, after *Magill*, the CJEU further applied the exceptional circumstances doctrine in the *Bronner* case, which *IMS Health* also refers to. The *Bronner* case concerned the refusal of a newspaper publisher in a dominant position to include a newspaper publisher with a smaller share in the market in its home-delivery scheme service in return for a reasonable remuneration. Judgment of 26 November 1998, *Oscar Bronner GmbH & Co. KG v Mediaprint Zeitungs- und Zeitschriftenverlag GmbH & Co. KG, Mediaprint Zeitungsvertriebsgesellschaft mbH & Co. KG and Mediaprint Anzeigengesellschaft mbH & Co. KG*, C-7/97, EU:C:1998:569. See Judgment of 29 April 2004, *IMS Health*, C-418/01, EU:C:2004:257, para. 40.

[43] Judgment of 26 November 1998, *Oscar Bronner GmbH & Co. KG v Mediaprint Zeitungs- und Zeitschriftenverlag GmbH & Co. KG, Mediaprint Zeitungsvertriebsgesellschaft mbH & Co. KG and Mediaprint Anzeigengesellschaft mbH & Co. KG*, C-7/97, EU:C:1998:569, para. 32.

[44] Judgment of 26 November 1998, *Oscar Bronner GmbH & Co. KG v Mediaprint Zeitungs- und Zeitschriftenverlag GmbH & Co. KG, Mediaprint Zeitungsvertriebsgesellschaft mbH & Co. KG and Mediaprint Anzeigengesellschaft mbH & Co. KG*, C-7/97, EU:C:1998:569, paras. 34–35.

indispensable.'[45] In *Bronner*, it was further explained that 'for such an access to be regarded as indispensable, it would be necessary at the very least to establish (...) that it is not economically viable to create a second home-delivery scheme for the distribution of daily newspapers with a circulation comparable to that of the daily newspapers distributed by the existing scheme'.[46,47] Thus, 'it is determinative that two different stages of production may be identified and that they are interconnected, inasmuch as the upstream product is indispensable for the supply of the downstream product'.[48] If that is the case, then the refusal to license might have the capability of excluding all competition.[49]

In short, after *IMS Health*, the conditions establishing the exceptional circumstances, in their essence, may be identified as four separate conditions: (i) indispensability of the protected product or service for carrying on a particular business, (ii) the new product's condition, (iii) absence of an objective justification and (iv) elimination of competition on the downstream market.

It was left for further discussion to assess whether these conditions are the most appropriate for determining the existence of exceptional circumstances and whether they were sufficiently elaborated within the reasoning of the judgment in *IMS Health*. Also, it was left unclear whether the listed conditions are exhaustive or non-exhaustive and whether they should necessarily be fulfilled cumulatively to

---

[45] Judgment of 29 April 2004, *IMS Health*, C-418/01, EU:C:2004:257, para. 44.

[46] Judgment of 26 November 1998, *Oscar Bronner GmbH & Co. KG v Mediaprint Zeitungs- und Zeitschriftenverlag GmbH & Co. KG, Mediaprint Zeitungsvertriebsgesellschaft mbH & Co. KG and Mediaprint Anzeigengesellschaft mbH & Co. KG*, C-7/97, EU:C:1998:569, para. 46.

[47] Judgment of 26 November 1998, *Oscar Bronner GmbH & Co. KG v Mediaprint Zeitungs- und Zeitschriftenverlag GmbH & Co. KG, Mediaprint Zeitungsvertriebsgesellschaft mbH & Co. KG and Mediaprint Anzeigengesellschaft mbH & Co. KG*, C-7/97, EU:C:1998:569, paras. 41–47.

In relation to that, in his Opinion, AG Tizzano argued:

> Thus, in applying the case-law cited on the refusal to grant a licence I consider it to be sufficient that it is possible to identify a market in upstream inputs, even where the market is a 'potential' one only, in the sense that operating within it is a monopoly undertaking which decides not to market independently the inputs in question (not withstanding that there is an actual demand for them) but to assert exclusive rights over a downstream market by restricting or eliminating all competition on that market.

Opinion of Advocate General Tizzano of 2 October 2003, *IMS Health*, C-418/01, EU:C:2003:537, para. 57.

To support his conclusion, AG Tizzano provides a comparison with an example of the essential facility doctrine, in which a maritime port owner refuses to provide necessary access for maritime transport services. See Opinion of Advocate General Tizzano of 2 October 2003, *IMS Health*, C-418/01, EU:C:2003:537, para. 58.

[48] Judgment of 29 April 2004, *IMS Health*, C-418/01, EU:C:2004:257, para. 45.

[49] It was not discussed before the CJEU whether the conditions were fulfilled or not in the particular case, considering that the case was discussed as a preliminary question. Following the CJEU ruling, in the later procedure, the Regional Court Frankfurt am Main rejected the complaint of IMS Health, arguing that the NDC structure was not an anti-competitive takeover, nor did it interfere with IMS Health's copyright rights. See The Commission, Case COMP/38.044, *National Data Corporation/ IMS Global Services*, C(2009)5222, 25.6.2009.

constitute exceptional circumstances. Namely, the wording of the judgment seems to imply that the conditions should be cumulatively satisfied for the refusal to license copyright to constitute an abuse of a dominant position.[50] However, confusingly, in the same sentence, the CJEU also stated that the conditions are 'sufficient',[51] which, on the other hand, may imply that the list of conditions was non-exhaustive and that, in some other situations, different conditions may be required to form exceptional circumstances.

Besides, some criticism was directed towards the lack of general filters and an insufficient degree of flexibility.[52]

Nonetheless, having in mind that this may still be considered an early phase in the development of the exceptional circumstances doctrine, the interpretation provided in *IMS Health* seems sound and a solid basis for the further development of the issue of refusal to license copyright as an abuse of a dominant position. Thus, in a paper from 2004, Derclaye considered: 'The decision is crucial to the area of competition law dealing with abuses of dominant position by copyright holders as it clarifies the Community courts' rather murky case law in this field. (...) The decision strikes an adequate balance between competition and copyright laws by making a difference between copyright and other forms of property in the conditions required for abuse.'[53]

5.2.2.2.3 *Microsoft*: Deviation from the Exceptional Circumstances Doctrine

After the gradual development of the exceptional circumstances doctrine through prior case law, the *Microsoft*[54] case seemed to be a turning point in the further development of such doctrine. The *Microsoft* case concerned two kinds of conduct that constitute an abuse of a dominant position by Microsoft: (1) refusal to supply and authorise the use of interoperability information and (2) tying of the Windows client PC operating system and Windows Media Player.

In the first stage of the procedure, the Commission found an abuse of a dominant position for both conduct. Interestingly, in deciding on the refusal to supply, the Commission did not base its reasoning on the exceptional circumstances doctrine but instead adopted a new method, 'the entirety of circumstances' analysis.[55] In doing

[50] Some commentators agree that according to *IMS Health*, the conditions should be fulfilled cumulatively to constitute exceptional circumstances. Derclaye (2004), pp. 687, 691.

[51] Judgment of 29 April 2004, *IMS Health*, C-418/01, EU:C:2004:257, para. 38.

[52] There is still an ongoing discussion in theory on how much flexibility a competition rule should optimally allow (from an economic perspective); see Evans and Padilla (2005), pp. 97–122.

[53] Derclaye (2004), p. 687.

[54] Judgment of 17 September 2007, *Microsoft v Commission*, T-201/04, EU:T:2007:289.

[55] The Commission, Case COMP/C-3/37.792, *Microsoft*, C(2004)900 final, 24.3.2004, para. 558. See Ahlborn et al. (2005), p. 1127.

so, the Commission entered uncharted waters and based its reasoning on the effects of dynamic efficiency evoked by the refusal to supply and introduced the incentive balance test.[56] Thus, according to the Commission, to determine whether a refusal to license is abusive, all particular circumstances surrounding that refusal must be taken into consideration. Such circumstances need not necessarily be the same as those identified in *Magill* and *IMS Health*. For the *Microsoft* case, the Commission's analysis was based on three factors: (i) the refusal implicating software interoperability and being part of a general pattern of conduct,[57] (ii) Microsoft's leveraging of its extraordinary power in the client PC operating system market to eliminate competition in the adjacent work group server operating system market[58] and (iii) the disruption of previous supply.[59,60] Ultimately, the Commission's analysis concluded that refusal to license on the part of Microsoft limited technical development, to the prejudice of consumers.

The CFI acknowledged that the refusal at issue constituted a refusal to license an intellectual property right;[61] however, it did not follow the Commission's approach in its decision.[62] The CFI disagreed with the criteria that the Commission used and instead reinstated the approach established in previous case law.[63] Thus, the CFI

---

[56] Microsoft complained that the Commission 'advanced a new and legally defective balancing test invoking public interest in disclosure'. See Case T-201/04: Action brought on 7 June 2004 by Microsoft Corporation against the Commission of the European Communities, OJ C 179, 10.7.2004, pp. 18–19.

The Commission's approach received lots of criticism. Thus, Czapracka comments:

> To my mind the balancing test is flawed, even if we assume that antitrust authorities and judges have the prophetic skills required to apply it.

Czapracka (2009), pp. 91–93.

[57] The Commission, Case COMP/C-3/37.792, *Microsoft*, C(2004)900 final, 24.3.2004, paras. 573–577.

[58] The Commission, Case COMP/C-3/37.792, *Microsoft*, C(2004)900 final, 24.3.2004, paras. 585–692.

[59] The Commission, Case COMP/C-3/37.792, *Microsoft*, C(2004)900 final, 24.3.2004, paras. 578–584.

[60] Judgment of 17 September 2007, *Microsoft v Commission*, T-201/04, EU:T:2007:289, paras. 314–317.

[61] Judgment of 17 September 2007, *Microsoft v Commission*, T-201/04, EU:T:2007:289, paras. 283–290.

[62] See Judgment of 17 September 2007, *Microsoft v Commission*, T-201/04, EU:T:2007:289, paras. 316–336.

[63] However, the CFI did not completely reject the Commission's approach but rather left it as a backup option if one of the established exceptional circumstances conditions was absent. See Judgment of 17 September 2007, *Microsoft v Commission*, T-201/04, EU:T:2007:289, para. 336.

Later on, in the *Microsoft II* case, concerning the penalty payment for not complying with the decision in *Microsoft* (in relation to the pricing of interoperability information), the GC acknowledged the exceptional circumstances approach as the criterion for the determination of an abuse of a dominant position and noted that the conditions from *IMS Health* were fulfilled in *Microsoft*. Judgment of 27 June 2012, *Microsoft Corp. v European Commission*, T-167/08, EU:T:2012:323, paras. 139–140.

based its reasoning on the exceptional circumstances doctrine but in a rather extensive interpretation developed for purposes of the case at hand. In its assessment, the CFI applied the four conditions constituting the exceptional circumstances situation but with a modified interpretation compared to that previously established. Also, with regard to the exhaustivity issue that was left hanging after *IMS Health*, the CFI left room for the identification of further conditions that could form the exceptional circumstances required to determine a refusal to license conduct as an abuse of a dominant position—if one or more of the established conditions was absent.[64] Still, it was left unclear what alternative sets of circumstances would suffice to demonstrate an abusive refusal since in *Microsoft*, the CFI concluded that the four recognised conditions were satisfied—hence, there was no need to further seek other conditions for exceptional circumstances.

Firstly, the CFI discussed the indispensability condition—the indispensable nature of the interoperability information. The indispensability criterion, as established in previous case law, seemed to be one of the stringent conditions forming the exceptional circumstances. Namely, in *IMS Health*, it was elaborated that 'in order to determine whether a product or service is indispensable for enabling an undertaking to carry on business in a particular market, it must be determined whether there are products or services which constitute alternative solutions, even if they are less advantageous, and whether there are technical, legal or economic obstacles capable of making it impossible or at least unreasonably difficult for any undertaking seeking to operate in the market to create, possibly in cooperation with other operators, the alternative products or services'.[65] In *Microsoft*, there were additional alternative methods other than disclosure of the information at issue that may have ensured sufficient interoperability (but not perfect substitutability) between different suppliers' operating systems, which was necessary for effective competition. However, the CFI concluded that none of such methods or solutions made it possible to achieve the high degree of client/server and server/server interoperability required. Thus, *Microsoft*'s indispensability criteria were practically degraded to require only some competitive disadvantage on the part of the undertaking requesting the intellectual property owners' right as a consequence of a dominant undertaking's refusal to license.[66]

Secondly, regarding the elimination of competition in the downstream market, the *Microsoft* case again lowered the criteria established in previous case law. In *Magill* and *IMS Health*, the standard used in the evaluation of the second condition was 'likely to eliminate competition'. However, the CFI did not follow the established standards and accepted the Commission's stricter test of high probability using the terminology 'risk of elimination of competition'. Although the CFI argued that the distinction between terminology is irrelevant, having in mind that 'risk of' is

[64] Judgment of 17 September 2007, *Microsoft v Commission*, T-201/04, EU:T:2007:289, para. 336.

[65] Judgment of 29 April 2004, *IMS Health*, C-418/01, EU:C:2004:257, para. 28.

[66] See Judgment of 17 September 2007, *Microsoft v Commission*, T-201/04, EU:T:2007:289, paras. 345–346, 434–435.

certainly not a synonym for 'likely to', it seems pretty apparent that the use of new terminology lowers the standard for the fulfilment of the second condition to even maybe a mere possibility of eliminating competition.[67] Further on, the CFI replaced 'elimination of all competition' with a lower standard, which is 'elimination of all effective competition', and argued that 'the fact that the competitors of the dominant undertaking retain a marginal presence in certain niches on the market cannot suffice to substantiate the existence of such competition'.[68] Taking that into consideration, the CFI's interpretation of the elimination of competition condition very much lowers the standards established in the previous case law. Instead of this condition remaining strict and hard to prove, using standards like 'risk of elimination' and 'effective competition' makes such a condition seem easy to satisfy. Especially if the previous condition of indispensability is satisfied, the satisfaction of this condition practically follows automatically.

Thirdly, the new product criterion also departed from the prior interpretation. In *IMS Health*, it was established that the undertaking requesting a licence must 'not intend to limit itself essentially to duplicating the goods or services already offered on the secondary market by the owner of the intellectual property right, but intends to produce new goods or services not offered by the owner of the right and for which there is a potential consumer demand'.[69] With the wording of this explanation, it seems that an undertaking must have a clear vision of and plan for why it is seeking a licence and what it intends to do with it to create some improvement in the secondary market. Nevertheless, in *Microsoft*, the CFI concluded that the circumstances relating to the appearance of a new product, envisaged in the previous case law, cannot be the only parameters determining whether a refusal to license is capable of causing prejudice to consumers within Article 102b TFEU.[70] Thus, the CFI construed the new product criterion to embrace technical development. However, it failed to define the scope and meaning of such a standard. From the wording of this part of the decision, it seems that the CFI required competitor undertakings to 'differentiate their products from Microsoft's products with respect to certain parameters and certain features'. What those parameters and features are and what their significance should be within the meaning of the new product criterion were left unexplained. It can be read from the previous paragraph that some of the parameters in the case in question may be security, reliability, ease of use or operating performance speed, but that does not help a lot for future assessments.[71] Quite the opposite, in *Microsoft*, the CFI again distorted the solid and strict criteria established in previous case law

[67] See Judgment of 17 September 2007, *Microsoft v Commission*, T-201/04, EU:T:2007:289, paras. 560–562; see also para. 439.

[68] Judgment of 17 September 2007, *Microsoft v Commission*, T-201/04, EU:T:2007:289, paras. 563–564.

[69] Judgment of 29 April 2004, *IMS Health*, C-418/01, EU:C:2004:257, para. 48.

[70] Judgment of 17 September 2007, *Microsoft v Commission*, T-201/04, EU:T:2007:289, para. 647.

[71] Judgment of 17 September 2007, *Microsoft v Commission*, T-201/04, EU:T:2007:289, para. 653, 658.

against intellectual property rights holders. This condition seems especially more lenient in connection with the notion of consumer harm, under which practically anything may be placed.[72]

Fourthly, regarding the objective justification condition, an intriguing new interpretation was introduced as well. According to the CFI, the burden of proving the existence of circumstances that constitute an infringement of Article 102 TFEU is borne by the Commission. However, it is for the dominant undertaking holding an intellectual property right to raise any plea of objective justification and to support it with arguments and evidence, all before the end of the administrative procedure. Afterwards, it falls on the Commission to show that abuse of a dominant position (if found) prevails over the raised justification.[73] Having in mind that through the established case law acknowledged by the CJEU in *Microsoft* the objective justification condition is made part of the exceptional circumstances doctrine, it seems rational that in such a case, the competent body evaluating the potential infringement of Article 102 TFEU should also take into consideration the fourth condition constituting the exceptional circumstances. It is logical and expected that a concerned undertaking will almost always try to defend itself and counter the competent body's findings. However, that does not mean that the competent body should be exempt from investigating the existence of potential objective justifications. According to established case law (including *Microsoft*), in general, the exceptional circumstances doctrine consists of four conditions. Only if all four conditions are satisfied can a particular conduct be determined as contrary to the competition rules on abuse of dominance. Thus, in *Microsoft*, the Commission should have evaluated the fourth condition as well. Nevertheless, the fact is that throughout the case, Microsoft based its justification for its refusal to license primarily on the fact that intellectual property rights covered the technology in question and that the technology was secret and of great value to Microsoft.[74] With regard to that argument, the CFI rightly noted that intellectual property rights in themselves could not constitute objective justification since in that case, this exception established by the case law, where the exercise of intellectual property rights may constitute an abuse of a dominant position, could never apply.[75] Also, the Court further observed a potential negative impact on Microsoft's incentives to innovate but upheld the Commission's reasoning that Microsoft's incentives to

[72] Judgment of 17 September 2007, *Microsoft v Commission*, T-201/04, EU:T:2007:289, para. 665. In regard to this condition, Katz and Veel also commented:

> Arguably, this lower standard can be satisfied in any circumstance where the licensing of the IPR will not simply result in a competitor creating a copy of the IP owner's product.

Katz and Veel (2013), p. 151.

[73] Judgment of 17 September 2007, *Microsoft v Commission*, T-201/04, EU:T:2007:289, para. 688.

[74] Judgment of 17 September 2007, *Microsoft v Commission*, T-201/04, EU:T:2007:289, paras. 689, 692.

[75] Judgment of 17 September 2007, *Microsoft v Commission*, T-201/04, EU:T:2007:289, paras. 690–691.

innovate were outweighed by its positive impact on the level of innovation of the whole industry (including Microsoft).[76] Although Microsoft failed to justify its conduct, from the wording of the judgment, it seems that the incentive balancing test, if favourable to the intellectual property holder, could constitute an objective justification, even when the other conditions constituting exceptional circumstances were identified in a particular case. At first sight, an incentive balance test may introduce more economic thinking into an evaluation of such cases. However, considering that justification is the last step before the determination of the exceptional circumstances situation and that previously the first three conditions are already supposed to have been determined as fulfilled, it is hard to imagine that any justification could be accepted on the basis of the incentive balance test. Namely, if it had already been determined that certain conduct causes competitive disadvantage, that there is a risk of eliminating all effective competition and that there may be technical benefits in favour of consumers in the secondary market, it is completely unclear how it could even be possible for the incentive balance test to turn out in favour of the intellectual property holder to establish justification, particularly since in none of the decided cases was objective justification ever successfully pleaded. Therefore, after *Microsoft*, this condition practically turned out to be only symbolic.

After *Microsoft*, the exceptional circumstances doctrine, established for the evaluation of cases concerning refusal to license copyright as an abuse of a dominant position, seemed more confusing than ever—definitely not worthy of the title 'judgment of the decade', as some called the *Microsoft* case.[77] Generally, infringement of competition law provisions is seen only as an exception from the exercise of intellectual property rights since it is well established that the mere fact of holding intellectual property cannot constitute abuse in itself.[78] However, under the interpretation provided in *Microsoft*, the determination that refusal to license copyright is contrary to Article 102 TFEU seems more the rule than the exception in cases of copyright-competition interaction. Namely, after *Microsoft*, the conditions constituting the exceptional circumstance looked relatively easy to satisfy.

Thus, the exceptional circumstances doctrine, as set up in *Microsoft*, received much criticism. Some observed *Microsoft* as unhealthy interventionism into the field of intellectual property and free market, at the ultimate expense of the European economy and the consumers,[79] while others think it is an application of the ordoliberal approach, which is inconsistent with modern economic theory and evidence.[80] Some claimed *Microsoft* as a protectionist trade policy that disadvantages foreign firms doing business in Europe,[81] while some criticism was directed at

---

[76] Judgment of 17 September 2007, *Microsoft v Commission*, T-201/04, EU:T:2007:289, paras. 696–710.

[77] See Ahlborn and Evans (2009), p. 927.

[78] See OECD (2018).

[79] See Briard (2007), p. 4. (Note: The article was written before the CFI decision; however, the result is the same, and criticism remains).

[80] Ahlborn and Evans (2009), pp. 909–917.

[81] See Spulber (2008), pp. 283–284.

focusing on plain market power rather than on an economic analysis of the (anti-) competitive effects on the market.[82]

5.2.2.2.4 The Transatlantic Approach to Refusal to License Cases

Especially for US commentators, the CFI's interpretation of *Microsoft* seemed somewhat controversial.[83] In response to the decision in *Microsoft*, even the US Assistant Attorney General for the Antitrust Division took an unorthodox approach and publicly criticised the Court of First Instance's decision only hours after it was released.[84] In general, US commentators argued that imposing competition law liability on refusals to license intellectual property rights undercuts a fundamental constituent of intellectual property rights—the right to exclude others.[85] Also, imposing such liability for violations of competition rules could potentially undermine the goal of individual intellectual property rights to provide incentives for further creation, originality and innovation—as well as, indirectly, competition law objectives in view of consumer welfare and dynamic efficiency.[86] Thus, especially after *Microsoft*, by comparatively analysing the standpoints of the EU and US competent authorities on refusal to license copyright, it seems that there is a rather interesting paradox. In the EU, where the Member States generally provide more substantial protection for copyright holders,[87] competition authorities are more likely to view an undertaking's refusal to license copyright as abusive than in the United States, where competition authorities are less prone to determine such conduct as contrary to competition law provisions (see also *supra*, Sect. 2.1).[88]

---

[82] See Spulber (2008), pp. 285–300. On criticism on *Microsoft*, see also Larouche (2009), pp. 948–952; Lévêque (2005), pp. 71–91; Schmidt (2010), p. 35.

[83] Spulber even questions the independence of the EU judiciary. See Spulber (2008), p. 284.

[84] The US Assistant Attorney General for the Antitrust Division stated:

> (…) We are, however, concerned that the standard applied to unilateral conduct by the CFI, rather than helping consumers, may have the unfortunate consequence of harming consumers by chilling innovation and discouraging competition (…).

US Department of Justice (2017).

[85] The right to exclude others is considered one of the essential sticks in the bundle of copyright. (Note: Within the continental approach, it would not be appropriate to say that copyright is a bundle of rights due to its open-ended character.). The existence of this right is crucial in preventing the free-riding problem. See Kwok (2011), p. 262; Pessach (2011), p. 9.

[86] See Katz and Veel (2013), pp. 140–141.

[87] See Katz and Veel (2013), p. 142.

[88] See, for example, US Supreme Court, *Aspen Skiing Co. v. Aspen Highlands Skiing Corp.*, 472 U.S. 585 (1985); The Supreme Court of the United States, *Verizon Communications, Petitioner v. Law Offices of Curtis V. Trinko, LLP*, 540 U.S. 398 (2004); The Supreme Court of the United States, *Pacific Bell Telephone Co. v. linkLine Communications, Inc.*, 555 U.S. 438 (2009).

Thus, Katz and Veel observe:

To understand better the difference between the EU and US approaches and why the reaction of the United States, which generally has a weaker copyright protection system, to the EU decision was so intense, it is useful to provide a brief background of the US approach to cases on refusal to license.

The United States has a somewhat different approach to cases concerning refusals to deal in general—from an antitrust perspective, it in a way follows the essential facilities doctrine.[89] Interestingly, some copyright-competition interaction situations are completely dealt with within copyright doctrines without invoking competition rules. Under the essential facilities doctrine, an undertaking in a monopolisation

---

> The above demonstrates that EU courts are more willing than their American counterparts to find that a refusal to license an IPR can constitute an antitrust violation. While liability for refusal to deal stands on very tenuous ground in the United States, it is firmly established in European jurisprudence and has been used to compel the licensing of IPRs on a number of occasions.

Katz and Veel (2013), p. 151.

Coco comments:

> A comparative analysis of the current European and American systems—the two most mature for both antitrust and IP—shows that the former tends to downplay IP rights in favor of competition, whereas the latter tends to curtail the imperative of competition to preserve the exclusivity based upon IP rights.

Coco (2008), p. 4; Katz and Veel (2013), p. 140.

Kwok also notes that the EU approach is competition trumping intellectual property rights, while the US approach is intellectual property rights trumping competition. Kwok (2011), pp. 261–286, pp. 263–270.

Briard writes:

> The economic and legal principles that form the foundation of free market competition are the same in Europe and the United States, yet the EC has taken a very different approach to regulation. In the United States, a fruitful dialogue between Microsoft and the government produced a legitimate and reasonable result that enables Microsoft's rivals to access Windows technologies. As a result, numerous companies have taken out licenses that provide this access while also upholding the value of Microsoft's intellectual property. In Brussels, by contrast, heavy artillery and unilateralism dominate: first a fine of € 497.2 million in 2004, another fine of € 280.5 million in 2006; a new Statement of Objections before Microsoft had the opportunity to bring its licensing program to the marketplace; legal summons; formal notices; a threat of new fines retroactive to December 2005 for € 3 million per day—more than one billion per year!

Briard (2007).

[89] The essential facilities doctrine was initially introduced in *United States v. Terminal R.R. Ass'n*. Later on, it was further developed through cases like *Associated Press v. United States* and *Otter Tail Power Co. v. United States*. However, the term essential facilities was initially coined by Neale in 1970 and was first used in practice in *Hecht v. Pro- Football, Inc.* See *United States v. Terminal R.R. Ass'n*, 224 U.S. 383 (1912); *Associated Press v. United States*, 326 U.S. 1 (1945); *Otter Tail Power Co. v. United States*, 410 U.S. 366 (1973); *Hecht v. Pro- Football, Inc.*, 570 F.2d 982 (D.C. Cir. 1977).

See Waller (2008), p. 361; Neale (1970); Leaffer (2005), pp. 625–629.

However, within the US system, it still remains unclear what the status and importance of the essential facilities doctrine is to the refusal to deal cases.

position that is found to own a facility essential to other competitors is required to provide a reasonable use of that facility, unless some aspect of it precludes shared access. Copyright, as well as other intellectual property rights, is considered to be an essential facility if certain conditions are met. The conditions establishing liability under competition rules on the prohibition of monopolisation are as follows: control of the essential facility by a monopolist, competitor's inability to practically or reasonably duplicate the essential facility, denial of the use of the facility to a competitor, the feasibility of providing the facility to competitors and absence of regulatory oversight by an agency.[90]

These conditions are very difficult to establish for several reasons. Firstly, it is quite difficult to demonstrate that a particular facility is 'essential' for entry into and/or competition within the relevant market. Secondly, it must be demonstrated that the 'facility' must be something so indispensable to entry or competition that it would be impossible for smaller firms to compete with the market leader. Thirdly, it must be shown that compelling the dominant firm to permit others to use the facility would not interfere with the dominant firm's ability to serve its own customers.[91]

Indeed, US courts have been very reluctant in finding refusals by dominant undertakings to license intellectual property rights as contrary to competition rules prohibiting monopolisation. The considered leading case on this point is often *Verizon Communications v. Law Offices of Curtis V. Trinko, LLP*.[92,93] The case concerned an allegation that Verizon's refusal to provide adequate network access to its competitors constituted a violation of Section 2 of the Sherman Act. The US Supreme Court rejected the plaintiff's claim, refusing to find Verizon's anti-competitive liability. The Supreme Court noted that there is no general obligation for an undertaking in a dominant position to deal with its competitors.[94] However, there are two exceptions to that rule. One is the so-called *Aspen Skiing*[95] exception, under which an undertaking may be held responsible for a refusal to deal if it terminates a previously existing, profitable and voluntary course of dealing with the other party to achieve an anti-competitive end. If there is no previous dealing, there can be no liability. The other exception relates to the essential facilities

[90] The standard analysis of the elements for the essential facilities doctrine was set forth in *MCI Communications Corp. v. AT&T Co.* and continued to develop in further practice. See *MCI Communications Corp. v. AT&T Co.*, 708 F.2d 1081 (7th Cir. 1983).
See Waller (2008), pp. 362–365.

[91] In his notable work on the essential facilities doctrine, Areeda criticised its application and advocated to more rigorously define its limits. His work is often cited by scholars and influenced later case law, including the *Trinko* case. See Areeda (1990), pp. 841–854; Waller (2008).

[92] The Supreme Court of the United States, *Verizon Communications, Petitioner v. Law Offices of Curtis V. Trinko, LLP*, 540 U.S. 398 (2004).

[93] See Katz and Veel (2013), p. 144.

[94] See The Supreme Court of the United States, *Verizon Communications, Petitioner v. Law Offices of Curtis V. Trinko, LLP*, 540 U.S. 398 (2004), 407–408.

[95] See The Supreme Court of the United States, *Aspen Skiing Co. v. Aspen Highlands Skiing Corp.*, 472 U.S. 585 (1985).

doctrine, under which it is, as previously mentioned, extremely difficult to establish a violation of competition rules prohibiting monopolisation.[96] Thus, the US approach on refusals to deal distinguishes situations where a dominant undertaking has already dealt with the undertaking requesting a deal and where there were no prior relationships.[97] Later on, the Supreme Court reaffirmed the restrictive interpretation of the refusal to deal with anti-competitive liability in the case *Pacific Bell Telephone Co. v. linkLine Communications, Inc.*[98] Herein, the Supreme Court additionally noted: 'a firm with no duty to deal in the wholesale market has no obligation to deal under terms and conditions favourable to its competitors'.[99] Also, interestingly, when discussing situations in which a dominant undertaking might be held responsible for a refusal to deal, the Supreme Court only mentioned the *Aspen Skiing* exception and not the essential facilities doctrine.[100] Nevertheless, although practice on this matter is scarce, similarly, lower courts have affirmed that refusal to license will only be exceptionally held as being contrary to competition rules prohibiting monopolisation. Thus, in *Data General Corporation, et al. v. Grumman Systems Support Corporation*,[101] concerning a refusal to license a software program for diagnosing problems, the Court considered that valid business justification could rebut anti-competitive concerns of a refusal to license. The Court further noted: 'an author's desire to exclude others from use of its copyrighted work is a presumptively valid business justification for any immediate harm to consumers'.[102] Probably the most extreme example was the case *In Re Independent Service*

[96] In *Trinko*, the Supreme Court avoided discussing the essential facilities doctrine but simply held that even if the doctrine exists, it would not be applicable to the case. See The Supreme Court of the United States, *Verizon Communications, Petitioner v. Law Offices of Curtis V. Trinko, LLP*, 540 U.S. 398 (2004), 410–411.

[97] In the EU *Microsoft* case, the Commission did not consider it particularly important to distinguish between the situations of new entrants and established relationships within the market. See Judgment of 17 September 2007, *Microsoft v Commission*, T-201/04, EU:T:2007:289, para. 307.

[98] See The Supreme Court of the United States, *Pacific Bell Telephone Co. v. linkLine Communications, Inc.*, 555 U.S. 438 (2009).

[99] See The Supreme Court of the United States, *Pacific Bell Telephone Co. v. linkLine Communications, Inc.*, 555 U.S. 438 (2009), 450–451.

[100] The Supreme Court of the United States, *Pacific Bell Telephone Co. v. linkLine Communications, Inc.*, 555 U.S. 438 (2009), 448.

[101] See *Data General Corporation, et al. v. Grumman Systems Support Corporation*, 36 F.3d 1147 (1st Cir. 1994).

[102] See *Data General Corporation, et al. v. Grumman Systems Support Corporation*, 36 F.3d 1147 (1st Cir. 1994), 1187.

The restrictive *Data General*'s interpretation of the refusal to license was acknowledged in *Image Tech. Services, Inc. v. Eastman Kodak*, one of the rare cases in which it was established that refusal to deal violated Section 2 of the Sherman Act. However, here, it was determined that Kodak's intention was not to protect its intellectual property rights but to exclude competition from the market. Hence, it seems that the subjective element was decisive in resolving that case. See *Image Tech. Services, Inc. v. Eastman Kodak*, 125 F.3d 1195 (9th Cir. 1997).

Organizations Antitrust Litigation v. Xerox Corporation, concerning patented parts and copyrighted manuals, where the Federal Circuit held that, subject to certain enumerated exceptions, a refusal to license an intellectual property right cannot practically give rise to antitrust liability.[103]

However, aside from the essential facilities doctrine and the *Aspen Skiing* exception, which are mainly applied from an antitrust perspective, in relation to the copyright-competition interaction issue, the US system also applies other approaches from a copyright perspective. This stems from the generally more economical and pro-competitive approach to copyright with a practically open-ended concept of limitations and exceptions (if certain conditions are met). As a result, unlike in most of Europe, in the US system, there is no such clear distinction between copyright law and antitrust law—sometimes they overlap, bringing in questions of whether a particular matter should be dealt with from an antitrust or a copyright perspective.[104] Thus, in dealing with copyright-competition interaction, the US system also applies the copyright misuse doctrine,[105] the fair use doctrine[106] and the merger doc-

---

[103]See *In Re Independent Service Organizations Antitrust Litigation v. Xerox Corporation*, 203 F.3d 1322 (Fed. Cir. 2000).

See Katz and Veel (2013), p. 147.

[104]On the differences between the US and the EU approaches in relation to the licensing of intellectual property rights in view of competition law, see the Letter from Hartmut Johannes, Directorate General IV, Commission of the European Communities, Brussels, Belgium, to Chairman Kastenmeier, April 26, 1988, with attachments, in: Hearing before the Subcommittee on Courts, Civil Liberties, and the Administration of Justice of the Committee on the Judiciary House of Representatives, One Hundredth Congress, Second Session, on H.R. 4086 Patent Licensing Reform Act of 1988, Serial No. 103, May 11, 1988, pp. 201–268, pp. 201–211.

Thus, Czapracka observes:

> The analysis of the relevant case law points to the conclusion that EU competition law is applied to remedy the consequences of imperfect IP laws. In contrast, the U.S. antitrust agencies and courts note flaws in the IP system, but are much more reserved when it comes to remedying their negative effects; instead they defer such problems to the authorities responsible for IP policy.

Czapracka (2009), p. 47.

[105]Under one formulation, the copyright misuse doctrine prevents copyright holders from leveraging their limited monopoly to allow them control in areas outside the monopoly (see *A&M Records, Inc. v. Napster, Inc.*, 239 F.3d 1004 (9th Cir. 2001), 1026), and it has a wide application where the copyright holder had in some way acted improperly. The seminal case on this doctrine is *Lasercomb America, Inc. v. Reynolds* concerning die-making software (*Lasercomb America, Inc. v. Reynolds*, 911 F.2d 970 (4th Cir. 1990)). The differentiation between antitrust violations and copyright misuse can be seen from *Alcatel USA, Inc. v. DGI Techs*., Inc., 166 F.3d 772, 787 (5th Cir. 1999).

[106]Under the fair use doctrine, certain copying for legitimate purposes is permitted, thereby serving pro-competitive interests. See *Atari Games Corp. v. Nintendo of America Inc.*, 975 F.2d 832 (Fed. Cir. 1992); *Sega Enterprises Ltd. v. Accolade, Inc.*, 977 F.2d 1510 (9th Cir. 1992).

trine.[107,108] Generally, under those doctrines, which are still not fully developed, certain anti-competitive uses of copyright and other intellectual property rights can be resolved without invoking antitrust law and the enforcement system. Europe is not familiar with such an approach, and it would therefore be required to apply stricter standards and the rules of competition law.[109]

By observing US case law and doctrine, it is easier to understand why the United States so fiercely criticised *Microsoft*, where liability for refusal to license copyright stands on very tenuous grounds, particularly considering that the *Microsoft* case in the United States ended in a settlement much more lenient than in the EU case.[110] In that sense, it seems that the paradox remains that the less pro-copyright-protective US system is not prone to perceiving refusals to license copyright as contrary to competition rules on abuse of dominance, while the more pro-copyright EU is. However, considering that the United States partially deals with the copyright-competition interaction matter exclusively within the copyright domain, the ultimate outcome is not that different. Under copyright doctrines dealing with anti-competitive behaviour, violations were more often found.

Nonetheless, some influence of the US approach might be found in European case law concerning copyright-competition interaction. Although it has never explicitly been stated, some consider that the essential facilities doctrine is closely associated with the exceptional circumstances doctrine in *Magill*, *Tiercé Ladbroke*,[111] *Bronner*[112] and *IMS Health*, particularly with regard to the indispensability

---

[107] The merger doctrine can be perceived as a further manifestation of the idea-expression dichotomy, under which the author is denied exclusivity over his/her expression where such protection would inevitably give the author exclusivity over the idea itself. See *Regos v. Associated Press*, 937 F.2d 700 (2d Cir. 1991), 705; *Computer Associates International, Inc. v. Altai, Inc.*, 982 F.2d 693 (2d Cir. 1992); *New York Mercantile Exchange v. Intercontinental Exchange*, 323 F. Supp. 2d 559. (S.D.N.Y. 2004); *Lexmark International, Inc. v. Static Control Components, Inc.*, 387 F.3d 522 (6th Cir. 2004).

[108] See also Goldstein (1989), pp. 38–39; Goldstein (2024), pp. 11:1–11:61.

[109] See Katz and Veel (2013), pp. 163–173; Coco (2008), pp. 7–10.

[110] *United States v. Microsoft Corporation*, 253 F.3d 34 (D.C. Cir. 2001). Nevertheless, had the European *Microsoft* case been decided in the United States, liability under Section 2 of the Sherman Act may even have been found under the *Aspen Skiing* exception, if it was established that Microsoft was already dealing with the undertaking requesting a licence. The Commission explicitly claimed that Microsoft's initial policy was to disclose interoperability information but changed its strategy and stopped sharing that information after its server products were sufficiently established in the market. See Judgment of 17 September 2007, *Microsoft v Commission*, T-201/04, EU:T:2007:289, paras. 307–308.

[111] In *Tiercé Ladbroke*, some consider that the requirement of an essential facility function was introduced as an alternative to the new product criterion. See Schmidt (2010), p. 14.

[112] In *Bronner*, Oscar Bronner explicitly referred to the essential facilities doctrine and argued that 'under the doctrine of 'essential faculties' as established by the Court of Justice in Joined Cases C-241/91 P and C-242/91 P RTE and ITP v Commission [1995] ECR I-743 (the 'Magill judgment'), the service performed by placing a facility at the disposal of others and that supplied by using that facility in principle constitute separate markets. It therefore maintains that, as the owner of such an 'essential facility', in this case the only economically viable home-delivery scheme

criteria.[113] This is certainly debatable, having in mind the particularities and the individual development of EU competition law and copyright in Europe; nevertheless, some resemblance indeed exists.

5.2.2.2.5 Further Development of the Exceptional Circumstances Doctrine

Practically nothing very significant occurred in the exceptional circumstances doctrine after *Microsoft*. The confusion still remains. However, case law on refusal to license, as dealt with under the exceptional circumstances doctrine, has evidently influenced the definition of the general criteria for refusal to supply cases. This influence is particularly visible within the Guidance on the Commission's Enforcement Priorities in Applying Article 82 of the EC Treaty to Abusive Exclusionary Conduct by Dominant Undertakings,[114] which provides a general framework for dealing with abuse of dominance situations. Thus, the Guidance defined the existence of the following conditions as potentially problematic in cases of refusal to supply: the refusal relates to a product or service that is objectively necessary to enable competing effectively in a downstream market, the refusal is likely to lead to the elimination of effective competition in the downstream market and the refusal is likely to lead to consumer harm.[115] The defined conditions clearly resemble the exceptional circumstances conditions as established in *Magill*, *Bronner* and *IMS Health*. However, differences obviously exist,[116] which is not strange, having in mind that the Guidance provides a general framework and does not take into consideration the specificities of particular intellectual property rights.

With regard to case law, the CJEU once again discussed the exceptional circumstances doctrine in a patent-related case on abuse of a dominant position—*Astra*

---

existing in Austria on a national scale, Mediaprint is obliged to allow access to the scheme by competing products on market conditions and at market prices.' However, in the reasoning of the CJEU, there is no further mention of the essential facilities doctrine. See Judgment of 26 November 1998, *Oscar Bronner GmbH & Co. KG v Mediaprint Zeitungs- und Zeitschriftenverlag GmbH & Co. KG, Mediaprint Zeitungsvertriebsgesellschaft mbH & Co. KG and Mediaprint Anzeigengesellschaft mbH & Co. KG*, C-7/97, EU:C:1998:569, para. 24.

[113] See Schmidt (2010), p. 25.

Some commentators address the refusal to license situation as 'essential facilities' even for cases in Europe. See Brison (2005); Czapracka (2009); Firth (2021), pp. 44–73; Lamping (2015), p. 125; Martin (2005), pp. 613–618.

[114] Communication from the Commission—Guidance on the Commission's enforcement priorities in applying Article 82 of the EC Treaty to abusive exclusionary conduct by dominant undertakings, OJ C 45, 24.2.2009, pp. 7–20.

[115] Communication from the Commission—Guidance on the Commission's enforcement priorities in applying Article 82 of the EC Treaty to abusive exclusionary conduct by dominant undertakings, OJ C 45, 24.2.2009, pp. 7–20, paras. 81–88.

[116] See Schmidt (2010), pp. 42–45.

Zeneca v Commission.[117] In the case in question, the CJEU rejected the applicant's claim and concluded that its conduct is in no way comparable to the compulsory licensing of a particular intellectual property right and to the *IMS Health* case. Although the case in question did not make any further contribution to the exceptional circumstances doctrine, it is still significant that, therein, the CJEU once again endorsed the idea of the special status of intellectual property rights and that liability exists only exceptionally.[118]

Also noteworthy for the refusal to license in the context of copyright-competition interaction is the development of case law in the field of standard-essential patents. First of all, it should be recalled that this specific case law concerns patents and that the patents at issue are essential for a standard laid down by a standardisation body. However, it is still a fact that this matter concerns refusals to license a particular intellectual property right and is based on the exceptional circumstances doctrine. Thus, in *Huawei*,[119] the CJEU firstly acknowledged that the exercise of an exclusive right linked to a particular intellectual property right involves abuse of a dominant position only in exceptional circumstances.[120] However, the CJEU explicitly distinguished this case from cases on classical interaction between intellectual property rights and competition law due to the particular circumstances of the case.[121] From the reasoning of the judgment in *Huawei*, it is apparent that the CJEU preserved the concept that intellectual property rights have a special status in view of competition rules and that the exercise of intellectual property rights may infringe competition

---

[117] Judgment of 6 December 2012, *AstraZeneca AB and AstraZeneca plc v European Commission*, C-457/10 P, EU:C:2012:770. The case concerned the potential abuse of patent systems and the procedures for marketing pharmaceutical products in order to prevent or delay the arrival of competing generic medicinal products on the market and to impede parallel trade.

According to Petit, this case is often 'overlooked in the antitrust and IP literature because the impugned conduct did not involve an IP-instrumented strategy'. Petit (2017), p. 101.

[118] See Judgment of 6 December 2012, *AstraZeneca AB and AstraZeneca plc v European Commission*, C-457/10 P, EU:C:2012:770, paras. 148, 150.

[119] Judgment of 16 July 2015, *Huawei Technologies Co. Ltd v ZTE Corp. and ZTE Deutschland GmbH*, C-170/13, EU:C:2015:477.

[120] Judgment of 16 July 2015, *Huawei Technologies Co. Ltd v ZTE Corp. and ZTE Deutschland GmbH*, C-170/13, EU:C:2015:477, para. 47.

[121] Firstly, 'the patent at issue is essential to a standard established by a standardisation body, rendering its use indispensable to all competitors which envisage manufacturing products that comply with the standard to which it is linked. That feature distinguishes SEPs from patents that are not essential to a standard and which normally allow third parties to manufacture competing products without recourse to the patent concerned and without compromising the essential functions of the product in question.' Secondly, 'the case in the main proceedings may be distinguished by the fact, as is apparent from paragraphs 15 to 17 and 22 of the present judgment, that the patent at issue obtained SEP status only in return for the proprietor's irrevocable undertaking, given to the standardisation body in question, that it is prepared to grant licences on FRAND terms'. Judgment of 16 July 2015, *Huawei Technologies Co. Ltd v ZTE Corp. and ZTE Deutschland GmbH*, C-170/13, EU:C:2015:477, paras. 49–51.

rules (in particular Article 102 TFEU) only exceptionally.[122] Due to the specific circumstances of the case, for a dominant holder of the standard-essential patent to abuse the dominant position when seeking an injunction prohibiting the infringement of its patent or seeking the recall of products for the manufacture of which that patent has been used, it must be established that the holder has failed to do the following:

- prior to bringing that action, the proprietor has, first, alerted the alleged infringer of the infringement complained about by designating that patent and specifying the way in which it has been infringed, and, secondly, after the alleged infringer has expressed its willingness to conclude a licensing agreement on FRAND terms, presented to that infringer a specific, written offer for a licence on such terms, specifying, in particular, the royalty and the way in which it is to be calculated, and
- where the alleged infringer continues to use the patent in question, the alleged infringer has not diligently responded to that offer, in accordance with recognised commercial practices in the field and in good faith, this being a matter which must be established on the basis of objective factors and which implies, in particular, that there are no delaying tactics.

Some commentators see the notion of the 'particular circumstances' in Paragraph 48 of *Huawei* as a shift from the exceptionalism concept.[123] However, it seems more likely that the notion of 'particular circumstances' is not a departure from the exceptional circumstances doctrine but rather indicates that the case in question is not a standard case of an interaction between intellectual property rights and competition law due to the particular circumstances, which are clearly elaborated in the further reasoning. Therefore, in such a situation, the holder of the standard-essential patent clearly has the special obligation to license on fair, reasonable and non-discriminatory (FRAND) terms. The exercise of rights stemming from standard-essential patents may still only exceptionally constitute an abuse of a dominant position. However, for this specific situation, the conditions mentioned above substantially represent an alternative set of conditions constituting exceptional circumstances, as implied in *IMS Health* and *Microsoft*.

Although this case law cannot be directly applicable to the general issue of the refusal to license copyright as an abuse of a dominant position, it is still noteworthy considering it further contributes to the general understanding of the interaction between particular intellectual property rights and competition law. The contribution is particularly notable with regard to the acknowledgement of the specific status of intellectual property rights, the establishment of the non-exhaustiveness of the conditions forming the exceptional circumstances situation and an emphasis on the need for a more economical approach.

---

[122] Judgment of 16 July 2015, *Huawei Technologies Co. Ltd v ZTE Corp. and ZTE Deutschland GmbH*, C-170/13, EU:C:2015:477, paras. 45–47.

[123] See Petit (2017), pp. 17–18. Rato and English (2016), pp. 103–112.

5.2.2.3 Concluding Remarks Regarding the Exceptional Circumstances Doctrine

The exceptional circumstances doctrine probably had the most substantial influence on the CJEU's case law on refusal to license under Article 102 TFEU, as opposed to other theoretical fundaments. However, the exceptional circumstances doctrine is far from settled or universally accepted.

Generally, the idea behind the exceptional circumstances doctrine is that copyright (as well as other intellectual property rights) has a special status from a competition law perspective, as opposed to other non-IPR rights.[124] Competition law can intervene in the exercise of copyright, however only in exceptional circumstances. Although the CJEU confirmed the special status of intellectual property rights on several occasions, the fact is that there is also case law that applied the exceptional circumstances doctrine in non-IPR cases under Article 102 TFEU. The most prominent example of that is the *Bronner* case. Also, the concept of 'wholly exceptional circumstances' was applied for assessing whether the use of legal remedies may constitute abuse of a dominant position in both IPR[125] and non-IPR cases.[126] Besides that, the CJEU used the notion of exceptional circumstances in the determination of large market shares as evidence of the existence of a dominant position.[127] On the other hand, in *Tiercé Ladbroke SA*, a case that came shortly after *Magill* and is quite comparable to it, involving a refusal to license copyright rights over televised pictures and sound commentaries on horse racing, the CFI clearly refused to discuss the case through the exceptional circumstances doctrine[128] and

---

[124] See, for instance, Judgment of 17 September 2007, *Microsoft v Commission*, T-201/04, EU:T:2007:289, para. 284.

[125] See Judgment of 13 September 2012, *Protégé International Ltd v European Commission*, T-119/09, EU:T:2012:421, paras. 48–49.

[126] See Judgment of 17 July 1998, *ITT Promedia NV v Commission of the European Communities*, T-111/96, EU:T:1998:183, para. 60.

[127] See Judgment of 13 February 1979, *Hoffmann-La Roche & Co. AG v Commission of the European Communities*, C-85-76, ECLI:EU:C:1979:36, para. 41. Judgment of 6 December 2012, *AstraZeneca AB and AstraZeneca plc v European Commission*, C-457/10 P, EU:C:2012:770, para. 176.

[128] The CFI concluded that *Magill* was a specific case in which the dominant undertaking prevented the applicant from entering the market with a new product:

> The applicant cannot rely on the *Magill* judgement to demonstrate the existence the alleged abuse, since the decision is not in point. In contrast to the position in *Magill*, where the refusal to grant a licence to the applicant prevented it from entering the market in comprehensive guides, in this case the applicant is not only present in, but has the largest share, of the main betting market on which the product in question, namely sound and pictures, is offered to consumers whilst the *sociétés de courses*, the owners of the intellectual property rights, are not present on that market. Accordingly, in the absence of direct or indirect exploitation by the *sociétés de courses* of their intellectual property rights on the Belgian market, their refusal to supply cannot be regarded as involving any restriction of competition on the Belgian market.

decided the case through a standard abuse of dominant position assessment.[129] Hence, some commentators do not see the exceptional circumstances doctrine as IPR specific.[130] However, if that is the case, given Article 102 TFEU, it remains unclear in which situations the exceptional circumstances doctrine should be applied—only to a certain kind of refusal to deal cases or to refusal to deal cases in general or even maybe beyond refusal to deal cases?!

Furthermore, even if we put aside the scope of the applicability of the exceptional circumstances doctrine, probably the most problematic issue whatsoever is the conditions forming the exceptional circumstances. Generally, four conditions have been recognised in practice: indispensability, a new product, the elimination of competition and objective justification. First of all, there is an issue regarding the exhaustivity of those conditions. Having in mind the reasoning in *IMS Health* and *Microsoft*, it seems more likely that the conditions are not exhaustive. However, if that is the case, it remains completely uncertain what the other possible conditions could be that might constitute the exceptional circumstances situation. Moreover, even the content of the identified conditions is questionable, let alone the content of the other possible (as yet unidentified) conditions. *IMS Health* provided one version of the exceptional circumstances conditions, while *Microsoft* provided another much looser version, which, in some moments, seems to have been created only to justify a finding of the infringement.[131] For future reference, if the exceptional circumstances doctrine is to be used, it is of the utmost importance to have clear criteria for determining the exceptional circumstances situation that may constitute an infringement of Article 102 in cases of the exercise of copyright.

In any case, the idea that competition law may intervene in copyright only in exceptional circumstances is practical and seems a proper basis for the further development of the refusal to license issue, particularly as opposed to other abstract solutions. However, to ensure consistency and legal security, it is necessary to have clear and solid criteria for establishing the exceptional circumstances situation—this is not the case at the moment. Moreover, concerning the case law that applied the exceptional circumstances doctrine, criticism is also directed at the neglect of the importance of copyright and the lack of economic analysis.

Judgment of 12 June 1997, *Tiercé Ladbroke SA v Commission of the European Communities*, T-540/93, EU:T:1997:84, para. 130.

[129] See Judgment of 12 June 1997, *Tiercé Ladbroke SA v Commission of the European Communities*, T-540/93, EU:T:1997:84, paras. 123–134. Nevertheless, the CFI's decision seems plausible since from the factsheet of the case, it does not seem that there was an infringement of competition rules on abuse of a dominant position even if the case were decided through different methods of assessment.

[130] See, for instance, discussion in Petit (2017), p. 102.

[131] That is particularly indicative in Paragraph 336 of *Microsoft*, where the Court essentially states that 'if the infringement cannot be established through the (exceptional circumstances) test applied, then another test (the Commission's) would apply that would more likely find the infringement' (paraphrased). See Judgment of 17 September 2007, *Microsoft v Commission*, T-201/04, EU:T:2007:289, para. 336.

5.2.3 The Theory of Complementarity

As already discussed earlier (see *supra*, Sect. 4.2.3), in the EU, the complementarity theory was initially introduced within the Guidelines on Technology Transfer Agreements—hence primarily for dealing with licensing agreements under Article 101 TFEU. Interestingly, in the EU, no legal document concerning Article 102 TFEU later acknowledged the complementarity concept within its text.

Nonetheless, the idea that copyright and competition law should jointly strive to achieve complementary (or, according to some, even joint) goals of dynamic efficiency and consumer welfare attracted many proponents, who additionally often advocate the wider application of the complementarity concept.[132] Thus, Drexl writes: 'The Commission would be well advised to extend its concept of complementary goals of IP law and competition law from the field of technology transfer agreements to the area of abuse of dominance and merger control.'[133]

Still, the practical application of complementarity concepts has been scarce, even with regard to the exercise of copyright (or other intellectual property rights) under the competition rules on prohibited agreements. With respect to the abuse of a dominant position, some consider that *Huawei* endorsed the theory of complementarity by referring to the paragraph stating:[134]

> (...) the Court must strike a balance between maintaining free competition—in respect of which primary law and, in particular, Article 102 TFEU prohibit abuses of a dominant position—and the requirement to safeguard that proprietor's intellectual property rights and its right to effective judicial protection guaranteed by Article 17(2) and Articles 47 of the Charter, respectively.[135]

Such an interpretation seems to be a little too extensive. This judicial pronouncement looks somewhat too general to be considered as endorsing the complementarity theory, particularly since immediately in the further text, the CJEU refers to the standard case law related to the inherency theory (*Volvo v Veng*) and the exceptional circumstances doctrine (*Magill, IMS Health*).[136] The complementarity theory indeed advocates balancing the different interests involved but is not solely about balancing between copyright and competition law. Also, the need for balancing between different interests is not unbreakably connected to the complementarity theory. On the contrary, it is one of the basic methods integrated into several different approaches.

The idea that copyright and competition do not collide but rather complement one another and that competition law may intervene in the exercise of copyright but the

---

[132] See Apostolopoulos (2007), p. 238; Kwok (2011), pp. 262–263.

[133] Drexl (2008), p. 53.

[134] See Petit (2017), pp. 107–108.

[135] Judgment of 16 July 2015, *Huawei Technologies Co. Ltd v ZTE Corp. and ZTE Deutschland GmbH*, C-170/13, EU:C:2015:477, para. 42.

[136] Judgment of 16 July 2015, *Huawei Technologies Co. Ltd v ZTE Corp. and ZTE Deutschland GmbH*, C-170/13, EU:C:2015:477, paras. 46–47.

interests must be balanced may be applied to Article 102 TFEU as well as to Article 101 TFEU. Criticism of the complementarity theory remains (see *supra*, Sect. 4.2.3); however, the complementarity theory undoubtedly contributed to the general understanding of the copyright-competition interaction and should be taken into consideration in the further development of this matter.

5.2.4 The Theory of Absolutism

Generally, what has already been discussed before on the 'theory of absolutism' concerning competition rules on prohibited agreements can also be applied to abuse of dominance (see *supra*, Sect. 4.2.4). Generally, copyright is conceptually an absolute property right. However, this does not mean that the use of copyright is unlimited in scope. Literally taken, the idea that the exercise of copyright rights is absolute and cannot be limited at all is not a realistic approach.[137] The CJEU has also never rejected competition claims altogether on the ground that competition law cannot, under any circumstances, interfere with conduct that involves the exercise of copyright. The possibility of interference between copyright law and competition law is a reality, but the question is, at what point does it happen? What is the appropriate situation when competition law should intervene with conduct involving the exercise of copyright?

'The theory of absolutism', as a clearly pro-copyright approach, still deserves further discussion and the development of the copyright-competition interaction issue. Notably, it plays a role in preserving the substance of copyright when there is a need for competition law interventions, that is, to maintain a proper balance between copyright law and competition law. It can be inferred from the theory of absolutism that copyright has a specific status in competition interventions. Namely, in dealing with cases on the copyright-competition interaction, the CJEU has clearly acknowledged the special status of copyright, as well as of other intellectual property rights. This is especially noticeable in cases concerning the abuse of dominance. Thus, regardless of the approach that was taken, in the vast majority of cases, the CJEU recognised the specific status of copyright and the need for a specific method of assessment (see *CICRA v Renault*, *Volvo v Veng*, *Magill*, *IMS Health*, *Microsoft*,[138] *Huawei*, etc.). Still, all things considered, 'the theory of absolutism' has more of a theoretical than a practical value.

---

[137] From a comparative perspective, somewhat in line with that approach might be the US case *In Re Independent Service Organizations Antitrust Litigation v. Xerox Corporation*, in which the District Circuit held that a refusal to license an intellectual property right practically cannot give rise to antitrust liability. See *In Re Independent Service Organizations Antitrust Litigation v. Xerox Corporation*, 203 F.3d 1322 (Fed. Cir. 2000).

[138] In *Microsoft*, for example, the CFI states that among the refusal to supply as an abuse of dominance cases, the refusal to license an intellectual property right is the strictest legal test (the

5.2.5 *Standard Competition Law Approach in Copyright Matters*

Not everyone agrees that copyright and other intellectual property rights should have a specific status from the perspective of competition law. Also, when dealing with cases concerning the refusal to license a particular intellectual property right from the perspective of competition rules on abuse of dominance, the CJEU did not always acknowledge the specific status of intellectual property rights.

For instance, in the *DSD*[139] case, the CJEU discussed the matter as a conventional exploitative abuse case, although the case at issue involved the exercise of a trademark. DSD, a German waste collection system in a dominant position, required payment of a fee for all packaging bearing its trademark, even if customers had not used their system. The CJEU found abuse of a dominant position without applying any specific intellectual property-competition interaction assessment. Moreover, in support of its reasoning, the CJEU did not refer to any IP-related case law either.[140]

Nevertheless, this example seems more of an exception than the rule, especially since in *DSD*, the CJEU explicitly refused to discuss the intellectual property aspect of the particular case[141] and did not oppose the general idea of granting intellectual

---

one most favourable to Microsoft). See Judgment of 17 September 2007, *Microsoft v Commission*, T-201/04, EU:T:2007:289, para. 284.

[139] Judgment of 16 July 2009, *Der Grüne Punkt - Duales System Deutschland GmbH v Commission of the European Communities*, C-385/07 P, EU:C:2009:456.

[140] See Judgment of 16 July 2009, *Der Grüne Punkt - Duales System Deutschland GmbH v Commission of the European Communities*, C-385/07 P, EU:C:2009:456, paras. 142–143:

> In the same paragraph of the judgment under appeal, the Court of First Instance noted the settled case-law, according to which an undertaking abuses its dominant position where it charges for its services fees which are disproportionate to the economic value of the service provided (see, inter alia, Case 226/84 British Leyland v Commission [1986] ECR 3263, paragraph 27, and Case C-340/99 TNT Traco [2001] ECR I-4109, paragraph 46). As the Court of First Instance held at paragraph 164 of the judgment under appeal, following its analysis set out at paragraphs 119 to 163 of that judgment, the conduct of DSD which is objected to in Article 1 of the decision at issue and which consists in requiring payment of a fee for all packaging bearing the DGP logo and put into circulation in Germany, even where customers of the company show that they do not use the DGP system for some or all of that packaging, must be considered to constitute an abuse of a dominant position within the meaning of the provision and the case-law referred to above. It is also apparent from paragraphs 107 to 117 and 126 to 133 of this judgment that the findings made by the Court of First Instance are sufficiently reasoned and are not vitiated by the errors of fact or law invoked by DSD as regards the exclusive rights attached to the DGP logo.

[141] See Judgment of 16 July 2009, *Der Grüne Punkt - Duales System Deutschland GmbH v Commission of the European Communities*, C-385/07 P, EU:C:2009:456, paras. 129–133, 138–139.

property rights special status in competition law assessments.[142] Therefore, in conclusion, it is widely accepted that copyright and intellectual property rights should have a specific status from the perspective of competition law (see discussion *supra*, Sect. 3.2).[143]

5.3 The More Traditional Approach to the Copyright-Competition Interaction Issue: Refusal to License Copyright as an Abuse of Dominance

5.3.1 Introduction: Theoretical Foundation

The overall situation with the issue of refusal to license copyright, from the perspective of the competition rules on abuse of dominance, is not much more settled than it is with the issue of the exercise of copyright under competition rules on prohibited agreements. Namely, for both issues of copyright-competition interaction, several approaches can be identified. With regard to the refusal to license copyright under Article 102 TFEU, the first cases were also influenced by the inherency theory. However, due to the questionable practical value of that approach, soon after, the CJEU shifted to the exceptional circumstances doctrine, which has left a significant mark on the general understanding of the refusal to license copyright under the competition rules on abuse of dominance. The influence of the exceptional circumstances doctrine was certainly much more significant than it was for the issue of the exercise of copyright under the competition rules on prohibited agreements, where it remained mostly on the theoretical level. Thus, the CJEU discussed most of the cases dealing with the copyright-competition interaction issue under Article 102 TFEU, applying some variation of the exceptional circumstances approach. Afterwards, there was a tendency to apply the complementarity concept to the issue of refusal to license copyright, which was advocated by the Commission and some scholars. However, in practice, that idea never came to life for any of the copyright-competition interaction cases (dealt with under Article 101 or 102 TFEU). Also, the uttermost approaches of the theory of absolutism and the standard competition evaluation should not be completely neglected. Both of these approaches also have a certain value in the

[142] The previously discussed case *Tiercé Ladbroke SA* (see *supra*, Sect. 5.2.2.3) can potentially be considered another example of a case concerning the refusal to license that was discussed through a standard abuse of dominance assessment. See Judgment of 12 June 1997, *Tiercé Ladbroke SA v Commission of the European Communities*, T-540/93, EU:T:1997:84, paras. 123–134.

[143] See also Derclaye (2004), pp. 693–694.

overall understanding of cases concerning the refusal to license copyright discussed under the competition rules on abuse of dominance.

In the academic society, many criticised the approaches applied throughout the case law concerning refusals to license copyright under the competition rules on abuse of dominance. Some scholars even suggested certain new solutions. For instance, Apostolopoulos suggests the application of a two-step test where the first step examines 'whether there is the possibility of competition by substitution and a *de facto* monopoly on the downstream market', while 'the second step of the proposed analysis would consist of an economic balancing between the pro- and anti-competitive effects of the IP owner's refusal to deal'.[144] Schmidt considers the incentive balance test 'as an optimal instrument to analyse whether a refusal to license an intellectual property right impedes innovation and competition'.[145] However, he ultimately concludes that the incentive balance test is not yet practical due to its complexity and the amount of information it requires; hence, he suggests the innovation effects and appropriability test.[146]

However, after analysing different approaches formulated in practice and theory, it can be inferred that none of the identified approaches is entirely satisfactory. However, this does not mean that any of them should be completely dismissed. The appropriate comprehensive approach that provides the proper balance between all the rationales and interests involved should be found somewhere in between.

Competition law must not disturb the substance of copyright. Nonetheless, the reality is that in certain situations, it is justified for competition law to intervene in conduct involving the exercise of an economic copyright right. As has already been explained (see *supra*, Sect. 2.1.2), such situations represent a factual outside limitation on the exercise of copyright. Even in such cases, the intervention of competition law may take place only exceptionally under specific circumstances. Thus, copyright, as a specific intangible property right, has a special status from a competition law perspective, and a specific assessment should be applied.

For the case of refusal to license copyright, dealt with under competition rules on abuse of a dominant position, practice and theory have already identified particular conditions constituting the exceptional circumstances situations under which competition interventions against conduct involving economic copyright rights are justified. However, the exact meaning and scope of those conditions must yet be clarified. Finally, in defining the appropriate approach, balancing between the

[144] See Apostolopoulos (2007), pp. 251, 258.

[145] Schmidt views the three exceptional circumstances conditions (without objective justification) as mere filters. See Schmidt (2010), pp. 66–69.

[146] Schmidt (2010), pp. 153–184.

rationales and interests of those concerned in a particular case must always be taken into consideration,[147] and the economic aspect should also be addressed appropriately.[148]

Therefore, to adequately address the issue of refusal to license copyright, dealt with under the competition rules on abuse of dominance, and thereby maintain legal security, it is essential to have a clear rule book—guidelines for both competition authorities and stakeholders. The issue is undoubtedly very complex and requires an effects-based approach and a certain dose of flexibility. Hence, a comprehensive assessment of anti-competitive effects is necessary, whereas the use of particular standards is desirable if the standards are well defined to serve their purpose—of course, all within the boundaries of the rule book. A good example is the set of conditions establishing exceptional circumstances. The four identified conditions may serve as a general guideline in determining whether such an exceptional situation exists. However, room should be left for an alternative set of conditions, such as the case with the standard-essential patents (see *supra*, Sect. 5.2.2.2.5). The important thing is that competition interventions in the exercise of copyright occur only exceptionally, but when they occur, they must provide harmonised and well-balanced results in maintaining competition and preserving the copyright protection of rights holders.

---

[147] Many commentators have addressed the importance of balancing in refusal to deal cases; however, it seems that none of them have yet suggested a comprehensive and sustainable solution to settle the issue. Thus, Apostolopoulos, within the suggested two-step test, advocates for an economic balancing between the pro- and anti-competitive effects of the IP owner's refusal to deal. See Apostolopoulos (2007), pp. 251, 258.

Crane argued for a flexible, balancing approach to determine whether property rules or liability rules should govern the legality of a conduct at the antitrust-IPR interface. See Crane (2009), pp. 253–300.

Kaplow suggested a framework for balancing objectives of antitrust and intellectual property rights advocating qualitative application of the ratio test 'to prohibit at least those practices that exhibit a serious potential for substantial loss'. Thereat, Kaplow took into consideration: the extent to which the reward is pure transfer; the portion of reward accruing to the patentee; and the degree to which the reward serves as an incentives.; Kaplow (1984).

Kwok advocates that a balance can be struck by weighing anti-competitive effects against pro-competitive effects if refusal and, accordingly, allocative efficiency losses against dynamic efficiency gains, thereat, focusing on circumstantial factors including market power, network effects, monopoly leveraging, predatory intent, degree of follow-on innovation, and the casual connection between IPR protection and innovation incentives.; See Kwok (2011), pp. 270–286.

Schmidt considers the incentives balance test not only as an objective justification but as the central criterion of the interplay between intellectual property rights and competition policy.; See Schmidt (2010), p. 68.

[148] Many commentators have also criticised the existing case-law for lack of reliable economic foundations. Thus, Apostolopoulos states that both the EU and the US Courts 'do not use any economic arguments at all, although the US law facilitates an economic efficiency test and the EU law intends to adopt an economical approach for the application of Art. 82 EC'. See Apostolopoulos (2007), pp. 240, 253–254.

5.3.2 *The Method of Assessing Cases Concerning Refusal to License Copyright and Competition Rules on Abuse of Dominance*

For cases concerning the refusal to license copyright under the scrutiny of Article 102 TFEU, a specific approach is required to acknowledge the particularities characteristic of copyright-competition interaction situations (see *supra*, Sect. 3.2). To do so, the method of assessment must be well structured and defined, theoretically founded and practically applicable.

Similarly, as the method of assessment suggested for cases concerning the exercise of copyright under the competition rules on prohibited agreements, for refusal to license cases, the competition assessment should follow a well-defined structure. The core of the assessment is again the tailor-made test of reasonableness (see *infra*, *Ch. V*, *Section III.2.4*). The test is designed to satisfy the particularities of the copyright-competition interaction issue in an accurate and administrable manner.

Thus, as a result of the previous discussion, the method of assessment appropriate for cases concerning the refusal to license copyright under Article 102 TFEU is divided into the following stages, which will be elaborated upon in detail later:

1. Analysis of the copyright right involved in the conduct
2. Definition of the relevant market
3. Determination of a dominant position
4. Abuse of dominance
5. Exoneration

5.3.2.1 Analysis of the Copyright Right Involved Within the Conduct

The general competition rule on abuse of dominance, incorporated into Article 102 TFEU, states:

> Any abuse by one or more undertakings of a dominant position within the internal market or in a substantial part of it shall be prohibited as incompatible with the internal market in so far as it may affect trade between the Member States.
>
> Such abuse may, in particular, consist in:
>
> (a) directly or indirectly imposing unfair purchase or selling prices or other unfair trading conditions;
> (b) limiting production, markets or technical development to the prejudice of consumers;
> (c) applying dissimilar conditions to equivalent transactions with other trading parties, thereby placing them at a competitive disadvantage;
> (d) making the conclusion of contracts subject to acceptance by the other parties of supplementary obligations which, by their nature or according to commercial usage, have no connection with the subject of such contracts.

In a standard competition assessment, logically, the first stage would be to define the relevant market and then to determine whether the undertaking under investigation is in a dominant position in the relevant market in question. However, when copyright and other intellectual property rights are involved, that fact undoubtedly affects the definition of the relevant market and, consequently, the existence of dominance in the market. The specific nature and economics of copyright ought not to be neglected.

For instance, in *Microsoft*, the one extraordinarily significant and somewhat controversial case, where only the CFI's judgment was written on over 400 pages, the CFI completely neglected the potential presence of copyright and other intellectual property rights.[149] The disregard of the presence of intellectual property rights can clearly be read from the following paragraphs, in which the CFI quite explicitly stated that it does not see the need to determine an intellectual property right:

> Although the parties devoted lengthy argument, both in their written pleadings and at the hearing, to the question of the intellectual property rights which cover Microsoft's communication protocols or the specifications of those protocols, the Court considers that there is no need to decide that question in order to resolve the present case.
>
> The arguments which Microsoft derives from the alleged intellectual property rights cannot, as such, affect the lawfulness of the contested decision. The Commission did not take a position on the merits of those arguments but adopted the decision on the assumption that Microsoft was able to rely on such rights in the present case. In other words, it proceeded on the premiss that, so far as it relates to the interoperability information, the conduct at issue in the present case might not be a mere refusal to supply a product or a service indispensable to the exercise of a specific activity but a refusal to license intellectual property rights, and thus chose the strictest legal test and therefore the one most favourable to Microsoft (see paragraphs 312 to 336 below). The Commission did not therefore decide whether or not Microsoft's impugned conduct constituted a refusal to grant a licence or whether or not the remedy prescribed by Article 5 of the contested decision entailed compulsory licensing.
>
> (…)
>
> Furthermore, the Commission confirmed, in answer to one of the written questions put by the Court, that the contested decision did not establish that the interoperability information was not covered by a patent or by copyright or, on the contrary, that it was. There was no need to decide that issue since, in any event, 'the conditions for finding an abuse and for imposing the remedy [prescribed by Article 5 of the contested decision] were satisfied whether or not the information is protected by any patent or copyright'.[150]

The existence of copyright is not only crucial for deciding what kind of legal test to choose when it comes to determining abuse. The presence of copyright-protected works is also pertinent for defining the relevant market and, consequently, determining dominance, which competent authorities failed to adequately take into consideration in *Microsoft*. Reference to intellectual property rights in general cannot provide adequate results, considering the particularities of each intellectual

---

[149] The Commission and the CFI proceeded on the assumption that Microsoft's interoperability information was protected by some intellectual property rights, without actually carrying out a proper analysis and a conclusion on that point. See also Whish and Bailey (2021), p. 844.

[150] Judgment of 17 September 2007, *Microsoft v Commission*, T-201/04, EU:T:2007:289, paras. 283, 284, 288.

property right. The notion of 'intellectual property rights' can only be used for practical purposes as an umbrella term (which indeed it is) and only after every concerned right is adequately acknowledged and included in the assessment.

Nonetheless, the CFI, in *Microsoft*, at least emphasised the special status of intellectual property rights in the competition assessment.

Although such interpretation may be criticised for different reasons (*see supra*, Sect. 5.2.2.2), with regard to the importance of copyright in competition assessments, the Commission, in *Magill*, stated:

> The Commission points out that, in order to resolve the conflict referred to in the preceding paragraph, between copyright on the one hand and the rules on, inter alia, freedom of competition on the other, the proper approach is, as has consistently been held, to identify in each particular case the 'specific subject-matter' of the intellectual property right, which alone merits special protection within the Community legal order and thereby justifies certain encroachments on the Community rules. In that connection, the Commission first reflects on the legitimacy of copyright in programme listings and the underlying reasons for the maintenance thereof, which it describes as unusual. It is necessary, the Commission submits, to appraise the legal and economic 'value' and 'well-foundedness' of the copyright in the weekly listings in the present case, having regard to the objectives normally attributed to such a right. In that light, it asserts, it is necessary to take into consideration, inter alia, the nature of the property protected from the technological, cultural or innovative point of view, together with the purpose and justification in domestic law of the copyright in listings.[151]

The determination of the existence of copyright in competition law proceedings is essential for further assessment. As already discussed, copyright has a special status in the perspective of competition law. Thus, in a competition law assessment, the existence of copyright influences practically every step; therefore, it is necessary to first determine whether the conduct observed involves the exercise of a right stemming from copyright, what the characteristics of that copyright are and how it affects the market.[152] This, naturally, also includes the evaluation of the applicable national copyright framework.

Having in mind the vast array of different objects enjoying copyright protection, even within copyright, to adequately address the particular case, it is important to analyse the specific copyright in question and the rights exercised. Different objects of copyright, such as books, music, films and software, do not produce the same

---

[151] 89/205/EEC: Commission Decision of 21 December 1988 relating to a proceeding under Article 86 of the EEC Treaty (IV/31.851 - Magill TV Guide/ITP, BBC and RTE), OJ L 78, 21.3.1989, pp. 43–51. For citation, see Judgment of 10 July 1991, *RTE v Commission*, T-69/89, EU:T:1991:39, para. 45; Judgment of 10 July 1991, *BBC v Commission*, T-70/89, EU:T:1991:40, para. 29; Judgment of 10 July 1991, *ITP v Commission*, EU:T:1991:41, para. 28.

[152] AG Gulmann, in his Opinion in *Magill*, also considered that copyright should be taken as a starting point in refusal to license copyright cases:

> Thus in considering these cases the starting point must be a definition of the specific subject-matter of copyright, which is used synonymously in the Court's case-law with the concepts of the actual substance of copyright and the essential rights of the copyright proprietor.

Opinion of Advocate General Gulmann of 1 June 1994, *RTE and ITP v Commission*, Joined Cases C-241/91 P and C-242/91 P, EU:C:1994:210, para. 32.

economic effects and differently affect the structure of a relevant market. After the copyright is adequately analysed, only then is the competent authority set to move to the next stage of the assessment, starting from defining the relevant market and then determining the dominance of the undertaking exercising the copyright right.

Here, some may argue that competition authorities are not competent in deciding on copyright matters.[153] In general, such an argument might be convincing from a strictly one-sided perspective; however, this does not prevent the competent authority from assessing the case comprehensively. Quite the opposite, in copyright-competition interaction cases, competition authorities are required to adequately analyse the related exercise of copyright for purposes of the case. Keeping in mind the vast powers of competition authorities, both national authorities and the Commission, such conduct should not be problematic from a jurisdictional perspective. The competent authority's findings with regard to copyright only have an *inter partes* effect in relation to the discussed case and do not disturb the general structure of competence over copyright matters. On the contrary, if there is a decision with respect to the exercise of the copyright concerned, the competition authority should take it into consideration in the competition assessment. In addition, competition authorities are empowered to seek additional expert opinions in relation to the copyright at issue. Unlike the general courts, competition authorities, in combining the role of an investigator and a decision-maker, have the discretion to devote their efforts to what they deem the most socially important and harmful infringements[154]—this makes them just the right authorities to tackle the copyright-competition interaction issue.

Overall, in assessing refusals to license under Article 102 TFEU, it is necessary to begin with an analysis of copyright. If the exercise of a right stemming from copyright is involved, a specific assessment applies; if not, a standard competition assessment can be conducted.

5.3.2.2 Definition of the Relevant Market

Before determining whether an undertaking under a competition investigation is in a dominant position, which is a prerequisite for finding an infringement under Article 102 TFEU, it is necessary to define the relevant market.

Almost everything already discussed in the previous chapter concerning the definition of the relevant market in the context of the copyright-competition interaction (see *supra*, Sect. 4.3.2.3) also applies to an assessment of a refusal to license copyright under Article 102 TFEU. Market definition is certainly an important element in any competition assessment. This is particularly the case in situations of abuse of dominance since the definition of the relevant market will largely affect the determination of an undertaking's dominant position.[155]

---

[153] See Myrick (1992), pp. 301, 304.

[154] See Ibáñez Colomo (2018), p. 5.

[155] See Maher (2005), pp. 578–584.

How the relevant market is defined affects the relationship among competitors on the market, the market shares and the power of the undertaking under competition investigation. Thus, if a market is defined too narrowly, an undertaking may be considered to hold a dominant position, while in a broader definition, the same undertaking could avoid scrutiny under competition rules on abuse of dominance, and *vice versa*. A perfect example of this is the *Magill* case. In *Magill*, the relevant market was defined so narrowly that one product (TV programme listing) represented one whole market. If the market had been defined differently, possibly none of the undertakings involved would have even been subject to competition assessment under Article 102 TFEU.[156]

Thus, the definition of the relevant market is certainly vital and must be accurate and based on a comprehensive, well-reasoned analysis. Otherwise, the entire competition assessment can be called into question. Another example of a somewhat questionable market definition can be found in *Microsoft*. In that case, three different product markets were defined: client PC operating systems,[157] work group server operating systems[158] and streaming media players.[159,160] During the proceedings before the CFI, Microsoft raised a complaint that the second market was defined too restrictively, specifically by including only server operating systems used to supply services, known as work group services, and that such definition or terminology did not align with the industry in question.[161] However, the CFI rejected Microsoft's complaint, arguing that the Commission's definition was based on a complex

---

[156] Thus, Czapracka also questions the definition of the relevant market in *Magill*:

> Though the Court upheld the market definition and the finding of dominance on the relevant market, an interesting question is whether such a narrow market definition was correct. The question is particularly interesting taken the fact that the Court explicitly rejected the possibility that a dominant position could be implied from the possession of an IP right (see below).

Czapracka (2009), p. 79.
Myrick also considers the following in analysing *Magill*:

> With markets so narrowly defined, one can easily identify competing but different products also in other areas, such as pharmaceuticals and data processing, or treat raw 'technology' (that is the patent right) as a separate market. This would substantially affect intellectual property protection.

Myrick (1992).

[157] The Commission, Case COMP/C-3/37.792, *Microsoft*, C(2004)900 final, 24.3.2004, paras. 324–342.

[158] The Commission, Case COMP/C-3/37.792, *Microsoft*, C(2004)900 final, 24.3.2004, paras. 343–401.

[159] The Commission, Case COMP/C-3/37.792, *Microsoft*, C(2004)900 final, 24.3.2004, paras. 402–425.

[160] Judgment of 17 September 2007, *Microsoft v Commission*, T-201/04, EU:T:2007:289, para. 23.

[161] Judgment of 17 September 2007, *Microsoft v Commission*, T-201/04, EU:T:2007:289, para. 481.

economic assessment with emphasis on supply-side and demand-side substitutability.[162] After going through both the Commission's and the CFI's reasoning, it is not entirely convincing that the market was not, in fact, defined too narrowly. In any case, earlier examples show that the size of the relevant market might influence the direction of the whole case.

The existence of copyright may make things more difficult in the process of defining the relevant market (*see Ch IV, Section III.2.3*). Nevertheless, the presence of copyright and its effect on both primary and secondary markets[163] must be taken into consideration. For this reason, it is necessary to begin with an analysis of the exercise of the copyright concerned before even defining the relevant market. Unfortunately, by analysing existing case law on this matter, it was found that the effect of copyright within the relevant market seems often neglected. It appears that the two previously mentioned cases represent two opposite approaches to defining the relevant market, neither of which ultimately seemed to be plausible. On the one hand, in *Magill*, the relevant market was defined based on the existence of copyright in television programmes and the limited substitutability of the work in question. On the other hand, in the case of *Microsoft*, it would be interesting to analyse whether and how the definition of the relevant market would differ if the Commission had evaluated in detail the effect of copyright on such a market.[164]

In any case, without a comprehensive acknowledgement of copyright particularities in the assessment of the relevant market, the entire competition procedure can justifiably be called into question, leaving behind legal insecurity rather than maintaining market competition and protecting the interests of copyright holders.

5.3.2.3 Determination of a Dominant Position

The existence of an undertaking's dominant position in a competition investigation is a necessary precondition for the application of Article 102 TFEU.[165] If an undertaking does not hold a dominant position in the relevant market, the competi-

[162] Judgment of 17 September 2007, *Microsoft v Commission*, T-201/04, EU:T:2007:289, paras. 480–532.

[163] For a discussion on the dependant secondary markets, see Anderman and Schmidt (2019), pp. 49–53.

[164] The Commission acknowledges the existence of copyright; however, there is no adequate analysis of copyright in the matter. See The Commission, Case COMP/C-3/37.792, *Microsoft*, C (2004)900 final, 24.3.2004, para. 71.

[165] See, for instance, Judgment of the Court of 21 February 1973, *Europemballage Corporation and Continental Can Company Inc. v Commission of the European Communities*, C-6/71, EU:C:1973:22, para. 32; Judgment of 1 July 2010, *AstraZeneca AB and AstraZeneca plc v European Commission*, T-321/05, EU:T:2010:266, para. 30.

tion rules on abuse of dominance do not apply. In *United Brands v Commission*,[166] the CJEU laid down the test of what is considered to be a dominant position:

> The dominant position referred to in this article relates to a position of economic strength enjoyed by an undertaking which enables it to prevent effective competition being maintained on the relevant market by giving it the power to behave to an appreciable extent independently of its competitors, customers and ultimately of its consumers.[167]

Such a definition of a dominant position was later acknowledged by the Commission, which further explained the concept of dominance in its Guidance on the Enforcement Priorities in Applying Article [102 TFEU]:[168]

> (...) This notion of independence is related to the degree of competitive constraint exerted on the undertaking in question. Dominance entails that these competitive constraints are not sufficiently effective and hence that the undertaking in question enjoys substantial market power over a period of time. This means that the undertaking's decisions are largely insensitive to the actions and reactions of competitors, customers and, ultimately, consumers. (...)[169]

Usually, if the undertaking's market share in the relevant market is below 40%, it is unlikely that there is dominance.[170] However, for the determination of a dominant position, it is not sufficient to only calculate market shares. A finding of a dominant position derives from a combination of several factors, which, taken separately, are not necessarily determinative.[171] According to Paragraph 12 of the Guidance on the Enforcement Priorities in Applying Article [102 TFEU],

> The assessment of dominance will take into account the competitive structure of the market, and in particular the following factors:
> - constraints imposed by the existing supplies from, and the position on the market of, actual competitors (the market position of the dominant undertaking and its competitors),
> - constraints imposed by the credible threat of future expansion by actual competitors or entry by potential competitors (expansion and entry),
> - constraints imposed by the bargaining strength of the undertaking's customers (countervailing buyer power).

One should be especially cautious when determining an undertaking's dominant position, bearing in mind that, unlike other competitors in the market, such a position

---

[166] Judgment of the Court of 14 February 1978, *United Brands Company and United Brands Continentaal BV v Commission of the European Communities (Chiquita Bananas)*, C-27/76, EU:C:1978:22.

[167] Judgment of the Court of 14 February 1978, *United Brands Company and United Brands Continentaal BV v Commission of the European Communities (Chiquita Bananas)*, C-27/76, EU:C:1978:22, para. 65.

[168] Communication from the Commission—Guidance on the Commission's enforcement priorities in applying Article 82 of the EC Treaty to abusive exclusionary conduct by dominant undertakings, OJ C 45, 24.2.2009, pp. 7–20.

[169] Guidance on the enforcement priorities in applying Article [102 TFEU], para. 10.

[170] Guidance on the enforcement priorities in applying Article [102 TFEU], para. 14.

[171] Guidance on the enforcement priorities in applying Article [102 TFEU]. para. 14.

carries a special responsibility with regard to how to behave in the market.[172] An undertaking in a dominant position must abstain from certain behaviour that would normally be allowed for a normal (non-dominant) market competitor. Otherwise, the conduct of an undertaking in a dominant position would fall under the scrutiny of competition rules on abuse of dominance.

With regard to copyright-competition interaction cases involving abuse of dominance, there was some confusion earlier regarding the concept of monopoly and the impact of particular intellectual property rights on the relevant market. Especially from a common law perspective, copyright is frequently described as a monopoly.[173] Indeed, copyright, as well as most other intellectual property rights, confers certain exclusive rights that may be argued to have a certain monopolistic character in the use of individual work.[174] Thus, there was confusion with regard to the distinction between (i) the legal monopoly granted by intellectual property rights and (ii) the forms of economic monopoly and market power relevant to competition law.[175] In this respect, it should be clarified, on the one hand, that according to Posner, 'A firm that is the only seller of a product or service having no close substitutes is said to enjoy a monopoly'.[176] It follows that the characteristics of a monopoly are the absence of competition and the lack of substitute goods, resulting in a single seller controlling the market. On the other hand, copyright merely entitles holders to an exclusive right over their copyright-protected work; therefore, copyright does not constitute a monopoly.[177]

Thus, a single copyright-protected work almost never constitutes a complete market. Otherwise, practically every copyright holder would automatically be in a dominant position and, quite contradictory to the concept of copyright, more prone to violate competition rules on abuse of dominance. For this reason, it is vital to have a reliable, comprehensive definition of the relevant market in the prior phase of the assessment (see Sect. 5.3.2.2). The scope of the relevant market directly affects the market power of the competitors involved. For instance, in *Magill*, the relevant market was defined quite narrowly, whereas one copyright-protected work

---

[172]The concept of 'special responsibility' of the dominant undertaking can be traced back to the ordoliberal school of thought with the interpretation that a dominant undertaking cannot use its market power to unfairly exclude its rivals on the market. See Vansberg (2004).

[173]See Patterson (1968), p. 17; Strowel (1994), p. 236; Borghart (2008), pp. 32–33; Vernet (2008), p. 154.

[174]European Commission, Glossary of terms used in EU competition policy: Antitrust and control of concentrations, Brussels. July 2002. https://publications.europa.eu/en/publication-detail/-/publication/100e1bc8-cee3-4f65-9b30-e232ec3064d6. Accessed 24 Oct 2024, p. 26; OECD (1993), para. 106.

[175]See OECD (2018) Scoping Note, p. 6. On the different usage of the word 'monopoly' in the context of competition law and intellectual property rights from the US perspective, see also Leslie (2011), pp. 54–56.

[176]Posner (1969), p. 548.

[177]See Skone James et al. (1991), pp. 1–3; Max Planck Institute for Intellectual Property and Competition Law (2013), p. 74.

constituted the whole relevant market.[178] If the relevant market were defined more broadly,[179] not all undertakings under investigation would likely be in a dominant position and, consequently, would not fall under the scrutiny of competition rules on abuse of dominance. Nevertheless, such a narrow definition of the market, where a single copyright forms the entire relevant market, is an exception.

Fortunately, nowadays, the view that IPR equates to market monopoly has been firmly replaced by the understanding that the legal monopoly conferred by intellectual property rights does not translate into economic market power. In that sense, the CJEU made it clear that, in general, individual copyright does not *per se* confer dominance in a market.[180] However, copyright protection can still lead to market dominance.[181] Copyright is undoubtedly relevant for the assessment of market power and should be adequately considered.[182]

5.3.2.4 Abuse of Dominance

5.3.2.4.1 General Remarks

Article 102 TFEU generally prescribes:

> Any abuse by one or more undertakings of a dominant position within the internal market or in a substantial part of it shall be prohibited as incompatible with the internal market in so far as it may affect trade between Member States.

[178] See Judgment of 10 July 1991, *RTE v Commission*, T-69/89, EU:T:1991:39, paras. 41, 61–63; Judgment of 10 July 1991, *BBC v Commission*, T-70/89, EU:T:1991:40, paras. 26, 48–51; Judgment of 10 July 1991, *ITP v Commission*, EU:T:1991:41, paras. 25, 47–49.

[179] The undertakings argued (unsuccessfully) that the diverse sources of information on television programmes, such as daily or weekly newspapers, trailers, teletext services and previous knowledge of programme times, are substitutable for television guides and that the legal monopoly deriving from its copyright in the listings must not be confused with the economic concept of a dominant position. See Judgment of 10 July 1991, *RTE v Commission*, T-69/89, EU:T:1991:39, paras. 30–32; Judgment of 10 July 1991, *BBC v Commission*, T-70/89, EU:T:1991:40, para. 17; Judgment of 10 July 1991, *ITP v Commission*, EU:T:1991:41, para. 17.

[180] See Judgment of 18 February 1971, *Sirena S.r.l. v Eda S.r.l. and Others*, C-40/70, EU:C:1971:18, para. 16; Judgment of 8 June 1971, *Deutsche Grammophon v Metro SB*, C-78/70, EU:C:1971:59, para. 16; Judgment of 6 April 1995, *RTE and ITP v Commission*, Joined Cases C-241/91 P and C-242/91 P, EU:C:1995:98, para. 46; Judgment of 6 December 2012, *AstraZeneca AB and AstraZeneca plc v European Commission*, C-457/10 P, EU:C:2012:770, para. 186.

[181] Max Planck Institute for Intellectual Property and Competition Law (2013), p. 7.

[182] On intellectual property and market power, see Apostolopoulos (2007), pp. 240–242; Katz (2007), pp. 860–871; Stazi (2011), pp. 2–3.

OECD (2018) Scoping Note, pp. 4–7. DG Competition discussion paper on the application of Article 82 of the Treaty to exclusionary abuses, Brussels. December 2005. https://ec.europa.eu/competition/antitrust/art82/discpaper2005.pdf. Accessed 24 Oct 2024, paras. 20–42.

The subsequent paragraph of Article 102 TFEU provides a non-exhaustive list of what abuse may consist.[183]

The competition rules on abuse of dominance impose special obligations for undertakings in a dominant position in the relevant market to behave with more caution than other competitors with less market power. An undertaking in a dominant position has a special responsibility 'not to allow its conduct to impair genuine undistorted competition on the common market'.[184]

However, as repeatedly emphasised within this thesis, due to its particularities and special economics, copyright (and other intellectual property rights) has a special status from the perspective of competition law. Hence, in the competition assessments of conduct involving an exercise of copyright, a specific tailor-made approach should be taken. Special features of this approach are present in practically all stages of competition assessment, where the determination of abuse is undoubtedly the central issue and, in essence, the subject of most discussion.

During the development of this specific issue, where refusal to license copyright is the most common situation, several approaches have been recognised through both practice and theory—from the inherency concepts and the existence v. exercise dichotomy, through variations of the exceptional circumstances concept, to the complementarity concept. However, not one approach has provided a clear and balanced criterion for determining abuse of dominance in cases of copyright-competition interaction. It seems that the exceptional circumstances conditions from *IMS Health* are the most reliable solution that theory and practice have developed. However, they are still far from adequate to fully settle the issue.

To establish appropriate criteria for addressing refusal to license copyright cases, several things should be clarified. Due to the special status of copyright in competition assessments, abuse of dominance should only be found in exceptional circumstances. Such a situation may occur when the exercise of copyright goes beyond the 'normal' exercise of copyright. Although abuse of dominance is predominantly an objective concept, especially in cases concerning copyright-competition interaction, the subjective elements are not irrelevant.[185] In the assessment of conduct, it must be determined whether the exercise of a right stemming from copyright was directed to

---

[183] Article 102(2) TFEU:

Such abuse may, in particular, consist in:

(a) directly or indirectly imposing unfair purchase or selling prices or other unfair trading conditions;
(b) limiting production, markets or technical development to the prejudice of consumers;
(c) applying dissimilar conditions to equivalent transactions with other trading parties, thereby placing them at a competitive disadvantage;
(d) making the conclusion of contracts subject to acceptance by the other parties of supplementary obligations which, by their nature or according to commercial usage, have no connection with the subject of such contracts.

[184] Judgment of the Court of 9 November 1983, *NV Nederlandsche Banden Industrie Michelin v Commission of the European Communities*, C-322/81, EU:C:1983:313, para. 57.

[185] See also Chirita (2011), pp. 83–89, 96–98.

harm competition in the relevant market rather than simply to enjoy the copyright. This implies not necessarily an awareness of the distortion of competition but rather an intention to engage in conduct that falls within the scope of competition rules on abuse of dominance, in this case in the context of the copyright-competition interaction.

In any case, the appropriate theory of harm must be clearly articulated and possess the following characteristics:

- It should clearly explain how competition and, ultimately, consumers will be harmed in relation to an appropriately defined counterfactual.
- It should be internally logically consistent.
- It should be consistent with the incentives that the various parties face.
- It should be consistent with (or at least not inconsistent with) available empirical evidence[186] (see *supra, Ch IV, Section III.2.5*).

It should be borne in mind that articulating a reasonable theory of harm has been especially problematic from the aspect of the competition rules on abuse of dominance. Zenger and Walker observe: 'Arguably, the area of European competition law in which the Commission has been most reluctant to formulate and investigate a reasonable theory of harm is the assessment of potentially exclusionary conduct under Article 102.'[187] They further note: 'Prohibiting unilateral conduct without a convincing theory of harm is therefore harmful to competition itself.'[188]

In articulating the proper theory of harm, the specificity of copyright-competition interaction must also be taken into consideration. Thus, certain exceptional circumstances must be present for the exercise of copyright to constitute an infringement of competition rules on abuse of dominance. To adequately determine abuse of dominance, a specific test is required that would respect the particularities of copyright and find abuse only exceptionally. In *Microsoft*, it was generally acknowledged that the copyright-competition interaction test is the strictest legal test in competition evaluations.[189] However, from the solutions provided in practice and theory, the exceptional circumstances test provided in *IMS Health* seems to be the most suitable starting point. In itself, the *IMS Health* test is certainly not wholly developed and is too superficial. Nonetheless, in comparison with the approach provided in *Microsoft*, it seems to be a more universal and sustainable solution rather than a one-time-only test clearly designed only to establish abuse.

---

[186] See Zenger and Walker (2012), p. 185.

[187] Zenger and Walker attribute this to the ordoliberal origins of European competition law. Namely, the ordoliberal doctrine is formulated in accordance with the formal characteristics of perfect competition, which have little in common with reality. Thus, many unilateral conduct sometimes creates substantial efficiencies rather than competitive harm; see Zenger and Walker (2012), pp. 202–209.

[188] Zenger and Walker (2012), p. 203.

[189] See Judgment of 17 September 2007, *Microsoft v Commission*, T-201/04, EU:T:2007:289, para. 284.

In *IMS Health*, a set of four conditions was identified that, if fulfilled, would constitute the exceptional circumstances situation in which competition intervention in an exercise of copyright is necessary. Taking everything into consideration, such a set of conditions generally does seem like an appropriate test for the determination of refusal to license copyright as an abuse of dominance; however, further improvements are required. Therefore, the test of reasonableness presented below modifies the *IMS Health* exceptional circumstances test to fit the requirements of copyright-competition interaction.

5.3.2.4.2 The Conditions Constituting an Exceptional Circumstances Situation in View of the Copyright-Competition Interaction Issue

After it has been established that the assessed conduct concerns the exercise of copyright and the relevant market has been comprehensively defined and it has been determined that the undertaking under competition investigation is indeed in a dominant position in the relevant market, the next step is to perform the test of reasonableness. The rationale of the test of reasonableness is to establish whether there are exceptional circumstances that justify limiting the exercise of copyright by means of competition law.

In practice, the conditions constituting exceptional circumstances situations are identified as follows:

i) Indispensability of the protected product or service for carrying on a particular business
ii) The new product condition
iii) Absence of objective justification
iv) Elimination of competition in the downstream market

What each particular condition entails has been differently interpreted. Probably the best example is a comparison of the *IMS Health* and *Microsoft* interpretations of exceptional circumstances criteria, which clearly shows how significant different interpretations of a particular condition can be (see *supra*, Sect. 5.2.2.2). However, for a convincing and founded understanding of the copyright-competition interaction, such deviations in interpretation are unacceptable. Above all, there is a need for consistency and security in dealing with this specific issue.

This research considers that, in general, the concept of exceptional circumstances is plausible and founded. However, the existing understanding of exceptional circumstances certainly needs to be modified to be in line with the general understanding of the relationship between copyright law and competition law (see *supra*, Sect. 3.2). The *IMS Health* interpretation might be used as a starting point; however, the suggested test of reasonableness clearly differs from the established concept of exceptional circumstances.

The research suggests the following structure of the exceptional circumstances test, specifically tailored to assess the refusal to license copyright as an abuse of dominance:

1. New original and creative work
2. Indispensability of the refused copyright licence
3. Refusal directed towards eliminating competition in the downstream market
4. The 'three-step test'

1. New Original and Creative Work

This condition is usually discussed under the so-called new product criterion. In *IMS Health*, the interpretation of the new product criterion was that the undertaking requesting a licence must 'not intend to limit itself essentially to duplicating the goods or services already offered on the secondary market by the owner of the intellectual property right, but intends to produce new goods or services not offered by the owner of the right and for which there is a potential consumer demand'.[190] In *Microsoft*, the interpretation of the new product criterion was lessened and extended to other factors that may cause consumer harm, such as the limitation of technical development, making it much easier for competition authorities to establish the exceptional circumstances situation.[191]

However, neither interpretation of the 'new product' seems to be suitable for the copyright-competition interaction issue.[192] Namely, the complementarity between copyright law and competition law can be found in the effects of copyright and the objectives of competition law—both provide incentives to further creation and originality: copyright law through the protection of authorship and competition law through the protection of dynamic competition.

Thus, a 'new product' should not be any new product but a new original and creative work—one that is protected by copyright law.[193] From the perspective of competition law and competition rules on abuse of dominance, the exercise of copyright can only be limited if the refusal to license by a copyright holder in a dominant position negatively impacts the competitive process that enhances creativity and originality. However, in limiting the exercise of copyright, competition law should not encourage competition by imitation[194] and competition by extension,[195] considering that such limitation would interfere with the very substance of copyright.[196]

---

[190] Judgment of 29 April 2004, *IMS Health*, C-418/01, EU:C:2004:257, para. 48.

[191] See Judgment of 17 September 2007, *Microsoft v Commission*, T-201/04, EU:T:2007:289, paras. 643–665.

[192] Some even consider that the new product criterion should be omitted from the refusal to deal analysis. See Apostolopoulos (2007), p. 251; Leistner (2005), p. 161.

[193] It should remain an open question whether it would be acceptable if a request for a licence under this condition is required for a new patent or some other intellectual property right. However, any new (not creative/original/innovative) product ought not to be considered sufficient to satisfy this exceptional circumstances condition.

[194] See Drexl (2004), pp. 788–808.

[195] See Firth (2021), pp. 53–54.

[196] See also Max Planck Institute for Intellectual Property and Competition Law (2013), p. 75.

Hence, for the fulfilment of this criterion, the conduct of the undertaking must prevent the creation of new creative and original work(s). Since such work is new and original, the implication is that it is not already offered by the undertaking in a dominant position and that there is some potential customer demand for such work.

For instance, and without yet addressing the other exceptional circumstances conditions, if an undertaking is asking for a license to create new software that would provide a solution to improve car safety, predict the spread of COVID-19 disease or offer something else that is potentially interesting for a certain linked market, then there might be indications of exceptional circumstances in that particular case. If an undertaking is asking for a license to read floppy disks, then it may be less likely that there would be potential customer demand for such work (even if protected by copyright) and that the new original and creative work condition would be fulfilled. However, there is no straightforward answer to what kind of work would be acceptable under this condition and whether there would be a potential customer demand for such a product. Theoretically, the refusal to grant a licence for a derivative copyright work (i.e. film adaptation of a novel) might as well satisfy this condition *per se*.[197] However, such conduct would still have to satisfy the other conditions constituting exceptional circumstances. Hence, it is probably not very likely that such a situation (i.e. film adaptation of a novel) would ultimately establish the abuse entailed in competition rules on abuse of dominance.

This criterion of a new original and creative work should be evaluated on a case-by-case basis through a detailed legal-economic analysis. Under existing case law, it is likely that a weekly television guide in a particular system represented a new original and creative work for which there was a potential customer demand (*Magill*), it is less likely that a modified brick structure constituting a database represented a new and original work for which there was a potential customer demand (*IMS Health*), while it remains questionable whether there was a concrete new and original work behind the request to license Microsoft's interoperability information (*Microsoft*).

Therefore, in the exceptional circumstances test, the 'new product' criterion ought to be replaced by the 'new original and creative work' criterion. This should also be the first condition to be evaluated when testing the existence of exceptional circumstances in a particular case.

2. Indispensability of the Refused Copyright Licence

In *IMS Health*, the indispensability criterion was explained in the following way: 'in order to determine whether a product or service is indispensable for enabling an undertaking to carry on business in a particular market, it must be determined whether there are products or services which constitute alternative solutions, even if they are less advantageous, and whether there are technical, legal or economic

[197] In that sense, Firth argues that, for instance, copyright holders of *Harry Potter* stories might even be subject to Article 102 TFEU if they refuse to license copyright to creators of 'fan fiction' in situations where no substitutes for the exceptional work exist. See Firth (2021), pp. 65–66.

obstacles capable of making it impossible or at least unreasonably difficult for any undertaking seeking to operate in the market to create, possibly in cooperation with other operators, the alternative products or services'.[198] In *Microsoft*, this condition was practically diminished, requiring only some competitive disadvantage on the part of the undertaking requesting a copyright licence as a consequence of the dominant undertaking's refusal to license.[199]

Regarding this condition, the interpretation provided in *IMS Health* seems a tenable solution. Indeed, if there are other means and ways for an undertaking to carry on business in a particular market, there is no justifiable reason to force the copyright holder to license copyright rights if the copyright holder does not want to license them willingly. This would be considered unjustified interference with guaranteed copyright protection.

Still, to be fully in line with the understanding of copyright-competition interaction, there is a need to amend the interpretation provided in *IMS Health*. A more appropriate way to formulate the indispensability criterion would be to acknowledge the involvement of copyright. Thus, an improved definition of the indispensability criterion should be as follows: 'indispensability of the refused copyright license means that besides the requested copyright license, there are no other alternative means or ways that would reasonably enable the undertaking requesting the license to carry on business in a particular market'. The situation of the undertaking requesting the licence must be analysed comprehensively, and the technical, legal and economic obstacles must be considered, as well as the possibility of cooperating with other operators. If there are other means or ways to enable the undertaking to carry on its business, even if they are less advantageous, the copyright licence should not be considered indispensable.

From previous case law, a solid example of an indispensable licence can be drawn, for example from *Magill*, where a weekly television guide could not indeed be created without the licence requested from TV and radio broadcasters found to be in a dominant position.[200]

3. Refusal Directed Towards the Elimination of Competition in the Downstream Market

Throughout practice, there have been different interpretations regarding the criterion for the elimination of competition. Mainly, this condition concerns competition in the downstream market; however, discussions focus on the degree of elimination of competition. In *Magill*, it was merely required that the undertakings refusing to license had eliminated all competition in the secondary market,[201] while

---

[198] Judgment of 29 April 2004, *IMS Health*, C-418/01, EU:C:2004:257, para. 28.

[199] See Judgment of 17 September 2007, *Microsoft v Commission*, T-201/04, EU:T:2007:289, paras. 345–346, 434–435.

[200] To note, in *Magill*, the CJEU brought together the indispensability and elimination of competition criteria. See Judgment of 6 April 1995, *RTE and ITP v Commission*, Joined Cases C-241/91 P and C-242/91 P, ECLI:EU:C:1995:98., para. 56.

[201] Judgment of 6 April 1995, *RTE and ITP v Commission*, Joined Cases C-241/91 P and C-242/91 P, ECLI:EU:C:1995:98., para. 56.

in *IMS Health*, where it was more thoroughly discussed, this condition was said to have been fulfilled if the refusal were 'likely to eliminate all competition'.[202] *Microsoft*, on the other hand, used a more lenient interpretation and concluded that this condition would be satisfied if there were a 'risk of elimination of all effective competition',[203] which clearly makes it much easier to establish the exceptional circumstances situation.

In the context of the copyright-competition interaction issue, the elimination of competition is surely a condition that needs to be satisfied in order to establish the existence of an exceptional circumstances situation. If the refusal is not directed towards eliminating competition in the downstream market, then the situation is not exceptional, even if some of the other conditions are fulfilled. Thus, the question remains what the appropriate interpretation of this condition is.

The 'risk to eliminate all effective competition' truly seems a feeble standard to be satisfied in order to fulfil the elimination of competition condition. Particularly, nowadays, when undertakings are acting in a dynamic environment and most business schools teach that creating barriers is good and scaling and strengthening one's own position as much as possible is encouraged, the 'risk' of something happening seems an open-ended criterion. Instead, when it is objectively likely that a particular instance of refusal to license copyright is eliminating all competition in the downstream market or that it is destroying the connected relevant market, then, indeed, there might be a need to intervene. In such a situation, it makes sense to conclude that copyright is being exercised under exceptional circumstances that justify competition intervention (of course, if the other conditions are also satisfied). Concerning the addition of 'effective' before competition—most likely referencing a concept introduced by Clark and discussed under the name 'workable competition'[204]—such an addition might be accepted, although it does not seem necessary. Also, what was not discussed in the case law on refusal to license was the rare but possible anti-competitive impact that may also occur in the upstream market due to the refusal of the dominant undertaking.[205] Hence, concerning the potential specific situation, it might be advisable to substitute 'downstream market' with the notion 'linked market'.

Therefore, the appropriate interpretation of the elimination of competition condition in exceptional circumstances seems to be that the refusal to license is 'likely to eliminate all (effective) competition on the linked market'.

4. Objective Justification

---

[202] See Judgment of 29 April 2004, *IMS Health*, C-418/01, EU:C:2004:257, paras 37–47.

[203] See Judgment of 17 September 2007, *Microsoft v Commission*, T-201/04, EU:T:2007:289, paras. 560–564.

[204] Clark (1940), pp. 241–256.

[205] See European Commission, Directorate for Financial and Enterprise Affairs Competition Committee, Roundtable on Refusals to Deal, a Note by the European Commission, DAF/COMP/WD (2007)100, October 4, 2007, pp. 3–5.

In practice and academia, the (absence of the) objective justification criterion is commonly discussed as one of the conditions necessary for establishing exceptional circumstances situations. However, it was never explained what the objective justification truly is in essence. In *Magill*, it was merely noted that 'there was no justification for such refusal either in the activity of television broadcasting or in that of publishing television magazines'.[206] In *IMS Health*, the CJEU stated that the condition should be examined, 'if appropriate, in light of the facts before it, whether the refusal of the request for a licence is justified by objective considerations'.[207] However, no objective considerations were found or even discussed. In that sense, Czapracka considers: 'It is reasonable to expect that the value of IP at stake and the cost of research and development could be considered as an objective "justification" for a refusal to license.'[208] In *Microsoft*, the existence of an intellectual property right and the secrecy of technology were rejected as possible objective justifications. Instead, the incentive balance test was considered as a possible objective justification.[209]

Indeed, the existence of copyright *per se* is not a valid 'objective justification' in the context of copyright-competition interaction. This is precisely because the existence of copyright itself necessitates a special competition law approach to conduct involving its exercise. If the existence of copyright was taken as a valid objective justification, then there would be no copyright-competition interaction issue, and every conduct involving the exercise of copyright would automatically be exempted from the scope of competition law. Such an approach would be in line with the so-called theory of absolutism (see *supra*, Sect. 5.2.4), which considers that copyright should be completely immune from the application of competition law. However, this approach is neither well founded nor realistic.

Besides that, balancing the negative impact that the imposition of the requirement to license copyright might have on the dominant undertaking's incentives to create against the positive impact of that obligation on industry-wide innovation does not seem to be an appropriate element for the objective justification criterion.[210] Namely, balancing interests seems reasonable and useful for a comprehensive approach; however, it should be integrated throughout the entire assessment rather than applied separately at the very end. In copyright-competition interaction, it is not

---

[206] Judgment of 6 April 1995, *RTE and ITP v Commission*, Joined Cases C-241/91 P and C-242/91 P, ECLI:EU:C:1995:98, para. 55.

[207] Judgment of 29 April 2004, *IMS Health*, C-418/01, EU:C:2004:257, para. 51.

[208] However, she makes that comment after questioning whether the approach taken in *Magill* and *IMS Health* would apply to a valid patent. See Czapracka (2009), pp. 86–87.

[209] See Judgment of 17 September 2007, *Microsoft v Commission*, T-201/04, EU:T:2007:289, paras. 688–712.

[210] See Judgment of 17 September 2007, *Microsoft v Commission*, T-201/04, EU:T:2007:289, para. 710.

about two conflicting laws and deciding which of the two should prevail. Quite the opposite, with a proper comprehensive and balanced assessment of the copyright-competition interaction issue, both copyright law and competition law stay in line with their rationales. Hence, the isolated balancing test does not seem to be an acceptable 'objective justification' either.

All things considered, it seems that objective justification should not be regarded as one of the conditions constituting an exceptional circumstances situation. Instead, even after the establishment of exceptional circumstances, the conduct may still be defended (exonerated) for a limited number of reasons, which are discussed below (see *infra*, *Ch V, Section III.2.5*).

4. The 'Three-Step Test'

The objective justification criterion was rejected as part of the anti-competitiveness test. It does not seem to be an appropriate criterion for assessing the potential exceptional circumstances situation that would justify competition intervention in the exercise of copyright.

Instead, the copyright 'three-step test' should be considered an alternative fourth condition in the anti-competitiveness test.[211] Thus, as the final criterion, it should be necessary to establish whether the situation constitutes a special case, which does not conflict with the 'normal' exploitation of the copyright-protected work and does not unreasonably prejudice the legitimate interests of authors or rights holders. As was already indicated, evidently, the three-step test is part of the copyright framework; hence, it is not directly applicable to competition law as an outside limitation on the exercise of copyright. However, considering the content of the three-step test, it seems adequate to apply this test *per analogiam* to establish whether the competition intervention in the exercise of copyright is indeed justified.

If the 'three-step test' shows that, regardless of some competition concerns, competition law intervention would conflict with the 'normal' exploitation of copyright-protected work[212] and unreasonably prejudice the legitimate interest of the authors and rights holders,[213] this should be considered a genuine objective justification in the context of the copyright-competition interaction. Incorporating such a criterion should serve as an additional mechanism for balancing all the interests involved and ensuring competition law assessment is aligned with copyright law.

---

[211] Firth also considers the application of the three-step test in the context of copyright-competition interaction matters. See Firth (2021), p. 66.

[212] In relation to the copyright three-step test, Ginsburg and Treppoz consider that 'exceptions and limitations would be presumed not to conflict with normal exploitation if they are confined to a scope that does not enter into economic competition with non-exempted uses'. See Ginsburg and Treppoz (2015), p. 464.

[213] Considering 'the unreasonable prejudice of legitimate interests of authors and other right holders', Ginsburg and Treppoz explain that this condition implies several steps: first is to define the interests of the right holders at stake and which attributes make them legitimate; second is to develop an interpretation of the term 'prejudice' and establish what degree of it reaches a level that should be considered 'unreasonable'. See Ginsburg and Treppoz (2015), p. 467.

5.3.2.4.3 Some Further Remarks on the Comprehensive Exceptional Circumstances Test as the Criterion for Determining the Exercise of Copyright as an Abuse of a Dominant Position

Within the sphere of copyright-competition interaction, refusal to deal is one of the standard potential abuses of dominance—arguably the most characteristic of the copyright-competition interaction issue and convincingly the most discussed within case law and academia.[214] The earlier-described set of conditions establishing exceptional circumstances is primarily designed to evaluate whether a particular refusal to license by an undertaking in a dominant position distorts competition contrary to competition rules on abuse of dominance. Thus, this test should be appropriate for the assessment of that specific situation. Other anti-competitive conduct involving the exercise of copyright, such as price discrimination, product tying or others, can interfere with competition rules on abuse of dominance as well. For the assessment of those situations, this set of conditions would possibly not always be appropriate. Within the patent-competition interaction, a good analogue example is the standard-essential patent (SEP) case of *Huawei*. The practice has evolved that SEPs must be licensed under FRAND terms. For several reasons (see *supra*, Sect. 5.2.2.2.5), this situation is clearly different from a classic refusal to license particular intellectual property cases. Thus, in *Huawei*, by referring to established case law (*Magill, IMS Health*), the CJEU plainly acknowledged the recognised understanding that the exercise of an intellectual property right may infringe competition rules on abuse of dominance only in exceptional circumstances.[215] However, due to the specific characteristics of the situation at issue, the CJEU established another set of conditions to define exceptional circumstances.[216]

Therefore, the list provided above is generally cumulative but is not universal for all cases involving the exercise of copyright under Article 102 TFEU. If certain situations require the identification of another set of conditions, that should be acknowledged.[217] Nevertheless, the relationship between copyright law and competition law and the main principles of this matter should always stay the same—copyright has a special status in competition assessments, and the infringement of rules may only take place exceptionally as an outside limitation on the exercise of copyright. Thus, the only variable in the competition assessment can be the set of conditions establishing exceptional circumstances, while the rest of the assessment remains the same. For the refusal to license situation, probably the most common one, the set of conditions is clearly listed and explained above, while for other

[214] See Max Planck Institute for Intellectual Property and Competition Law (2013), pp. 8, 118; Firth (2021), p. 47.

[215] See Judgment of 16 July 2015, *Huawei Technologies Co. Ltd v ZTE Corp. and ZTE Deutschland GmbH*, C-170/13, EU:C:2015:477, para. 47.

[216] Judgment of 16 July 2015, *Huawei Technologies Co. Ltd v ZTE Corp. and ZTE Deutschland GmbH*, C-170/13, EU:C:2015:477, paras. 48–71.

[217] See Anderman and Schmidt (2019), pp. 109–110.

particular situations, such as excessive pricing or tying, some other set of conditions might be more appropriate.

Also, with regard to other intellectual property rights, the findings from and the main principles of this research may be applied *per analogiam*. Still, due to the unique nature of each right encompassed within the notion of intellectual property rights, it is necessary to analyse the interaction between each intellectual property right and competition law separately.

5.3.2.5 Exoneration

The competition rules on abuse of dominance generally do not include exemption provisions, like those set out in Article 101(3) TFEU, or different block exemptions related to prohibited agreements. Still, through practice, the so-called objective justification concept was developed. As its name indicates, it allows for the possibility of justifying particular abuses of dominance for specific objective reasons.[218]

However, it is still not clear what those objective reasons are that might justify conduct representing abuse of dominance.[219] In relation to copyright-competition interaction, it is certain that the existence of copyright *per se* is not sufficient to objectively justify the abusive conduct of dominant undertakings. Otherwise, any conduct involving the exercise of copyright would immediately be immune from the enforcement of competition rules on abuse of dominance. Aside from the pure existence of copyright, the balancing of incentives was also discussed as a possible objective justification in the context of exceptional circumstances conditions. However, practice has shown that the balancing of incentives seems not a realistic objective justification for exonerating any abusive conduct of a dominant undertaking (see discussion *supra*, Sect. 5.3.2.4.2).

Nonetheless, in the Guidance on the Commission's Enforcement Priorities in Applying Article 82 of the EC Treaty [Article 102 TFEU] to Abusive Exclusionary Conduct by Dominant Undertakings, the Commission acknowledged the possibility of exonerating the prohibition in Article 102 TFEU, even if the conduct of a dominant undertaking leads to the foreclosure of competitors. To do so, and to

---

[218] See, for instance, Judgment of 14 February 1978, *United Brands Company and United Brands Continentaal BV v Commission of the European Communities (Chiquita Bananas)*, Case 27/76, EU:C:1978:22, para. 184; Judgment of 3 October 1985, *Centre belge d'études de marché - Télémarketing (CBEM) v SA Compagnie luxembourgeoise de télédiffusion (CLT) and Information publicité Benelux (IPB)*, Case 311/84, EU:C:1985:394, para. 27; Judgment of 12 December 1991, *Hilti AG v Commission of the European Communities*, T-30/89, EU:T:1991:70, paras. 102–119; Judgment of 6 October 1994, *Tetra Pak International SA v Commission of the European Communities*, T-83/91, EU:T:1994:246, paras. 136, 207; Judgment of 15 March 2007, *British Airways plc v Commission of the European Communities*, C-95/04 P, EU:C:2007:166, paras. 69, 86; Judgment of 27 March 2012, *Post Danmark A/S v Konkurrencerådet*, C-209/10, EU:C:2012:172, paras. 41–43.

[219] Some scholars consider that the protection of moral (or personality) rights might represent an objective justification in the context of refusal to license copyright cases. See Burke (2002); Firth (2021), pp. 60–61, 66.

justify its conduct, the dominant undertaking would have to demonstrate that its conduct is objectively necessary or produces substantial efficiencies that outweigh any anti-competitive effects on consumers. In assessing such claims by a dominant undertaking, the Commission will have to assess whether the conduct in question is indispensable and proportionate to the goal allegedly pursued by the dominant undertaking.[220]

Thus, the Commission recognises two grounds for the justification of the abusive conduct of dominant undertakings. On the first ground, the assessment of whether the conduct is objectively necessary and proportionate must be determined on the basis of factors external to the dominant undertaking.[221] Concerning the second ground—that efficiencies are sufficient to guarantee that no net harm to consumers is likely to arise—the Commission requires demonstration of the existence of specific conditions ('with a sufficient degree of probability, and on the basis of verifiable evidence').[222] The conditions, recognised as follows, are expected to be fulfilled cumulatively:

- The efficiencies have been, or are likely to be, realised as a result of the conduct. They may, for example, include technical improvements in the quality of goods, or a reduction in the cost of production or distribution.
- The conduct is indispensable to the realisation of those efficiencies: there must be no less anti-competitive alternatives to the conduct that are capable of producing the same efficiencies.
- The likely efficiencies brought about by the conduct outweigh any likely negative effects on competition and consumer welfare in the affected markets.
- The conduct does not eliminate effective competition, by removing all or most existing sources of actual or potential competition. Rivalry between undertakings is an essential driver of economic efficiency, including dynamic efficiencies in the form of innovation. In its absence the dominant undertaking will lack adequate incentives to continue to create and pass on efficiency gains. Where there is no residual competition and no foreseeable threat of entry, the protection of rivalry and the competitive process outweighs possible efficiency gains. In the Commission's view, exclusionary conduct which maintains, creates or strengthens a market position approaching that of a monopoly can normally not be justified on the grounds that it also creates efficiency gains.[223]

[220]Communication from the Commission—Guidance on the Commission's enforcement priorities in applying Article 82 of the EC Treaty to abusive exclusionary conduct by dominant undertakings, OJ C 45, 24.2.2009, pp. 7–20, para. 28.

[221]The Commission provides examples of health and safety reasons related to the nature of the product in question and further notes that, generally, it is the task of public authorities to set and enforce public health and safety standards and not of undertakings in their own discretion. See Communication from the Commission—Guidance on the Commission's enforcement priorities in applying Article 82 of the EC Treaty to abusive exclusionary conduct by dominant undertakings, OJ C 45, 24.2.2009, pp. 7–20, para. 29.

[222]See Communication from the Commission—Guidance on the Commission's enforcement priorities in applying Article 82 of the EC Treaty to abusive exclusionary conduct by dominant undertakings, OJ C 45, 24.2.2009, pp. 7–20, para. 30.

[223]See Communication from the Commission—Guidance on the Commission's enforcement priorities in applying Article 82 of the EC Treaty to abusive exclusionary conduct by dominant undertakings, OJ C 45, 24.2.2009, pp. 7–20, para. 30.

Generally, the Commission considers that it is incumbent upon the dominant undertaking to provide all the evidence necessary to demonstrate that the conduct concerned is objectively justified. Only after the undertaking provides sufficient evidence will it fall to the Commission to make the ultimate assessment of whether the conduct concerned is not objectively necessary and, through a weighing up of any apparent anti-competitive effects against any advanced and substantiated efficiencies, is likely to result in consumer harm.[224]

Thus, although the concept of competition rules on abuse of dominance does not explicitly provide exoneration clauses, clearly there is a possibility to justify the abusive conduct of a dominant undertaking for specific reasons. Anderman and Schmidt consider: 'In a sense, the values and structure of Article 101(3) are built into the objective justification test.'[225]

The value and meaning of such exoneration remain certainly doubtful. Still, especially for future developments, it is desirable to leave the window open for such a possibility—particularly in the context of copyright-competition interaction, where the concept of exoneration might have significance. As we can see from prior practice, attempts to acknowledge the possibility of exoneration through the concept of objective justification have been made. However, those attempts were not reasoned in a sufficiently skilful way. Firstly, the balancing of interests and the consideration of efficiency should be integrated throughout the assessment of the conduct under investigation. Secondly, the exoneration test should rather be conducted at the end of the assessment and not as part of the exceptional circumstances test, which is specific for copyright-competition interaction. Moreover, the Commission has refrained from considering the possibility of exoneration *ex officio*. However, if there is already sufficient evidence that indicates the possibility of exoneration, it might be a more reasonable approach to immediately include such evidence in the assessment, particularly having in mind the vast powers of competition authorities (and the fact that the undertaking under investigation would, in any case, try to prove its innocence during the whole procedure).

5.3.2.6 Algorithm of the Suggested Copyright-Competition Interaction Assessment Method for Cases Concerning Refusal to License Under Competition Rules on Abuse of Dominance

See Fig. 5.1.

---

[224] See Communication from the Commission—Guidance on the Commission's enforcement priorities in applying Article 82 of the EC Treaty to abusive exclusionary conduct by dominant undertakings, OJ C 45, 24.2.2009, pp. 7–20, para. 31.

[225] Anderman and Schmidt (2019), p. 323. Still, the application of Article 101(3) TFEU is clearly separate from Article 102 TFEU. See Colino (2019), p. 249.

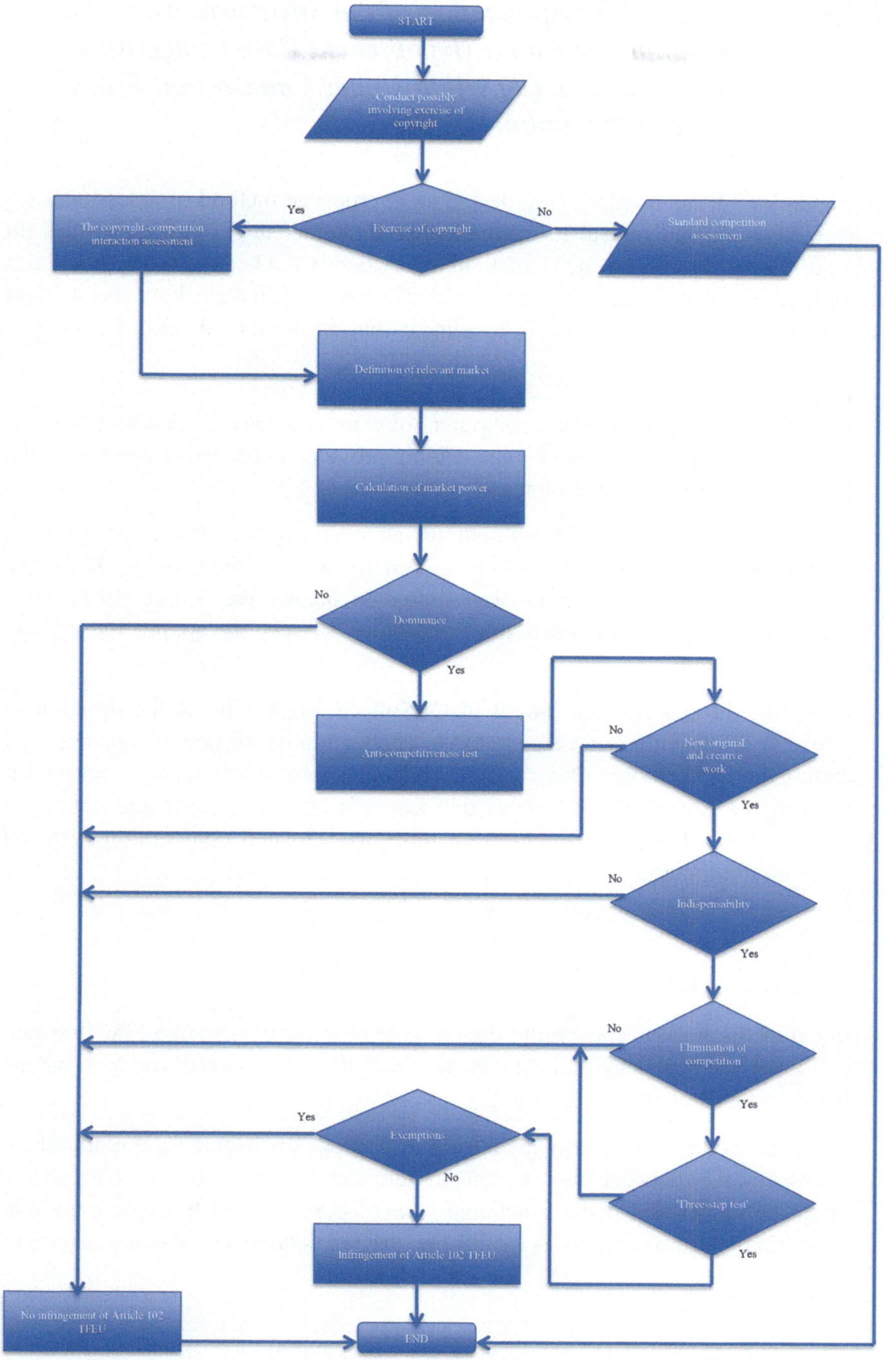

Fig. 5.1 Algorithm of the suggested copyright-competition interaction method of assessment for cases concerning refusal to license under competition rules on abuse of dominance

5.3.3 *Case Study: The Application of the Structured Test of Reasonableness on a Hypothetical Case Concerning Refusal to License Copyright Under Competition Rules on Abuse of Dominance*

The intention of this research is to design an appropriate method of assessment for cases concerning the refusal to license copyright under the competition rules on abuse of dominance. Since such a method has evidently not been tested in practice, a simplified hypothetical situation is provided below to illustrate how the method should be applied. The factsheet is, to some extent, inspired by *Microsoft*.

Factsheet

Qi-Soft GmbH is an Austrian computer software company specialising in operating systems. Qi-Soft GmbH is the leading provider of operating systems in the territory of the European Union.

For an application to be functional on an operating system, there must be interoperability between the operating system and the application. Thus, the holder of the operating system is required to license the source code to the application developer to ensure interoperability between the application and the operating system.

However, the management board of Qi-Soft GmbH has made the decision to refuse to disclose the source code to the application developers competing with their own applications. One of the application developers whose request for licensing Qi-Soft GmbH's source code was refused filed a complaint to the EU Commission, claiming that Qi-Soft GmbH has violated competition rules on abuse of dominance.

Test

1) Analysis of Copyright

In competition cases concerning the possible exercise of copyright, the first step in the assessment should be to establish if the investigated conduct indeed involves the exercise of copyright.

The described case concerns the refusal to disclose the source code required for interoperability between the operating system and the application. In that sense, it might be questioned if the functional source code could even enjoy copyright protection.[226] However, if it is established that the conduct could enjoy copyright

[226] In that sense, see Judgment of 2 May 2012, *SAS Institute Inc. v World Programming Ltd.*, C-406/10, EU:C:2012:259, and The Supreme Court of the United States, *Google LLC v. Oracle America, Inc.*, argued October 7, 2020, decided April 5, 2021, No. 18-956.

protection, then the specific method should apply within the complete assessment.

In the particular case, the subject matter of copyright protection is refusal to license the software source code to a third party. Hence, establishing a possible violation of the competition rules on abuse of dominance would surely present a limitation to the exercise of copyright on software. In that sense, it is vital that the limitation remains only an outside restriction to the exercise of copyright and does not interfere with the substance of the right. To do so, it would further be necessary to analyse the relevant copyright framework and discuss the particularities of the software that is the object of copyright protection.

2) Definition of the Relevant Market

After establishing that the investigated conduct involves the exercise of copyright, the next step is to define the relevant market. The fact that the conduct involves an exercise of copyright generates specific economic effects due to the exclusivity of the rights and affects both the product and the geographical dimension of the market.

In the described case, the object of the investigation is, in essence, the refusal to license software. In defining the relevant product market, it is vital to properly define the scope of the market. In the context of the case, the relevant product market can comprise operating systems in general, or it can be narrowed to specific types of operating systems (like in the *Microsoft* case), depending on the particular circumstances of the case.

With regard to the relevant geographical market, due to the universal character of software programs, software commonly has a worldwide application. In the factsheet of the case, it was stated that Qi-Soft's operating system is provided mainly in the territory of the EU. This fact would imply that in the case in question, the geographical market may be narrowed to the territory of the EU Member States. However, in determining the scope of the geographical market, other factors than pure supply and demand should be considered. Thus, according to the Commission's Notice on the definition of relevant markets, the definition of the relevant geographical market is also affected by the homogeneous conditions of competition, which can be distinguished from neighbouring areas because the conditions of competition are appreciably different in those areas.[227] In that sense, differences between national copyright systems can also play a part. If one system recognises copyright protection for a source code that might be considered functional while others do not, it is reasonable to distinguish such markets. Namely, the conditions of competition are obviously not the same if in one system such software enjoys copyright protection while in others the copyright holder could not oppose disclosing the source code.

[227] Commission Notice on the definition of relevant market for the purposes of Community competition law, OJ C 372, 9.12.1997, pp. 5–13, para. 8.

Many factors must be assessed to properly define the product and the geographic components of the relevant markets, among which the presence of copyright rights might have a significant effect.

3) Determination of a Dominant Position

Following the definition of the market structure, the next thing is to establish whether the undertaking is indeed in a dominant market position. Such a position confers a special responsibility in terms of how to behave in the market and makes the undertaking vulnerable to competition rules on abuse of dominance.

To determine dominance, it is not sufficient to merely calculate market shares, but it should be established that the undertaking indeed enjoys the economic strength to prevent effective competition from being maintained in the relevant market, giving it the power to behave, to an appreciable extent, independently of its competitors, customers and, ultimately, consumers.

In the case, it was stated that Qi-Soft GmbH is the leading operating system provider in the territory of the EU. Firstly, if the undertaking is the leading market player in the EU, that does not mean that it is also one of the leading market players on the global scale if the geographical scope of the market is worldwide. Secondly, even if the relevant market is narrowed to the territory of the EU, being the leading market player does not automatically imply the dominance of that undertaking. In diversified markets, the strongest market player might only have a small market share in comparison to the whole market. However, for the purpose of the example, even if we state that Qi-Soft GmbH has a more significant market share, for instance 37%, still other factors would have to be considered, such as the following:

- The constraints imposed by existing supplies from, and the position in the market of, actual competitors (the market position of the dominant undertaking and its competitors)
- The constraints imposed by the credible threat of future expansion by actual competitors or entry by potential competitors (expansion and entry)
- The constraints imposed by the bargaining strength of the undertaking's customers (countervailing buyer power)

Hence, the establishment of the individual case would also depend on the particular situation. However, in any case, the fact that the software is protected by copyright would not *per se* confer the dominant position on the right holder. The market power of that undertaking would be compared with the overall power of other undertakings holding rights on other comparable software, ultimately depending on the definition of the relevant market. Still, exclusive copyright rights might help lock out competitors and lock in customers.

4) Anti-competitiveness Test

The core of the competition assessment is the anti-competitiveness test. In accordance with the test of reasonableness suggested within this work, in establishing anti-competitive conduct, the first step is to establish that the refused licence was requested for the creation of a new original and creative work. In the context of the described case, this means the licence of the operating system's source code was required for the creation of an application that will represent a copyrighted work *per se* when created.

If the first criterion were established, the second condition would be the indispensability of the licence. This condition entails that besides the requested licensing of the source code, there are no other alternative means or ways that would reasonably enable the undertaking requesting the licence to make the application fit to perform on Qi-Soft GmbH's operating system.

The third criterion is fulfilled if the conduct of Qi-Soft GmbH is likely to eliminate all (effective) competition in the linked market. Thus, to establish anti-competitive behaviour, it is not sufficient that the refusal to license was directed towards an individual situation, but it must eliminate effective competition in the entire specific market for the application that is related to the relevant market.

Finally, if the three conditions are fulfilled, the final condition evaluates if the possible competition intervention conflicts with the 'normal' exploitation of copyright and does not unreasonably prejudice the legitimate interests of authors or right holders. In other words, the establishment of abuse of dominance must not affect copyright protection for software.

5) Potential Exemptions

Considering that competition rules on abuse of dominance generally do not include exemption provisions and, in light of the test of reasonableness, the exemption phase in this case holds theoretical value only, it is unlikely that the conduct of the undertaking would be exempted, and it would be determined that Qi-Soft GmbH had abused its dominant position by refusing to license the source code of the operating system.

5.3.4 Conclusion

In the context of the copyright-competition interaction issue, the situation with abuse of dominance cases is not much better than that with prohibited agreements—maybe even worse, keeping in mind that the cases themselves and their interpretations have been far more controversial. Here, again, substantial unresolved issues concerning the relationship between copyright law and competition law lie at the core of the problem. Furthermore, in practice and academia, there is no formulated structured approach or reasonable theory of harm to deal with the issue; the quality of economic analysis is low. Practice has shown to be extremely inconsistent and confusing, leaving undertakings and other stakeholders nothing but frustrated with the situation at hand.

Ongoing technological and legal developments may especially affect the issue of the exercise of copyright under the competition rules on abuse of dominance, particularly refusal to license situations. With the development of new technologies and digital industries in the new creative and dynamic environment, there is an ongoing trend of encouraging different kinds of platforms, often holding a dominant position on a market, that create another market exposed to fierce competition. Considering that this concept of competition commonly includes an undertaking in a dominant on one market and lots of competitors on related market exploiting copyright-protected works, it is imaginable that the copyright-competition interaction cases will appear more often before the competent authorities.

In any case, it is unacceptable that the issue of exercising copyright under competition rules on abuse of dominance has not yet been settled. The solution provided in this work tried to stay within the fundamental principles and rules of copyright law and competition law while providing an appropriate approach and a structured assessment test for the issue at hand.

References

Ahlborn C, Evans DS (2009) The Microsoft judgment and its implications for competition policy towards dominant firms in Europe. Antitrust Law J 75(3):887–932

Ahlborn C, Evans DS, Padilla J (2005) The logic & limits of the "exceptional circumstances test" in Magill and IMS Health. Fordham Int Law J 28(4):1109–1156

Anderman S, Schmidt H (2019) EU competition law and intellectual property rights: the regulation of innovation, 3rd edn. Oxford University Press, Oxford

Apostolopoulos H (2007) Refusal-to-deal cases of IP rights in the aftermarket of US and EU law: convergence of both law systems through speaking the same language of law and economics. DePaul Bus Commer Law J 5(2):237–263

Areeda P (1990) Essential facilities: an epithet in need of limiting principles. Antitrust Law J 58(4): 841–854

Borghart M (2008) An antitrust perspective. In: Lidgard HH, Atik J (eds) The intersection of IPR and competition law: studies of recent developments in European and U.S. Law, Chapter I: history and context. Intellecta docysus, Gothenburg, pp 28–38

Briard F-H (2007) A costly and suspect offensive. International Herald Tribune, 28–29 Apr 2007

Brison F (2005) Application of the essential facilities theory to intellectual property: comparative analysis - a European approach. In: Exploring the Sources of Copyright. ALAI Congress, Paris, 18–21 Sept 2005, pp 596–605

Burke A (2002) On the relationship between copyright and antitrust law: Economic versus moral rights. University of Warwick Centre for Small- and Medium-sized Enterprises, Working Paper No 74, October 2002. http://www2.warwick.ac.uk/fac/soc/wbs/research/ei/research/working_papers. Accessed 22 Oct 2024

Chirita AD (2011) The German and Romanian abuse of market dominance in the light of Article 102 TFEU. Nomos, Baden-Baden

Clark JM (1940) Toward a concept of workable competition. Am Econ Rev 1940:241–256

Coco R (2008) Antitrust liability for refusal to license intellectual property: a comparative analysis and the international setting. Marquette Intellect Prop Law Rev 12(1):1–47

Colino SM (2019) Competition law of the EU and UK. 8th edn. Oxford University Press, Oxford

Crane DA (2009) Intellectual liability. Texas Law Rev 88(2):253–300

Czapracka K (2009) Intellectual property and the limits of antitrust: a comparative study of US and EU approaches. Edward Elgar Publishing Ltd, Cheltenham

Derclaye E (2004) The IMS Health decision and the reconciliation of copyright and competition law. Eur Law Rev 29(5):687–697

Drexl J (2004) IMS Health and Trinko – antitrust placebo for consumers instead of sound economics in refusal-to-deal cases. Int Rev Intellect Prop Compet Law 35(7):788–808

Drexl J (2008) Is there a 'more economic approach' to intellectual property and competition law? In: Drexl J (ed) Research handbook on intellectual property and competition law. Max Planck Institute for Innovation and Competition, Munich, pp 27–53

Evans DS, Padilla AJ (2005) Excessive prices: using economics to define administrable legal rules. J Compet Law Econ 1(1):97–122

Firth A (2021) The essential facilities principle and other issues of competition. In: Stamatoudi I, Torremans P (eds) EU copyright law: a commentary, 2nd edn. Edward Elgar Publishing, Cheltenham, pp 44–73

Ginsburg JC, Treppoz E (2015) International copyright law: U.S. and E.U perspectives - text and cases. Edward Elgar Publishing, Cheltenham

Goldstein P (1989) Copyright. Vol. I. Little, Brown and Company, Boston

Goldstein P (2024) Goldstein on Copyright. Vol. II. Wolters Kluwer, New York

Hull DW, Strowel A (2005) Exploring the Sources of Copyright. In: ALAI Congress, Paris, 18-–21 September 2005, pp 678–688

Ibáñez Colomo P (2018) The shaping of EU competition law. Cambridge University Press, Cambridge

Kaplow L (1984) The patent-antitrust intersection: a reappraisal. Harv Law Rev 97:1813–1897

Katz A (2007) Making sense of nonsense: intellectual property rights, antitrust and market power. Arizona Law Rev 49(4):839–909

Katz A, Veel P-E (2013) Beyond refusal to deal: a cross-Atlantic view of copyright, competition and innovation policies. Antitrust Law J 79(1):139–184

Kwok KHF (2011) A new approach to resolving refusal to license intellectual property disputes. World Compet 34(2):261–286

Lamping M (2015) Refusal to licence as an abuse of market dominance: from commercial solvents to Microsoft. In: Hilty RM, Liu K-C (eds) Compulsory licensing: practical experiences and ways forward. Springer, Heidelberg, pp 121–145

Larouche P (2009) The European Microsoft Case at the crossroads of competition policy and innovation: comment on Ahlborn and Evans. Antitrust Law J 75(3):933–963

Leaffer M (2005) Application of the essential facilities theory to intellectual property: comparative analysis - the essential facilities doctrine in U.S. law. In: Exploring the Sources of Copyright. ALAI Congress, Paris, 18–21 September 2005, pp 625–629

Leistner M (2005) Intellectual property and competition law: the European development from Magill to IMS health compared to recent German and US case law. Zeitschrift für Wettbewerbsrecht 3(2):138–162

Leslie CR (2011) Antitrust law and intellectual property rights. Oxford University Press, Oxford

Lévêque F (2005) Innovation, leveraging and essential facilities: interoperability licensing in the EU Microsoft case. World Compet 28(1):71–91

Maher I (2005) The market definition in competition law: repercussions of copyright law. In: Exploring the Sources of Copyright. ALAI Congress, 18–21 Paris, September 2005, pp 569–584

Martin S (2005) Application of the essential facilities theory to intellectual property: comparative analysis - reconciling copyright with the essential facilities doctrine. In: Exploring the Sources of Copyright. ALAI Congress, Paris, 18–21 September 2005, pp 613–618

Max Planck Institute for Intellectual Property and Competition Law, Munich (2013) Report: Copyright, Competition and Development. December 2013. https://www.ip.mpg.de/fileadmin/ipmpg/content/forschung_aktuell/02_copyright_competition/report_copyright-competition-development_december-2013.pdf. Accessed 22 Oct 2024

Myrick RE (1992) Will intellectual property on technology still be viable in a unitary market. Eur Intellect Prop Rev 14(9):298–304

Neale AD (1970) The antitrust laws of the United States of America: a study of competition enforced by law. Cambridge University Press, Cambridge

OECD (1993) Glossary of Industrial Organisation Economics and Competition Law. compiled by Khemani RS, Shapiro DM (ed) http://www.oecd.org/regreform/sectors/2376087.pdf. Accessed 22 Oct 2024

OECD (2018) Scoping Note on Competition and Intellectual Property Rights as a long-term theme for 2019-2020, 6–8 June 2018, OECD Conference Centre, DAF/COMP/WD(2018)4

Patterson LR (1968) Copyright and Author's Rights. Harv Libr Bull XVI(4):370–384

Pessach G (2011) Reverse exclusion in copyright law – reconfiguring users' rights. In: WIPO, Fifth Advanced Research Forum on Intellectual Property Rights; Selected Topics on the Balance of Intellectual Property, 23–25 May 2011, Geneva, Topic 14. https://www.wipo.int/meetings/en/doc_details.jsp?doc_id=167806. Accessed 12 Oct 2024

Petit N (2017) The antitrust and intellectual property intersection in European Union law. In: Blair RD, Sokol DD (eds) Handbook of antitrust, intellectual property and high tech. Cambridge University Press, Cambridge, pp 92–11

Posner RA (1969) Natural monopoly and its regulation. Stanford Law Rev 21(3):548–643

Rato M, English M (2016) An assessment of injunctions, patents, and standards following the Court of Justice's Huawei/ZTE Ruling. J Eur Compet Law Pract 7(2):103–112

Schmidt C (2010) Refusal to license intellectual property rights as abuse of dominance, political economics competition and regulation. Vol. 11. Peter Lang GmbH Internationaler Verlag der Wissenschaften, Frankfurt am Main

Skone James EP, Mummery J, Rayner James JE, Garnett KM, Nimmer D, Silman S, Skone James R (1991) Copinger and Skone James on Copyright. Sweet & Maxwell, London

Spulber DF (2008) Competition policy and the incentive to innovate. Yale J Regul 25(2):247–301

Stazi A (2011) Intellectual property rights and market power in the European Union: The Fil Rouge of Consumer Welfare. Comparazione e Diritto Civile, June 2011. https://papers.ssrn.com/sol3/papers.cfm?abstract_id=1898185. Accessed 24 Oct 2024

Strowel A (1994) Droit d'auteur and Copyright. In: Sherman B, Strowel A (eds) Of authors and origins: essays on copyright law. Claredon Press, Oxford, pp 235–253

US Department of Justice (2017) Press Release, Assistant Attorney General for Antitrust, Thomas O. Barnett, Issues Statement on European Microsoft Decision. 17 September 17. https://www.justice.gov/archive/atr/public/press_releases/2007/226070.htm. Accessed 24 Oct 2024

Vansberg VV (2004) The Freiburg School: Walter Eucken and Ordoliberalism, Freiburger Diskussionspapiere zur Ordnungsökonomik, No. 04/11, AlbertLudwigs-Universität Freiburg, Institut für Allgemeine Wirtschaftsforschung, Abteilung für Wirtschaftspolitik, Freiburg i. Br

Vernet R (2008) The existence/exercise distinction: helpful, confusing or merely obsolete. In: Lidgard HH, Atik J (eds) The intersection of IPR and competition law: studies of recent developments in European and U.S. law. Chapter IV: IPR and Dominance. Intellecta docysus, Gothenburg, pp 153–164

Waller SW (2008) Areeda, epithets, and essential facilities. Wis Law Rev 2008(2):359–386

Whish R, Bailey D (2021) Competition law, 10th edn. Oxford University Press, Oxford

Zenger H, Walker M (2012) Theories of harm in European competition law: a progress report. In: Bourgeois J, Waelbroeck D (eds) Ten years of effects-based approach in EU competition law: state of play and perspectives. GCLC Annual Conference Series, Bruylant, pp 185–209

Chapter 6
The Implementation of the Suggested Approach to the Copyright-Competition Interaction Issue

The discussion on how to settle the copyright-competition interaction issue is still ongoing. Relevant decisions made by competent authorities were mostly criticised for various reasons. Some solutions were suggested through academic works. However, the copyright-competition interaction issue still remains unsettled.

This research aims to identify the flaws in the previous understanding of this specific matter and to present a comprehensive and founded understanding of the copyright-competition interaction issue. In doing so, the research starts from the fundamentals of copyright law and competition law (see *supra*, *Chap. 2*) to set the grounds for defining the relationship between those two laws in cases of their interaction (see *supra*, *Chap. 3*).

After establishing a fundamental understanding of the copyright-competition interaction, the next step was to discuss the specific situations occurring within the scope of the copyright-competition interaction issue. The research focused on the exercise of copyright as a prohibited agreement (see *supra*, *Chap. 4*) and the refusal to license copyright as an abuse of dominance (see *Chap. 5*). In both situations, the general understanding and approach to copyright-competition interaction should remain the same. However, due to the particularities of those specific situations, one is assessed under the competition rules on prohibited agreements (Article 101 TFEU) while the other under the competition rules on abuse of dominance (Article 102 TFEU), and the method of assessment accordingly differs. After an analysis of the relevant case law and theory, Chaps. 4 and 5 provide suggestions for the specific methods of assessment that are supposed to acknowledge the rationales of the copyright-competition interaction issue properly. With respect to other possible situations covered by the copyright-competition interaction that were not discussed herein (e.g. mergers and acquisitions, collective organisations), the presented understanding of copyright-competition interaction is believed to be equally applicable to all such matters. Nonetheless, the particular method of assessment might differ accordingly.

Considering all of the above, this chapter explores the appropriate legislative framework to implement the suggested comprehensive approach to the

D. Gliha, *The Copyright-Competition Interaction within the EU*,
https://doi.org/10.1007/978-3-031-94402-4_6

copyright-competition interaction issue. In that sense, it discusses the general need for legislative interventions in the field of copyright law or competition law to address this issue. Also, the chapter provides a discussion on the application of the suggested approach on the national level of Member States and provides observations of possible future developments with regard to the copyright-competition interaction issue.

6.1 Exploring the Appropriate Legislative Framework to Implement the Suggested Comprehensive Approach to the Copyright-Competition Interaction Issue

The understanding of copyright-competition interaction provided in this work is probably somewhat different from the other solutions presented in the existing body of knowledge on copyright-competition interaction. The approach suggested here is believed to be founded on and developed from the established principles of copyright law and competition law. Hence, it ought to be immediately applicable to concrete real-life situations without any legislative interventions.

Nonetheless, to ensure the uniform application of law and legal security, further consideration should be given to the potential need to codify the suggested approach to copyright-competition interaction. In that sense, there should be discussion of a need and basis for the legal implementation of the suggested interpretation within copyright law and/or competition law. If necessary, there should be an analysis of whether the implementation should occur at the EU or national level.

6.1.1 Examining the Need for Legislative Interventions Within Copyright Law and/or Competition Law

Copyright-competition interaction is an interdisciplinary issue that can be observed from the aspect of copyright law and competition law.

From the general perspective of copyright law, the copyright-competition interaction situation is perceived as an outside limitation to the exercise of copyright (see *supra*, Sect. 3.2). Thus, such a situation falls outside the framework of copyright, and there is no need for national or international legislative intervention to deal with this matter.[1] The crucial point is to acknowledge and remain aligned with the existing

[1] From a comparative perspective of systems following the Anglo-Saxon copyright tradition, particularly in the United States, the situation might be perceived somewhat differently. In such system(s), copyright-competition interaction is likely to be observed through the 'fair use' and 'misuse' doctrines—thus, possibly even within the copyright framework. Nonetheless, due to a

rules and principles of copyright law when dealing with the copyright-competition interaction issue.

From the general perspective of competition law, copyright-competition interaction is perceived as a specific situation in which the focus should mainly be on the effects of copyright instead of on allocation and productiveness. At the same time, the concept of authorship should be considered in light of consumer welfare (see *supra*, Sect. 3.2). Thus, the situation concerning copyright-competition interaction can be dealt with under the general principles and rules of competition law through an adjusted method of assessment. Given that, in recent times, the legal framework of competition policy has become more economically sophisticated, there is now an even better basis for accommodating competition rules in the exercise of copyright.[2] This applies to EU competition law as well as to Member States' national competition laws.

As understood within this research, the copyright-competition issue can be immediately dealt with through existing rules and principles of copyright law and competition law. It is only a matter of applying the proper interpretation to particular situations. Nonetheless, the question of how to ensure legal security and the uniform application of the law remains open.

6.1.2 A Need for Guidelines on the Matter of Copyright-Competition Interaction

EU competition law commonly supplements the fundamental understanding of complex competition rules with soft law instruments, making the system more transparent and efficient.

Thus, considering the anarchic situation concerning the copyright-competition interaction issue in the EU, it seems that there is indeed a need for a comprehensive soft law document providing guidance for dealing with the issue. Case law is inconsistent; scholars are in continuous disagreement, while stakeholders are left in a situation of insecurity.

Some EU soft law documents already address, to some extent, the matter of copyright-competition interaction.[3] However, there are no comprehensive guidelines

---

more flexible approach, it is likely that even in such system(s) there is no need for intervention in copyright law to deal with the copyright-competition interaction issue.

[2] See Anderman and Schmidt (2019), p. 5.

[3] Communication from the Commission — Guidance on the Commission's enforcement priorities in applying Article 82 of the EC Treaty to abusive exclusionary conduct by dominant undertaking, C 45, 24.2.2009, pp. 7–20.; Communication from the Commission — Guidelines on the application of Article 101 of the Treaty on the Functioning of the European Union to technology transfer agreements, OJ C 89, 28.3.2014, pp. 3–50.; Commission Regulation (EU) No 316/2014 of 21 March 2014 on the application of Article 101(3) of the Treaty on the Functioning of the European Union to categories of technology transfer agreements, OJ L 93, 28.3.2014, pp. 17–23.

on the copyright-competition interaction issue within the EU. Some other comparative systems, such as the United States,[4] Japan[5] and Singapore,[6] have issued guidelines on the interaction between intellectual property rights and competition law. Nevertheless, none of them substantially settle the issue of interaction between intellectual property rights and competition law. They mainly deal with licensing practices only.

To establish firm grounds, ensure consistency and provide legal security regarding the copyright-competition interaction situation, the only reasonable solution seems to be comprehensive guidelines.[7] These guidelines should provide greater clarity and predictability regarding the specific framework of analysis to be employed by competent authorities in their decision-making process and also help undertakings that exercise copyright understand better whether their particular behaviour is likely to result in competition intervention. A soft law document should suffice for such guidelines since grounds have already been set within copyright law and competition law. Interventions in secondary legislation would undoubtedly be questionable from the perspective of copyright law and possibly even from the perspective of competition law.

The appropriate content for such a guideline-type soft law document is still undetermined. Drafting guidelines in accordance with the fundamental understanding of the copyright-competition interaction as presented within this research would provide the desired legal security and uniform application of the law. Otherwise, the problem remains.

Above all, the guidelines should define the relationship between copyright law and competition law. This fundamental issue is often overlooked in discussions on the copyright-competition interaction, resulting in non-sustainable solutions that disturb the substance of copyright law and competition law. Copyright law and competition law coexist peacefully. In the case of interaction, possible competition law intervention represents an outside limitation on the exercise of copyright, evaluated through the specific method of assessment.

After the fundaments of copyright-competition interaction have been elaborated, the guidelines should set the framework for the specific methods of assessment designed for dealing with copyright-competition interaction. The basic rules and principles applicable to copyright-competition interaction remain the same regardless of the particular situation. However, considering the differences between the competition rules on prohibited agreements and the competition rules on abuse of

[4] 2017 Antitrust Guidelines for the Licensing of Intellectual Property, issued by the U.S. Department of Justice and the Federal Trade Commission, January 12, 2017. https://www.justice.gov/atr/IPguidelines/download. Accessed 23 Oct 2024.

[5] Guidelines for the Use of Intellectual Property under the Antimonopoly Act (2016) https://www.jftc.go.jp/en/legislation_gls/imonopoly_guidelines_files/IPGL_Frand.pdf. Accessed 23 Oct 2024.

[6] Guidelines on the Treatment of Intellectual Property Rights in Competition Cases 2016. https://www.cccs.gov.sg/legislation/competition-act. Accessed 23 Oct 2024.

[7] On the universal need for guidance see Max Planck Institute for Intellectual Property and Competition Law (2013), p. 20.

dominance, each method of assessment should be elaborated separately. The methods of assessment suggested for dealing with the exercise of copyright under Article 101 TFEU (see *supra*, Sect. 4.3.2) and the refusal to license under Article 102 TFEU (see *supra*, Sect. 5.3.2) were discussed in detail above.[8] This part of the soft law document would be the most critical one as it provides practical guidelines for dealing with specific situations concerning the copyright-competition interaction.

For practical purposes, the guidelines might also contain a visual representation of the suggested methods of assessment through the algorithms suggested in this research (see *supra*, Sects. 4.3.2.7 and 5.3.2.6).

In discussing the need for guidelines on copyright-competition interaction, one additional question arises—whether such guidelines should address all intellectual property rights collectively or deal with each one separately. Most countries that provided guidelines on this matter have dealt with all intellectual property rights in the same document. In general, there is nothing wrong with such an approach. All intellectual property rights indeed share some similarities due to their intangible character and demand specific acknowledgement when interacting with competition law.

However, a problem emerges when there is no distinction between particular intellectual property rights. As mentioned on several occasions in the work, it is vital to maintain a clear distinction between intellectual property rights (see *supra*, Sects. 2.1.3 and 3.2). Each intellectual property right interacts with competition law in a specific way, and the particularities and substance of such interaction must be acknowledged when addressing the specific issue. Thus, the solution is either to clearly distinguish how different intellectual property rights interact with competition law or to issue separate guidelines for each intellectual property right affected by this issue.

6.2 The Comprehensive Approach to the Copyright-Competition Interaction Issue and Member States' National Competition Laws

The work mainly focuses on the copyright-competition interaction issue through the lenses of EU law. However, the copyright-competition interaction issue may also arise as a solely national matter discussed before the national authorities. The findings from this research should equally apply in such cases.

The EU has indeed made (effective) attempts to harmonise copyright law among its Member States to a certain degree.[9] Nonetheless, each Member State preserved its own systems of national copyright laws, among which differences are respected.

---

[8] Note: Concentrations are not discussed within this work; however, it might also be useful to include concentrations within the guidelines.

[9] Clark (2022).

From the aspect of copyright, as a territorial right, nothing substantially changes whether the copyright-competition interaction issue is discussed at the regional (the EU) or national level. Even when the case is discussed as a matter of EU law, the relevant national copyright system still applies to the copyright concerned.

In relation to competition law, the core EU competition rules are integrated within the treaties of the EU—the Treaty on the Functioning of the European Union.[10] EU competition law is applied by EU institutions and by national authorities.[11] In parallel, Member States also have their own national competition laws; however, those laws have mainly been developed under the influence of EU competition law and follow the same principles. Hence, there is no reason why the copyright-competition interaction issue should not be dealt with in the same way even if it affects trade between Member States.

All in all, there are no justifiable reasons why the particular Member States should not fully recognise the copyright-competition interaction issue and follow the approach suggested within this research. In that sense, it would be even more beneficial to have appropriate guidelines on the EU level for dealing with the matter of copyright-competition interaction.

6.3 A View to the Future: General Observations

At the current state of affairs in the copyright-competition interaction issue, a view to the future seems somewhat frightening. The overall understanding of the issue is not convincing, there is no consensus at all on how to deal with particular situations and general insecurity subsists among stakeholders.

Although there have not been many cases dealing with the copyright-competition interaction issue, the ones that were discussed were monumental. Many situations in everyday commercial activities might be qualified as copyright-competition interaction matter. However, for various reasons, most of them were never brought before the competent authorities. Still, that does not mean that copyright-competition interaction did occur more often.

For healthy undertakings performing in competitive creative-industry markets, it is crucial to have certainty concerning the exceptional circumstances under which their commercial exploitation of copyright might be limited for distorting competition. A good, or perhaps a bad, example of this is surely the case of *Microsoft*. In that case, after the whole procedure and the draconian punishment were imposed, the undertaking was still not convinced that what they did was actually wrong and why. As late as more than a decade after the decision, in an interview in 2019, Bill Gates

[10]Consolidated version of the Treaty on the Functioning of the European Union, OJ C 326, 26.10.2012, pp. 47–390.

[11]Council Regulation (EC) No 1/2003 of 16 December 2002 on the implementation of the rules on competition laid down in Articles 81 and 82 of the Treaty, OJ L 1, 4.1.2003, pp. 1–25, Art 6.

was asked to comment if Microsoft should have been prosecuted for abuse of monopoly (dominant position). He replied in the following way: 'If monopoly means extremely high market shares with short term market power, the answer is yes, if it means that we had an unchallengeable position where new and better technology didn't have a chance to replace us, the answer is no.'[12] And indeed, from a more objective academic perspective, the assessment of such complex markets and conducts requires a deep and comprehensive understanding focused on long-term effects. It is not uncommon for big industries to force their interests to the detriment of individual creators. However, big players often derive their overall business models from the concept of authorship. In essence, in the case of copyright-competition interaction, it should not be about how big or small an undertaking is[13]—it should be about strengthening copyright law by strictly limiting extreme anti-competitive behaviour. To some extent, the more powerful an undertaking is, the more closely it should be scrutinised for competition rules. It should be sanctioned not because it took a big share of the market but because it abuses the copyright protection it enjoys.

In any case, when dealing with the copyright-competition interaction issue, regardless of the object of copyright or industry involved, it is vital to approach the matter in a consistent and founded way while acknowledging the substance of copyright law and of competition law.

References

Anderman S, Schmidt H (2019) EU competition law and intellectual property rights: the regulation of innovation, 3rd edn. Oxford University Press, Oxford

Clark B (2022) Harmonisation of EU copyright law – a long and winding road. In: Allgrove B (ed) International copyright: a practical global guide, 2nd edn. Global Law and Business, Surrey, pp 29–49

Max Planck Institute for Intellectual Property and Competition Law, Munich (2013) Report: Copyright, Competition and Development. December 2013. https://www.ip.mpg.de/fileadmin/ipmpg/content/forschung_aktuell/02_copyright_competition/report_copyright-competition-development_december-2013.pdf. Accessed 22 Oct 2024

Netflix (2019) Inside Bill's Brain: Decoding Bill Gates. Netflix TV Mini-Series, Ep. 3

[12] See Netflix (2019), Ep. 3.

[13] While not forgetting that market power can play an important role in establishing the potential competition liability.

Chapter 7
The Copyright-Competition Interaction Issue: A View to the Future in Digital Surroundings

Nowadays, we are going through an intense period of digital and technological revolution that is affecting all pores of human society—the economic, social and cultural domains. Copyright law and competition law are no exceptions to this.

This chapter provides a specific analysis of the digital industry in the context of the copyright-competition interaction issue. The possible copyright-competition interaction issues are examined within the scope of the EU Digital Single Market and, in particular, the Directive on Copyright in the Digital Single Market. The particular emphasis is set on the functioning of digital platforms, which is identified as a situation that could, in future, be especially considered a possible copyright-competition interaction issue.

7.1 Introduction

Nowadays, things are rapidly changing. We are clearly going through an intense period of digital and technological revolution that is affecting all pores of human society—the economic, social and cultural domains.[1] Both copyright law and competition law are affected as well. The new economy is increasingly driven by creativity and originality; technological complexity has increased significantly. The ways in which works and other protected subject matters are created, produced, distributed and exploited have changed. New uses, actors and business models have emerged. Cross-border uses have also intensified, and new opportunities for consumers to access copyright-protected content have materialised. In such an economic

[1] Indicatively, according to the analysis preceding the issuing of the Digital Single Market Strategy (6 May 2015), 90% of all data circulating on the Internet were created less than 2 years before that time. See Communication from the Commission to the European Parliament, the Council, the European Economic and Social Committee and the Committee of the Regions, 'A Digital Single Market Strategy', COM(2015) 192 final, p. 11.

D. Gliha, *The Copyright-Competition Interaction within the EU*,
https://doi.org/10.1007/978-3-031-94402-4_7

environment, businesses seem to be born and die more easily than before in traditional markets. Thus, due to such developments, the importance of dynamic competition has overcome the need for static competition, and the importance of the comprehensive interdisciplinary approach is greater than ever.

There is a higher possibility of interaction between copyright law and competition law in such a dynamic environment. With the inflation of works and the increase in competitors in the market, in the fight for their survival in the market, the chances that some undertakings would enter into arrangements that might be considered prohibited agreements (i.e. anti-competitive software licensing agreements[2]) are significant. Also, there is a growing tendency for the platformisation of the economy and the concentration of markets. Such business models are commonly based on the exploitation of copyrighted works. Due to their specific concept, online platforms often lead to the disruption of traditional business models and present a severe challenge to competition authorities. They create new markets, which may ultimately displace earlier markets.[3]

The digital development of commerce has undoubtedly brought many benefits for both businesses and consumers. Many individuals have started to create and launch their businesses exclusively due to digital development, and there has probably never in history been more creative content available than there is now. However, the opening of the digital world also opens many new concerns and leaves a kind of state of chaos. Both copyright law and competition law are facing the emerging challenges and concerns of digitising social, economic and cultural life. The intense involvement of copyright in the dynamic and sometimes ruthless competition in the market will, in some situations, indeed necessitate the intervention of competition law and raise the copyright-competition interaction issue. Hence, it can reasonably be expected that the copyright-competition interaction issue will more often be a matter of on- and off-court discussions. How to approach such a situation has been discussed in this work, while some specific situations regarding the copyright-competition interaction issue in the digital environment will be discussed further in this chapter.

---

[2]E.g., cross-licensing (an agreement between two parties to grant rights to their IP rights to the other), conditional licensing (imposing restrictions on licensees as to the customers to whom the goods or services can be supplied or the technical fields or territories in which they can supply the licensed goods or services; imposing conditions as to the price, or placing restrictions on the geographical territory, of the services or goods produced pursuant to the licence); grant back in open-source licences (copyleft—the requirement to grant back all development improvements to other market participants without any fee). See Ibáñez Colomo (2017), pp. 339–357. Valimaki (2006), pp. 130–136.

[3]See Graef (2019), pp. 6–12; Firth (2021), p. 54.

7.2 The EU Digital Single Market Strategy and the (New) Copyright Directives

On 15 July 2014, as part of his political programme as a candidate for the president of the European Commission, Jean-Claude Juncker delivered his Opening Statement to the European Parliament Plenary Session, titled 'A New Start for Europe: My Agenda for Jobs, Growth, Fairness and Democratic Change'. In that speech he identified the connected digital market as the second priority and stated the following:

> I believe that we must make much better use of the great opportunities offered by digital technologies, which know no borders. To do so, we will need to have the courage to break down national silos in telecoms regulation, in copyright and data protection legislation, in the management of radio waves and in the application of competition law.
>
> If we do this, we can ensure that European citizens will soon be able to use their mobile phones across Europe without having to pay roaming charges. We can ensure that consumers can access services, music, movies and sports events on their electronic devices wherever they are in Europe and regardless of borders. We can create a fair level playing field where all companies offering their goods or services in the European Union are subject to the same data protection and consumer rules, regardless of where their server is based. By creating a connected digital single market, we can generate up to € 250 billion of additional growth in Europe in the course of the mandate of the next Commission, thereby creating hundreds of thousands of new jobs, notably for younger job-seekers, and a vibrant knowledge-based society.
>
> To achieve this, I intend to take, within the first six months of my mandate, ambitious legislative steps towards a connected digital single market, notably by swiftly concluding negotiations on common European data protection rules; by adding more ambition to the ongoing reform of our telecom's rules; by modernising copyright rules in the light of the digital revolution and changed consumer behaviour; and by modernising and simplifying consumer rules for online and digital purchases. This should go hand-in-hand with efforts to boost digital skills and learning across society and to facilitate the creation of innovative start-ups. Enhancing the use of digital technologies and online services should become a horizontal policy, covering all sectors of the economy and of the public sector.

Indeed, in 2015, as part of the EU Digital Agenda,[4] the EU Commission published the Digital Single Market Strategy,[5] which defines the critical areas in need of specific intervention to fit the twenty-first-century digital surroundings. Copyright law and competition law were included as well. For competition law,

---

[4]European Commission, Digital Single Market: Europe 2020 Strategy, 20.2.2015. https://ec.europa.eu/digital-single-market/en/europe-2020-strategy. Accessed 23 Oct 2024. See also Communication from the Commission to the European Parliament, the Council, the European Economic and Social Committee and the Committee of the Regions, 'Towards a modern, more European copyright framework', COM(2015) 626, final.

[5]Communication from the Commission to the European Parliament, the Council, the European Economic and Social Committee and the Committee of the Regions, 'A Digital Single Market Strategy', COM(2015) 192 final.

the Digital Single Market Strategy did not aim to amend the existing rules and principles, considering its flexible and open-ended concept; however, it did require the acknowledgement of new processes and developments within the digital-based economy. Thus, the idea was to create a more business- and consumer-friendly playing field that provides incentives for increasing competition within the Single Market and for removing unnecessary legal and territorial barriers, to the ultimate benefit of consumers.[6] Concerning copyright law, the Digital Market Strategy identified the need for 'a modern, more European copyright framework'.[7] Namely, the Commission recognised the fact that copyright underpins creativity and the cultural industry in Europe and that copyright-protected digital content is one of the main drivers of the growth of the digital economy. Hence, they proposed the following legislative interventions in copyright law at the EU level: '(i) portability of legally acquired content; (ii) ensuring cross-border access to legally purchased online services while respecting the value of rights in the audiovisual sector; (iii) greater legal certainty for the cross-border use of content for specific purposes (e.g. research, education, text and data mining, etc.) through harmonised exceptions; (iv) clarifying the rules on the activities of intermediaries in relation to copyright-protected content and, in 2016; (v) modernising enforcement of intellectual property rights, focusing on commercial-scale infringements (the "follow-the-money" approach) as well as its cross-border applicability'.[8] To implement these measures, the EU introduced Regulation 2017/1128 on cross-border portability of online content services in the Single Internal Market,[9] Directive (EU) 2019/790 on copyright and related rights in the Digital Single Market[10] and Directive (EU) 2019/789 laying down rules on the exercise of copyright and related rights applicable to certain online transmissions of broadcasting organisations and retransmissions of television and radio programmes.[11]

---

[6] See Communication from the Commission to the European Parliament, the Council, the European Economic and Social Committee and the Committee of the Regions, 'A Digital Single Market Strategy', COM(2015) 192 final, pp. 4–6, 9–11, 13–16.

[7] See Communication from the Commission to the European Parliament, the Council, the European Economic and Social Committee and the Committee of the Regions, 'A Digital Single Market Strategy', COM(2015) 192 final, pp. 6–7.

[8] See Communication from the Commission to the European Parliament, the Council, the European Economic and Social Committee and the Committee of the Regions, 'A Digital Single Market Strategy', COM(2015) 192 final, p. 8.

[9] Regulation (EU) 2017/1128 of the European Parliament and of the Council of 14 June 2017 on cross-border portability of online content services in the internal market, OJ L 168, 30.6.2017, pp. 1–11.

[10] Directive (EU) 2019/790 of the European Parliament and of the Council of 17 April 2019 on copyright and related rights in the Digital Single Market and amending Directives 96/9/EC and 2001/29/EC, PE/51/2019/REV/1, OJ L 130, 17.5.2019, pp. 92–125.

[11] Directive (EU) 2019/789 of the European Parliament and of the Council of 17 April 2019 laying down rules on the exercise of copyright and related rights applicable to certain online transmissions of broadcasting organisations and retransmissions of television and radio programmes, and amending Council Directive 93/83/EEC, PE/7/2019/REV/1, OJ L 130, 17.5.2019, pp. 82–91.

Considering the shift in the EU policy and the recognition of digital processes and surroundings, the question arises: how have these developments affected the copyright-competition interaction issue?

In the communication titled 'Towards a modern, more European copyright framework',[12] which is part of the Digital Single Market Strategy, the Commission acknowledged that both EU competition rules and copyright are integral components of the set of rules governing the circulation of creative content across the EU. Thus, the Commission recognised that the interaction between copyright and competition law (alongside other policies) determines how value is generated from the production and dissemination of works and how it is shared among market participants.[13]

On the one hand, competition law did not undergo substantial changes to adapt to the digital environment. Even the recent enactment of the Digital Markets Act does not alter EU competition rules.[14] Still, digital surroundings demand competition law to acknowledge the particularities of new types of business models, markets and undertakings on markets and focus more on dynamic competition and the preservation of creative and innovative processes to benefit consumers. Copyright law, on the other hand, went through more significant (and controversial) changes, particularly with the enactment of Directive (EU) 2019/790 on copyright and related rights in the Digital Single Market (hereinafter 'the EU Copyright Directive').

However, despite the Commission recognising, in some way, the importance of the copyright-competition interaction issue, none of the Digital Single Market interventions directly addressed this issue.[15] Probably the most important product of the Digital Single Market Strategy—the EU Copyright Directive—recognised that a harmonised legal framework contributes to the proper functioning of the internal market and stimulates innovation, creativity, investment and the production

[12] Communication from the Commission to the European Parliament, the Council, the European Economic and Social Committee and the Committee of the Regions, 'Towards a modern, more European copyright framework', COM(2015) 626 final, 9.12.2015.

[13] Communication from the Commission to the European Parliament, the Council, the European Economic and Social Committee and the Committee of the Regions, 'Towards a modern, more European copyright framework', COM(2015) 626 final, 9.12.2015.

[14] Regulation (EU) 2022/1925 of the European Parliament and of the Council of 14 September 2022 on contestable and fair markets in the digital sector and amending Directives (EU) 2019/1937 and (EU) 2020/1828 (Digital Markets Act) (Text with EEA relevance), PE/17/2022/REV/1, OJ L 265, 12.10.2022, pp. 1–66, Article 1(6).

[15] Some argue that certain provisions of the Digital Markets Act implicitly address the copyright-competition issue, which can be seen as a sign that the EU is moving toward regulating this matter. Although new regulation will certainly affect the behaviour of digital market leaders, an understanding that the Act directly regulates the copyright-competition interaction seems an overextended interpretation of its scope. Within the Digital Markets Act, there are no direct references to the copyright-competition issue. Paemen (2023), pp. 34–35.

of new content and that legislation needs to be future-proof. Also, it recognised that there is legal uncertainty among stakeholders with regard to the specific uses of works in the digital environment.[16] However, the EU Copyright Directive did not further address the copyright-competition interaction issue, and indeed, there was no need to. Considering that competition law represents an external constraint on the exercise of copyright, the copyright-competition interaction issue falls outside the framework of copyright (see *supra*, Sect. 3.2).

Still, the Digital Single Market Strategy was well placed to produce guidelines on the copyright-competition interaction (see *supra*, Sect. 4.2.1.2), at least with regard to the digital sector.

The Digital Single Market is a fruitful field, not only for encouraging the development of copyright-protected content but also for enabling potential abuses in the exploitation of copyrighted works, to the detriment of consumers and future creators. When acting on the market based on the concept of free (and fair) competition, copyright holders must have sufficient copyright protection in the exploitation of their copyright rights. This also includes clarity on what kind of exercise of copyright could potentially surpass 'normal' exploitation and warrant the scrutiny of competition law.

In that sense, particularly online platforms, which ground their business models on exploiting copyright, have already attracted the increasing attention of competition authorities. Although the concept of online platforms as a way of exploiting copyright most likely concerns competition rules on abuse of dominance, this does not necessarily exclude the potential application of competition rules on prohibited agreements. On the one hand, online platforms (not necessarily in a dominant position) might engage in potentially anti-competitive licensing arrangements between them, closing the market for other competitors. On the other hand, online platform models might also encourage undertakings operating within on-platform markets (e.g. app developers) to engage in anti-competitive licensing agreements in an attempt to dominate on-platform markets.

Nonetheless, despite the copyright-competition interaction issue remaining unresolved, even at the current state of the art, there are grounds to apply the approach suggested above when dealing with the issue. Even in the digital environment, the approach suggested in this work should provide sufficient flexibility to acknowledge the particularities of digital markets, thus preserving the substance of copyright law and competition law.

---

[16]Directive (EU) 2019/790 of the European Parliament and of the Council of 17 April 2019 on copyright and related rights in the Digital Single Market and amending Directives 96/9/EC and 2001/29/EC, PE/51/2019/REV/1, OJ L 130, 17.5.2019, pp. 92–125, paras. 2–3.

7.3 Online Platforms and the Copyright-Competition Interaction Issue

The Digital Single Market Strategy recognised the importance of online (digital) platforms (e.g. search engines, social media platforms, e-commerce platforms, app stores, price comparison websites).[17] Indeed, the rise of online platforms is changing the face of the economy throughout the world.[18] Online platforms are playing a central role in economic and social life. By using advances in technology and global connectivity, they facilitate fundamental and basic activities, such as buying, selling, creative expression and access to tools and resources. Today's world is almost unimaginable without online platforms such as Google, YouTube, Amazon, eBay, Facebook, LinkedIn, etc. The holders of dominant online platforms are now the most valuable companies in the world, and their growing power in the economy is enabling them to rewrite the rules of business strategy. The majority of those platforms are created and controlled by private enterprises.[19] Without entering into discussion about whether that is generally a good thing or a bad thing, the fact is that both social life and economic life have become highly dependent on online platforms.[20]

The impact of a particular online platform differs depending on its type,[21] content and market power. Nevertheless, the common characteristics of online platforms are

[17] See Communication from the Commission to the European Parliament, the Council, the European Economic and Social Committee and the Committee of the Regions, 'A Digital Single Market Strategy', COM(2015) 192 final, pp. 11–13.

However, online platforms were mainly discussed, as online-content-sharing service providers, in the context of liability for the uploaded content. See Directive (EU) 2019/790 of the European Parliament and of the Council of 17 April 2019 on copyright and related rights in the Digital Single Market and amending Directives 96/9/EC and 2001/29/EC, PE/51/2019/REV/1, OJ L 130, 17.5.2019, pp. 92–125, paras. 61–71.

[18] See Parker et al. (2016), pp. 7–20.

[19] Evans and Gawer (2016), p. 13. In that sense, it should be borne in mind that online platforms are not companies but, in essence, technologies that can be products and services. Private companies stand behind online platforms as their developers and/or holders. See Gawer (2015), p. 2.

[20] However, the concept of what are considered platforms is not a novelty. Thus, some examples of offline platforms—serving two or more distinct sets of users that interact in at least one direction through the service—are traditional print newspapers (the advertisers interact with readers by paying the newspaper to place advertisements, which at least some of the readers see), stock exchange (stock buyers and stock sellers interact through the exchange by signalling the prices at which they are willing to buy and sell), radio platforms (the listeners interact with advertisers), etc. See OECD (2019), pp. 20–21. See also Bundeskartellamt Decision, *Funke/Springer Programmzeitschriften*, Case B6-98/13, 25 April 2014, para. 138; Bundeskartellamt Decision, *Zeitungsverlag Schwäbisch Hall*, Case B6-150/08, 21 April 2009, para. 33; The Commission, Case AT.39398, *VISA MIF*, C(2014)1199 final, 26.2.2014, para. 16.

[21] Thus, there is a difference between transaction platforms—technology, products or services that act as a conduit (or intermediary) facilitating exchange or transactions between different users, buyers, or suppliers (e.g. Uber, Airbnb, PayPal, LinkedIn, Snapchat, Badu); innovation platforms—technology, products or services that serve as a foundation on top of which other firms (loosely

that they are a digital service that facilitates interactions between two or more distinct but interdependent sets of users (whether businesses or individuals), which interact through the service via the Internet.[22] Thus, after establishing their position on a relevant market, platforms commonly attract and serve at least two different sets of users simultaneously, bringing them together and enabling interactions between them that can benefit the users and the platform itself.[23] That stems from the two- or multi-sided nature of such creations.[24]

In understanding the concept of online platforms and their effect on the market, of particular interest are their positive, indirect network effects—a group of users (for instance, third-party sellers on Amazon) benefits more as the number of people in another group of users (buyers using the same platform) increases, and possibly *vice versa*.[25] Thus, if a platform provides a better service to one side of the market, it increases the demand for its service on the other side(s). In other words, if there are more providers on one side, the platforms become more attractive to users on the other side(s); if there are more users on that other side(s), the attractiveness of the platform will further grow on the providers' side.[26] For instance, more drivers on a taxi transportation platform will attract more customers to use the app—more customers using the app will attract more taxi drivers to join the platform. The same example can be made with restaurants and diners on a food delivery platform,

---

organised into an innovative ecosystem) develop complementary technologies, products or services (e.g. Microsoft, Oracle, Intel, SAP, Salesforce); and integrated platforms—technology, products or services that are both a transaction platform and an innovation platform. This category includes companies such as Apple, which has both matching platforms—like the App Store and a large third-party developer ecosystem that supports content creation on the platform (e.g. Apple, Google, Facebook, Amazon, Alibaba, Xiaomi)—and investment platforms—consisting of companies that have developed a platform portfolio strategy and act as a holding company, an active platform investor or both (e.g. Priceline Group, Softbank, Naspers, IAC Interactive, Rocket Internet). See Evans and Gawer (2016), pp. 9, 14–17.

[22] See OECD (2019), p. 21.

According to the European Commission's report on public consultations on platforms, stakeholders are not inclined to have a one-size-fits-all definition of online platforms, nor do they see a justifiable reason for that. See European Commission (2016).

[23] Rochet and Tirole consider two-sided (or multi-sided) markets as those in which one or several platforms enable interactions between end users and try to get the two (or multiple) sides 'on board' by appropriately charging each side. See Rochet and Tirole (2006), pp. 645–646.

[24] See Shelanski et al. (2018), p. 190.

[25] Generally, economists began developing the theory of network effects already in the 1970s. The basic idea of the network effect is that in some cases, a service is more valuable if more customers are using it because customers want to interact with each other. Some customers attract more customers—more customers make the network more attractive. Finally, explosive growth results in a single undertaking firmly holding the market—the winner takes all. In comparison to indirect network effects (between different kinds of users), which are characteristic of multi-sided markets, direct network effects are between the same kind of users (for instance, characteristic of the concept of landline telephone services, fax machines, the standard for videocassette recorders (VCRs)). See Evans and Schmalensee (2017–2018), pp. 36–38.

[26] See OECD (2019), pp. 22, 23.

buyers and sellers on an e-commerce platform, application developers and users on an application platform, etc. Although this is generally correct, it should be considered that it is not all about the number of users—it is more important to get the right users, not just attract more users (i.e. platforms create value when customers find suitable matches and enter into exchanges).[27] In other words, platforms enable or facilitate interaction between two or more sides only if they indeed want to interact.[28] Consequently, it is vital to figure out how to deal with the chicken-and-egg strategy problem and get all sides on board[29] and how to determine the appropriate strategy formation[30] and monetisation of the platform, especially at the beginning of its operation.[31] The start is tough, and commonly, only a few players survive.[32] However, once established, an online platform business can be gratifying and lucrative.[33]

The platformisation of the economy is prevalent in all kinds of industries (transport, food, tourism, accommodation, education, audiovisual, recruiting, etc.) and has profoundly challenged traditional business models, given its possibilities and

---

[27] See Evans and Schmalensee (2017–2018), p. 38.

[28] See Rochet and Tirole (2006). At that point, it seems that users are not looking for a particular seller or someone that carefully selects and assures the quality of suppliers; instead, they crowdsource recommendations and only ask that they be able to search for, or be introduced by an algorithm to, the best possible match. See OECD (2018), p. 3.

[29] See Ott et al. (2018), pp. 2, 12, 19–20. Rochet and Tirole (2003), p. 990.

[30] According to Ott, Bremner and Eisenhardt, strategy formation is the process by which executives create a unique set of interdependent activities to create and capture value. See Ott et al. (2018), p. 2.

[31] In the monetisation strategy of an online platform business, not all users must necessarily pay the same price for using the platform. Some platforms successfully function without directly charging their users. Sometimes, only one side of the platform is charged. Some platforms charge their services on the basis of a prescription fee while others by taking a share or a fixed amount (e.g. CarLotz, thePowerMBA). Due to the specificities of online platforms, each and every platform needs to find its own business model and monetisation strategy appropriate for its concept. Rochet and Tirole note that the choice of a business model seems to be the key to success and receives much corporate attention. Ott, Bremner and Eisenhardt deem that in finding the appropriate strategy formation, the 'get big fast' strategy is commonly ineffective because it is too difficult to figure out how to both fit together the correct pieces of a complex strategy and kick-start network effects. Evans, Hagiu and Schmalensee believe that in order for online platforms to succeed, they have to get the pricing structure right; they must balance the demands of the various customer groups and nurture the several sides of the market. In doing so, getting the balance right seems to be more important than building shares. See Rochet and Tirole (2003), pp. 991, 1007–1008; Ott et al. (2018), p. 11; Evans et al. (2006), pp. 63–67. See also Büge and Ozcan (2021), pp. 17–23.

[32] Even platforms that have succeeded network effects can also work in reverse—each lost user induces other users to leave (e.g. AOL, MSN Messenger, Friendster, Myspace). See Evans and Schmalensee (2017–2018), p. 38.

[33] Contrary to what may even be the prevailing viewpoint, the business of online platforms is not all about winner takes all (see, for instance, Frank and Cook 1996; Iansiti and Lakhani 2017, pp. 84–92). Indeed, only a few online platforms manage to enjoy the benefits of indirect network effects. The success of online platforms is often short (less than a decade), and many platforms struggle with the monetisation of their business. Thus, with a few exceptions, many 'winners' success is only for a short term. See Evans and Schmalensee (2017–2018), pp. 38–39.

exponential growth.[34] Online platforms have reorganised markets and industries and redefined value creation and competition dynamics, thereby substantially changing the very nature of competition.[35] They are commonly considered drivers of creativity and innovation and have proven to encourage and facilitate smaller businesses to move online and reach new markets.[36] Thus, the existence of online platforms has evidently encouraged many authors to create—many of whom might not have otherwise—and has provided them with new ways of distributing their works. It is worthwhile to take examples of platforms like YouTube, Instagram, Facebook and AppSumo. Not going into the qualitative assessment of such digital content, the online platforms induced inflation of copyright works (although the ultimate benefits of such developments are questionable for authors[37]). Consequently, online platforms enabled consumers to access much more content than was available before their emergence.[38]

However, aside from its evident benefits—mainly stemming from network effects—such an intriguing concept of online platforms has raised some regulatory concerns, particularly regarding competition law.[39] Thus, a key point of discussion is how to assess the common tendency of platforms to concentrate their core competing market and lock-in consumers within 'vertical silos with lack of interoperability',[40] while simultaneously diversifying and encouraging the development of the related market(s). In this case, it is even questionable how to define relevant markets properly. On the one hand, due to indirect network effects, (successful) online platforms tend to establish a strong, commonly even dominant, market position with high barriers to entry.[41] They have the power to control access to online markets and can exercise significant influence over how various players in the market are remunerated. This includes a lack of transparency as to how they use the

[34] In that sense, Evans, Hagiu and Schmalensee state:

> Creative destruction has been a hallmark of economic progress for millennia, but it has proceeded at a glacial pace for most of history. The Industrial Revolution sped this process up. Even so, it took decades for change to filter through the economy following innovations such as the spinning jenny, steam engine, and electric generator. The information technology revolution has quickened the pace of industrial change greatly. The plummeting costs of computer processing and storage make it possible to create products and industries that were not only infeasible but also unimaginable a few years earlier. Software platforms further accelerate the process of creative destruction, mainly because code is digital and malleable.

Evans et al. (2006), p. 338. See also Parker et al. (2016), pp. 62–78.

[35] See Parker et al. (2016), pp. 190–211.

[36] See Communication from the Commission to the European Parliament, the Council, the European Economic and Social Committee and the Committee of the Regions, 'A Digital Single Market Strategy', COM(2015) 192 final, p. 11.

[37] See Mazziotti (2020), pp. 1027–1032.

[38] See Freeman (2015), pp. 17–18.

[39] See Cusumano et al. (2019), pp. 131–140.

[40] See European Commission (Online Platforms), p. 19.

[41] See Evans and Schmalensee (2017–2018), p. 39; Gawer (2015), p. 3.

information they acquire; their strong bargaining power compared to their users, which is often evident in unilaterally imposed or non-negotiable terms and conditions (particularly for small and medium-sized enterprises (SMEs)); the promotion of their own services to the disadvantage of their competitors; non-transparent pricing policies; and restrictions on pricing and sales conditions.[42] There is still no firm understanding of how these occurrences can be approached and their effects on the overall competition in relevant markets. Such problems are made worse by the fact that online platforms play a dual role *vis-a-vis* other businesses—some online platforms do not only transact with them in the capacity of supplier/buyer, but they also compete with them in vertical markets. That is why it is challenging to disentangle competition issues from supplier-buyer trade issues as the two overlap and interact. Moreover, the power of online platforms dramatically constrains the freedom of businesses to devise and pursue competitive strategies. Namely, in the case of platform-dependent businesses, online platforms limit the construction of a unique value proposition, strategic pricing flexibility, customer relationships and room for manoeuvre.[43] Hence, considering the concept and vast powers of online platforms, it is clear that there is not much room for many successful players in the online platform business. However, those that manage to establish their position often have the special responsibility 'not to allow its conduct to impair genuine undistorted competition on the common market'.[44,45]

Taking all these into consideration, one of the central benefits of online platforms (diversified related market(s) on platforms), is, in a way, also increasingly becoming one of its biggest downsides (concentrated main platform market). Hence, it is not surprising that authorities (particularly competition authorities) are still struggling to take a position on the issue of online platforms, notwithstanding that, by now, there is much empirical evidence on the matter. It is particularly challenging to evaluate the pro- and anti-competitive effects of specific platforms—to distinguish between legitimate benefits arising from network effects and deliberate efforts to deny competitors from accessing those same effects.

In the context of this research, things can get even more complicated if the competition concerns of online platforms also include possible limitations to the exercise of copyright. In this case, the situation should be observed as a copyright-competition interaction matter. Indeed, such a scenario is very likely to happen,

---

[42] See Communication from the Commission to the European Parliament, the Council, the European Economic and Social Committee and the Committee of the Regions, 'A Digital Single Market Strategy', COM(2015) 192 final, p. 11; Reyna (2015), p. 13. Keeping in mind that online platforms often control critical access points (such as operating systems, app stores, and popular apps), especially in the music industry, songwriters and composers feel forced to accept unfair licensing terms from online platforms, and if these terms were not accepted, they threaten to simply not license at all and rely instead on 'Safe harbour'. See European Commission (2016), pp. 17–18.

[43] See Cutolo et al. (2021), pp. 3–4.

[44] Judgment of the Court of 9 November 1983, *NV Nederlandsche Banden Industrie Michelin v Commission of the European Communities*, C-322/81, EU:C:1983:313, para. 57.

[45] See Sauter (2020), pp. 406–427.

considering that at the heart of an online platform is a software engine that runs on a computer code.[46] Given that software is protected by copyright, the operation of online platforms fundamentally relies on the use and exploitation of copyrighted works, particularly software source code.[47] Hence, competition concerns arising from an online platform's conduct are—or should primarily be—understood as issues of copyright-competition interaction. From older case law, a good example of such a situation is the *Microsoft* case, which can be considered an innovation platform case (see *supra*, Sect. 5.2.2.2.3).[48]

Recently, online platforms have indeed attracted the attention of competition authorities. Google has been of particular interest to them. Since 2010, the Commission has initiated several cases against Google and has found infringements of competition law in three of those cases: for promoting its own vertical search results over general content search results,[49] for preventing websites that used its search bar and ads from showing competing ads[50] and for managing Android.[51] In the United States, there is an ongoing extensive antitrust investigation against Google. Similarly, the Commission has initiated proceedings against Amazon, focusing on the treatment of third-party retailers[52] and whether the company uses sellers' data to gain an advantage in favour of the products it directly sells.[53,54] Apple also faces competition issues before the Commission, concerning the terms governing the use of Apple's App Store by developers offering apps (or certain content within these apps) that directly compete with apps or services offered by Apple[55]—in other

[46] See Evans et al. (2006), pp. 1–4, 39.

[47] See de Lima Assafin (2018), pp. 24–25.

[48] See Cusumano et al. (2019), pp. 136–138.

[49] The Commission, Case AT.39740, *Google Search (Shopping)*; Judgement of 10 September 2024, *Google and Alphabet v Commission (Google Shopping)*, C-48/22 P, ECLI:EU:C:2024:726 (appeal dismissed).

[50] The Commission, Case AT.40411, *Google Search (AdSense)*; Judgement of 18 September 2024, *Google and Alphabet v Commission (Google AdSense for Search)*, T-334/19, ECLI:EU:T:2024:634 (Commission decision annulled).

[51] The Commission, Case AT.40099, *Google Android*; Judgement of 14 September 2022, *Google and Alphabet v Commission (Google Android)*, T-604/18, ECLI:EU:T:2022:541 (Commission decision partly annulled).

[52] The Commission, Case AT.40703, *Amazon - Buy Box*.

[53] The Commission, Case AT.40462, *Amazon Marketplace*.

[54] In late 2022, the Commission accepted commitments by Amazon, barring it from using marketplace seller data and ensuring equal access to Buy Box and Prime; Commission Decision of 20 December 2022 relating to a proceeding under Article 102 of the Treaty on the Functioning of the European Union and Article 54 of the EEA Agreement (Cases AT.40462 – Amazon Marketplace and AT.40703 – Amazon Buy Box) (Text with EEA relevance), 2023/C 87/05, C/2022/9442, OJ C 87, 9.3.2023, pp. 7–11.

[55] The Commission, Case AT.40437, *Apple - App Store Practices (music streaming)*; The Commission, Case AT.40652, *Apple - App Store Practices (e-books/audiobooks)*; The Commission, Case AT.40716, *Apple - App Store Practices*.

words, for allegedly limiting choice and stifling innovation by acting as both a player and a referee, thereby gaining an unfair advantage and causing disadvantages to other application developers.[56] In March 2024, the Commission fined Apple for alleged anti-competitive conduct related to music streaming.[57] At the EU level, online platforms have also attracted the attention of national competition authorities. Worth mentioning in this regard are certainly the Belgian *Immoweb*[58] case and the Swedish *Booking.com*[59] and *Expedia*[60] cases.

However, it seems that aside from *Microsoft*, the cases mentioned did not address the copyright-competition interaction issue as no limitation on the exercise of copyright was found. Perhaps those cases did not impact the exercise of copyright in any way. Still, in competition assessments, it should be taken into account that online platforms are, in essence, the product of copyright exploitation. Hence, in such assessments, it should first be analysed whether there is a possible exercise of copyright involved in the conduct under investigation, as suggested in the presented methods of assessment (see *supra*, Sects. 4.3.2.2 and 5.3.2.1). If an exercise of copyright is found, the specific method of assessment should apply. Nevertheless, although the cases mentioned above did not discuss the matter of copyright-competition interaction, it is still indicative that online platforms are increasingly falling under the scrutiny of competition rules.

Bearing in mind that much of the content offered through the platform marketplace is, in essence, copyright-protected work, it is also possible that the copyright-competition interaction issue could arise in the platform market—among undertakings competing on online platforms.[61]

In the online platform world, it is reasonable to expect that some of the online platform cases will actually be discussed as a copyright-competition interaction issue before competition authorities. Thus, the grounds for dealing with the copyright-competition interaction issue must be set.[62] The conduct of online platforms may fall under the scrutiny of competition rules on prohibited agreements and abuse of dominance, while for undertakings competing on platforms, the main concerns are

[56] UNCTAD (2019), p. 7.

[57] Commission Decision of 4 March 2024 relating to a proceeding under Article 102 of the Treaty on the Functioning of the European Union and Article 54 of the EEA Agreement (Case AT.40437 – Apple – App Store Practices (Music Streaming)), C/2024/1307, OJ C, C/2024/3554, 7.6.2024.

[58] Belgian Competition Authority (BCA), Case MEDE-I/0-15/0002, *Immoweb*, 7 November 2016.

[59] Decision of the Swedish Competition Authority of 15 April 2015, file ref. 596/2013.

[60] Decision of the Swedish Competition Authority of 5 October 2015, file ref. 595/2013.

[61] To some extent in that sense, see Graef (2019); Firth (2021), pp. 68–69.

[62] According to the European Commission's survey on online platforms, intellectual property rights and competition concerns were identified as one of the main issues of online platforms. Many stakeholders expressed the need for the harmonisation of rules on that matter at the EU level. See European Commission (2016), pp. 11, 26. For different perspectives on the balancing of competition law and copyright in digital surroundings, see Boliek (2017), pp. 47–49.

'only' prohibited agreements.[63] In any case, it is essential that in assessing the conduct of or on online platforms, the specific concept and effects of an online platform should be acknowledged on a case-by-case basis.[64]

In addition to the particularities of copyright-competition interaction regarding online platforms, as elaborated above (see *supra*, Sects. 4.3 and 5.3), the main principles and standard tools of competition law generally seem to fit the purpose.[65] Still, regardless of the type of assessment, the conduct of or on online platforms should be analysed as a potential violation 'by effect' rather than 'by object'. The economy of online-platform-related markets is different from the economy of traditional markets, especially considering the specificity of network effects.[66] Ignoring those particularities most likely leads to bad decision-making.[67] Thus, already at the stage of market definition, it is first necessary to determine how many markets are to be defined in a particular case, then apply the appropriate method and include all the relevant factors in the market definition.[68] Further, in establishing market power and the possible dominant position of an undertaking holding an online platform, it should be considered that such 'recent and fast-growing sectors which is characterized by short innovation cycles in which large market shares may turn out to be ephemeral'.[69] Thus, it is vital to recognise the network effects and their impact on the potential competitors and consumers in a dynamic context for the assessment of online platform market power. It is necessary to observe what the pattern of use says about substitutability on either side of the market and what substitutability on one side of the market implies for the platform's market power, which needs to be evaluated across all sides of the market. Brekke and Collyer, and Mullan and Timan, consider that in the assessment of market power, it is necessary to take into consideration consumers' elasticities and diversion ratios. Still, market shares, barriers to entry and exit, measures of concentration or profitability, and patterns of use (e.g. single or multi-homing) remain the primary tools for assessing market power.[70] Also, in determining exclusionary conduct, it should not be assumed to be harmless simply because there was another side of the market.[71] On the contrary, several commentators consider that exclusionary conduct is even

[63] Other competition concerns, such as concentration and state aid, are not discussed in this work. Nevertheless, conduct concerning online platforms may surely evoke other competition concerns as well.

[64] See Graef et al. (2014); Pike (2018); Reyna (2015), p. 13; Shelanski et al. (2018), pp. 192–194.

[65] See de Lima Assafin (2018), p. 38; Pike (2018), pp. 25–26.

[66] See Pike (2018), pp. 9–12.

[67] See Jenny (2018), p. 4.

[68] See Fillistrucchi (2018), pp. 37–51; Pike (2018), pp. 12–16; Wismer and Rasek (2018), pp. 55–67.

[69] Wording from *Cisco Systems and Messagenet v Commission* on the consumer communications sector; Judgment of 11 December 2013, *Cisco Systems and Messagenet v Commission*, T-79/12, EU:T:2013:635, para. 69.

[70] See Brekke (2018), pp. 87–99; Collyer et al. (2018), pp. 16–20.

[71] See Jenny (2018), p. 4.

more likely to happen in markets where multi-sided platforms operate than in traditional markets. There, also, users on the other side of the platform are particularly affected. Hence, the examination of such markets should be given greater priority.[72] The same goes for vertical restraints.[73] In such cases, some scholars have recognised the importance of formulating and explaining (preferably explicitly) an adequate and convincing theory of harm.[74]

7.4 Concluding Remarks

The main question with regard to the copyright-competition interaction issue is—what happens next? Will the situation remain in its *status quo*, or are we finally ready to tackle the issue and settle it once and for all? The digital revolution is gathering speed and is not expected to end soon. It seems that the most exciting and challenging matters are still in front of us—like the further development of artificial intelligence, cloud computing, blockchain technology, etc.

A vital part of digital evolution is rooted in creative content—in other words, copyright-protected works of authors—although there is not always an awareness of this. This is particularly the case for online platforms, which are substantially built upon copyright-protected works (software). Copyright is copyright regardless of the object of copyright protection. If the conduct of an online platform holder under competition scrutiny involves the exercise of copyright, it is a matter of copyright-competition interaction. Thus, the potential application of competition law represents a possible external limitation on the exercise of copyright, so the specific method of assessment should apply.

In dynamic digital surroundings, the copyright-competition interaction issue seems even more challenging. At the moment, there is no uniform case law on the matter, and there is obviously significant confusion on how to deal with the issue. The authorities do not know how to approach the issue in a convincing and grounded manner, while copyright holders do not know where the limit of 'normal exploitation' lies and at what moment they will fall under the scrutiny of competition authorities for exercising their copyright.

Nowadays, competition authorities have shifted their attention to the winners of digital evolution, such as Google, Apple, Amazon and others. However, the purpose of investigation against these businesses should not be prosecution *per se* but a genuine evaluation of their impact on markets and how they affect the further

[72] See Amelio et al. (2018), pp. 131–147; de Lima Assafin (2018), pp. 22–23; Katz (2018), pp. 103–129.

[73] See Caffarra and Kühn (2018), pp. 213–228; Johnson (2018), pp. 201–211; Pike (2018), pp. 26–29.

[74] See Caffarra and Kühn (2018), pp. 224–225; Collyer et al. (2018), pp. 73–74; Johnson (2018), pp. 205–206.

development of the creative industry in general. Although not explicitly addressed, many of the issues concerning those investigations might be considered a matter of copyright-competition interaction. Thus, it is one minute to midnight to adopt a comprehensive and fundamentally sustainable approach to the copyright-competition interaction issue and apply it to situations where competition law potentially limits the exercise of copyright.

References

Amelio A, Karlinger L, Valetti T (2018) Exclusionary practices and two-sided platforms. In: OECD, Rethinking Antitrust Tools for Multi-Sided Platforms, available via https://www.oecd.org/competition/rethinking-antitrust-tools-for-multi-sided-platforms.htm. Accessed 22 Oct 2024, pp 131–147

Boliek BE (2017) The economics of the internet. In: Blair RD, Sokol DD (eds) The Cambridge handbook of antitrust, intellectual property, and high tech. Cambridge University Press, Cambridge, pp 43–57

Brekke KR (2018) Measuring market power in multi-sided markets. In: OECD, Rethinking Antitrust Tools for Multi-Sided Platforms. https://www.oecd.org/competition/rethinking-antitrust-tools-for-multi-sided-platforms.htm. Accessed 22 Oct 2024, pp 87–99

Büge M, Ozcan P (2021) Platform scaling, fast and slow. MIT Sloan Management Review, special edition, New Strategies for the Platform Economy, Spring 2021, pp 17–23

Caffarra C, Kühn KU (2018) The competition analysis of vertical restraints in multi-sided markets. In: OECD, Rethinking Antitrust Tools for Multi-Sided Platforms. https://www.oecd.org/competition/rethinking-antitrust-tools-for-multi-sided-platforms.htm. Accessed 22 Oct 2024, pp 213–228

Collyer K, Mullan H, Timan N (2018) Measuring market power in multi-sided markets. In: OECD, Rethinking Antitrust Tools for Multi-Sided Platforms. https://www.oecd.org/competition/rethinking-antitrust-tools-for-multi-sided-platforms.htm. Accessed 22 Oct 2024, pp 71–86

Cusumano MA, Gawer A, Yoffie DB (2019) The business of platforms: strategy in the age of digital competition, innovation, and power. Harper Business, New York

Cutolo D, Hargadon A, Kenney M (2021) Competing on platforms. MIT Sloan Management Review, special edn, New Strategies for the Platform Economy, Spring 2021, pp 1–8

de Lima Assafin M (2018) International Report. In: Kilpatrick B, Kobel P, Këllezi P (eds) Anti-trust analysis of online sales platforms & copyright limitations and exceptions. Springer, Cham, pp 3–40

European Commission (2016) Online Platforms: Contrasting perceptions of European stakeholders - A qualitative analysis of the European Commission's Public Consultation on the Regulatory Environment for Platforms. Final report. A study prepared for the European Commission DG Communications Networks, Content & Technology by: Prof. Annabelle Gawer. https://www.surrey.ac.uk/sites/default/files/2018-11/online-platforms-contrasting-perceptions-european-stakeholders-report.pdf. Accessed 22 Oct 2024

Evans PC, Gawer A (2016) The rise of the platform enterprise - a global survey. The Emerging Platform Economy Series No. 1, The Center for Global Enterprise. https://www.thecge.net/wp-content/uploads/2016/01/PDF-WEB-Platform-Survey_01_12.pdf. Accessed 22 Oct 2024

Evans DS, Schmalensee S (2017–2018) Debunking the 'Network Effects' Boogeyman: policymakers need to march to the evidence, not to slogans. Regulation - Cato Rev Bus Gov 40(4):36–39

Evans DS, Hagiu A, Schmalensee R (2006) Invisible engines: how software platforms drive innovation and transform industries. The MIT Press, Cambridge

Fillistrucchi L (2018) Market definition in multi-sided markets. In: OECD, Rethinking Antitrust Tools for Multi-Sided Platforms. https://www.oecd.org/competition/rethinking-antitrust-tools-for-multi-sided-platforms.htm. Accessed 22 Oct 2024, pp 37–51

Firth A (2021) The essential facilities principle and other issues of competition. In: Stamatoudi I, Torremans P (eds) EU copyright law: a commentary, 2nd edn. Edward Elgar Publishing, Cheltenham, pp 44–73

Frank RH, Cook PJ (1996) The Winner-Take-All Society. Penguin Books, New York

Freeman J (2015) Evidence to the UK House of Lords, Inquiry into Online Platforms and the EU Digital Single Market. 12 Oct 2015. http://data.parliament.uk/writtenevidence/committeeevidence.svc/evidencedocument/eu-internal-market-subcommittee/online-platforms-and-the-eu-digital-single-market/oral/23234.pdf. Accessed 22 Oct 2024

Gawer A (2015) Evidence to the UK House of Lords, inquiry into online platforms and the EU Digital Single Market. 12 October 2015. https://committees.parliament.uk/oralevidence/4789/pdf/. Accessed 22 Oct 2024

Graef I (2019) Rethinking the essential facilities doctrine for the EU digital economy. TILEC Discussion Paper No. DP2019-028, 4 April 2019. https://papers.ssrn.com/sol3/papers.cfm?abstract_id=3371457. Accessed 22 Oct 2024

Graef I, Wahyuningtyas SY, Valcke P (2014) How Google and others upset competition analysis: disruptive innovation and European competition law. Conference paper, 25th European Regional Conference of the International Telecommunications Society (ITS): "Disruptive Innovation in the ICT Industries: Challenges for European Policy and Business", Brussels, Belgium, 22–25 June 2014, International Telecommunications Society (ITS), Calgary

Iansiti M, Lakhani KR (2017) Managing our hub economy. Harvard Business Rev, September-October issue, pp 84–92

Ibáñez Colomo P (2017) Copyright licensing and the EU Digital Single Market Strategy. In: Blair RD, Sokol DD (eds) The Cambridge handbook of antitrust, intellectual property, and high tech. Cambridge University Press, Cambridge, pp 339–357

Jenny F (2018) Foreword. In: OECD, Rethinking Antitrust Tools for Multi-Sided Platforms. https://www.oecd.org/competition/rethinking-antitrust-tools-for-multi-sided-platforms.htm. Accessed: 22 Oct 2024

Johnson PA (2018) Suggestions for competition authorities when assessing vertical restraints in multi-sided platforms. In: OECD, Rethinking Antitrust Tools for Multi-Sided Platforms. https://www.oecd.org/competition/rethinking-antitrust-tools-for-multi-sided-platforms.htm. Accessed 22 Oct 2024, pp 201–211

Katz ML (2018) Exclusionary conduct in multi-sided markets. In: OECD, Rethinking Antitrust Tools for Multi-Sided Platforms. https://www.oecd.org/competition/rethinking-antitrust-tools-for-multi-sided-platforms.htm. Accessed 22 Oct 2024, pp 103–129

Mazziotti G (2020) What is the future of creators' rights in an increasingly platform-dominated economy? Int Rev Intellect Prop Compet Law 51:1027–1032

OECD (2018) Rethinking antitrust tools for multi-sided platforms. https://www.oecd.org/competition/rethinking-antitrust-tools-for-multi-sided-platforms.htm. Accessed 22 Oct 2024

OECD (2019) An introduction to online platforms and their role in the digital transformation. OECD Publishing, Paris

Ott TE, Bremner RP, Eisenhardt KM (2018) Beyond the chicken and egg: strategy formation in two-sided marketplace ventures. Research paper, UNC Kenan-Flagler Business School, Chapel Hill, NC, 20 March 2018. https://www.kenaninstitute.unc.edu/wp-content/uploads/2018/05/Beyond-the-Chicken-and-Egg-Ott-1.pdf. Accessed 22 Oct 2024

Paemen D (2023) European Union. In: Paemen D (ed) The intellectual property and antitrust review. Law Business Research, London, pp 16–35

Parker GG, Van Alstyne MW, Choudary SP (2016) Platform revolution: how networked markets are transforming the economy - and how to make them work for you. W. W. Norton & Company, New York and London

Pike C (2018) Introduction and key findings. In: OECD, Rethinking Antitrust Tools for Multi-Sided Platforms. https://www.oecd.org/competition/rethinking-antitrust-tools-for-multi-sided-platforms.htm. Accessed 22 Oct 2024, pp 9–34

Reyna A (2015) Evidence to the UK House of Lords, inquiry into online platforms and the EU Digital Single Market. 12 October 2015. https://committees.parliament.uk/oralevidence/4789/pdf/. Accessed 22 Oct 2024

Rochet JC, Tirole J (2003) Platform competition in two-sided markets. J Eur Econ Assoc 1(4): 990–1029

Rochet JC, Tirole J (2006) Two-sided markets: a progress report. RAND J Econ 35(3):645–667

Sauter W (2020) A duty of care to prevent online exploitation of consumers? Digital dominance and special responsibility in EU competition law. J Antitrust Enforce 8(2):406–427

Shelanski H, Knox S, Dhilla A (2018) Network effects and efficiencies in multi-sided markets. In: OECD, Rethinking Antitrust Tools for Multi-Sided Platforms. https://www.oecd.org/competition/rethinking-antitrust-tools-for-multi-sided-platforms.htm. Accessed 22 Oct 2024

UNCTAD (2019) Competition issues in the digital economy. 1 May. TD/B/C.I/CLP/54. https://unctad.org/system/files/official-document/ciclpd54_en.pdf. Accessed 22 Oct 2024

Valimaki M (2006) Copyleft licensing and EU competition law. Eur Compet Law Rev 27(3): 130–136

Wismer S, Rasek A (2018) Market definition in multi-sided markets. In: OECD, Rethinking Antitrust Tools for Multi-Sided Platforms. https://www.oecd.org/competition/rethinking-antitrust-tools-for-multi-sided-platforms.htm. Accessed 22 Oct 2024, pp 55–67

Chapter 8
Afterthought

From the beginning of the issue, the interaction between copyright and competition law has been intriguing. There were already several remarkable cases in the EU concerning the copyright-competition interaction, and many different approaches have been applied in practice and discussed in theory throughout the years. Still, neither practice nor theory has demonstrated an adequate approach to dealing with the copyright-competition interaction, and the issue remains unsettled until now.

The copyright-competition interaction issue represents, in essence, a situation in which competition rules are applied to conduct involving an exercise of copyright. Those situations are exceptional yet significant.

The relationship between copyright law and competition law seems to be a logical starting point for dealing with such an issue. Copyright law and competition law peacefully co-exist, and we must observe and respect the rules and principles of both laws. From the perspective of copyright law, an application of competition law represents a *de facto* limitation to the exercise of copyright. It is a limitation in a broader sense, originating outside of copyright law. From the perspective of competition law, the presence of copyright should be understood as a specific situation. In an analysis of such a situation, the focus should mainly be on the effects of copyright instead of allocation and productiveness. At the same time, consumer welfare *per se*, as one of the main objectives of competition law, cannot be used as a justification for limiting the exercise of copyright.

Therefore, dealing with copyright-competition interaction requires a specific assessment method that respects the individual rules and rationales of copyright law and competition law. This research suggests a method of assessment explicitly designed for matters dealing with the exercise of copyright under competition rules on prohibited agreements and for cases dealing with the refusal to license copyright under competition rules on abuse of dominance. The suggested method of assessment follows the structure of a standard competition law analysis, adapted to embrace the particularities of copyright in the matter. The adaptation is present in all stages of the analysis, from the determination of the agreement or the determination of a dominant position to the establishment of anti-competitive behaviour.

D. Gliha, *The Copyright-Competition Interaction within the EU*,
https://doi.org/10.1007/978-3-031-94402-4_8

This research does not cover all possible situations concerning the copyright-competition interaction. Nonetheless, the main findings from the research are also applicable to situations not directly covered by this research. In those other situations, the main rules and principles of copyright law and competition law must still be respected in the same manner. The main difference is that an appropriate method for assessing cases must be adapted to satisfy the needs of a particular situation. Such adaptation would involve modifying the analysis structure and the conditions establishing anti-competitive behaviour. In any case, conduct involving an exercise of copyright can only infringe competition rules under exceptional circumstances—in essence, the principle of exceptionality remains the same.

Even if we acknowledge the approach suggested in this research, the question remains how to implement such an approach in practice. As discussed before, the suggested approach does not fundamentally change copyright law or competition law. Copyright law and competition law already contain everything necessary to recognise the issue and to appropriately deal with situations concerning copyright-competition interaction. Solid grounds have already been set in the rationales and rules of those laws. Hence, there is no need for substantive legislative interventions in copyright law or competition law but rather for proper interpretation of the law. On the one hand, copyright law tolerates particular *de facto* limitations to the exercise of copyright, although such limitations are external and are not part of the copyright law framework. On the other hand, competition law has a flexible and open-ended character, adjustable to specific situations. The copyright-competition interaction is no exception and should be perceived as one of the specific situations requiring a special approach. Therefore, the suggested method of assessment can immediately be applied to cases concerning copyright-competition interaction.

However, to ensure the uniform application of law as well as predictability and clarity in the market, it is almost necessary to elaborate the suggested approach within an appropriate soft law document. Up until now, practice has shown to be highly inconsistent. Considering there is no need for substantial legislative interventions in law, creating an interpretative document that would provide a clear and adequate interpretation of the law in situations concerning the copyright-competition interaction seems proper. In general, such a document should include the definition of the relationship between copyright law and competition law to set the grounds for dealing with the copyright-competition interaction. In a specific section, there should be a detailed elaboration of the method of assessment, separately for cases concerning the exercise of copyright under competition rules on prohibited agreements and separately for cases concerning the refusal to license copyright under competition rules on abuse of dominance. The elaboration should follow the structure of the analysis, elaborating the particularities of every stage in the assessment. The section on the exercise of copyright and the competition rules on prohibited agreement should be structured as follows: 1) determining the existence of an agreement, 2) analysing the copyright right involved in the conduct, 3) defining the relevant market, 4) assessing market share, 5) evaluating anti-competitive behaviour and 6) considering exemptions to prohibited agreements in light of the exercise of copyright. Similarly, the section on the refusal to license copyright as abuse of dominance should be structured in the following way: 1) analysing the copyright right involved in the conduct, 2) defining the relevant market, 3) determining a dominant position, 4) assessing abuse of dominance and 5) evaluating exoneration.

The research mainly focuses on the copyright-competition interaction within the EU, so it can be debated whether intervention should come at the level of the EU. Having in mind the exclusive competencies of the EU with regard to competition law and the continuous efforts of the EU to harmonise national copyright laws within the internal market, intervention at the level of the EU seems indeed appropriate. The copyright-competition issue likely affects the internal market. Moreover, the most significant cases had an effect on intra-EU trade. However, considering that there is no need for direct intervention in law, legislative acts such as regulations and directives do not seem appropriate instruments to deal with the copyright-competition interaction, but rather, a soft law instrument such as interpretative guidelines would be more suitable.

Even when the issue only concerns a Member State's national market, national authorities must still follow the interpretation and principles of EU law, at least when it comes to competition law, which is an inherent part of this issue. Firstly, EU competition law has a direct effect on national legislation; secondly, the Member States have aligned their national competition laws with EU competition law. Hence, in any case, the findings from the research are applicable among the Member States regardless of whether a situation has an effect on the internal market. Therefore, having a soft law instrument at the level of the EU seems the most appropriate solution to ensure a uniform approach in dealing with the copyright-competition interaction within the EU. Interpretative guidelines on the application of competition law to situations concerning the exercise of copyright would contribute to the overall legal security in the internal market and ensure that EU and national authorities have comprehensive instructions on how to apply the law in those situations.

Until the day the EU intervention comes (or even afterwards in parallel), there is no obstacle for the Member States to issue guidelines accordingly at a national level (or use some other appropriate national instrument). As we already discussed, cases concerning copyright-competition interaction can also come as an utterly national matter, not affecting intra-EU trade. Thus, regardless of the EU intervention, Member States surely have an interest in maintaining legal security and ensuring the uniform application of their national law when it comes to situations concerning copyright-competition interaction. Interpretative guidelines at the level of the EU, if appropriately drafted, would be sufficient to satisfy the needs of the internal market and national markets. However, with respect to copyright, EU guidelines can only address the particularities of copyright in general due to the diversity of copyright laws among the Member States. Copyright has a territorial nature, and each Member State has a specific national regime on copyright. The particularities of each copyright law cannot be fully acknowledged within an EU soft law document. At the same time, any direct or indirect intervention in substantial law would not be necessary from the perspective of competition law and would be inappropriate from the perspective of copyright law, considering the lack of competence of the

EU and the fact that the application of competition law to conduct can only be perceived as an external limitation to the exercise of copyright. Thus, in addition to EU guidelines, national guidelines drafted in accordance with this research, where necessary, could allow certain adjustments within the suggested approach with respect to a Member State's specific culture and tradition.

The differences among Member States' copyright regimes might especially have relevance in several stages of the analysis of cases concerning copyright-competition interaction. Although particularities of copyright are relevant throughout the entire assessment, the specific features of national regimes are especially evident during the analysis of the copyright right involved in the conduct and in defining the relevant market. In the stage concerning the analysis of a copyright right involved in conduct, it is vital to observe the applicable copyright law. Different copyright regimes have different criteria regarding what is protected under copyright law and to what extent. These differences can particularly be seen among the Member States, which adhere to different copyright traditions. For instance, works that were discussed in *Magill* might not be considered copyright-protected works in the copyright regime of some other Member State. If that were the case, then a specific copyright-competition analysis would not apply to such a situation but rather a standard competition law evaluation. Different copyright traditions, market structure and customer culture in the Member States might also have an effect on the definition of the relevant market. Concerning competition rules on abuse of dominance, in an entirely comparable situation, an undertaking might be considered in a dominant position in one Member State while not in another due to a different definition of a relevant national market.

Besides having potential relevance in addressing national law in the analysis, the existence of national guidelines might also have a positive effect on the acceptance of the suggested approach by national authorities. Particularly when applying national law, competent national authorities might be reluctant to address non-binding EU guidelines in strictly national matters. The EU guidelines serve a legitimate purpose of ensuring legal certainty and should be taken into consideration by national authorities regardless of whether a case concerns the internal market or only a national market. Nonetheless, creating national guidelines could help eliminate any doubt regarding the requirement for implementing the suggested approach to copyright-competition interaction in practice.

With the rise of creative industries and the dynamism of competition in markets, it is rational to expect more matters concerning copyright-competition interaction in future. The cases that were decided in the past years were significant with far-reaching consequences. It is easily imaginable that future cases concerning the copyright-competition interaction will have even greater significance, particularly in the digital industry. In any case, the important thing is to be prepared for upcoming developments and to learn from prior experience.

Whatever happens in the years to come, we will eagerly be observing new developments in the copyright-competition interaction within the EU. The most exciting cases are yet to come.

List of Case Law

European Union

- Judgment of 5 October 1988, AB Volvo v Erik Veng (UK) Ltd, C-238/87, EU: C:1988:477
- Judgment of 15 July 1970, ACF Chemiefarma NV v Commission of the European Communities, Case 41/69, EU:C:1970:71
- Judgment of 10 February 2011, Activision Blizzard Germany GmbH v European Commission, C-260/09 P, EU:C:2011:62
- The Commission, Case AT.40703, Amazon - Buy Box
- The Commission, Case AT.40462, Amazon Marketplace
- Commission Decision of 20 December 2022 relating to a proceeding under Article 102 of the Treaty on the Functioning of the European Union and Article 54 of the EEA Agreement (Cases AT.40462 - Amazon Marketplace and AT.40703 - Amazon Buy Box) (Text with EEA relevance), 2023/C 87/05, C/2022/9442, OJ C 87, 9.3.2023, pp. 7–11
- 2000/146/EC: Commission Decision of 14 December 1999 relating to a proceeding pursuant to Article 15(1)(b) of Council Regulation No. 17 (Case No. IV/34.237/F3 - Anheuser-Busch Incorporated - Scottish & Newcastle) (notified under document number C(1999) 4499), OJ L 49, 22.2.2000, pp. 37–44
- The Commission, Case AT.40716, Apple - App Store Practices
- The Commission, Case AT.40652, Apple - App Store Practices (e-books/audiobooks)
- The Commission, Case AT.40437, Apple - App Store Practices (music streaming)
- Commission Decision of 4 March 2024 relating to a proceeding under Article 102 of the Treaty on the Functioning of the European Union and Article 54 of the EEA Agreement (Case AT.40437 - Apple - App Store Practices (music streaming)), C/2024/1307, OJ C, C/2024/3554, 7.6.2024

D. Gliha, *The Copyright-Competition Interaction within the EU*,
https://doi.org/10.1007/978-3-031-94402-4

- Judgment of 23 November 2006, Asnef-Equifax, Servicios de Información sobre Solvencia y Crédito, SL v Asociación de Usuarios de Servicios Bancarios (Ausbanc), C-238/05, EU:C:2006:734
- Judgment of 10 January 1985, Association des Centres distributeurs Édouard Leclerc and Others v SARL 'Au blé vert' and Others, C-229/83, EU:C:1985:1
- Judgment of 1 July 2010, AstraZeneca AB and AstraZeneca plc v European Commission, T-321/05, EU:T:2010:266
- Judgment of 6 December 2012, AstraZeneca AB and AstraZeneca plc v European Commission, C-457/10 P, EU:C:2012:770
- Judgment of the Court of 28 February 2002, Atlantic Container Line AB and Others v Commission of the European Communities, T-395/94, EU:T:2002:49
- Judgment of the Court of 24 October 1995, Bayerische Motorenwerke AG v ALD Auto-Leasing D GmbH, C-70/93, EU:C:1995:344
- Judgment of 10 July 1991, BBC v Commission, T-70/89, EU:T:1991:40
- Judgment of 25 November 1971, Béguelin Import Co. v S.A.G.L. Import Export, C-22/71, EU:C:1971:113
- Judgment of the Court of 30 January 1974, Belgische Radio en Televisie and société belge des auteurs, compositeurs et éditeurs v SV SABAM and NV Fonior, Case 127/73, EU:C:1974:6
- Judgment of 16 February 2012, Belgische Vereniging van Auteurs, Componisten en Uitgevers CVBA (SABAM) v Netlog NV, C-360/10
- Judgment of the Court of 8 July 2008, BPB plc v Commission of the European Communities, T-53/03, EU:T:2008:254
- Judgment of 15 March 2007, British Airways plc v Commission of the European Communities, C-95/04 P, EU:C:2007:166
- Judgment of 17 November 1993, Bundesanstalt für den Güterfernverkehr v Gebrüder Reiff GmbH & Co. KG, C-185/91, EU:C:1993:886
- Judgment of 30 January 1985, Bureau national interprofessionnel du cognac v Guy Clair, C-123/83, EU:C:1985:33
- Judgment of 21 January 1999, Carlo Bagnasco and Others v Banca Popolare di Novara soc. coop. arl. (BNP) (C-215/96) and Cassa di Risparmio di Genova e Imperia SpA (Carige) (C-216/96), Joined Cases C-215/96 and C-216/96, EU:C:1999:12
- Judgment of 30 April 2009, CD-Contact Data GmbH v Commission of the European Communities, T-18/03, EU:T:2009:132
- Judgment of 3 October 1985, Centre belge d'études de marché - Télémarketing (CBEM) v SA Compagnie luxembourgeoise de télédiffusion (CLT) and Information publicité Benelux (IPB), Case 311/84, EU:C:1985:394
- Judgment of the Court of 31 October 1974, Centrafarm BV and Adriaan de Peijper v Sterling Drug Inc., C-15/74, EU:C:1974:114
- Judgment of 31 October 1974, Centrafarm BV and Adriaan de Peijper v Winthrop BV, C-16/74, EU:C:1974:115
- Judgment of 11 December 2013, Cisco Systems and Messagenet v Commission, T-79/12, EU:T:2013:635

- Judgment of 6 October 1982, Coditel SA, Compagnie générale pour la diffusion de la télévision, and Others v Ciné-Vog Films SA and Others, Case 262/81, ECLI:EU:C:1982:334
- Judgment of 28 February 2002, Compagnie générale maritime and Others v Commission of the European Communities, T-86/95, EU:T:2002:50
- Judgment of 5 October 1988, Consorzio italiano della componentistica di ricambio per autoveicoli and Maxicar v Régie nationale des usines Renault, C-53/87, EU:C:1988:472
- Judgment of 17 November 1993, Criminal proceedings against Ohra Schadeverzekeringen NV, C-245/91, EU:C:1993:887
- Judgment of 2 February 2012, Denki Kagaku Kogyo Kabushiki Kaisha and Denka Chemicals GmbH v European Commission, T-83/08, EU:T:2012:48
- Judgment of 16 July 2009, Der Grüne Punkt - Duales System Deutschland GmbH v Commission of the European Communities, C-385/07 P, EU:C:2009:456
- Judgment of 8 June 1971, Deutsche Grammophon Gesellschaft mbH v Metro-SB-Großmärkte GmbH & Co. KG, C-78/70, EU:C:1971:59
- Judgment of 1 June 1999, Eco Swiss China Time Ltd v Benetton International NV, C-126/87, EU:C:1999:269
- Judgment of 15 June 1976, EMI Records Limited v CBS Grammofon A/S, C-86/75, EU:C:1976:86
- Judgment of 15 June 1976, EMI Records Limited v CBS United Kingdom Limited, C-51/75, EU:C:1976:85
- 87/3/EEC: Commission Decision of 4 December 1986 in proceedings under Article 85 of the EEC Treaty (IV/31.055 - ENI/Montedison), OJ L 5, 7.1.1987, pp. 13–22
- Judgment of 13 July 1966, Établissements Consten S.à.R.L. and Grundig-Verkaufs-GmbH v Commission of the European Economic Community, Joined Cases 56 and 58–64, EU:C:1966:41
- Judgment of the Court of 21 February 1973, Europemballage Corporation and Continental Can Company Inc. v Commission of the European Communities, C-6/71, EU:C:1973:22
- Judgment of 13 December 2012, Expedia Inc. v Autorité de la concurrence and Others, C-226/22, EU:C:2012:795
- 89/536/EEC: Commission Decision of 15 September 1989 relating to a proceeding under Article 85 of the EEC Treaty (IV/31.734 - Film purchases by German television stations), OJ L 284, 3.10.1989, pp. 36–44
- Judgment of 4 October 2011, Football Association Premier League Ltd and Others v QC Leisure and Others and Karen Murphy v Media Protection Services Ltd, Joined Cases C-403/08 and C-429/08, EU:C:2011:631
- Judgment of 9 July 1969, Franz Völk v S.P.R.L. Ets J. Vervaecke, C-5/69, EU:C:1969:35
- Judgment of the Court of 2 March 1983, Gesellschaft zur Verwertung von Leistungsschutzrechten mbH (GVL) v Commission of the European Communities, Case 7/82, EU:C:1983:52

- Judgment of 6 October 2009, GlaxoSmithKline Services Unlimited v Commission of the European Communities (C-501/06 P) and Commission of the European Communities v GlaxoSmithKline Services Unlimited (C-513/06 P) and European Association of Euro Pharmaceutical Companies (EAEPC) v Commission of the European Communities (C-515/06 P) and Asociación de exportadores españoles de productos farmacéuticos (Aseprofar) v Commission of the European Communities (C-519/06 P), Joined Cases C-501/06 P, C-513/06 P, C-515/06 P and C-519/06 P, EU:C:2009:610
- The Commission, Case AT.40099, Google Android
- Judgment of 14 September 2022, Google and Alphabet v Commission (Google Android), T-604/18, ECLI:EU:T:2022:541
- The Commission, Case AT.40411, Google Search (AdSense)
- Judgment of 18 September 2024, Google and Alphabet v Commission (Google AdSense for Search), T-334/19, ECLI:EU:T:2024:634
- The Commission, Case AT.39740, Google Search (Shopping)
- Judgment of 10 September 2024, Google and Alphabet v Commission (Google Shopping), C-48/22 P, ECLI:EU:C:2024:726
- Judgment of the Court of 29 October 1980, Heintz van Landewyck SARL and Others v Commission of the European Communities, Joined Cases 209 to 215 and 218/78, EU:C:1980:248
- Judgment of 12 December 1991, Hilti AG v Commission of the European Communities, T-30/89, EU:T:1991:70
- Judgment of 23 May 1978, Hoffmann-La Roche & Co. AG v Centrafarm Vertriebsgesellschaft Pharmazeutischer Erzeugnisse mbH, C-102/77, EU:C:1978:108
- Judgment of 13 February 1979, Hoffmann-La Roche & Co. AG v Commission of the European Communities, C-85-76, ECLI:EU:C:1979:36
- 94/210/EC: Commission Decision of 29 March 1994 relating to a proceeding pursuant to Articles 85 and 86 of the EC Treaty (IV/33.941 - HOV SVZ/MCN), OJ L 104, 23.4.1994, pp. 34–57
- Judgment of 16 July 2015, Huawei Technologies Co. Ltd v ZTE Corp. and ZTE Deutschland GmbH, C-170/13, EU:C:2015:477
- Judgment of 12 July 1984, Hydrotherm Gerätebau GmbH v Compact del Dott. Ing. Mario Andreoli & C. Sas., C-170/83, EU:C:1984:271
- Judgment of the Court of 14 July 1972, Imperial Chemical Industries Ltd. v Commission of the European Communities, C-48/69, EU:C:1972:70
- Opinion of Advocate General Tizzano of 2 October 2003, IMS Health, C-418/01, EU:C:2003:537
- Judgment of 29 April 2004, IMS Health, C-418/01, EU:C:2004:257
- Judgment of 16 July 2009, Infopaq International A/S v Danske Dagblades Forening, C-5/08, EU:C:2009:465
- Judgment of 12 April 2013, International Confederation of Societies of Authors and Composers (CISAC) v European Commission, T-442/08, EU:T:2013:188
- Judgment of 10 July 1991, ITP v Commission, EU:T:1991:41

- Judgment of 17 July 1998, ITT Promedia NV v Commission of the European Communities, T-111/96, EU:T:1998:183
- Judgment of 19 February 2002, J. C. J. Wouters, J. W. Savelbergh and Price Waterhouse Belastingadviseurs BV v Algemene Raad van de Nederlandse Orde van Advocaten, intervener: Raad van de Balies van de Europese Gemeenschap, C-309/99, EU:C:2002:98
- Judgment of 28 April 1998, Javico International and Javico AG v Yves Saint Laurent Parfums SA (YSLP), C-306/96, EU:C:1998:173
- Judgment of 28 May 1998, John Deere Ltd v Commission of the European Communities, C-7/95 P, EU:C:1998:256
- Judgment of 14 May 1975, Kali und Salz AG and Kali-Chemie AG v Commission of the European Communities, Joined Cases 19 and 20/74, EU:C:1975:58
- 79/68/EEC: Commission Decision of 12 December 1978 relating to a proceeding under Article 85 of the EEC Treaty (IV/29.430 - Kawasaki), OJ L 16, 23.1.1979
- Judgment of 14 September 1982, Keurkoop BV v Nancy Kean Gifts BV, C-144/81, EU:C:1982:289
- Judgment of 17 February 2011, Konkurrensverket v TeliaSonera Sverige AB, C-52-09, EU:C:2011:83
- The Commission, Case AT.39226, Lundbeck, C(2013) 3803 final, 19.6.2013
- Judgment of 8 September 2016, *Lundbeck v Commission*, Case T-472/13, ECLI: EU:T:2016:449
- Judgment of 25 March 2021, Case C-591/16 P, *Lundbeck v. Commission*, ECLI: EU:C:2021:243
- 89/205/EEC: Commission Decision of 21 December 1988 relating to a proceeding under Article 86 of the EEC Treaty (IV/31.851 - Magill TV Guide/ITP, BBC and RTE), OJ L 78, 21.3.1989, pp. 43–51
- Judgment of 9 February 2012, Martin Luksan v Petrus van der Let, C-277/10, EU:C:2012:65
- Judgment of 15 July 1994, Matra Hachette SA v Commission of the European Communities, T-17/93, EU:T:1994:89
- Opinion of Advocate General Cosmas of 16 May 2000, Masterfoods and HV, Case C-344/98, EU:C:2000:249
- Judgment of 25 October 1977, Metro SB-Großmärkte GmbH & Co. KG v Commission of the European Communities, C-26/76, EU:C:1977:167
- Judgment of 18 September 2001, Métropole télévision (M6), Suez-Lyonnaise des eaux, France Télécom and Télévision française 1 SA (TF1) v Commission of the European Communities, T-112/99, EU:T:2001:215
- Judgment of 16 December 1999, Micro Leader Business v Commission of the European Communities, T-198/98, EU:T:1999:341
- The Commission, Case COMP/C-3/37.792, Microsoft, C(2004)900 final, 24.3.2004
- Case T-201/04: Action brought on 7 June 2004 by Microsoft Corporation against the Commission of the European Communities, OJ C 179, 10.7.2004, pp. 18–19
- Judgment of 17 September 2007, Microsoft v Commission, T-201/04, EU: T:2007:289

- Judgment of 27 June 2012, Microsoft Corp. v European Commission, T-167/08, EU:T:2012:323
- Judgment of 13 July 1989, Ministère public v Jean-Louis Tournier, Case 395/87, EU:C:1989:319
- The Commission, Case COMP/38.044, *National Data Corporation/IMS Global Services*, C(2009)5222, 25.6.2009
- 82/853/EEC: Commission Decision of 7 December 1982 relating to a proceeding under Article 85 of the EEC Treaty (IV/30.070 - National Panasonic), OJ L 354, 16.12.1982, pp. 28–35
- Judgment of 8 June 1982, L.C. Nungesser KG and Kurt Eisele v Commission of the European Communities, Case 258/78, ECLI:EU:C:1982:211
- 84/191/EEC: Commission Decision of 30 March 1984 relating to a proceeding under Article 85 of the EEC Treaty (IV/30.804 - Nuovo CEGAM), OJ L 99, 11.4.1984, pp. 29–37
- Judgment of 9 November 1983, NV Nederlandsche Banden Industrie Michelin v Commission of the European Communities, C-322/81, EU:C:1983:313
- Opinion of Advocate General Jacobs of 28 May 1998, Oscar Bronner, C-7/97, EU:C:1998:264
- Judgment of 26 November 1998, Oscar Bronner GmbH & Co. KG v Mediaprint Zeitungs und Zeitschriftenverlag GmbH & Co. KG, Mediaprint Zeitungsvertriebsgesellschaft mbH & Co. KG and Mediaprint Anzeigengesellschaft mbH & Co. KG, C-7-97, EU:C:1998:569
- Judgment of 7 June 2006, Österreichische Postsparkasse and Bank für Arbeit und Wirtschaft v Commission, Joined Cases T-213/01 and T-214/01, EU:T:2006:151
- Judgment of 29 February 1968, Parke, Davis and Co. v Probel, Reese, Beintema-Interpharm and Centrafarm, C-24/67, EU:C:1968:11
- Judgment of 2 April 2009, Pedro IV Servicios SL v Total España SA, C260/07, EU:C:2009:215
- Judgment of 20 October 1993, Phil Collins v Imtrat Handelsgesellschaft mbH and Patricia Im- und Export Verwaltungsgesellschaft mbH and Leif Emanuel Kraul v EMI Electrola GmbH, Joined Cases C-92/92 and 263/92, EU:C:1993:847
- 2003/675/EC: Commission Decision of 30 October 2002 relating to a proceeding pursuant to Article 81 of the EC Treaty and Article 53 of the EEA Agreement (COMP/35.587 PO Video Games, COMP/35.706 PO Nintendo Distribution and COMP/36.321 Omega - Nintendo) (notified under document number C(2002) 4072), OJ L 255, 8.10.2003, pp. 33–100
- Judgment of 27 March 2012, Post Danmark A/S v Konkurrencerådet, C-209/10, EU:C:2012:172
- 1999/60/EC: Commission Decision of 21 October 1998 relating to a proceeding under Article 85 of the EC Treaty (Case No IV/35.691/E-4 - Pre-Insulated Pipe Cartel) (notified under number C(1998) 3117), OJ L 24, 30.1.1999, pp. 1–70
- Judgment of 13 September 2012, Protégé International Ltd v European Commission, T-119/09, EU:T:2012:421
- Judgment of 7 February 2013, Protimonopolný úrad Slovenskej republiky v Slovenská sporiteľňa a.s., C-68/12, U:C:2013:71

- 89/44/EEC: Commission Decision of 12 December 1988 relating to a proceeding under Article 85 of the EEC Treaty (IV/27.393 and IV/27.394, Publishers Association - Net Book Agreements), OJ L 22, 26.1.1989, pp. 12–35
- Judgment of 9 July 1992, Publishers Association v Commission of the European Communities, T-66/89, EU:T:1992:84
- Judgment of 17 January 1995, The Publishers Association v Commission of the European Communities, C-360/92 P, EU:C:1995:6
- Judgment of 10 July 1991, RTE v Commission, T-69/89, EU:T:1991:39
- Opinion of Advocate General Gulmann of 1 June 1994, RTE and ITP v Commission, Joined Cases C-241/91 P and C-242/91 P, EU:C:1994:210
- Judgment of 6 April 1995, RTE and ITP v Commission, Joined Cases C-241/91 P and C-242/91 P, ECLI:EU:C:1995:98
- Judgment of 18 March 1980, SA Compagnie générale pour la diffusion de la télévision, Coditel, and Others v Ciné Vog Films and Others, C-62/79, EU: C:1980:84
- Judgment of 16 November 1977, SA G.B.-INNO-B.M. v Association des détaillants en tabac (ATAB), C-13/77, EU:C:1977:185
- Judgment of 17 December 1991, SA Hercules Chemicals NV v Commission of the European Communities, T-7/89, EU:T:1991:75
- Judgment of 11 January 1990, Sandoz prodotti farmaceutici SpA v Commission of the European Communities, C-277/87, EU:C:1990:6
- Judgment of 2 May 2012, *SAS Institute Inc. v World Programming Ltd.*, C-406/ 10, EU:C:2012:259
- Judgment of 24 November 2011, Scarlet Extended SA v Société belge des auteurs, compositeurs et éditeurs SCRL (SABAM), C-70/10, EU:C:2011:771
- Judgment of 8 October 2008, Schunk GmbH and Schunk Kohlenstoff-Technik GmbH v Commission of the European Communities, T-69-04, EU:T:2008:415
- Judgment of 18 February 1971, Sirena S.r.l. v Eda S.r.l. and Others, C-40/70, EU: C:1971:18
- Judgment of 10 December 1985, Stichting Sigarettenindustrie and Others v Commission of the European Communities, Joined Cases 240, 241, 242, 261, 262, 268 and 269/82, EU:C:1985:488
- Notice published pursuant to Article 19(3) of Council Regulation No. 17 concerning an application for negative clearance or exemption under Article 81(3) of the EC Treaty (Case COMP/C2/38.287 - Telenor/Canal+/Canal Digital), OJ C 149, 26.6.2003, pp. 16–17
- The Commission, Case COMP/C.2-38.287 ñ Telenor/Canal+/Canal Digital, C (2003) 5192 final, 29.12.2003
- Judgment of 20 June 1978, Tepea BV v Commission of the European Communities, C-28-77, EU:C:1978:133
- Judgment of 6 October 1994, Tetra Pak International SA v Commission of the European Communities, T-83/91, EU:T:1994:246
- Judgment of 12 June 1997, Tiercé Ladbroke SA v Commission of the European Communities, T-540/93, EU:T:1997:84

- Judgment of 14 February 1978, United Brands Company and United Brands Continentaal BV v Commission of the European Communities (Chiquita Bananas), C-27/76, EU:C:1978:22
- Judgment of 17 January 1984, Vereniging ter Bevordering van het Vlaamse Boekwezen, VBVB, and Vereniging ter Bevordering van de Belangen des Boekhandels, VBBB, v Commission of the European Communities, Joined Cases 43/82 and 63/82, EU:C:1984:9
- 91/532/EEC: Commission Decision of 5 June 1991 relating to a proceeding under Article 85 of the EEC Treaty (Case No IV/32.879 - Viho/Toshiba), OJ L 287, 17.10.1991, pp. 39–43
- The Commission, Case AT.39398, VISA MIF, C(2014)1199 final, 26.2.2014
- 2001/711/EC: Commission Decision of 29 June 2001 relating to a proceeding under Article 81 of the EC Treaty (Case COMP/F-2/36.693 - Volkswagen) (notified under document number C(2001) 1698), OJ L 262, 2.10.2001, pp. 14–37
- Judgment of 3 December 2003, Volkswagen AG v Commission of the European Communities, T-208/01, EU:T:2003:326
- Judgment of 13 July 2006, Commission of the European Communities v Volkswagen AG, C-75/04 P, EU:C:2006:460
- Judgment of 13 February 1969, Walt Wilhelm and Others v Bundeskartellamt, C-14/68, EU:C:1969:4
- Judgment of 17 May 1988, Warner Brothers Inc. and Metronome Video ApS v Erik Viuff Christiansen, C-158/86, EU:C:1988:242
- Judgment of 25 February 1986, Windsurfing International Inc. v Commission of the European Communities, C-193/83, EU:C:1986:75

National

Belgium

- Belgian Competition Authority (BCA), Case MEDE-I/0-15/0002, Immoweb, 7 November 2016

Germany

- Reisgericht, Decision of 4 February 1897, 38 RGZ 155, 157
- Bundeskartellamt Decision, Funke/Springer Programmzeitschriften, Case B6-98/13, 25 April 2014
- Bundeskartellamt Decision, Zeitungsverlag Schwäbisch Hall, Case B6-150/08, 21 April 2009

South Africa

- The Competition Appeal Court, Primedia Limited, Capricorn Capital Partners (Pty) Ltd., New Africa Investments Limited v The Competition Commission, Decision of 9 May 2008, Case 39/AM/MAY06. https://www.comptrib.co.za/other-court-judgments. Accessed 22 October 2024

Sweden

- Decision of the Swedish Competition Authority of 15 April 2015, file ref. 596/2013
- Decision of the Swedish Competition Authority of 5 October 2015, file ref. 595/2013

United Kingdom

- Darcy v Allin (1602) 11 Co Rep 84b
- East India Company v Sandys (1685) St.Tr. 371

United States

- Adams v. Burke, 84 U.S. 453 (1873)
- Alcatel USA, Inc. v. DGI Techs., Inc., 166 F.3d 772, 787 (5th Cir. 1999)
- A&M Records, Inc. v. Napster, Inc., 239 F.3d 1004 (9th Cir. 2001)
- Associated Press v. United States, 326 U.S. 1 (1945)
- US Supreme Court, Aspen Skiing Co. v. Aspen Highlands Skiing Corp., 472 U.S. 585, 1985
- Atari Games Corp. v. Nintendo of America Inc., 975 F.2d 832 (Fed. Cir. 1992)
- Bobbs-Merrill Co. v. Straus, 210 U.S. 339 (1908)
- Computer Associates International, Inc. v. Altai, Inc., 982 F.2d 693 (2d Cir. 1992)
- Data General Corporation, et al. v. Grumman Systems Support Corporation, 36 F.3d 1147 (1st Cir. 1994)
- Dr. Miles Medical Co. v. John D. Park & Sons Co., 220 U. S. 373, 400–401 (1911)
- The Supreme Court of the United States, Google LLC v. Oracle America, Inc., argued October 7, 2020, decided April 5, 2021, No. 18-956
- Hecht v. Pro- Football, Inc., 570 F.2d 982 (D.C. Cir. 1977)

- Image Tech. Services, Inc. v. Eastman Kodak, 125 F.3d 1195 (9th Cir. 1997)
- In Re Independent Service Organizations Antitrust Litigation v. Xerox Corporation, 203 F.3d 1322 (Fed. Cir. 2000)
- Lasercomb America v. Reynolds, 911 F.2d 970, 973, 979 (4th Cir. 1990)
- Lexmark International, Inc. v. Static Control Components, Inc., 387 F.3d 522 (6th Cir. 2004)
- M. Witmark & Sons v. Jensen, 80 F. Supp. 843, 850, 79 U.S.P.Q. 6 (D. Minn. 1948), appeal dismissed, 177 F.2d 515, 84 U.S.P.Q. 41 (8th Cir. 1949)
- MCI Communications Corp. v. AT&T Co., 708 F.2d 1081 (7th Cir. 1983)
- New York Mercantile Exchange v. Intercontinental Exchange, 323 F. Supp. 2d 559 (S.D.N.Y. 2004)
- Otter Tail Power Co. v. United States, 410 U.S. 366 (1973)
- The Supreme Court of the United States, Pacific Bell Telephone Co. v. linkLine Communications, Inc., 555 U.S. 438 (2009)
- Regos v. Associated Press, 937 F.2d 700 (2d Cir. 1991)
- Sega Enterprises Ltd. v. Accolade, Inc., 977 F.2d 1510 (9th Cir. 1992)
- US Feist Publications, Inc. v. Rural Telephone Service Company, Inc., 499 U.S. 340, 345 (1991)
- United States v. Microsoft Corporation, 253 F.3d 34 (D.C. Cir. 2001)
- The Supreme Court of the United States, United States v. Paramount Pictures, Inc. et al. 334 U.S. 131, 68 S. Ct. 915; 92 L. Ed. 1260; 1948 U.S. LEXIS 2850; 77 U.S.P.Q. (BNA) 243; 1948 Trade Cas. (CCH), 62, 244
- United States v. Terminal R.R. Ass'n, 224 U.S. 383 (1912)
- The Supreme Court of the United States, Verizon Communications, Petitioner v. Law Offices of Curtis V. Trinko, LLP, 540 U.S. 398 (2004)

Legislation

European Union

- Anti-counterfeiting Trade Agreement (ACTA), European Parliament Resolution of 24 November 2010 on the Anti-counterfeiting Trade Agreement (ACTA), OJ C 99E, 3.4.2012, pp. 27–29
- Antitrust: Commission adopts revised safe harbours for minor agreements ('De Minimis Notice') and provides guidance on 'by object' restrictions of competition - European Commission, Frequently asked questions, MEMO, 25 June 2014. https://ec.europa.eu/commission/presscorner/detail/en/MEMO_14_440. Accessed 24 October 2024
- The Charter of Fundamental Rights of the European Union, OJ C 326, 26.10.2012, pp. 391–407
- The Commission, Fourth Report on Competition Policy (Addendum to the 'Eighth General Report on the Activities of the Communities'), Brussels - Luxemburg, April 1975. https://ec.europa.eu/competition/publications/annual_report/ar_1974_en.pdf. Accessed 24 October 2024
- Commission Notice—Guidelines on the effect on trade concept contained in Articles 81 and 82 of the Treaty, C 101, 27.4.2004
- Commission Notice on agreements of minor importance which do not appreciably restrict competition under Article 81(1) of the Treaty establishing the European Community (De Minimis), OJ C 368, 22.12.2001
- Commission Notice on the definition of relevant market for the purposes of Community competition law, OJ C 372, 9.12.1997, pp. 5–13
- Commission Regulation (EU) No. 316/2014 of 21 March 2014 on the application of Article 101(3) of the Treaty on the Functioning of the European Union to categories of technology transfer agreements, OJ L 93, 28.3.2014, pp. 17–23
- Commission Staff Working Paper Accompanying the Report from the Commission on Competition Policy 2011, COM(2012) 253 final

D. Gliha, *The Copyright-Competition Interaction within the EU*,
https://doi.org/10.1007/978-3-031-94402-4

- Communication from the Commission—Guidelines on the applicability of Article 101 of the Treaty on the Functioning of the European Union to horizontal co-operation agreements, OJ C 11, 14.1.2011, pp. 1–72
- Communication from the Commission—Guidelines on the applicability of Article 101 of the Treaty on the Functioning of the European Union to horizontal co-operation agreements, C/2023/4752, OJ C 259, 21.7.2023, pp. 1–125
- Communication from the Commission—Guidelines on the application of Article 101 of the Treaty on the Functioning of the European Union to technology transfer agreements, OJ C 89, 28.3.2014, pp. 3–50
- Communication from the Commission—Guidance on the Commission's enforcement priorities in applying Article 82 of the EC Treaty to abusive exclusionary conduct by dominant undertaking, C 45, 24.2.2009, pp. 7–20
- Communication from the Commission—Notice on agreements of minor importance which do not appreciably restrict competition under Article 101(1) of the Treaty on the Functioning of the European Union (De Minimis Notice), OJ C 291, 30.8.2014, pp. 1–4
- Communication from the Commission to the European Parliament, the Council, the European Economic and Social Committee and the Committee of the Regions, a Digital Single Market Strategy, COM(2015) 192 final
- Communication from the Commission to the European Parliament, the Council, the European Economic and Social Committee and the Committee of the Regions, 'Towards a modern, more European copyright framework', COM (2015) 626, final
- Council Directive 91/250/EEC of 14 May 1991 on the legal protection of computer programs, OJ L 122, 17.5.1991, pp. 42–46
- Council Directive 92/100/EEC of 19 November 1992 on rental right and lending right and on certain rights related to copyright in the field of intellectual property, OJ L 346, 27.11.1992, pp. 61–66
- Council Directive 93/83/EEC of 27 September 1993 on the coordination of certain rules concerning copyright and rights related to copyright applicable to satellite broadcasting and cable retransmission, OJ L 248, 6.10.1993, pp. 15–21
- Council Directive 93/98/EEC of 29 October 1993 harmonizing the term of protection of copyright and certain related rights, OJ L 290, 24.11.1993, pp. 9–13
- Commission Notice—Guidelines on the application of Article 81 of the EC Treaty to technology transfer agreements, OJ C 101, 27.4.2004, pp. 2–42
- Commission Regulation (EU) No. 316/2014 of 21 March 2014 on the application of Article 101(3) of the Treaty on the Functioning of the European Union to categories of technology transfer agreements, OJ L 93, 28.3.2014, pp. 17–23
- Commission Regulation (EU) 2022/720 of 10 May 2022 on the application of Article 101(3) of the Treaty on the Functioning of the European Union to categories of vertical agreements and concerted practices (Text with EEA relevance), C/2022/3015, OJ L 134, 11.5.2022, pp. 4–13
- Consolidated version of the Treaty on the Functioning of the European Union, *OJ C 326, 26.10.2012, pp. 47–390*

- Council Regulation (EEC) No. 4064/89 of 21 December 1989 on the control of concentrations between undertakings, OJ L 395/89, pp. 1–12
- Council Regulation (EC) No. 139/2004 of 20 January 2004 on the control of concentrations between undertakings (the EC Merger Regulation), OJ L 24, 29.1.2004, pp. 1–22
- Council Regulation (EC) No. 1/2003 of 16 December 2002 on the implementation of the rules on competition laid down in Articles 81 and 82 of the Treaty, OJ L 1, 4.1.2003, pp. 1–25
- DG Competition discussion paper on the application of Article 82 of the Treaty to exclusionary abuses, Brussels. December 2005. https://ec.europa.eu/competition/antitrust/art82/discpaper2005.pdf. Accessed 24 October 2024
- Directive 96/9/EC of the European Parliament and of the Council of 11 March 1996 on the legal protection of databases, OJ L 77, 27.3.1996, pp. 20–28
- Directive 2001/29/EC of the European Parliament and of the Council of 22 May 2001 on the harmonisation of certain aspects of copyright and related rights in the information society, OJ L 167, 22.06.2001, pp. 10–19
- Directive 2001/84/EC of the European Parliament and of the Council of 27 September 2001 on the resale right for the benefit of the author of an original work of art, OJ L 272, 13.10.2001, pp. 32–36
- Directive 2006/115/EC of the European Parliament and of the Council of 12 December 2006 on rental right and lending right and on certain rights related to copyright in the field of intellectual property (codified version), OJ L 376, 27.12.2006, pp. 28–35
- Directive 2006/116/EC of the European Parliament and of the Council of 12 December 2006 on the term of protection of copyright and certain related rights (codified version), OJ L 372, 27.12.2006, pp. 12–18
- Directive 2009/24/EC of the European Parliament and of the Council of 23 April 2009 on the legal protection of computer programs (Codified version), OJ L 111, 5.5.2009, pp. 16–22
- Directive 2011/77/EU of the European Parliament and of the Council of 27 September 2011 amending Directive 2006/116/EC on the term of protection of copyright and certain related rights, OJ L 265, 11.10.2011, pp. 1–5
- Directive 2012/28/EU of the European Parliament and of the Council of 25 October 2012 on certain permitted uses of orphan works, OJ L 299, 27.10.2012, pp. 5–12
- Directive 2014/26/EU of the European Parliament and of the Council of 26 February 2014 on collective management of copyright and related rights and multi-territorial licensing of rights in musical works for online use in the internal market, OJ L 84, 20.3.2014, pp. 72–98
- Directive (EU) 2017/1564 of the European Parliament and of the Council of 13 September 2017 on certain permitted uses of certain works and other subject matter protected by copyright and related rights for the benefit of persons who are blind, visually impaired or otherwise print-disabled and amending Directive 2001/29/EC on the harmonisation of certain aspects of copyright and related rights in the information society, OJ L 242, 20.9.2017, pp. 6–13

– Directive (EU) 2019/789 of the European Parliament and of the Council of 17 April 2019 laying down rules on the exercise of copyright and related rights applicable to certain online transmissions of broadcasting organisations and retransmissions of television and radio programmes, and amending Council Directive 93/83/EEC, PE/7/2019/REV/1, OJ L 130, 17.5.2019, pp. 82–91
– Directive (EU) 2019/790 of the European Parliament and of the Council of 17 April 2019 on copyright and related rights in the Digital Single Market and amending Directives 96/9/EC and 2001/29/EC, PE/51/2019/REV/1, OJ L 130, 17.5.2019, pp. 92–125
– EEC Council: Regulation No. 17: First Regulation implementing Articles 85 and 86 of the Treaty, OJ 13, 21.2.1962, pp. 204–211
– EU Commission Staff Working Document Accompanying the Document Report from the Commission to the European Parliament, the Council, the European Economic and Social Committee and the Committee of the Regions Report on Competition Policy 2014, COM(2015) 247 final
– EU Commission Staff Working Document Accompanying the Document Report from the Commission to the European Parliament, the Council, the European Economic and Social Committee and the Committee of the Regions Report on Competition Policy 2015, COM(2016) 393 final
– EU Commission Staff Working Document Accompanying the Document Report from the Commission to the European Parliament, the Council, the European Economic and Social Committee and the Committee of the Regions Report on Competition Policy 2017, COM(2018) 482 final
– EU Communication from the Commission Europe 2020: A strategy for smart, sustainable and inclusive growth, COM(2010) 2020
– EU Communication from the Commission—Guidance on the Commission's enforcement priorities in applying Article 82 of the EC Treaty to abusive exclusionary conduct by dominant undertakings, OJ C 45, 24.2.2009, pp. 7–20
– EU Communication from the Commission—Notice—Guidelines on the application of Article 81(3) of the Treaty, OJ C 101, 27.4.2004, pp. 97–118
– EU Green Paper on Vertical Restraints in EC Competition Policy, COM (96) 721 final, 22 January 1997
– European Commission, Digital Single Market: Europe 2020 Strategy, 20.2.2015. https://ec.europa.eu/digital-single-market/en/europe-2020-strategy. Accessed 23 October 2024
– European Commission, Glossary of terms used in EU competition policy: Antitrust and control of concentrations, Brussels. July 2002. https://publications.europa.eu/en/publication-detail/-/publication/100e1bc8-cee3-4f65-9b30-e232ec3064d6. Accessed 24 October 2024
– European Commission, Study on judges' training needs in the field of European competition law, Final Report, January 2016. https://op.europa.eu/en/publication-detail/-/publication/bfe6ccba-9a94-11e6-9bca-01aa75ed71a1/language-en. Accessed 24 October 2024
– European Parliament, Briefing paper on addressing unfair practices in business-to-business relations in the internal market, IP/A/IMCO/NT/2010-18, PE

457.364, May 2011. https://www.europarl.europa.eu/RegData/etudes/note/join/2011/457364/IPOL-IMCO_NT(2011)45736_EN.pdf. Accessed 24 October 2024
- Green paper on Copyright and the Challenges of Technology issues requiring immediate action, 7 June 1988, COM (88) 172 final
- Memorandum of Understanding, Key Principles on the Digitisation and Making Available of Out-of-Commerce Works, MEMO/11/619, Brussels, 20.9.2011
- Regulation (EU) 2017/1128 of the European Parliament and of the Council of 14 June 2017 on cross-border portability of online content services in the internal market, OJ L 168, 30.6.2017, pp. 1–11
- Regulation (EU) 2022/1925 of the European Parliament and of the Council of 14 September 2022 on contestable and fair markets in the digital sector and amending Directives (EU) 2019/1937 and (EU) 2020/1828 (Digital Markets Act) (Text with EEA relevance), PE/17/2022/REV/1, OJ L 265, 12.10.2022, pp. 1–66
- The Treaty establishing the European Coal and Steel Community (The Treaty of Paris), 18 April 1951. https://www.cvce.eu/content/publication/1997/10/13/11a21305-941e-49d7-a171-ed5be548cd58/publishable_en.pdf. Accessed 22 October 2024
- Treaty establishing the European Economic Community (EEC) (Treaty of Rome), 25 March 1957. https://eur-lex.europa.eu/legal-content/EN/TXT/?uri=CELEX:11957E/TXT. Accessed 22 October 2024
- Treaty of Amsterdam amending the Treaty on European Union, the Treaties establishing the European Communities and certain related acts, OJ C 340, 10.11.1997, pp. 1–144
- Treaty of Lisbon amending the Treaty of European Union and the Treaty establishing the European Community, OJ C 306, 17.12.2007
- Treaty of Nice amending the Treaty on European Union, the Treaties establishing the European Communities and certain related acts, OJ C 80, 10.3.2001, pp. 1–87
- Treaty on European Union (Maastricht Treaty), OJ C 191, 29.7.1992, pp. 1–112
- White Paper on Modernisation of the Rules Implementing Articles 85 and 86 of the EC Treaty, COM(1999) 101 final, 28.4.1999, OJ C 132, 12.5.1999, pp. 1–33

International

- The Agreement on Trade-Related Aspects of Intellectual Property Rights (TRIPS), 1 January 1995. https://www.wto.org/english/docs_e/legal_e/27-trips.pdf. Accessed 22 October 2024
- Beijing Treaty on Audiovisual Performances, 24 June 2012. https://www.wipo.int/edocs/mdocs/copyright/en/avp_dc/avp_dc_20.pdf. Accessed 22 October 2024
- Berne Convention for the Protection of Literary and Artistic Works, September 9, 1886, as revised at Paris on July 24, 1971 and amended in 1979, S. Treaty Doc. No. 99-27 (1986)

- Brussels Convention Relating to the Distribution of Programme-Carrying Signals Transmitted by Satellite, 21 May 1974. Accessed 23 October 2024
- The Convention for the Protection of Human Rights and Fundamental Freedoms, as amended by Protocols Nos. 11 and 14, supplemented by Protocols Nos. 1, 4, 6, 7, 12, 13 and 16. https://www.echr.coe.int/documents/convention_eng.pdf. Accessed 22 October 2024
- Convention for the Protection of Producers of Phonograms Against Unauthorized Duplication of Their Phonograms, 29 October 1971. https://wipolex.wipo.int/en/text/288579. Accessed 23 October 2024
- Convention on Literary and Artistic Works Copyright (The Buenos Aires Convention), 11 August 1910. https://www.wipo.int/edocs/lexdocs/treaties/en/bac/trt_bac_001en.pdf. Accessed 22 October 2024
- International Covenant on Economic, Social and Cultural Rights Adopted and opened for signature, ratification and accession by General Assembly Resolution 2200A (XXI) of 16 December 1966, entry into force 3 January 1976, in accordance with Article 27. https://www.ohchr.org/Documents/ProfessionalInterest/cescr.pdf. Accessed 22 October 2024
- International Convention for the Protection of Performers, Producers of Phonograms and Broadcasting Organisations (Rome Convention), Rome, October 26, 1961. https://www.wipo.int/edocs/pubdocs/en/wipo_pub_328.pdf. Accessed 22 October 2024
- Marrakesh Treaty to Facilitate Access to Published Works for Persons Who Are Blind, Visually Impaired, or Otherwise Print Disabled, 27 June 2013. https://wipolex.wipo.int/en/treaties/textdetails/13169. Accessed 22 October 2024
- Paris Convention for the Protection of Industrial Property of March 20, 1883, as revised at Brussels on December 14, 1900, at Washington on June 2, 1911, at The Hague on November 6, 1925, at London on June 2, 1934, at Lisbon on October 31, 1958, and at Stockholm on July 14, 1967, and as amended on September 28, 1979. https://www.unido.org/sites/default/files/2014-04/Paris_Convention_0.pdf. Accessed 22 October 2024
- Universal Copyright Convention, with Appendix Declaration relating to Articles XVII and Resolution concerning Article XI, 1952. https://www.unesco.org/en/legal-affairs/universal-copyright-convention-appendix-declaration-relating-article-xvii-and-resolution-concerning. Accessed 22 October 2024
- The Universal Declaration of Human Rights, adopted by the United Nations General Assembly of its 183rd meeting, held in Paris on 10 December 1948. https://www.un.org/en/universal-declaration-human-rights/. Accessed 22 October 2024
- The WIPO Copyright Treaty (WCT), 20 December 1996. https://wipolex.wipo.int/en/treaties/textdetails/12740. Accessed 22 October 2024
- The WIPO Performance and Phonogram Treaty (WPPT), 20 December 1996. https://wipolex.wipo.int/en/treaties/textdetails/12743. Accessed 22 October 2024

National

Austria

- Verordnung des Bundesministeriums für Justiz vom 14. September 1951 zur Durchführung des Kartellgesetzes (KartellG.-DV.), BGBI Nr. 173/1951, Bundesgesetblatt für die Republik Österreich, 3.11.1951, 53. Stück

Canada

- An Act for the Prevention and Suppression of Combinations Formed in Restraint of Trade, 1889, 52, Vict. c. 42

Croatia

- The Constitution of the Republic of Croatia (Official Gazette No. 56/90, 135/97, 08/98, 113/00, 124/00, 28/01, 41/01, 55/01, 76/10, 85/10, 05/14

France

- The Constitution of France 1958. https://www.conseil-constitutionnel.fr/sites/default/files/as/root/bank_mm/anglais/constiution_anglais_oct2009.pdf. Accessed 23 October 2024
- Decree of the King's Council of State, containing regulations on book trade privileges and counterfeitings, 30 July 1778 (orig. *Arrêt du Conseil d'Etat du Roi portant réglement sur les privilèges en librairie et les contrefaçons*, Du 30 juillet 1778). Paris (1778). Primary Sources on Copyright (1450–1900). eds L. Bently & M. Kretschmer. www.copyrighthistory.org. Accessed 23 October 2024
- Decree of the King's Council of State, containing regulations on the duration of book trade privileges, 30 August 1777 (orig. *Arrest du Conseil d'Etat du Roi, Portant Règlement sur la durée des Priviléges en Librairie. Du 30 août 1777*). Paris (1777). Primary Sources on Copyright (1450–1900). eds L. Bently & M. Kretschmer. www.copyrighthistory.org. Accessed 23 October 2024
- Decree of the National Convention, 19 July 1793, regarding the property rights of authors to writings of all kinds, of composers of music, of painters and illustrators (with the report of Lakanal) (orig. *Décret de la Convention Nationale du dix-neuf juillet 1793 relatif aux droits de propriété des Auteurs d'écrits en tout genre, des*

Compositeurs de musique, des Peintres et des Dessinateurs (avec le rapport de Lakanal)), Primary Sources on Copyright (1450–1900). eds L. Bently & M. Kretschmer. www.copyrighthistory.org. Accessed 23 October 2024
- Legislation French Law of 13 January 1791, concerning the works of living playwrights, Primary Sources on Copyright (1450–1900). eds L. Bently & M. Kretschmer. www.copyrighthistory.org. Accessed 23 October 2024
- Louis d'Héricourt's memorandum, Paris (1725–1726). Primary Sources on Copyright (1450–1900). eds L. Bently & M. Kretschmer. www.copyrighthistory.org. Accessed 23 October 2024
- Patent of 'Music Printers to the King', awarded by Henri II to Messrs Adrien Le Roy and Robert Ballard (orig. *Brevet d'Impression du Roy pour la musique accordé par Henri II aux Sieurs Adrien Le Roy et Robert Ballard*). Paris (1552). Primary Sources on Copyright (1450–1900). eds L. Bently & M. Kretschmer. www.copyrighthistory.org. Accessed 23 October 2024
- Privilege granted to Eloy d'Amerval for his poem 'Le Livre de la deablerie' (1507), Primary Sources on Copyright (1450–1900). eds L. Bently & M. Kretschmer. www.copyrighthistory.org. Accessed 23 October 2024
- Privilege granted to the printer Galliot Du Pré for 'Le Grand Coutumier de France' (1515). Primary Sources on Copyright (1450–1900). eds L. Bently & M. Kretschmer. www.copyrighthistory.org. Accessed 23 October 2024
- Report of Le Chapelier on Dramatic Author's property (with the Decree adopted by the National Assembly). Paris (1791). Primary Sources on Copyright (1450–1900). eds L. Bently & M. Kretschmer. www.copyrighthistory.org. Accessed 23 October 2024

Germany

- The Basic Law for the Federal Republic of Germany in the revised version published in the Federal Law Gazette Part III, classification number 100-1, as last amended by Article 1 of the Act of 28 March 2019 (Federal Law Gazette I, p. 404). https://www.gesetze-im-internet.de/englisch_gg/englisch_gg.html#p0019. Accessed 23 October 2024
- Privilege granted by Rudolf of Scherenberg, Prince-Bishop of Würzburg for the Printers Reyser, Dold and Beckenhub in a Breviary for the Würzburg Diocese (orig. *Breviarium Herbipolense*) (1479). Primary Sources on Copyright (1450–1900). eds L. Bently & M. Kretschmer. www.copyrighthistory.org. Accessed 23 October 2024
- Title, Dedications and Colophon with Reference to a Privilege of the Imperial Senate in Favour of the Sodalitas Celitica for an Edition of Works of Conrad Celtis, Nuremberg (orig. Quatuor libri amorum secundum quatuor latera Germanie) (1502). Primary Sources on Copyright (1450–1900). eds L. Bently & M. Kretschmer. www.copyrighthistory.org. Accessed 23 October 2024

- Title, Dedications and Colophon with Reference to a Privilege of the Imperial Senate in Favour of the Sodalitas Celitica for an Edition of Works of Hrotsvit, Nuremberg (orig. *OPERA HROSVITE ILLVSTRIS VIR||GINIS ET MONIALIS GERMANE GEN||TE SAXONICA ORTE NVPER A CONRA||DO CELTE INVENTA.||*) (1501). Primary Sources on Copyright (1450–1900). eds L. Bently & M. Kretschmer. www.copyrighthistory.org. Accessed 23 October 2024
- Verordnung gegen Missbrauch wirtschaftlicher Machtstellungen, November 2, 1923 (Kartell Verordnung) REICHSGESETZBLATT 1, 1067

Italy

- Privilege granted to Benedetto Bordon for 'Triumph of Caesar', Venice (1504). Primary Sources on Copyright (1450–1900). eds L. Bently & M. Kretschmer. www.copyrighthistory.org. Accessed 23 October 2024
- Printing monopoly granted to a German master printer, Johannes of Speyer, conceding a five-year exclusive right to print in Venice and its dominions, Venice (1469). Primary Sources on Copyright (1450–1900). eds L. Bently & M. Kretschmer. www.copyrighthistory.org. Accessed 23 October 2024
- Printing privilege granted to the author Marco Antonio Sabellico to print his 'Decades rerum Venetarum' (1486). Primary Sources on Copyright (1450–1900). eds L. Bently & M. Kretschmer. www.copyrighthistory.org. Accessed 23 October 2024

Japan

- Guidelines for the Use of Intellectual Property under the Antimonopoly Act (2016) https://www.jftc.go.jp/en/legislation_gls/imonopoly_guidelines_files/IPGL_Frand.pdf. Accessed 23 October 2024

Netherlands

- Bible: That is the entire Holy Scripture, thoroughly and faithfully translated into Dutch, Delft: Aelbert Hendricksz, 1579 (orig. *Biblia: dat is De gantsche Heylighe Schrift, grondelick ende trouwelick verduydtschet, Delft: Aelbert Hendricksz,* 1579). The Hague (1579), Primary Sources on Copyright (1450–1900). eds L. Bently & M. Kretschmer. www.copyrighthistory.org. Accessed 23 October 2024
- The Chronicle of Holland, Zealand and Frisia, starting from the time of Adam till the birth of our Lord Jesus, up until the year 1517, Leyden: Jan Severszoon, 1517

(orig. Die Chronyk van Hollandt, Zeelandt ende Vriesland, beghinnende van Adams tyden, tot die geboerte ons Heren Jhesu, voortgaende tot den jare 1517, Leyden: Jan Severszoon, 1517). Brussels (1516). Primary Sources on Copyright (1450–1900). eds L. Bently & M. Kretschmer. www.copyrighthistory.org Accessed 23 October 2024
- Simon du Chesne, Squaring of the circle or the manner of finding an equal square in a given circle, Delft: Albert Henry, 1584 (orig. *Simon du Chesne, Quadrature du cercle ou manière de trouver un quarre egual au cercle donne, Delft: Albert Henry*, 1584). Delft (1584). Primary Sources on Copyright (1450–1900). eds L. Bently & M. Kretschmer. www.copyrighthistory.org. Accessed 23 October 2024

Portugal

- The Constitution of the Portuguese Republic. https://dre.pt/constitution-of-the-portuguese-republic. Accessed 24 October 2024
- Order by Brás Afonso Correia, at the request of Valentim Fernandes, bookmaker (orig. Autos feitos por mandado de Brás Afonso Correia, a requerimento de Valentim Fernandes, livreiro), Lisbon, (1503). Primary Sources on Copyright (1450–1900). eds L. Bently & M. Kretschmer. www.copyrighthistory.org. Accessed 23 October 2024
- The Travels of Marco Polo written by Nicolau Vêneto, printed by Valentim Fernandes, containing a reference to the relevant royal privilege on the front cover (orig. *Marco Paulo. Ho liuro de Nycolao Veneto. Ho trallado da carta de huu[m] genoues das ditas terras*), Lisbon (1502). Primary Sources on Copyright (1450–1900). eds L. Bently & M. Kretschmer. www.copyrighthistory.org. Accessed 23 October 2024

Singapore

- Guidelines on the Treatment of Intellectual Property Rights in Competition Cases 2016. https://www.cccs.gov.sg/legislation/competition-act. Accessed 23 October 2024

Spain

- Don Quixote's Privilege (org. *Licencia y privilegio de impresión del Quijote*), Madrid (1605), Primary Sources on Copyright (1450–1900). eds L. Bently & M. Kretschmer. www.copyrighthistory.org. Accessed 23 October 2024

- Printing Privileges to the Monastery of San Pedro Mártir (Toledo) and Santa María de Prado (Valladolid) (orig. *Privilegios de impresión a los Monasterios de San Pedro Mártir (Toledo) y de Santa María de Prado (Valladolid)*) (1487), Primary Sources on Copyright (1450–1900). eds L. Bently & M. Kretschmer. www.copyrighthistory.org. Accessed 23 October 2024
- Privilege for printing music for the Indies (org. *Privilegio de impresión de libros corales con destino a las Indias*), Seville (1559). Primary Sources on Copyright (1450–1900). eds L. Bently & M. Kretschmer. www.copyrighthistory.org. Accessed 23 October 2024
- The Spanish Constitution. https://www.boe.es/buscar/pdf/1978/BOE-A-1978-40001-consolidado.pdf. Accessed 23 October 2024

Sweden

- The Constitution of Sweden. https://www.riksdagen.se/en/how-the-riksdag-works/democracy/the-constitution/. Accessed 23 October 2024
- Lagen om undersökning angående monopolistika företag och sammanslutningar, Svensk Författningssamling (SFS) 1925:223

United Kingdom

- An Act for the Encouragement of Learning, by Vesting the Copies of Printed Books in the Authors or Purchasers of such Copies, During the Times therein mentioned, 1710, 8 Anne, c.19 (1710). Primary Sources on Copyright (1450–1900). eds L. Bently & M. Kretschmer. www.copyrighthistory.org. Accessed 23 October 2024
- The Calendar (New Style) Act 1750, 24 Geo. II c.23 (Chesterfield's Act)
- John Day's Privilege for the Catechism, Westminster (1553). Primary Sources on Copyright (1450–1900). eds L. Bently & M. Kretschmer. www.copyrighthistory.org Accessed 23 October 2024
- Robert Calve's printing privilege for the 'Holsome and Catholick Doctrine' (30 April 1558), Westminster (1558). Primary Sources on Copyright (1450–1900). eds L. Bently & M. Kretschmer. www.copyrighthistory.org. Accessed 23 October 2024
- Thomas Phayer's lifetime privilege for Virgil's Aeneid in English (6 May 1558). Primary Sources on Copyright (1450–1900). eds L. Bently & M. Kretschmer. www.copyrighthistory.org. Accessed 23 October 2024

United States

- An Act to Protect Trade and Commerce Against Unlawful Restraints and Monopolies (The Sherman Antitrust Act of 1890), 26 Stat. 209, 15 U.S.C. §§ 1–38
- An Act to Supplement Existing Laws Against Unlawful Restraints and Monopolies, and for Other Purposes (The Clayton Antitrust Act of 1914), Pub.L. 63–212, 38 Stat. 730, enacted October 15, 1914, codified at 15 U.S.C. §§ 12–27, 29 U.S.C. §§ 52–53
- Antitrust Guidelines for the Licensing of Intellectual Property, issued by the U.S. Department of Justice and the Federal Trade Commission, April 6, 1995. https://www.justice.gov/atr/archived-1995-antitrust-guidelines-licensing-intellectual-property. Accessed 23 October 2024
- Antitrust Guidelines for the Licensing of Intellectual Property, issued by the U.S. Department of Justice and the Federal Trade Commission, January 12, 2017. https://www.justice.gov/atr/IPguidelines/download. Accessed 23 October 2024
- The Anti-Price Discrimination Act, Pub. L. No. 74-692, 49 Stat. 1526 (codified at 15 U.S.C. § 13
- The Constitution of the United States of America. https://www.senate.gov/civics/resources/pdf/US_Constitution-Senate_Publication_103-21.pdf. Accessed 23 October 2024
- The Federal Trade Commission Act of 1914, 15 U.S.C. §§ 41–58
- The Hart–Scott–Rodino Antitrust Improvements Act of 1976, Publ. L. No. 94-435, (codified at 15 U.S.C. § 18)
- John Usher's Printing Privilege, Massachusetts (1672). Primary Sources on Copyright (1450–1900). eds L. Bently & M. Kretschmer. www.copyrighthistory.org. Accessed 23 October 2024
- North Carolina Printing Privilege to Commissioners (Province) (1746), Primary Sources on Copyright (1450–1900). eds L. Bently & M. Kretschmer. www.copyrighthistory.org. Accessed 23 October 2024
- United States Copyright Office, Authors, Attribution, and Integrity: Examining Moral Rights in the United States, A Report of Register of Copyright, April 2019. https://www.copyright.gov/policy/moralrights/full-report.pdf. Accessed 24 October 2024
- William Bladen's Liberty to print in Maryland (1700). Primary Sources on Copyright (1450–1900). eds L. Bently & M. Kretschmer. www.copyrighthistory.org Accessed 23 October 2024

The manufacturer's authorised representative in the EU is Springer
Nature Customer Service Centre GmbH, Europaplatz 3, 69115 Heidelberg,
Germany. If you have any concerns regarding our products, please
contact ProductSafety@springernature.com

Printed and bound by CPI Group (UK) Ltd, Croydon, CR0 4YY
30/09/2026
02225572-0011